Here are six plays th  e modern drama:

Chekhov's THREE SISTERS

> repeats, in terms of a handful of people, the spasms of a dying society.

Ibsen's THE MASTER BUILDER

> is the tragedy of the modern romantic, caught between desire and reality.

Shaw's MRS. WARREN'S PROFESSION

> shocked England and America; this play was the first honest attempt in our era to deal with prostitution.

O'Casey's RED ROSES FOR ME

> is about a Protestant worker of Dublin who is a symbol of the ravaging conflicts in Ireland—and in man.

Williams' THE GLASS MENAGERIE

> is a tender, despairing portrait of two women, one lost in the past, the other in herself.

Miller's ALL MY SONS

> is a biting though compassionate, indictment of success through moral betrayal.

We call these plays "modern." But they are high art, and are written with devotion to truth, and those two qualities have already made them timeless.

CHEKHOV

IBSEN

SHAW

O'CASEY

WILLIAMS

MILLER

SIX

GREAT MODERN PLAYS

Dell

Published by
Dell Publishing
a division of
Random House, Inc.

Printed in the U. S. A.

ISBN: 0-440-37984-9

Previous Edition: #FE100 and 7984
New Dell Edition
October 1967
OPM 54 53 52 51 50 49 48 47 46

CONTENTS

THREE SISTERS   [*1900*]

---

by Anton Chekhov
[1860-1904]

CHARACTERS

PROZOROV, *Andrey Serghyevich*
NATASHA [*Natalia Ivanovna*], *his fiancée, afterwards his wife*
OLGA [*Olga Serghyevna, Olia*]
MASHA [*Maria Serghyevna*] } *his sisters*
IRENA [*Irena Serghyevna*]

KOOLYGHIN, *Fiodor Ilyich, master at the High School for boys, husband of Masha*

VERSHININ, *Alexandr Ignatyevich, Lieutenant-Colonel, Battery Commander*

TOOZENBACH, *Nigolai Lvovich, Baron, Lieutenant in the Army*

SOLIONY, *Vassily Vassilich, Captain*

CHEBUTYKIN, *Ivan Romanych, Army Doctor*

FEDOTIK, *Aleksey Petrovich, Second Lieutenant*

RODÉ, *Vladimir Karlovich, Second Lieutenant*

FERAPONT [*Ferapont Spiridonych*], *an old porter from the County Office*

ANFISA, *the Prozorovs' former nurse, an old woman of 80*

> *The action takes place in a county town*

ACT ONE

[*A drawing-room in the Prozorovs' house; it is separated from a large ballroom[1] at the back by a row of columns. It is midday; there is cheerful sunshine outside. In the ballroom the table is being laid for lunch.* OLGA, *wearing the regulation dark-blue dress of a secondary school mistress, is correcting her pupils' work, standing or walking about as she does so.* MASHA, *in a black dress, is sitting reading a book, her hat on her lap.* IRENA, *in white, stands lost in thought.*]

OLGA. It's exactly a year ago that Father died, isn't it? This very day, the fifth of May—your Saint's day, Irena. I remember it was very cold and it was snowing. I felt then as if I should never survive his death; and you had fainted and were lying quite still, as if you were dead. And now— a year's gone by, and we talk about it so easily. You're wearing white, and your face is positively radiant. . . . [*A clock strikes twelve.*] The clock struck twelve then, too. [*A pause.*] I remember when Father was being taken to the cemetery there was a military band, and a salute with rifle fire. That was because he was a general, in command of a brigade. And yet there weren't many people at the funeral. Of course, it was raining hard, raining and snowing.

IRENA. Need we bring up all these memories?

[1] A large room, sparsely furnished, used for receptions and dances in Russian houses.

[*Baron* TOOZENBACH, CHEBUTYKIN *and* SOLIONY *appear behind the columns by the table in the ballroom.*]

OLGA. It's so warm to-day that we can keep the windows wide open, and yet there aren't any leaves showing on the birch trees. Father was made a brigadier eleven years ago, and then he left Moscow and took us with him. I remember so well how everything in Moscow was in blossom by now, everything was soaked in sunlight and warmth. Eleven years have gone by, yet I remember everything about it, as if we'd only left yesterday. Oh, Heavens! When I woke up this morning and saw this flood of sunshine, all this spring sunshine, I felt so moved and so happy! I felt such a longing to get back home to Moscow!

CHEBUTYKIN [*to* TOOZENBACH]. The devil you have!

TOOZENBACH. It's nonsense, I agree.

MASHA [*absorbed in her book, whistles a tune under her breath*].

OLGA. Masha, do stop whistling! How can you? [*A pause.*] I suppose I must get this continual headache because I have to go to school every day and go on teaching right into the evening. I seem to have the thoughts of someone quite old. Honestly, I've been feeling as if my strength and youth were running out of me drop by drop, day after day. Day after day, all these four years that I've been working at the school. . . . I just have one longing and it seems to grow stronger and stronger. . . .

IRENA. If only we could go back to Moscow! Sell the house, finish with our life here, and go back to Moscow.

OLGA. Yes, Moscow! As soon as we possibly can.

[CHEBUTYKIN *and* TOOZENBACH *laugh.*]

IRENA. I suppose Andrey will soon get a professorship. He isn't likely to go on living here. The only problem is our poor Masha.

OLGA. Masha can come and stay the whole summer with us every year in Moscow.

MASHA [*whistles a tune under her breath*].

IRENA. Everything will settle itself, with God's help. [*Looks through the window.*] What lovely weather it is to-day! Really, I don't know why there's such joy in my heart. I remembered this morning that it was my Saint's day, and suddenly I felt so happy, and I thought of the time when we were children, and Mother was still alive. And then such wonderful thoughts came to me, such wonderful stirring thoughts!

OLGA. You're so lovely to-day, you really do look most attractive. Masha looks pretty to-day, too. Andrey could be good-looking, but he's grown so stout. It doesn't suit him. As for me, I've just aged and grown a lot thinner. I suppose it's through getting so irritated with the girls at school. But to-day I'm at home, I'm free, and my headache's gone, and I feel much younger than I did yesterday. I'm only twenty-eight, after all. . . . I suppose everything that God wills must be right and good, but I can't help thinking sometimes that if I'd got married and stayed at home, it would have been a better thing for me. [*A pause.*] I would have been very fond of my husband.

TOOZENBACH [*to* SOLIONY]. Really, you talk such a lot of nonsense, I'm tired of listening to you. [*Comes into the drawing-room.*] I forgot to tell you: Vershinin, our new battery commander, is going to call on you to-day. [*Sits down by the piano.*]

OLGA. I'm very glad to hear it.

IRENA. Is he old?

TOOZENBACH. No, not particularly. Forty, forty-five at the most. [*Plays quietly.*] He seems a nice fellow. Certainly not a fool. His only weakness is that he talks too much.

IRENA. Is he interesting?

TOOZENBACH. He's all right, only he's got a wife, a mother-in-law and two little girls. What's more, she's his second wife. He calls on everybody and tells them that he's got a wife and two little girls. He'll tell you about it, too, I'm sure of that. His wife seems to be a bit soft in the head. She wears a long plait like a girl, she is always philosophizing and talking in high-flown language, and then she often tries to commit suicide, apparently just to annoy her husband. I would have run away from a wife like that years ago, but he puts up with it, and just grumbles about it.

SOLIONY [*enters the drawing-room with* CHEBUTYKIN]. Now I can only lift sixty pounds with one hand, but with two I can lift two hundred pounds, or even two hundred and forty. So I conclude from that that two men are not just twice as strong as one, but three times as strong, if not more.

CHEBUTYKIN [*reads the paper as he comes in*]. Here's a recipe for falling hair . . . two ounces of naphthaline, half-a-bottle of methylated spirit . . . dissolve and apply once a day. . . . [*Writes it down in a notebook.*] Must make a note of it. [*To* SOLIONY.] Well, as I was trying to explain to you, you cork the bottle and pass a glass tube through the cork. Then you take a pinch of ordinary powdered alum, and . . .

IRENA. Ivan Romanych, dear Ivan Romanych!

CHEBUTYKIN. What is it, my child, what is it?

IRENA. Tell me, why is it I'm so happy to-day? Just as if I were sailing along in a boat with big white sails, and above me the wide, blue sky, and in the sky great white birds floating around?

CHEBUTYKIN [*kisses both her hands, tenderly*]. My little white bird!

IRENA. You know, when I woke up this morning, and after I'd got up and washed, I suddenly felt as if everything in the world had become clear to me, and I knew the way I ought to live. I know it all now, my dear Ivan Romanych. Man must work by the sweat of his brow whatever his class, and that should make up the whole meaning and purpose of his life and happiness and contentment. Oh, how good it must be to be a workman, getting up with the sun and breaking stones by the roadside—or a shepherd—or a schoolmaster teaching the children—or an engine-driver on the railway. Good Heavens! it's better to be a mere ox or horse, and work, than the sort of young woman who wakes up at twelve, and drinks her coffee in bed, and then takes two hours dressing. . . . How dreadful! You know how you long for a cool drink in hot weather? Well, that's the way I long for work. And if I don't get up early from now on and really work, you can refuse to be friends with me any more, Ivan Romanych.

CHEBUTYKIN [tenderly]. So I will, so I will. . . .

OLGA. Father taught us to get up at seven o'clock and so Irena always wakes up at seven—but then she stays in bed till at least nine, thinking about something or other. And with such a serious expression on her face, too! [Laughs.]

IRENA. You think it's strange when I look serious because you always think of me as a little girl. I'm twenty, you know!

TOOZENBACH. All this longing for work. . . . Heavens! how well I can understand it! I've never done a stroke of work in my life. I was born in Petersburg, an unfriendly, idle city—born into a family where work and worries were simply unknown. I remember a valet pulling off my boots for me when I came home from the cadet school. . . . I grumbled at the way he did it, and my mother looked on in admiration. She was quite surprised when other people looked at me in any other way. I was so carefully protected from work! But I doubt whether they succeeded in protecting me for good and all—yes, I doubt it very much! The time's come: there's a terrific thunder-cloud advancing upon us, a mighty storm is coming to freshen us up! Yes, it's coming all right, it's quite near already, and it's going to blow away all this idleness and indifference, and prejudice against work, this rot of boredom that our society is suffering from. I'm going to work, and in twenty-five or thirty years' time every man and woman will be working. Every one of us!

CHEBUTYKIN. I'm not going to work.

TOOZENBACH. You don't count.

SOLIONY. In twenty-five years' time you won't be alive, thank goodness. In a couple of years you'll die from a stroke—or I'll lose my temper with you and put a bullet in your head, my good fellow. [Takes a scent bottle from his pocket and *sprinkles the scent over his chest and hands.*]

CHEBUTYKIN [*laughs*]. It's quite true that I never have done any work. Not a stroke since I left the university. I haven't even read a book, only newspapers. [*Takes another newspaper out of his pocket.*] For instance, here. . . . I know from the paper that there was a person called Dobroliubov, but what he wrote about I've not the faintest idea. . . . God alone knows. . . . [*Someone knocks on the floor from downstairs.*] There! They're calling me to come down: there's someone come to see me. I'll be back in a moment. . . . [*Goes out hurriedly, stroking his beard.*]

IRENA. He's up to one of his little games.

TOOZENBACH. Yes. He looked very solemn as he left. He's obviously going to give you a present.

IRENA. I do dislike that sort of thing. . . .

OLGA. Yes, isn't it dreadful? He's always doing something silly.

MASHA. "A green oak grows by a curving shore, And round that oak hangs a golden chain" . . . [*Gets up as she sings under her breath.*]

OLGA. You're sad to-day, Masha.

MASHA [*puts on her hat, singing*].

OLGA. Where are you going?

MASHA. Home.

IRENA. What a strange thing to do.

TOOZENBACH. What! Going away from your sister's party?

MASHA. What does it matter? I'll be back this evening. Goodbye, my darling. [*Kisses* IRENA.] And once again— I wish you all the happiness in the world. In the old days when Father was alive we used to have thirty or forty officers at our parties. What gay parties we had! And to-day—what have we got to-day? A man and a half, and the place is as quiet as a tomb. I'm going home. I'm depressed to-day, I'm sad, so don't listen to me. [*Laughs through her tears.*] We'll have a talk later, but good-bye for now, my dear. I'll go somewhere or other. . . .

IRENA [*displeased*]. Really, you are a . . .

OLGA [*tearfully*]. I understand you, Masha.

SOLIONY. If a man starts philosophizing, you call that philosophy, or possibly just sophistry, but if a woman or a couple
of women start philosophizing you call that . . . what would
you call it, now? Ask me another!

MASHA. What are you talking about? You are a disconcerting
person!

SOLIONY. Nothing.
"He had no time to say 'Oh, oh!'
Before that bear had struck him low" . . .

[*A pause.*]

MASHA [*to* OLGA, *crossly*]. Do stop snivelling!

[*Enter* ANFISA *and* FERAPONT, *the latter carrying a large
cake.*]

ANFISA. Come along, my dear, this way. Come in, your boots
are quite clean. [*To* IRENA.] A cake from Protopopov, at
the Council Office.

IRENA. Thank you. Tell him I'm very grateful to him. [*Takes
the cake.*]

FERAPONT. What's that?

IRENA [*louder*]. Tell him I sent my thanks.

OLGA. Nanny, will you give him a piece of cake? Go along,
Ferapont, they'll give you some cake.

FERAPONT. What's that?

ANFISA. Come along with me, Ferapont Spiridonych, my dear.
Come along. [*Goes out with* FERAPONT.]

MASHA. I don't like that Protopopov fellow, Mihail Potapych,
or Ivanych, or whatever it is. It's best not to invite him
here.

IRENA. I haven't invited him.

MASHA. Thank goodness.

[*Enter* CHEBUTYKIN, *followed by a soldier carrying a silver
samovar. Murmurs of astonishment and displeasure.*]

OLGA [*covering her face with her hands*]. A samovar! But this
is dreadful! [*Goes through to the ballroom and stands by

the table.]

IRENA. My dear Ivan Romanych, what are you thinking about?

TOOZENBACH [*laughs*]. Didn't I tell you?

MASHA. Ivan Romanych, you really ought to be ashamed of yourself!

CHEBUTYKIN. My dear, sweet girls, I've no one in the world but you. You're dearer to me than anything in the world! I'm nearly sixty, I'm an old man, a lonely, utterly unimportant old man. The only thing that's worth anything in me is my love for you, and if it weren't for you, really I would have been dead long ago. [*To* IRENA.] My dear, my sweet little girl, haven't I known you since the very day you were born? Didn't I carry you about in my arms? . . . didn't I love your dear mother?

IRENA. But why do you get such expensive presents?

CHEBUTYKIN [*tearfully and crossly*]. Expensive presents! . . . Get along with you! [*To the orderly.*] Put the samovar over there. [*Mimics* IRENA.] Expensive presents!

[*The orderly takes the samovar to the ballroom.*]

ANFISA [*crosses the drawing-room*]. My dears, there's a strange colonel just arrived. He's taken off his coat and he's coming up now. Irenushka, do be nice and polite to him, won't you? [*In the doorway.*] And it's high time we had lunch, too. . . . Oh, dear! [*Goes out.*]

TOOZENBACH. It's Vershinin, I suppose.

[*Enter* VERSHININ.]

TOOZENBACH. Lieutenant-Colonel Vershinin!

VERSHININ [*to Masha and* IRENA]. Allow me to introduce myself—Lieutenant-Colonel Vershinin. I'm so glad, so very glad to be here at last. How you've changed! Dear, dear, how you've changed!

IRENA. Please, do sit down. We're very pleased to see you, I'm sure.

VERSHININ [*gayly*]. I'm so glad to see you, so glad! But there were three of you, weren't there?—three sisters. I remember there were three little girls. I don't remember their faces, but I knew your father, Colonel Prozorov, and I remember he had three little girls. Oh, yes, I saw them myself. I remember them quite well. How time flies! Dear, dear, how it flies!

TOOZENBACH. Alexandr Ignatyevich comes from Moscow.

IRENA. From Moscow? You come from Moscow?

VERSHININ. Yes, from Moscow. Your father was a battery commander there, and I was an officer in the same brigade. [*To* MASHA.] I seem to remember your face a little.

MASHA. I don't remember you at all.

IRENA. Olia, Olia! [*Calls towards the ballroom.*] Olia, do come!

[OLGA *enters from the ballroom.*]

IRENA. It seems that Lieutenant-Colonel Vershinin comes from Moscow.

VERSHININ. You must be Olga Serghyeevna, the eldest. And you are Maria. . . . And you are Irena, the youngest. . . .

OLGA. You come from Moscow?

VERSHININ. Yes. I studied in Moscow and entered the service there. I stayed there quite a long time, but then I was put in charge of a battery here—so I moved out here, you see. I don't really remember you, you know, I only remember that there were three sisters. I remember your father, though, I remember him very well. All I need to do is to close my eyes and I can see him standing there as if he were alive. I used to visit you in Moscow.

OLGA. I thought I remembered everybody, and yet . . .

VERSHININ. My Christian names are Alexandr Ignatyevich.

IRENA. Alexandr Ignatyevich, and you come from Moscow! Well, what a surprise!

OLGA. We're going to live there, you know.

IRENA. We hope to be there by the autumn. It's our home town, we were born there. . . . In Staraya Basmannaya Street.

[*Both laugh happily.*]

MASHA. Fancy meeting a fellow townsman so unexpectedly!

[*Eagerly.*] I remember now. Do you remember, Olga, there was someone they used to call "the lovesick Major"? You were a Lieutenant then, weren't you, and you were in love with someone or other, and everyone used to tease you about it. They called you "Major" for some reason or other.

VERSHININ [*laughs*]. That's it, that's it. . . . "The lovesick Major," that's what they called me.

MASHA. In those days you only had a moustache. . . . Oh, dear, how much older you look! [*Tearfully.*] How much older!

VERSHININ. Yes, I was still a young man in the days when they called me "the lovesick Major." I was in love then. It's different now.

OLGA. But you haven't got a single grey hair! You've aged, yes, but you're certainly not an old man.

VERSHININ. Nevertheless, I'm turned forty-two. Is it long since you left Moscow?

IRENA. Eleven years. Now what are you crying for, Masha, you funny girl? . . . [*Tearfully.*] You'll make me cry, too.

MASHA. I'm not crying. What was the street you lived in?

VERSHININ. In the Staraya Basmannaya.

OLGA. We did, too.

VERSHININ. At one time I lived in the Niemietzkaya Street. I used to walk from there to the Krasny Barracks, and I remember there was such a gloomy bridge I had to cross. I used to hear the noise of the water rushing under it. I remember how lonely and sad I felt there. [*A pause.*] But what a magnificently wide river you have here! It's a marvellous river!

OLGA. Yes, but this is a cold place. It's cold here, and there are too many mosquitoes.

VERSHININ. Really? I should have said you had a really good healthy climate here, a real Russian climate. Forest, river . . . birch-trees, too. The dear, unpretentious birch-trees— I love them more than any of the other trees. It's nice living here. But there's one rather strange thing, the station is fifteen miles from the town. And no one knows why.

SOLIONY. I know why it is. [*Everyone looks at him.*] Because if the station were nearer, it wouldn't be so far away, and as it is so far away, it can't be nearer. [*An awkward silence.*]

TOOZENBACH. You like your little joke, Vassily Vassilich.

OLGA. I'm sure I remember you now. I know I do.

VERSHININ. I knew your mother.

CHEBUTYKIN. She was a good woman, God bless her memory!

IRENA. Mamma was buried in Moscow.

OLGA. At the convent of Novo-Dievichye.

MASHA. You know, I'm even beginning to forget what she looked like. I suppose people will lose all memory of us in just the same way. We'll be forgotten.

VERSHININ. Yes, we shall all be forgotten. Such is our fate, and we can't do anything about it. And all the things that seem serious, important and full of meaning to us now will be forgotten one day—or anyway they won't seem important any more. [*A pause.*] It's strange to think that we're utterly unable to tell what will be regarded as great and important in the future and what will be thought of as just paltry and ridiculous. Didn't the great discoveries of Copernicus—or of Columbus, if you like—appear useless and unimportant to begin with?—whereas some rubbish, written up by an eccentric fool, was regarded as a revelation of great truth? It may well be that in time to come the life we live to-day will seem strange and uncomfortable and stupid and not too clean, either, and perhaps even wicked. . . .

TOOZENBACH. Who can tell? It's just as possible that future generations will think that we lived our lives on a very high plane and remember us with respect. After all, we no longer have tortures and public executions and invasions, though there's still a great deal of suffering!

SOLIONY [*in a high-pitched voice as if calling to chickens*]. Cluck, cluck, cluck! There's nothing our good Baron loves as much as a nice bit of philosophizing.

TOOZENBACH. Vassily Vassilich, will you kindly leave me alone? [*Moves to another chair.*] It's becoming tiresome.

SOLIONY [*as before*]. Cluck, cluck, cluck! . . .

TOOZENBACH [*to* VERSHININ]. The suffering that we see around us—and there's so much of it—itself proves that our society has at least achieved a level of morality which is higher. . . .

VERSHININ. Yes, yes, of course.

CHEBUTYKIN. You said just now, Baron, that our age will be called great; but people are small all the same. . . . [*Gets up.*] Look how small I am.

[*A violin is played off stage.*]

MASHA. That's Andrey playing the violin; he's our brother, you know.

IRENA. We've got quite a clever brother. . . . We're expecting him to be a professor. Papa was a military man, but Andrey chose an academic career.

OLGA. We've been teasing him to-day. We think he's in love, just a little.

IRENA. With a girl who lives down here. She'll be calling in to-day most likely.

MASHA. The way she dresses herself is awful! It's not that her clothes are just ugly and old-fashioned, they're simply pathetic. She'll put on some weird-looking, bright yellow skirt with a crude sort of fringe affair, and then a red blouse to go with it. And her cheeks look as though they've been scrubbed, they're so shiny! Andrey's not in love with her— I can't believe it; after all, he has got some taste. I think he's just playing the fool, just to annoy us. I heard yesterday that she's going to get married to Protopopov, the chairman of the local council. I thought it was an excellent idea. [*Calls through the side door.*] Andrey, come here, will you? Just for a moment, dear.

[*Enter ANDREY.*]

OLGA. This is my brother, Andrey Serghyeevich.

VERSHININ. Vershinin.

ANDREY. Prozorov. [*Wipes the perspiration from his face.*] I believe you've been appointed battery commander here?

OLGA. What do you think, dear? Alexandr Ignatyevich comes

from Moscow.

ANDREY. Do you, really? Congratulations! You'll get no peace from my sisters now.

VERSHININ. I'm afraid your sisters must be getting tired of me already.

IRENA. Just look, Andrey gave me this little picture frame today. [*Shows him the frame.*] He made it himself.

VERSHININ [*looks at the frame, not knowing what to say*]. Yes, it's . . . it's very nice indeed. . . .

IRENA. Do you see that little frame over the piano? He made that one, too.

[ANDREY *waves his hand impatiently and walks off.*]

OLGA. He's awfully clever, and he plays the violin, and he makes all sorts of things, too. In fact, he's very gifted all round. Andrey, please, don't go. He's got such a bad habit—always going off like this. Come here!

[MASHA *and* IRENA *take him by the arms and lead him back, laughing.*]

MASHA. Now just you come here!

ANDREY. Do leave me alone, please do!

MASHA. You are a silly! They used to call Alexandr Ignatyevich "the lovesick Major," and he didn't get annoyed.

VERSHININ. Not in the least.

MASHA. I feel like calling you a "lovesick fiddler."

IRENA. Or a "lovesick professor."

OLGA. He's fallen in love! Our Andriusha's in love!

IRENA [*clapping her hands*]. Three cheers for Andriusha! Andriusha's in love!

CHEBUTYKIN [*comes up behind* ANDREY *and puts his arms round his waist*]. "Nature created us for love alone." . . . [*Laughs loudly, still holding his paper in his hand.*]

ANDREY. That's enough of it, that's enough. . . . [*Wipes his face.*] I couldn't get to sleep all night, and I'm not feeling too grand just now. I read till four o'clock, and then I went to bed, but nothing happened. I kept thinking about one thing and another . . . and it gets light so early; the sun just pours into my room. I'd like to translate a book from the English while I'm here during the summer.

VERSHININ. You read English, then?

ANDREY. Yes. My father—God bless his memory—used to simply wear us out with learning. It sounds silly, I know, but I must confess that since he died I've begun to grow stout, as if I'd been physically relieved of the strain. I've grown quite stout in a year. Yes, thanks to Father, my sisters and I know French and German and English, and Irena here knows Italian, too. But what an effort it all cost us!

MASHA. Knowing three languages in a town like this is an unnecessary luxury. In fact, not even a luxury, but just a sort of useless encumbrance . . . it's rather like having a sixth finger on your hand. We know a lot of stuff that's just useless.

VERSHININ. Really! [*Laughs.*] You know a lot of stuff that's useless! It seems to me that there's no place on earth, however dull and depressing it may be, where intelligence and education can be useless. Let us suppose that among the hundred thousand people in this town, all of them, no doubt, very backward and uncultured, there are just three people like yourselves. Obviously, you can't hope to triumph over all the mass of ignorance around you; as your life goes by, you'll have to keep giving in little by little until you get lost in the crowd, in the hundred thousand. Life will swallow you up, but you'll not quite disappear, you'll make some impression on it. After you've gone, perhaps six more people like you will turn up, then twelve, and so on, until in the end most people will have become like you. So in two or three hundred years life on this old earth of ours will have become marvellously beautiful. Man longs for a life like that, and if it isn't here yet, he must imagine it, wait for it, dream about it, prepare for it, he must know and see more than his father and his grandfather did. [*Laughs.*] And you're complaining because you know a lot of stuff that's useless.

MASHA [*takes off her hat*]. I'll be staying to lunch.

IRENA [*with a sigh*]. Really, someone should have written all that down.

[ANDREY *has left the room, unnoticed.*]

TOOZENBACH. You say that in time to come life will be marvellously beautiful. That's probably true. But in order to share in it now, at a distance so to speak, we must prepare for it and work for it.

VERSHININ [*gets up*]. Yes. . . . What a lot of flowers you've got here! [*Looks round.*] And what a marvellous house! I do envy you! All my life I seem to have been pigging it in small flats, with two chairs and a sofa and a stove which always smokes. It's the flowers that I've missed in my life, flowers like these! . . . [*Rubs his hands.*] Oh, well, never mind!

TOOZENBACH. Yes, we must work. I suppose you're thinking I'm a sentimental German. But I assure you I'm not—I'm Russian. I don't speak a word of German. My father was brought up in the Greek Orthodox faith. [*A pause.*]

VERSHININ [*walks up and down the room*]. You know, I often wonder what it would be like if you could start your life over again—deliberately, I mean, consciously. . . . Suppose you could put aside the life you'd lived already, as though it was just a sort of rough draft, and then start another one like a fair copy. If that happened, I think the thing you'd want most of all would be not to repeat yourself. You'd try at least to create a new environment for yourself, a flat like this one, for instance, with some flowers and plenty of light. . . . I have a wife, you know, and two little girls; and my wife's not very well, and all that. . . . Well, if I had to start my life all over again, I wouldn't marry. . . . No, no!

[*Enter* KOOLYGHIN, *in the uniform of a teacher.*]

KOOLYGHIN [*approaches* IRENA]. Congratulations, dear sister—from the bottom of my heart, congratulations on your Saint's day. I wish you good health and everything a girl of your age ought to have! And allow me to present you with this little book. . . . [*Hands her a book.*] It's the history of our school covering the whole fifty years of its existence. I wrote it myself. Quite a trifle, of course—I wrote it in my spare time when I had nothing better to do—but I hope you'll read it nevertheless. Good morning to you all! [*To* VERSHININ.] Allow me to introduce myself. Koolyghin's the name; I'm a master at the secondary school here. And a town councillor. [*To* IRENA.] You'll find a list in the book of all the pupils who have completed their studies at our school during the last fifty years. *Feci quod potui, faciant meliora potentes.* [*Kisses* MASHA.]

IRENA. But you gave me this book last Easter!

KOOLYGHIN [*laughs*]. Did I really? In that case, give it me back— or no, better give it to the Colonel. Please do take it, Colonel. Maybe you'll read it some time when you've nothing better to do.

VERSHININ. Thank you very much. [*Prepares to leave.*] I'm so very glad to have made your acquaintance. . . .

OLGA. You aren't going are you? . . . Really, you mustn't.

IRENA. But you'll stay and have lunch with us! Please do.

OLGA. Please do.

VERSHININ [*bows*]. I see I've intruded on your Saint's day party. I didn't know. Forgive me for not offering you my congratulations. [*Goes into the ballroom with* OLGA.]

KOOLYGHIN. To-day is Sunday, my friends, a day of rest; let us rest and enjoy it, each according to his age and position in life! We shall have to roll up the carpets and put them away till the winter. . . . We must remember to put some naphthaline on them, or Persian powder. . . . The Romans enjoyed good health because they knew how to work *and* how to rest. They had *mens sana in corpore sano.* Their life had a definite shape, a form. . . . The director of the school says that the most important thing about life is form. . . . A thing that loses its form is finished—that's just as true of our ordinary, everyday lives. [*Takes* MASHA *by the waist and laughs.*] Masha loves me. My wife loves me. Yes, and the curtains will have to be put away with the carpets, too. . . .

I'm cheerful to-day, I'm in quite excellent spirits. . . . Masha, we're invited to the director's at four o'clock to-day. A country walk has been arranged for the teachers and their families.

MASHA. I'm not going.

KOOLYGHIN [*distressed*]. Masha, darling, why not?

MASHA. I'll tell you later. . . . [*Crossly.*] All right, I'll come, only leave me alone now. . . . [*Walks off.*]

KOOLYGHIN. And after the walk we shall all spend the evening at the director's house. In spite of weak health, that man is certainly sparing no pains to be sociable. A first-rate, thoroughly enlightened man! A most excellent person! After the conference yesterday he said to me: "I'm tired, Fiodor Ilyich. I'm tired!" [*Looks at the clock, then at his watch.*] Your clock is seven minutes fast. Yes, "I'm tired," he said.

[*The sound of the violin is heard off stage.*]

OLGA. Will you all come and sit down, please! Lunch is ready. There's a pie.

KOOLYGHIN. Ah, Olga, my dear girl! Last night I worked up to eleven o'clock, and I felt tired, but to-day I'm quite happy. [*Goes to the table in the ballroom.*] My dear Olga!

CHEBUTYKIN [*puts the newspaper in his pocket and combs his beard*]. A pie? Excellent!

MASHA [*sternly to* CHEBUTYKIN]. Remember, you mustn't take anything to drink to-day. Do you hear? It's bad for you.

CHEBUTYKIN. Never mind. I've got over that weakness long ago! I haven't done any heavy drinking for two years. [*Impatiently.*] Anyway, my dear, what does it matter?

MASHA. All the same, don't you dare to drink anything. Mind you don't now! [*Crossly, but taking care that her husband does not hear.*] So now I've got to spend another of these damnably boring evenings at the director's!

TOOZENBACH. I wouldn't go if I were you, and that's that.

CHEBUTYKIN. Don't you go, my dear.

MASHA. Don't go, indeed! Oh, what a damnable life! It's intolerable. . . . [*Goes into the ballroom.*]

CHEBUTYKIN [*follows her*]. Well, well! . . .

SOLIONY [*as he passes* TOOZENBACH *on the way to the ballroom*]. Cluck, cluck, cluck!

TOOZENBACH. Do stop it, Vassily Vassilich. I've really had enough of it. . . .

SOLIONY. Cluck, cluck, cluck! . . .

KOOLYGHIN [*gaily*]. Your health, Colonel! I'm a schoolmaster . . . and I'm quite one of the family here, as it were. I'm Masha's husband. She's got a sweet nature, such a very sweet nature!

VERSHININ. I think I'll have a little of this dark vodka. [*Drinks.*] Your health! [*To* OLGA.] I do feel so happy with you people!

[*Only* IRENA *and* TOOZENBACH *remain in the drawing-room.*]

IRENA. Masha's a bit out of humour to-day. You know, she got married when she was eighteen, and then her husband seemed the cleverest man in the world to her. It's different now. He's the kindest of men, but not the cleverest.

OLGA [*impatiently*]. Andrey, will you please come?

ANDREY [*off stage*]. Just coming. [*Enters and goes to the table.*]

TOOZENBACH. What are you thinking about?

IRENA. Oh, nothing special. You know, I don't like this man Soliony, I'm quite afraid of him. Whenever he opens his mouth he says something silly.

TOOZENBACH. He's a strange fellow. I'm sorry for him, even though he irritates me. In fact, I feel more sorry for him than irritated. I think he's shy. When he's alone with me, he can be quite sensible and friendly, but in company he's offensive and bullying. Don't go over there just yet, let them get settled down at the table. Let me stay beside you for a bit. Tell me what you're thinking about. [*A pause.*] You're twenty . . . and I'm not thirty yet myself. What years and years we still have ahead of us, a whole long succession of years, all full of my love for you! . . .

IRENA. Don't talk to me about love, Nikolai Lvovich.

TOOZENBACH [*not listening*]. Oh, I long so passionately for life, I long to work and strive so much, and all this longing is somehow mingled with my love for you, Irena. And just because you happen to be beautiful, life appears beautiful to me! What are you thinking about?

IRENA. You say that life is beautiful. Maybe it is—but what if it only seems to be beautiful? Our lives, I mean the lives of us three sisters, haven't been beautiful up to now. The truth is that life has been stifling us, like weeds in a garden. I'm afraid I'm crying. . . . So unnecessary. . . . [*Quickly dries her eyes and smiles.*] We must work, work! The reason we feel depressed and take such a gloomy view of life is that we've never known what it is to make a real effort. We're the children of parents who despised work. . . .

[*Enter* NATALIA IVANOVA. *She is wearing a pink dress with a green belt.*]

NATASHA. They've gone in to lunch already. . . . I'm late. . . . [*Glances at herself in a mirror, adjusts her dress.*] My hair seems to be all right. . . . [*Catches sight of* IRENA.] My dear Irena Serghyeevna, congratulations! [*Gives her a vigorous and prolonged kiss.*] You've got such a lot of visitors. . . . I feel quite shy. . . . How do you do, Baron?

OLGA [*enters the drawing-room*]. Oh, there you are, Natalia Ivanovna! How are you, my dear?

[*They kiss each other.*]

NATASHA. Congratulations! You've such a lot of people here, I feel dreadfully shy. . . .

OLGA. It's all right, they're all old friends. [*Alarmed, dropping her voice.*] You've got a green belt on! My dear, that's surely a mistake!

NATASHA. Why, is it a bad omen, or what?

OLGA. No, but it just doesn't go with your dress . . . it looks so strange. . . .

NATASHA [*tearfully*]. Really? But it isn't really green, you know, it's a sort of dull colour. . . . [*Follows* OLGA *to the ballroom.*]

[*All are now seated at the table; the drawing-room is empty.*]

KOOLYGHIN. Irena, you know, I do wish you'd find yourself a
good husband. In my view it's high time you got married.

CHEBUTYKIN. You ought to get yourself a nice little husband,
too, Natalia Ivanovna.

KOOLYGHIN. Natalia Ivanovna already has a husband in view.

MASHA [*strikes her plate with her fork*]. A glass of wine for me,
please! Three cheers for our jolly old life! We keep our end
up, we do!

KOOLYGHIN. Masha, you won't get more than five out of ten
for good conduct!

VERSHININ. I say, this liqueur's very nice. What is it made of?

SOLIONY. Black beetles!

IRENA. Ugh! ugh! How disgusting!

OLGA. We're having roast turkey for dinner to-night, and then
apple tart. Thank goodness, I'll be here all day to-day . . .
this evening, too. You must all come this evening.

VERSHININ. May I come in the evening, too?

IRENA. Yes, please do.

NATASHA. They don't stand on ceremony here.

CHEBUTYKIN. "Nature created us for love alone." . . . [*Laughs.*]

ANDREY [*crossly*]. Will you stop it, please? Aren't you tired of
it yet?

[*FEDOTIK and* RODÉ *come in with a large basket of flowers.*]

FEDOTIK. Just look here, they're having lunch already!

RODÉ [*in a loud voice*]. Having their lunch? So they are, they're
having lunch already.

FEDOTIK. Wait half a minute. [*Takes a snapshot.*] One! Just
one minute more! . . . [*Takes another snapshot.*] Two! All
over now.

[*They pick up the basket and go into the ballroom where
they are greeted uproariously.*]

RODÉ [*loudly*]. Congratulations, Irena Serghyeevna! I wish you
all the best, everything you'd wish for yourself! Gorgeous
weather to-day, absolutely marvellous. I've been out walk-

ing the whole morning with the boys. You do know that I teach gym at the high school, don't you? . . .

FEDOTIK. You may move now, Irena Serghyeevna, that is, if you want to. [*Takes a snapshot.*] You do look attractive to-day. [*Takes a top out of his pocket.*] By the way, look at this top. It's got a wonderful hum.

IRENA. What a sweet little thing!

MASHA. "A green oak grows by a curving shore, And round that oak hangs a golden chain." . . . A green chain around that oak. . . . [*Peevishly.*] Why do I keep on saying that? Those lines have been worrying me all day long!

KOOLYGHIN. Do you know, we're thirteen at table?

RODÉ [*loudly*]. You don't really believe in these old superstitions, do you? [*Laughter.*]

KOOLYGHIN. When thirteen people sit down to table, it means that some of them are in love. Is it you, by any chance, Ivan Romanych?

CHEBUTYKIN. Oh, I'm just an old sinner. . . . But what I can't make out is why Natalia Ivanovna looks so embarrassed.

[*Loud laughter.* NATASHA *runs out into the drawing-room,* ANDREY *follows her.*]

ANDREY. Please, Natasha, don't take any notice of them! Stop . . . wait a moment. . . . Please!

NATASHA. I feel so ashamed. . . . I don't know what's the matter with me, and they're all laughing at me. It's awful of me to leave the table like that, but I couldn't help it. . . . I just couldn't. . . . [*Covers her face with her hands.*]

ANDREY. My dear girl, please, please don't get upset. Honestly, they don't mean any harm, they're just teasing. My dear, sweet girl, they're really good-natured folks, they all are, and they're fond of us both. Come over to the window, they can't see us there. . . . [*Looks round.*]

NATASHA. You see, I'm not used to being with a lot of people.

ANDREY. Oh, how young you are, Natasha, how wonderfully, beautifully young! My dear, sweet girl, don't get so upset!

Do believe me, believe me. . . . I'm so happy, so full of love, of joy. . . . No, they can't see us here! They can't see us! How did I come to love you, when was it? . . . I don't understand anything. My precious, my sweet, my innocent girl, please—I want you to marry me! I love you, I love you as I've never loved anybody. . . . [*Kisses her.*]

[*Enter two officers and, seeing* NATASHA *and* ANDREY *kissing, stand and stare in amazement.*]

ACT TWO

[*The scene is the same as in Act 1.*
It is eight o'clock in the evening. The faint sound of an accordion is heard coming from the street.

The stage is unlit. Enter NATALIA IVANOVNA *in a dressing-gown, carrying a candle. She crosses the stage and stops by the door leading to* ANDREY'S *room.*]

NATASHA. What are you doing, Andriusha? Reading? It's all right, I only wanted to know. . . . [*Goes to another door, opens it, looks inside and shuts it again.*] No one's left a light anywhere. . . .

ANDREY [*enters with a book in his hand*]. What is it, Natasha?

NATASHA. I was just going round to see if anyone had left a light anywhere. It's carnival week, and the servants are so excited about it . . . anything might happen! You've got to watch them. Last night about twelve o'clock I happened to go into the dining-room, and—would you believe it?—there was a candle alight on the table. I've not found out who lit it. [*Puts the candle down.*] What time is it?

ANDREY [*glances at his watch*]. Quarter past eight.

NATASHA. And Olga and Irena still out. They aren't back from work yet, poor things! Olga's still at some teachers' conference, and Irena's at the post office. [*Sighs.*] This morning I said to Irena: "Do take care of yourself, my dear." But she won't listen. Did you say it was a quarter past eight? I'm afraid Bobik is not at all well. Why does he get so cold? Yesterday he had a temperature, but to-day he feels quite cold when you touch him. . . . I'm so afraid!

ANDREY. It's all right, Natasha. The boy's well enough.

NATASHA. Still, I think he ought to have a special diet. I'm so anxious about him. By the way, they tell me that some carnival party's supposed to be coming here soon after nine. I'd rather they didn't come, Andriusha.

ANDREY. Well, I really don't know what I can do. They've been asked to come.

NATASHA. This morning the dear little fellow woke up and looked at me, and then suddenly he smiled. He recognized me, you see. "Good morning, Bobik," I said, "good morning, darling precious!" And then he laughed. Babies understand everything, you know, they understand us perfectly well. Anyway, Andriusha, I'll tell the servants not to let that carnival party in.

ANDREY [*irresolutely*]. Well . . . it's really for my sisters to decide, isn't it? It's their house, after all.

NATASHA. Yes, it's their house as well. I'll tell them, too. . . . They're so kind. . . . [*Walks off.*] I've ordered sour milk for supper. The doctor says you ought to eat nothing but sour milk, or you'll never get any thinner. [*Stops.*] Bobik feels cold. I'm afraid his room is too cold for him. He ought to move into a warmer room, at least until the warm weather comes. Irena's room, for instance—that's just a perfect room for a baby: it's dry, and it gets the sun all day long. We must tell her: perhaps she'd share Olga's room for a bit. . . . In any case, she's never at home during the day, she only sleeps there. . . . [*A pause.*] Andriusha, why don't you say anything?

ANDREY. I was just day-dreaming. . . . There's nothing to say, anyway. . . .

NATASHA. Well. . . . What was it I was going to tell you? Oh, yes! Ferapont from the Council Office wants to see you about something.

ANDREY [*yawns*]. Tell him to come up.

[NATASHA *goes out.* ANDREY, *bending over the candle which she has left behind, begins to read his book. Enter* FERA-PONT *in an old shabby overcoat, his collar turned up, his ears muffled in a scarf.*]

ANDREY. Hullo, old chap! What did you want to see me about?

FERAPONT. The chairman's sent you the register and a letter or something. Here they are. [*Hands him the book and the letter.*]

ANDREY. Thanks. That's all right. Incidentally, why have you come so late? It's gone eight already.

FERAPONT. What's that?

ANDREY [*raising his voice*]. I said, why have you come so late? It's gone eight already.

FERAPONT. That's right. It was still daylight when I came first, but they wouldn't let me see you. The master's engaged, they said. Well, if you're engaged, you're engaged. I'm not in a hurry. [*Thinking that* ANDREY *has said something.*] What's that?

ANDREY. Nothing. [*Turns over the pages of the register.*] To-morrow's Friday, there's no meeting, but I'll go to the office just the same . . . do some work. I'm so bored at home! . . . [*A pause.*] Yes, my dear old fellow, how things do change, what a fraud life is! So strange! To-day I picked up this book, just out of boredom, because I hadn't anything to do. It's a copy of some lectures I attended at the University. . . . Good Heavens! Just think—I'm secretary of the local council now, and Protopopov's chairman, and the most I can ever hope for is to become a member of the council myself! I—a member of the local council! I, who dream every night that I'm a professor in Moscow University, a famous academician, the pride of all Russia!

FERAPONT. I'm sorry, I can't tell you. I don't hear very well.

ANDREY. If you could hear properly I don't think I'd be talking to you like this. I must talk to someone, but my wife doesn't seem to understand me, and as for my sisters . . . I'm afraid of them for some reason or other, I'm afraid of them laughing at me and pulling my leg. . . . I don't drink and I don't like going to pubs, but my word! how I'd enjoy an hour or so at Tyestov's, or the Great Moscow Restaurant! Yes, my dear fellow, I would indeed!

FERAPONT. The other day at the office a contractor was telling me about some business men who were eating pancakes in

Moscow. One of them ate forty pancakes and died. It was either forty or fifty, I can't remember exactly.

ANDREY. You can sit in some huge restaurant in Moscow without knowing anyone, and no one knowing you; yet somehow you don't feel that you don't belong there. . . . Whereas here you know everybody, and everybody knows you, and yet you don't feel you belong here, you feel you don't belong at all. . . . You're lonely and you feel a stranger.

FERAPONT. What's that? [*A pause.*] It was the same man that told me—of course, he may have been lying—he said that there's an enormous rope stretched right across Moscow.

ANDREY. Whatever for?

FERAPONT. I'm sorry, I can't tell you. That's what he said.

ANDREY. What nonsense! [*Reads the book.*] Have you ever been to Moscow?

FERAPONT [*after a pause*]. No. It wasn't God's wish. [*A pause.*] Shall I go now?

ANDREY. Yes, you may go. Good-bye. [FERAPONT *goes out.*] Good-bye. [*Reading.*] Come in the morning to take some letters. . . . You can go now. [*A pause.*] He's gone. [*A bell rings.*] Yes, that's how it is. . . . [*Stretches and slowly goes to his room.*]

[*Singing is heard off stage; a nurse is putting a baby to sleep. Enter* MASHA *and* VERSHININ. *While they talk together, a maid lights a lamp and candles in the ballroom.*]

MASHA. I don't know. [*A pause.*] I don't know. Habit's very important, of course. For instance, after Father died, for a long time we couldn't get accustomed to the idea that we hadn't any orderlies to wait on us. But, habit apart, I think it's quite right what I was saying. Perhaps it's different in other places, but in this town the military certainly do seem to be the nicest and most generous and best-mannered people.

VERSHININ. I'm thirsty. I could do with a nice glass of tea.

MASHA [*glances at her watch*]. They'll bring it in presently. You see, they married me off when I was eighteen. I was afraid of my husband because he was a school-master, and I had only just left school myself. He seemed terribly learned then, very clever and important. Now it's quite different, unfortunately.

VERSHININ. Yes. . . . I see. . . .

MASHA. I don't say anything against my husband—I'm used to him now—but there are such a lot of vulgar and unpleasant and offensive people among the other civilians. Vulgarity upsets me, it makes me feel insulted, I actually suffer when I meet someone who lacks refinement and gentle manners, and courtesy. When I'm with the other teachers, my husband's friends, I just suffer.

VERSHININ. Yes, of course. But I should have thought that in a town like this the civilians and the army people were equally uninteresting. There's nothing to choose between them. If you talk to any educated person here, civilian or military, he'll generally tell you that he's just worn out. It's either his wife, or his house, or his estate, or his horse, or something. . . . We Russians are capable of such elevated thoughts—then why do we have such low ideals in practical life? Why is it, why?

MASHA. Why?

VERSHININ. Yes, why does his wife wear him out, why do his children wear him out? And what about *him* wearing out his wife and children?

MASHA. You're a bit low-spirited to-day, aren't you?

VERSHININ. Perhaps. I haven't had any dinner to-day. I've had nothing to eat since morning. One of my daughters is a bit off colour, and when the children are ill, I get so worried. I feel utterly conscience-stricken at having given them a mother like theirs. Oh, if only you could have seen her this morning! What a despicable woman! We started quarrelling at seven o'clock, and at nine I just walked out and slammed the door. [*A pause.*] I never talk about these things in the ordinary way. It's a strange thing, but you're the only person I feel I dare complain to. [*Kisses her hand.*] Don't be angry with me. I've nobody, nobody but you. . . . [*A pause.*]

MASHA. What a noise the wind's making in the stove! Just before Father died the wind howled in the chimney just like that.

VERSHININ. Are you superstitious?

MASHA. Yes.

VERSHININ. How strange. [*Kisses her hand.*] You really are a wonderful creature, a marvellous creature! Wonderful, marvellous! It's quite dark here, but I can see your eyes shining.

MASHA [*moves to another chair*]. There's more light over here.

VERSHININ. I love you, I love you, I love you. . . . I love your eyes, I love your movements. . . . I dream about them. A wonderful, marvellous being!

MASHA [*laughing softly*]. When you talk to me like that, somehow I can't help laughing, although I'm afraid at the same time. Don't say it again, please. [*Half-audibly.*] Well, no . . . go on. I don't mind. . . . [*Covers her face with her hands.*] I don't mind. . . . Someone's coming. . . . Let's talk about something else. . . .

[*Enter* IRENA *and* TOOZENBACH *through the ballroom.*]

TOOZENBACH. I have a triple-barrelled name—Baron Toozenbach-Krone-Alschauer—but actually I'm a Russian. I was baptized in the Greek-Orthodox faith, just like yourself. I haven't really got any German characteristics, except maybe the obstinate patient way I keep on pestering you. Look how I bring you home every evening.

IRENA. How tired I am!

TOOZENBACH. And I'll go on fetching you from the post office and bringing you home every evening for the next twenty years—unless you send me away. . . . [*Noticing* MASHA *and* VERSHININ, *with pleasure.*] Oh, it's you! How are you?

IRENA. Well, here I am, home at last! [*To* MASHA.] A woman came into the post office just before I left. She wanted to send a wire to her brother in Saratov to tell him her son had just died, but she couldn't remember the address. So we had to send the wire without an address, just to Saratov. She was crying and I was rude to her, for no reason at all. "I've no time to waste," I told her. So stupid of me. We're having the carnival crowd to-day, aren't we?

MASHA. Yes.

IRENA [*sits down*]. How nice it is to rest! I am tired!

TOOZENBACH [*smiling*]. When you come back from work, you look so young, so pathetic, somehow. . . . [*A pause.*]

IRENA. I'm tired. No, I don't like working at the post office, I don't like it at all.

MASHA. You've got thinner. . . . [*Whistles.*] You look younger, too, and your face looks quite boyish.

TOOZENBACH. It's the way she does her hair.

IRENA. I must look for another job. This one doesn't suit me. It hasn't got what I always longed for and dreamed about. It's the sort of work you do without inspiration, without even thinking.

[*Someone knocks at the floor from below.*]

That's the Doctor knocking. [*To* TOOZENBACH.] Will you answer him, dear? . . . I can't. . . . I'm so tired.

TOOZENBACH [*knocks on the floor*].

IRENA. He'll be up in a moment. We must do something about all this. Andrey and the Doctor went to the club last night and lost at cards again. They say Andrey lost two hundred roubles.

MASHA [*with indifference*]. Well, what are we to do about it?

IRENA. He lost a fortnight ago, and he lost in December, too. I wish to goodness he'd lose everything we've got, and soon, too, and then perhaps we'd move out of this place. Good Heavens, I dream of Moscow every night. Sometimes I feel as if I were going mad. [*Laughs.*] We're going to Moscow in June. How many months are there till June? . . . February, March, April, May . . . nearly half-a-year!

MASHA. We must take care that Natasha doesn't get to know about him losing at cards.

IRENA. I don't think she cares.

[*Enter* CHEBUTYKIN. *He has been resting on his bed since*

dinner and has only just got up. He combs his beard, then sits down at the table and takes out a newspaper.]

MASHA. There he is. Has he paid his rent yet?

IRENA [*laughs*]. No. Not a penny for the last eight months. I suppose he's forgotten.

MASHA [*laughs*]. How solemn he looks sitting there!

[*They all laugh. A pause.*]

IRENA. Why don't you say something, Alexandr Ignatyevich?

VERSHININ. I don't know. I'm just longing for some tea. I'd give my life for a glass of tea! I've had nothing to eat since morning. . . .

CHEBUTYKIN. Irena Serghyeevna!

IRENA. What is it?

CHEBUTYKIN. Please come here. *Venez ici!* [IRENA *goes over to him and sits down at the table.*] I can't do without you.

[IRENA *lays out the cards for a game of patience.*]

VERSHININ. Well, if we can't have any tea, let's do a bit of philosophizing, anyway.

TOOZENBACH. Yes, let's. What about?

VERSHININ. What about? Well . . . let's try to imagine what life will be like after we're dead, say in two or three hundred years.

TOOZENBACH. All right, then. . . . After we're dead, people will fly about in balloons, the cut of their coats will be different, the sixth sense will be discovered, and possibly even developed and used, for all I know. . . . But I believe, life itself will remain the same; it will still be difficult and full of mystery and full of happiness. And in a thousand years' time people will still be sighing and complaining: "How hard this business of living is!"—and yet they'll still be scared of death and unwilling to die, just as they are now.

VERSHININ [*after a moment's thought*]. Well, you know . . . how shall I put it? I think everything in the world is bound to change gradually—in fact, it's changing before our very eyes. In two or three hundred years, or maybe in a thousand years—it doesn't matter how long exactly—life will be different. It will be happy. Of course, we shan't be able to enjoy that future life, but all the same, what we're living for now is to create it, we work and . . . yes, we suffer in order to create it. That's the goal of our life, and you might say that's the only happiness we shall ever achieve.

MASHA [*laughs quietly*].

TOOZENBACH. Why are you laughing?

MASHA. I don't know. I've been laughing all day to-day.

VERSHININ [*to* TOOZENBACH]. I went to the same cadet school as you did but I never went on to the Military Academy. I read a great deal, of course, but I never know what books I ought to choose, and probably I read a lot of stuff that's not worth anything. But the longer I live the more I seem to long for knowledge. My hair's going grey and I'm getting on in years, and yet how little I know, how little! All the same, I think I do know one thing which is not only true but also most important. I'm sure of it. Oh, if only I could convince you that there's not going to be any happiness for our own generation, that there mustn't be and won't be. . . . We've just got to work and work. All the happiness is reserved for our descendants, our remote descendants. [*A pause.*] Anyway, if I'm not to be happy, then at least my children's children will be.

[FEDOTIK *and* RODÉ *enter the ballroom; they sit down and sing quietly, one of them playing on a guitar.*]

TOOZENBACH. So you won't even allow us to dream of happiness! But what if I *am* happy?

VERSHININ. You're not.

TOOZENBACH [*flinging up his hands and laughing*]. We don't understand one another, that's obvious. How can I convince you?

MASHA [*laughs quietly*].

TOOZENBACH [*holds up a finger to her*]. Show a finger to her and she'll laugh! [*To* VERSHININ.] And life will be just the same as ever not merely in a couple of hundred years' time, but in a million years. Life doesn't change, it always goes on the same; it follows its own laws, which don't concern us, which we can't discover anyway. Think of the birds that migrate in the autumn, the cranes, for instance: they just fly on and on. It doesn't matter what sort of thoughts they've got in their heads, great thoughts or little thoughts, they just fly on and on, not knowing where or why. And they'll go on flying no matter how many philosophers they happen to have flying with them. Let them philosophize as much as they like, as long as they go on flying.

MASHA. Isn't there some meaning?

TOOZENBACH. Meaning? . . . Look out there, it's snowing. What's the meaning of that? [*A pause.*]

MASHA. I think a human being has got to have some faith, or at least he's got to seek faith. Otherwise his life will be empty, empty. . . . How can you live and not know why the cranes fly, why children are born, why the stars shine in the sky! . . . You must either know why you live, or else . . . nothing matters . . . everything's just wild grass. . . . [*A pause.*]

VERSHININ. All the same, I'm sorry my youth's over.

MASHA. "It's a bore to be alive in this world, friends," that's what Gogol says.

TOOZENBACH. And I feel like saying: it's hopeless arguing with you, friends! I give you up.

CHEBUTYKIN [*reads out of the paper*]. Balsac's marriage took place at Berdichev.[1]

IRENA [*sings softly to herself*].

CHEBUTYKIN. Must write this down in my notebook. [*Writes.*] Balsac's marriage took place at Berdichev. [*Reads on.*]

IRENA [*playing patience, pensively*]. Balsac's marriage took place at Berdichev.

TOOZENBACH. Well, I've thrown in my hand. Did you know that

[1] A town in Western Russia well known for its almost exclusively Jewish population.

I'd sent in my resignation, Maria Serghyeevna?

MASHA. Yes, I heard about it. I don't see anything good in it, either. I don't like civilians.

TOOZENBACH. Never mind. [Gets up.] What sort of a soldier do I make, anyway? I'm not even good-looking. Well, what does it matter? I'll work. I'd like to do such a hard day's work that when I came home in the evening I'd fall on my bed exhausted and go to sleep at once. [Goes to the ball-room.] I should think working men sleep well at nights!

FEDOTIK [to IRENA]. I've got you some coloured crayons at Pyzhikov's, in Moscow Street. And this little penknife, too. . . .

IRENA. You still treat me as if I were a little girl. I wish you'd remember I'm grown up now. [Takes the crayons and the penknife, joyfully.] They're awfully nice!

FEDOTIK. Look, I bought a knife for myself, too. You see, it's got another blade here, and then another . . . this thing's for cleaning your ears, and these are nail-scissors, and this is for cleaning your nails. . . .

RODÉ [in a loud voice]. Doctor, how old are you?

CHEBUTYKIN. I? Thirty-two.

[Laughter.]

FEDOTIK. I'll show you another kind of patience. [Sets out the cards.]

[The samovar is brought in, and ANFISA attends to it. Shortly afterwards NATASHA comes in and begins to fuss around the table.]

SOLIONY [enters, bows to the company and sits down at the table].

VERSHININ. What a wind, though!

MASHA. Yes. I'm tired of winter! I've almost forgotten what summer is like.

IRENA [playing patience]. I'm going to go out. We'll get to Moscow!

FEDOTIK. No, it's not going out. You see, the eight has to go on
   the two of spades. [*Laughs.*] That means you won't go to
   Moscow.

CHEBUTYKIN [*reads the paper*]. Tzitzikar. Smallpox is raging. . . .

ANFISA [*goes up to* MASHA]. Masha, the tea's ready, dear. [*To*
   VERSHININ.] Will you please come to the table, your Excel-
   lency? Forgive me, your name's slipped my memory. . . .

MASHA. Bring it here, Nanny. I'm not coming over there.

IRENA. Nanny!

ANFISA. Comi-ing!

NATASHA [*to* SOLIONY]. You know, even tiny babies understand
   what we say perfectly well! "Good morning, Bobik," I said
   to him only to-day, "Good morning, my precious!"—and
   then he looked at me in such a special sort of way. You may
   say it's only a mother's imagination, but it isn't, I do assure
   you. No, no! He really is an extraordinary child!

SOLIONY. If that child were mine, I'd cook him up in a frying
   pan and eat him. [*Picks up his glass, goes into the drawing-
   room and sits down in a corner.*]

NATASHA [*covers her face with her hands*]. What a rude, ill-
   mannered person!

MASHA. People who don't even notice whether it's summer or
   winter are lucky! I think I'd be indifferent to the weather
   if I were living in Moscow.

VERSHININ. I've just been reading the diary of some French
   cabinet minister—he wrote it in prison. He got sent to
   prison in connection with the Panama affair. He writes with
   such a passionate delight about the birds he can see through
   the prison window—the birds he never even noticed when
   he was a cabinet minister. Of course, now he's released he
   won't notice them any more. . . . And in the same way, you
   won't notice Moscow once you live there again. We're not
   happy and we can't be happy: we only want happiness.

TOOZENBACH [*picks up a box from the table*]. I say, where are
   all the chocolates?

IRENA. Soliony's eaten them.

TOOZENBACH. All of them?

ANFISA [*serving* VERSHININ *with tea*]. Here's a letter for you, Sir.

VERSHININ. For me? [*Takes the letter.*] From my daughter. [*Reads it.*] Yes, of course. . . . Forgive me, Maria Sergh-yeevna, I'll just leave quietly. I won't have any tea. [*Gets up, agitated.*] Always the same thing. . . .

MASHA. What is it? Secret?

VERSHININ [*in a low voice*]. My wife's taken poison again. I must go. I'll get away without them seeing me. All this is so dreadfully unpleasant. [*Kisses* MASHA'S *hand.*] My dear, good, sweet girl. . . . I'll go out this way, quietly. . . . [*Goes out.*]

ANFISA. Where's he off to? And I've just brought him some tea! What a queer fellow!

MASHA [*flaring up*]. Leave me alone! Why do you keep worrying me? Why don't you leave me in peace? [*Goes to the table, cup in hand.*] I'm sick and tired of you, silly old woman!

ANFISA. Why. . . . I didn't mean to offend you, dear.

ANDREY'S VOICE [*off stage*]. Anfisa!

ANFISA [*mimics him*]. Anfisa! Sitting there in his den! . . . [*Goes out.*]

MASHA [*by the table in the ballroom, crossly*]. Do let me sit down somewhere! [*Jumbles up the cards laid out on the table.*] You take up the whole table with your cards! Why don't you get on with your tea?

IRENA. How bad-tempered you are, Mashka!

MASHA. Well, if I'm bad-tempered, don't talk to me, then. Don't touch me!

CHEBUTYKIN [*laughs*]. Don't touch her! . . . Take care you don't touch her!

MASHA. You may be sixty, but you're always gabbling some damn nonsense or other, just like a child. . . .

NATASHA [*sighs*]. My dear Masha, need you use such expressions? You know, with your good looks you'd be thought so charming, even by the best people—yes, I honestly mean it—if only you wouldn't use these expressions of yours! Je vous prie, pardonnez moi, Marie, mais vous avez des manières un peu grossières.

TOOZENBACH [*with suppressed laughter*]. Pass me . . . I say, will you please pass me. . . . Is that cognac over there, or what? . . .

NATASHA. Il paraît que mon Bobik déjà ne dort pas. . . . I think he's awake. He's not been too well to-day. I must go and see him . . . excuse me. [*Goes out.*]

IRENA. I say, where has Alexandr Ignatyevich gone to?

MASHA. He's gone home. His wife's done something queer again.

TOOZENBACH [*goes over to* SOLIONY *with a decanter of cognac*]. You always sit alone brooding over something or other—though what it's all about nobody knows. Well, let's make it up. Let's have cognac together. [*They drink.*] I suppose I'll have to play the piano all night to-night—a lot of rubbishy tunes, of course. . . . Never mind!

SOLIONY. Why did you say "let's make it up"? We haven't quarrelled.

TOOZENBACH. You always give me the feeling that there's something wrong between us. You're a strange character, no doubt about it.

SOLIONY [*recites*]. "I am strange, but who's not so? Don't be angry, Aleko!"

TOOZENBACH. What's Aleko got to do with it? . . . [*A pause.*]

SOLIONY. When I'm alone with somebody I'm all right, I'm just like other people. But in company, I get depressed and shy, and . . . I talk all sorts of nonsense. All the same, I'm a good deal more honest and well-intentioned than plenty of others. I can prove I am.

TOOZENBACH. You often make me angry because you keep on pestering me when we're in company—but all the same, I do like you for some reason. . . . I'm going to get drunk to-night, whatever happens! Let's have another drink!

SOLIONY. Yes, let's. [*A pause.*] I've never had anything against you personally, Baron. But my temperament's rather like Lermontov's. [*In a low voice.*] I even look a little like Lermontov, I've been told. . . . [*Takes a scent bottle from his pocket and sprinkles some scent on his hands.*]

TOOZENBACH. I have sent in my resignation! Finished! I've been considering it for five years, and now I've made up my mind at last. I'm going to work.

SOLIONY [*recites*]. "Don't be angry, Aleko. . . . Away, away with all your dreams!"

[*During the conversation* ANDREY *enters quietly with a book in his hand and sits down by the candle.*]

TOOZENBACH. I'm going to work!

CHEBUTYKIN [*comes into the drawing-room with* IRENA]. And the food they treated me to was the genuine Caucasian stuff: onion soup, followed by chehartma—that's a meat dish, you know.

SOLIONY. Chereshma isn't meat at all; it's a plant, something like an onion.

CHEBUTYKIN. No-o, my dear friend. Chehartmá isn't an onion, it's roast mutton.

SOLIONY. I tell you chereshma is a kind of onion.

CHEBUTYKIN. Well, why should I argue about it with you? You've never been to the Caucasus and you've never tasted chehartma.

SOLIONY. I haven't tasted it because I can't stand the smell of it. Chereshma stinks just like garlic.

ANDREY [*imploringly*]. Do stop it, friends! Please stop it!

TOOZENBACH. When's the carnival crowd coming along?

IRENA. They promised to be here by nine—that means any moment now.

TOOZENBACH [*embraces* ANDREY *and sings*]. "Ah, my beautiful porch, my lovely new porch, my . . ." [1]

ANDREY [*dances and sings*]. "My new porch all made of maplewood. . . ."

CHEBUTYKIN [*dances*]. "With fancy carving over the door. . . ."

[*Laughter.*]

[1] A traditional Russian dance-song.

TOOZEBACH [*kisses* ANDREY]. Let's have a drink, the devil take it! Andriusha, let's drink to eternal friendship. I'll come with you when you go back to Moscow University.

SOLIONY. Which university? There are two universities in Moscow.

ANDREY. There's only one.

SOLIONY. I tell you there are two.

ANDREY. Never mind, make it three. The more the merrier.

SOLIONY. There are two universities in Moscow.

[*Murmurs of protest and cries of "Hush!"*]

There are two universities in Moscow, an old one and a new one. But if you don't want to listen to what I'm saying, if my conversation irritates you, I can keep silent. In fact I can go to another room. . . . [*Goes out through one of the doors.*]

TOOZENBACH. Bravo, bravo! [*Laughs.*] Let's get started, my friends, I'll play for you. What a funny creature that Soliony is! . . . [*Sits down at the piano and plays a waltz.*]

MASHA [*dances alone*]. The Baron is drunk, the Baron is drunk, the Baron is drunk. . . .

[*Enter* NATASHA.]

NATASHA [*To* CHEBUTYKIN]. Ivan Romanych! [*Speaks to him, then goes out quietly.* CHEBUTYKIN *touches* TOOZENBACH *on the shoulder and whispers to him.*]

IRENA. What is it?

CHEBUTYKIN. It's time we were going. Good-night.

IRENA. But really. . . . What about the carnival party?

ANDREY [*embarrassed*]. The carnival party's not coming. You see, my dear, Natasha says that Bobik isn't very well, and so . . . Anyway, I don't know . . . and I certainly don't care. . . .

IRENA [*shrugs her shoulders*]. Bobik's not very well! . . .

MASHA. Never mind, we'll keep our end up! If they turn us out, out we must go! [*To* IRENA.] It isn't Bobik who's not well, it's her. . . . There! . . . [*Taps her forehead with her finger.*] Petty little bourgeois housewife!

[ANDREY *goes to his room on the right.* CHEBUTYKIN *follows him. The guests say good-bye in the ballroom.*]

FEDOTIK. What a pity! I'd been hoping to spend the evening here, but of course, if the baby's ill. . . . I'll bring him some toys to-morrow.

RODÉ [*in a loud voice*]. I had a good long sleep after lunch to-day on purpose, I thought I'd be dancing all night. I mean to say, it's only just nine o'clock.

MASHA. Let's go outside and talk it over. We can decide what to do then.

[*Voices are heard saying "Good-bye! God bless you!" and* TOOZENBACH *is heard laughing gaily. Everyone goes out.* ANFISA *and a maid clear the table and put out the lights. The nurse sings to the baby off-stage. Enter* ANDREY, *wearing an overcoat and hat, followed by* CHEBUTYKIN. *They move quietly.*]

CHEBUTYKIN. I've never found time to get married, somehow . . . partly because my life's just flashed past me like lightning, and partly because I was always madly in love with your mother and she was married. . . .

ANDREY. One shouldn't marry. One shouldn't marry because it's so boring.

CHEBUTYKIN. That may be so, but what about loneliness? You can philosophize as much as you like, dear boy, but loneliness is a dreadful thing. Although, really . . . well, it doesn't matter a damn, of course! . . .

ANDREY. Let's get along quickly.

CHEBUTYKIN. What's the hurry? There's plenty of time.

ANDREY. I'm afraid my wife may try to stop me.

CHEBUTYKIN. Ah!

ANDREY. I won't play cards to-night, I'll just sit and watch. I'm not feeling too well. . . . What ought I to do for this breathlessness, Ivan Romanych?

CHEBUTYKIN. Why ask me, dear boy? I can't remember—I

simply don't know.

ANDREY. Let's go through the kitchen.

[*They go out. A bell rings. The ring is repeated, then voices and laughter are heard.*]

IRENA [*coming in*]. What's that?

ANFISA [*in a whisper*]. The carnival party.

[*The bell rings again.*]

IRENA. Tell them there's no one at home, Nanny. Apologize to them.

[ANFISA *goes out.* IRENA *walks up and down the room, lost in thought. She seems agitated. Enter* SOLIONY.]

SOLIONY [*puzzled*]. There's no one here. . . . Where is everybody?

IRENA. They've gone home.

SOLIONY. How strange! Then you're alone here?

IRENA. Yes, alone. [*A pause.*] Well . . . good-night.

SOLIONY. I know I behaved tactlessly just now, I lost control of myself. But you're different from the others, you stand out high above them—you're pure, you can see where the truth lies. . . . You're the only person in the world who can possibly understand me. I love you. . . . I love you with a deep, infinite . . .

IRENA. Do please go away. Good-night!

SOLIONY. I can't live without you. [*Follows her.*] Oh, it's such a delight just to look at you! [*With tears.*] Oh, my happiness! Your glorious, marvellous, entrancing eyes—eyes like no other woman's I've ever seen. . . .

IRENA [*coldly*]. Please stop it, Vassily Vassilich!

SOLIONY. I've never spoken to you of my love before . . . it makes me feel as if I were living on a different planet. . . . [*Rubs his forehead.*] Never mind! I can't force you to love me, obviously. But I don't intend to have any rivals—successful rivals, I mean. . . . No, no! I swear to you by everything I hold sacred that if there's anyone else, I'll kill him.

Oh, how wonderful you are!

[*Enter* NATASHA *carrying a candle.*]

NATASHA [*pokes her head into one room, then into another, but passes the door leading to her husband's room*]. Andrey's reading in there. Better let him read. Forgive me, Vassily Vassilich, I didn't know you were here. I'm afraid I'm not properly dressed.

SOLIONY. I don't care. Good-bye. [*Goes out.*]

NATASHA. You must be tired, my poor dear girl. [*Kisses* IRENA.] You ought to go to bed earlier.

IRENA. Is Bobik asleep?

NATASHA. Yes, he's asleep. But he's not sleeping peacefully. By the way, my dear, I've been meaning to speak to you for some time but there's always been something . . . either you're not here, or I'm too busy. . . . You see, I think that Bobik's nursery is so cold and damp. . . . And your room is just ideal for a baby. Darling, do you think you could move into Olga's room?

IRENA [*not understanding her*]. Where to?

[*The sound of bells is heard outside, as a "troika" is driven up to the house.*]

NATASHA. You can share a room with Olia for the time being, and Bobik can have your room. He is such a darling! This morning I said to him: "Bobik, you're my very own! My very own!" And he just gazed at me with his dear little eyes. [*The door bell rings.*] That must be Olga. How late she is!

[*A maid comes up to* NATASHA *and whispers in her ear.*]

NATASHA. Protopopov! What a funny fellow! Protopopov's come to ask me to go for a drive with him. In a troika! [*Laughs.*] Aren't these men strange creatures! . . .

[*The door bell rings again.*]

Someone's ringing. Shall I go for a short drive? Just for a

quarter of an hour? [*To the maid.*] Tell him I'll be down in a minute. [*The door bell rings.*] That's the bell again. I suppose it's Olga. [*Goes out.*]

[*The maid runs out;* IRENA *sits lost in thought. Enter* KOOLYGHIN *and* OLGA, *followed by* VERSHININ.]

KOOLYGHIN. Well! What's the meaning of this? You said you were going to have a party.

VERSHININ. It's a strange thing. I left here about half an hour ago, and they were expecting a carnival party then.

IRENA. They've all gone.

KOOLYGHIN. Masha's gone, too? Where has she gone to? And why is Protopopov waiting outside in a troika? Who's he waiting for?

IRENA. Please don't ask me questions. I'm tired.

KOOLYGHIN. You . . . spoilt child!

OLGA. The conference has only just ended. I'm quite worn out. The headmistress is ill and I'm deputizing for her. My head's aching, oh, my head, my head. . . . [*Sits down.*] Andrey lost two hundred roubles at cards last night. The whole town's talking about it.

KOOLYGHIN. Yes, the conference exhausted me, too. [*Sits down.*]

VERSHININ. So now my wife's taken it into her head to try to frighten me. She tried to poison herself. However, everything's all right now, so I can relax, thank goodness. . . . So we've got to go away? Well, good-night to you, all the best. Fiodor Illych, would you care to come along with me somewhere or other? I can't stay at home to-night, I really can't. . . . Do come!

KOOLYGHIN. I'm tired. I don't think I'll come. [*Gets up.*] I'm tired. Has my wife gone home?

IRENA. I think so.

KOOLYGHIN [*kisses* IRENA's *hand*]. Good-night. We can rest to-morrow and the day after to-morrow, two whole days! Well, I wish you all the best. [*Going out.*] How I long for some tea! I reckoned on spending the evening in congenial company, but—*o, fallacem hominum spem!* Always use the accusative case in exclamations.

VERSHININ. Well, it looks as if I'll have to go somewhere by myself. [*Goes out with* KOOLYGHIN, *whistling.*]

OLGA. My head aches, oh, my head. . . . Andrey lost at cards . . . the whole town's talking. . . . I'll go and lie down. [*Going out.*] To-morrow I'm free. Heavens, what a joy! To-morrow I'm free, and the day after to-morrow I'm free. . . . My head's aching, oh, my poor head. . . .

IRENA [*alone*]. They've all gone. No one's left.

[*Someone is playing an accordion in the street. The nurse sings in the next room.*]

NATASHA [*crosses the ballroom, wearing a fur coat and cap. She is followed by the maid*]. I'll be back in half an hour. I'm just going for a little drive. [*Goes out.*]

IRENA [*alone, with intense longing*]. Moscow! Moscow! Moscow!

ACT THREE

[*A bedroom now shared by* OLGA *and* IRENA. *There are two beds, one on the right, the other on the left, each screened off from the centre of the room. It is past two o'clock in the morning. Off-stage the alarm is being sounded on account of a fire which has been raging for some time. The inmates of the house have not yet been to bed.* MASHA *is lying on a couch, dressed, as usual, in black.* OLGA *and* ANFISA *come in.*]

ANFISA. Now they're sitting down there, under the stairs. . . . I keep telling them to come upstairs, that they shouldn't sit down there, but they just cry. "We don't know where our Papa is," they say, "perhaps he's got burned in the fire." What an idea! And there are people in the yard, too . . . half-dressed. . . .

OLGA [*takes a dress out of a wardrobe*]. Take this grey frock, Nanny. . . . And this one. . . . This blouse, too. . . . And this skirt. Oh, Heavens! what is happening! Apparently the whole of the Kirsanovsky Streets' been burnt down. . . . Take this . . . and this, too. . . . [*Throws the clothes into* ANFISA'S *arms.*] The poor Vershinins had a fright. Their house only just escaped being burnt down. They'll have to spend the night here . . . we mustn't let them go home. Poor Fedotik's lost everything, he's got nothing left. . . .

ANFISA. I'd better call Ferapont, Oliushka, I can't carry all this.

OLGA [*rings*]. No one takes any notice when I ring. [*Calls through the door.*] Is anyone there? Will someone come up, please!

[*A window, red with the glow of the fire, can be seen through the open door. The sound of a passing fire engine is heard.*]

How dreadful it all is! And how tired of it I am! [*Enter*
FERAPONT.] Take this downstairs please. . . . The Kolotilin
girls are sitting under the stairs . . . give it to them. And this,
too. . . .

FERAPONT. Very good, Madam. Moscow was burned down in
1812 just the same. Mercy on us! . . . Yes, the French were
surprised all right.

OLGA. Go along now, take this down.

FERAPONT. Very good. [*Goes out.*]

OLGA. Give it all away, Nanny, dear. We won't keep anything,
give it all away. . . . I'm so tired, I can hardly keep on my
feet. We mustn't let the Vershinins go home. The little girls
can sleep in the drawing-room, and Alexandr Ignatyevich
can share the downstairs room with the Baron. Fedotik can
go in with the Baron, too, or maybe he'd better sleep in the
ballroom. The doctor's gone and got drunk—you'd think
he'd done it on purpose; he's so hopelessly drunk that we
can't let anyone go into his room. Vershinin's wife will have
to go into the drawing-room, too.

ANFISA [*wearily*]. Don't send me away, Oliushka, darling! Don't
send me away!

OLGA. What nonsense you're talking, Nanny! No one's sending
you away.

ANFISA [*leans her head against* OLGA's *breast*]. My dearest girl!
I do work, you know, I work as hard as I can. . . . I suppose
now I'm getting weaker, I'll be told to go. But where can I
go? Where? I'm eighty years old. I'm over eighty-one!

OLGA. You sit down for a while, Nanny. . . . You're tired, you
poor dear. . . . [*Makes her sit down.*] Just rest a bit. You've
turned quite pale.

[*Enter* NATASHA.]

NATASHA. They're saying we ought to start a subscription in
aid of the victims of the fire. You know—form a society or
something for the purpose. Well, why not? It's an excellent
idea! In any case it's up to us to help the poor as best we
can. Bobik and Sofochka are fast asleep as if nothing had

happened. We've got such a crowd of people in the house; the place seems full of people whichever way you turn. There's 'flu about in the town. . . . I'm so afraid the children might catch it.

OLGA [*without listening to her*]. You can't see the fire from this room; it's quiet in here.

NATASHA. Yes. . . . I suppose my hair is all over the place. [*Stands in front of the mirror.*] They say I've got stouter, but it's not true! I'm not a bit stouter. Masha's asleep . . . she's tired, poor girl. . . . [*To* ANFISA, *coldly*.] How dare you sit down in my presence? Get up! Get out of here! [ANFISA *goes out. A pause.*] I can't understand why you keep that old woman in the house.

OLGA [*taken aback*]. Forgive me for saying it, but I can't understand how you . . .

NATASHA. She's quite useless here. She's just a peasant woman, her right place is in the country. You're spoiling her. I do like order in the home, I don't like having useless people about. [*Strokes* OLGA's *cheek*.] You're tired, my poor dear! Our headmistress is tired! You know, when my Sofochka grows up and goes to school, I'll be frightened of you.

OLGA. I'm not going to be a headmistress.

NATASHA. You'll be asked to, Olechka. It's settled.

OLGA. I'll refuse. I couldn't do it. . . . I wouldn't be strong enough. [*Drinks water.*] You spoke so harshly to Nanny just now. . . . You must forgive me for saying so, but I just can't stand that sort of thing . . . it made me feel quite faint. . . .

NATASHA [*agitated*]. Forgive me, Olia, forgive me. I didn't mean to upset you.

[MASHA *gets up, picks up a pillow and goes out in a huff.*]

OLGA. Please try to understand me, dear. . . . It may be that we've been brought up in a peculiar way, but anyway I just can't bear it. When people are treated like that, it gets me down, I feel quite ill. . . . I simply get unnerved. . . .

NATASHA. Forgive me, dear, forgive me! . . . [*Kisses her.*]

OLGA. Any cruel or tactless remark, even the slightest discourtesy, upsets me. . . .

NATASHA. It's quite true, I know I often say things which would be better left unsaid—but you must agree with me, dear, that she'd be better in the country somewhere.

OLGA. She's been with us for thirty years.

NATASHA. But she can't do any work now, can she? Either I don't understand you, or you don't want to understand me. She can't work, she just sleeps or sits about.

OLGA. Well, let her sit about.

NATASHA [in surprise]. What do you mean, let her sit about? Surely she is a servant! [Tearfully.] No, I don't understand you, Olia! I have a nurse for the children and a wet nurse and we share a maid and a cook. Whatever do we want this old woman for? What for?

[The alarm is sounded again.]

OLGA. I've aged ten years to-night.

NATASHA. We must sort things out, Olia. You're working at your school, and I'm working at home. You're teaching and I'm running the house. And when I say anything about the servants, I know what I'm talking about. . . . That old thief, that old witch must get out of this house to-morrow! . . . [Stamps her feet.] How dare you vex me so? How dare you? [Recovering her self-control.] Really, if you don't move downstairs, we'll always be quarrelling. This is quite dreadful!

[Enter KOOLYGHIN.]

KOOLYGHIN. Where's Masha? It's time we went home. They say the fire's getting less fierce. [Stretches.] Only one block got burnt down, but to begin with it looked as if the whole town was going to be set on fire by that wind. [Sits down.] I'm so tired, Olechka, my dear. You know, I've often thought that if I hadn't married Masha, I'd have married you, Olechka. You're so kind. I'm worn out. [Listens.]

OLGA. What is it?

KOOLYGHIN. The doctor's got drunk just as if he'd done it on purpose. Hopelessly drunk. . . . As if he'd done it on purpose. [*Gets up.*] I think he's coming up here. . . . Can you hear him? Yes, he's coming up. [*Laughs.*] What a fellow, really! . . . I'm going to hide myself. [*Goes to the wardrobe and stands between it and the wall.*] What a scoundrel!

OLGA. He's been off drinking for two years, and now suddenly he goes and gets drunk. . . . [*Walks with* NATASHA *towards the back of the room.*]

[CHEBUTYKIN *enters; walking firmly and soberly he crosses the room, stops, looks round, then goes to the wash-stand and begins to wash his hands.*]

CHEBUTYKIN [*glumly*]. The devil take them all . . . all the lot of them! They think I can treat anything just because I'm a doctor, but I know positively nothing at all. I've forgotten everything I used to know. I remember nothing, positively nothing. . . . [OLGA *and* NATASHA *leave the room without his noticing.*] The devil take them! Last Wednesday I attended a woman at Zasyp. She died, and it's all my fault that she did die. Yes. . . . I used to know a thing or two twenty-five years ago, but now I don't remember anything. Not a thing! Perhaps I'm not a man at all, but I just imagine that I've got hands and feet and a head. Perhaps I don't exist at all, and I only imagine that I'm walking about and eating and sleeping. [*Weeps.*] Oh, if only I could simply stop existing! [*Stops crying, glumly.*] God knows. . . . The other day they were talking about Shakespeare and Voltaire at the club. . . . I haven't read either, never read a single line of either, but I tried to make out by my expression that I had. The others did the same. How petty it all is! How despicable! And then suddenly I thought of the woman I killed on Wednesday. It all came back to me, and I felt such a swine, so sick of myself that I went and got drunk. . . .

[*Enter* IRENA, VERSHININ *and* TOOZENBACH. TOOZENBACH *is*

wearing a fashionable new civilian suit.]

IRENA. Let's sit down here for a while. No one will come in here.

VERSHININ. The whole town would have been burnt down but for the soldiers. They're a fine lot of fellows! [*Rubs his hands with pleasure.*] Excellent fellows! Yes, they're a fine lot!

KOOLYGHIN [*approaches them*]. What's the time?

TOOZENBACH. It's gone three. It's beginning to get light.

IRENA. Everyone's sitting in the ballroom and nobody thinks of leaving. That man Soliony there, too. . . . [*To* CHEBUTYKIN.] You ought to go to bed, Doctor.

CHEBUTYKIN. I'm all right. . . . Thanks. . . . [*Combs his beard.*]

KOOLYGHIN [*laughs*]. Half seas over, Ivan Romanych! [*Slaps him on the shoulder.*] You're a fine one! *In vino veritas,* as they used to say in Rome.

TOOZENBACH. Everyone keeps asking me to arrange a concert in aid of the victims of the fire.

IRENA. Well, who'd you get to perform in it?

TOOZENBACH. It could be done if we wanted to. Maria Serghyeevna plays the piano wonderfully well, in my opinion.

KOOLYGHIN. Yes, wonderfully well!

IRENA. She's forgotten how to. She hasn't played for three years. . . . or maybe it's four.

TOOZENBACH. Nobody understands music in this town, not a single person. But I do—I really do—and I assure you quite definitely that Maria Serghyeevna plays magnificently. She's almost a genius for it.

KOOLYGHIN. You're right, Baron. I'm very fond of Masha, She's such a nice girl.

TOOZENBACH. Fancy being able to play so exquisitely, and yet having nobody, nobody at all, to appreciate it!

KOOLYGHIN [*sighs*]. Yes. . . . But would it be quite proper for her to play in a concert? [*A pause.*] I don't know anything about these matters, my friends. Perhaps it'll be perfectly all right. But you know, although our director is a good man, a very good man indeed, and most intelligent, I know that he does hold certain views. . . . Of course, this doesn't really concern him, but I'll have a word with him about it, all the same, if you like.

CHEBUTYKIN [*picks up a china clock and examines it*].

VERSHININ. I've got my clothes in such a mess helping to put out the fire, I must look like nothing on earth. [*A pause.*] I believe they were saying yesterday that our brigade might be transferred to somewhere a long way away. Some said it was to be Poland, and some said it was Cheeta, in Siberia.

TOOZENBACH. I heard that, too. Well, the town will seem quite deserted.

IRENA. We'll go away, too!

CHEBUTYKIN [*drops clock and breaks it*]. Smashed to smithereens!

[*A pause. Everyone looks upset and embarrassed.*]

KOOLYGHIN [*picks up the pieces.*] Fancy breaking such a valuable thing! Ah, Ivan Romanych, Ivan Romanych! You'll get a bad mark for that!

IRENA. It was my mother's clock.

CHEBUTYKIN. Well, supposing it was. If it was your mother's, then it was your mother's. Perhaps I didn't smash it. Perhaps it only appears that I did. Perhaps it only appears to us that we exist, whereas in reality we don't exist at all. I don't know anything, no one knows anything. [*Stops at the door.*] Why are you staring at me? Natasha's having a nice little affair with Protopopov, and you don't see it. You sit here seeing nothing, and meanwhile Natasha's having a nice little affair with Protopopov. . . . [*Sings.*] Would you like a date? . . . [*Goes out.*]

VERSHININ. So. . . . [*Laughs.*] How odd it all is, really. [*A pause.*] When the fire started, I ran home as fast as I could. When I got near, I could see that our house was all right and out of danger, but the two little girls were standing there, in the doorway in their night clothes. Their mother wasn't there. People were rushing about, horses, dogs . . . and in the kiddies' faces I saw a frightened, anxious, appealing look, I don't know what! . . . My heart sank when I saw their faces. My God, I thought, what will these children have to go through in the course of their poor lives? And they may live a long time, too! I picked them up and ran back here with them, and all the time I was running, I was thinking the same thing: what will they have to go through? [*The alarm is sounded. A pause.*] When I got here, my wife was here already . . . angry, shouting!

[*Enter* MASHA *carrying a pillow; she sits down on the couch.*]

VERSHININ. And when my little girls were standing in the doorway with nothing on but their night clothes, and the street was red with the glow of the fire and full of terrifying noises, it struck me that the same sort of thing used to happen years ago, when armies used to make sudden raids on towns, and plunder them and set them on fire. . . . Anyway, is there any essential difference between things as they were and as they are now? And before very long, say, in another two or three hundred years, people may be looking at our present life just as we look at the past now, with horror and scorn. Our own times may seem uncouth to them, boring and frightfully uncomfortable and strange. . . . Oh, what a great life it'll be then, what a life! [*Laughs.*] Forgive me, I'm philosophizing my head off again . . . but may I go on, please? I'm bursting to philosophize just at the moment. I'm in the mood for it. [*A pause.*] You seem as if you've all gone to sleep. As I was saying: what a great life it will be in the future! Just try to imagine it. . . . At the present time there are only three people of your intellectual calibre in the whole of this town, but future generations will be more productive of people like you. They'll go on producing more and more of the same sort until at last the time will come when everything will be just as you'd wish it yourselves. People will live their lives in your way, and then even you may be outmoded, and a new lot will come along who will be even better than you are. . . . [*Laughs.*]

I'm in quite a special mood to-day. I feel full of a tremendous urge to live. . . . [*Sings.*]

"To Love all ages are in fee,
    The passion's good for you and me." . . . [*Laughs.*]

MASHA [*sings*]. Tara-tara-tara. . . .
VERSHININ. Tum-tum. . . .
MASHA. Tara-tara . . .
VERSHININ. Tum-tum, tum-tum. . . . [*Laughs.*]

[*Enter* FEDOTIK.]

FEDOTIK [*dancing about*]. Burnt, burnt! Everything I've got
burnt!

[*All laugh.*]

IRENA. It's hardly a joking matter. Has everything really been
burnt?
FEDOTIK [*laughs*]. Everything, completely. I've got nothing
left. My guitar's burnt, my photographs are burnt, all my
letters are burnt. Even the little note-book I was going to
give you has been burnt.

[*Enter* SOLIONY.]

IRENA. No, please go away, Vassily Vassilich. You can't come
in here.
SOLIONY. Can't I? Why can the Baron come in here if I can't?
VERSHININ. We really must go, all of us. What's the fire doing?
SOLIONY. It's dying down, they say. Well, I must say it's a pe-
culiar thing that the Baron can come in here, and I can't.

[*Takes a scent bottle from his pocket and sprinkles himself
with scent.*]

VERSHININ. Tara-tara.
MASHA. Tum-tum, tum-tum.
VERSHININ [*laughs, to* SOLIONY]. Let's go to the ballroom.
SOLIONY. Very well, we'll make a note of this. "I hardly need

to make my moral yet more clear: That might be teasing
geese, I fear!" [1] [*Looks at* TOOZENBACH.] Cluck, cluck, cluck!
[*Goes out with* VERSHININ *and* FEDOTIK.]

IRENA. That Soliony has smoked the room out. . . . [*Puzzled.*]
The Baron's asleep. Baron! Baron!

TOOZENBACH [*waking out of his doze*]. I must be tired. The
brick-works. . . . No, I'm not talking in my sleep. I really
do intend to go to the brick-works and start working there
quite soon. I've had a talk with the manager. [*To* IRENA, *tenderly.*] You are so pale, so beautiful, so fascinating. . . .
Your pallor seems to light up the darkness around you, as
if it were luminous, somehow. . . . You're sad, you're dissatisfied with the life you have to live. . . . Oh, come away
with me, let's go away and work together!

MASHA. Nikolai Lvovich, I wish you'd go away.

TOOZENBACH [*laughs*]. Oh, you're here, are you? I didn't see
you. [*Kisses* IRENA'S *hand.*] Good-bye, I'm going. You know
as I look at you now, I keep thinking of the day—it was
a long time ago, your Saint's day—when you talked to us
about the joy of work. . . . You were so gay and high-spirited
then. . . . And what a happy life I saw ahead of me! Where
is it all now? [*Kisses her hand.*] There are tears in your eyes.
You should go to bed, it's beginning to get light . . . it's almost morning. . . . Oh, if only I could give my life for you!

MASHA. Nikolai Lvovich, please go away! Really now. . . .

TOOZENBACH. I'm going. [*Goes out.*]

MASHA [*lies down*]. Are you asleep, Fiodor?

KOOLYGHIN. Eh?

MASHA. Why don't you go home?

KOOLYGHIN. My darling Masha, my sweet, my precious
Masha. . . .

IRENA. She's tired. Let her rest a while, Fyedia.

KOOLYGHIN. I'll go in a moment. My wife, my dear, good wife!
. . . How I love you! . . . only you!

MASHA [*crossly*]. *Amo, amas, amat, amamus, amatis, amant!*

¹From Krylov's fable *Geese* (translated by Bernard Pares.)

KOOLYGHIN [*laughs*]. Really, she's an amazing woman!— I've been married to you for seven years, but I feel as if we were only married yesterday. Yes, on my word of honour, I do! You really are amazing! Oh, I'm so happy, happy, happy!

MASHA. And I'm so bored, bored, bored! [*Sits up.*] I can't get it out of my head. . . . It's simply disgusting. It's like having a nail driven into my head. No, I can't keep silent about it any more. It's about Andrey. . . . He's actually mortgaged this house to a bank, and his wife's got hold of all the money—and yet the house doesn't belong to him, it belongs to all four of us! Surely, he must realize that, if he's got any honesty.

KOOLYGHIN. Why bring all this up, Masha? Why bother about it now? Andriusha owes money all round. . . . Leave him alone.

MASHA. Anyway, it's disgusting. [*Lies down.*]

KOOLYGHIN. Well, we aren't poor, Masha. I've got work, I teach at the county school, I give private lessons in my spare time. . . . I'm just a plain, honest man. . . . *Omnia mea mecum porto,* as they say.

MASHA. I don't ask for anything, but I'm just disgusted by injustice. [*A pause.*] Why don't you go home, Fiodor?

KOOLYGHIN [*kisses her*]. You're tired. Just rest here for a while. . . . I'll go home and wait for you. . . . Go to sleep. [*Goes to the door.*] I'm happy, happy, happy! [*Goes out.*]

IRENA. The truth is that Andrey is getting to be shallow-minded. He's ageing and since he's been living with that woman he's lost all the inspiration he used to have! Not long ago he was working for a professorship, and yet yesterday he boasted of having at last been elected a member of the County Council. Fancy him a member, with Protopopov as chairman! They say the whole town's laughing at him, he's the only one who doesn't know anything or see anything. And now, you see, everyone's at the fire, while he's just sitting in his room, not taking the slightest notice of it. Just playing his violin. [*Agitated.*] Oh, how dreadful it is, how dreadful, how dreadful! I can't bear it any longer, I can't, I really can't! . . .

[*Enter* OLGA. *She starts arranging things on her bedside table.*]

IRENA [*sobs loudly*]. You must turn me out of here! Turn me out; I can't stand it any more!

OLGA [*alarmed*]. What is it? What is it, darling?

IRENA [*sobbing.*] Where. . . . Where has it all gone to? Where is it? Oh, God! I've forgotten. . . . I've forgotten everything . . . there's nothing but a muddle in my head. . . . I don't remember what the Italian for "window" is, or for "ceiling." . . . Every day I'm forgetting more and more, and life's slipping by, and it will never, never come back. . . . We shall never go to Moscow. . . . I can see that we shall never go. . . .

OLGA. Don't, my dear, don't. . . .

IRENA [*trying to control herself*]. Oh, I'm so miserable! . . . I can't work, I won't work! I've had enough of it, enough! . . . First I worked on the telegraph, now I'm in the County Council office, and I hate and despise everything they give me to do there. . . . I'm twenty-three years old, I've been working all this time, and I feel as if my brain's dried up. I know I've got thinner and uglier and older, and I find no kind of satisfaction in anything, none at all. And the time's passing . . . and I feel as if I'm moving away from any hope of a genuine, fine life, I'm moving further and further away and sinking into a kind of abyss. I feel in despair, and I don't know why I'm still alive, why I haven't killed myself. . . .

OLGA. Don't cry, my dear child, don't cry. . . . It hurts me.

IRENA. I'm not crying any more. That's enough of it. Look, I'm not crying now. Enough of it, enough! . . .

OLGA. Darling, let me tell you something. . . . I just want to speak as your sister, as your friend. . . . That is, if you want my advice. . . . Why don't you marry the Baron?

IRENA [*weeps quietly*].

OLGA. After all, you do respect him, you think a lot of him. . . . It's true, he's not good-looking, but he's such a decent, clean-minded sort of man. . . . After all, one doesn't marry for love, but to fulfil a duty. At least, I think so, and I'd marry even if I weren't in love. I'd marry anyone that proposed to me, as long as he was a decent man. I'd even marry an old man.

IRENA. I've been waiting all this time, imagining that we'd be moving to Moscow, and I'd meet the man I'm meant for there. I've dreamt about him and I've loved him in my dreams. . . . But it's all turned out to be nonsense . . . nonsense. . . .

OLGA [*embracing her*]. My darling sweetheart, I understand everything perfectly. When the Baron resigned his commission and came to see us in his civilian clothes, I thought he looked so plain that I actually started to cry. . . . He asked me why I was crying. . . . How could I tell him? But, of course, if it were God's will that he should marry you, I'd feel perfectly happy about it. That's quite a different matter, quite different!

[NATASHA, *carrying a candle, comes out of the door on the right, crosses the stage and goes out through the door on the left without saying anything.*]

MASHA [*sits up*]. She goes about looking as if she'd started the fire.

OLGA. You're silly, Masha. You're the stupidest person in our family. Forgive me for saying so.

[*A pause.*]

MASHA. My dear sisters, I've got something to confess to you. I must get some relief, I feel the need of it in my heart. I'll confess it to you two alone, and then never again, never to anybody! I'll tell you in a minute. [*In a low voice.*] It's a secret, but you'll have to know everything. I can't keep silent any more. [*A pause.*] I'm in love, in love. . . . I love that man. . . . You saw him here just now. . . . Well, what's the good? . . . I love Vershinin. . . .

OLGA [*goes behind her screen*]. Don't say it. I don't want to hear it.

MASHA. Well, what's to be done? [*Holding her head.*] I thought he was queer at first, then I started to pity him . . . then I began to love him . . . love everything about him—his voice, his talk, his misfortunes, his two little girls. . . .

OLGA. Nevertheless, I don't want to hear it. You can say any nonsense you like, I'm not listening.

MASHA. Oh, you're stupid, Olia! If I love him, well—that's my fate! That's my destiny. . . . He loves me, too. It's all rather frightening, isn't it? Not a good thing, is it? [*Takes* IRENA *by the hand and draws her to her.*] Oh, my dear! . . . How are we going to live through the rest of our lives? What's going to become of us? When you read a novel, everything in it seems so old and obvious, but when you fall in love yourself, you suddenly discover that you don't really know anything, and you've got to make your own decisions. . . . My dear sisters, my dear sisters! . . . I've confessed it all to you, and now I'll keep quiet. . . . I'll be like that madman in the story by Gogol—silence . . . silence! . . .

[*Enter* ANDREY *followed by* FERAPONT.]

ANDREY [*crossly*]. What do you want? I don't understand you.

FERAPONT [*stopping in the doorway, impatiently*] I've asked you about ten times already, Andrey Serghyevich.

ANDREY. In the first place, you're not to call me Andrey Serghyevich—call me "Your Honour."

FERAPONT. The firemen are asking Your Honour if they may drive through your garden to get to the river. They've been going a long way round all this time—it's a terrible business!

ANDREY. All right. Tell them it's all right. [FERAPONT *goes out.*] They keep on plaguing me. Where's Olga? [OLGA *comes from behind the screen.*] I wanted to see you. Will you give me the key to the cupboard? I've lost mine. You know the key I mean, the small one you've got. . . .

[OLGA *silently hands him the key.* IRENA *goes behind the*

screen on her side of the room.]

ANDREY. What a terrific fire! It's going down though. That Ferapont annoyed me, the devil take him! Silly thing he made
me say. . . . Telling him to call me "Your Honour"! . . . [*A
pause.*] Why don't you say anything, Olia? [*A pause.*] It's
about time you stopped this nonsense . . . sulking like this
for no reason whatever. . . . You here, Masha? And Irena's
here, too. That's excellent! We can talk it over then, frankly
and once for all. What have you got against me? What
is it?

OLGA. Drop it now, Andriusha. Let's talk it over to-morrow
[*Agitated.*] What a dreadful night!

ANDREY [*in great embarrassment*]. Don't get upset. I'm asking
you quite calmly, what have you got against me? Tell me
frankly.

VERSHININ'S VOICE [*off stage*]. Tum-tum-tum!

MASHA [*in a loud voice, getting up*]. Tara-tara-tara! [*To* OLGA.]
Good-bye, Olia, God bless you! [*Goes behind the screen and
kisses* IRENA.] Sleep well. . . . Good-bye, Andrey. I should
leave them now, they're tired . . . talk it over to-morrow.
. . . [*Goes out.*]

OLGA. Really, Andriusha, let's leave it till to-morrow. . . . [*Goes
behind the screen on her side of the room.*] It's time to go
to bed.

ANDREY. I only want to say one thing, then I'll go. In a moment. . . . First of all, you've got something against my wife,
against Natasha. I've always been conscious of it from the
day we got married. Natasha is a fine woman, she's honest
and straightforward and high-principled. . . . That's my
opinion. I love and respect my wife. You understand that I
respect her, and I expect others to respect her, too. I repeat:
she's an honest, high-principled woman, and all your griev-
ances against her—if you don't mind my saying so—are
just imagination, and nothing more. . . . [*A pause.*] Secondly,
you seem to be annoyed with me for not making myself
a professor, and not doing any academic work. But I'm

working in the Council Office, I'm a member of the County Council, and I feel my service there is just as fine and valuable as any academic work I might do. I'm a member of the County Council, and if you want to know, I'm proud of it! [*A pause.*] Thirdly . . . there's something else I must tell you. . . . I know I mortgaged the house without asking your permission. . . . That was wrong, I admit it, and I ask you to forgive me. . . . I was driven to it by my debts. . . . I'm in debt for about thirty-five thousand roubles. I don't play cards any more, I've given it up long ago. . . . The only thing I can say to justify myself is that you girls get an annuity, while I don't get anything . . . no income, I mean. . . . [*A pause.*]

KOOLYGHIN [*calling through the door*]. Is Masha there? She's not there? [*Alarmed.*] Where can she be then? It's very strange. . . . [*Goes away.*]

ANDREY. So you won't listen? Natasha is a good, honest woman, I tell you. [*Walks up and down the stage, then stops.*] When I married her, I thought we were going to be happy, I thought we should all be happy. . . . But . . . oh, my God! . . . [*Weeps.*] My dear sisters, my dear, good sisters, don't believe what I've been saying, don't believe it. . . . [*Goes out.*]

KOOLYGHIN [*through the door, agitated*]. Where's Masha? Isn't Masha here? Extraordinary! [*Goes away.*]

[*The alarm is heard again. The stage is empty.*]

IRENA [*speaking from behind the screen*]. Olia! Who's that knocking on the floor?

OLGA. It's the doctor, Ivan Romanych. He's drunk.

IRENA. It's been one thing after another all night. [*A pause.*] Olia! [*Peeps out from behind the screen.*] Have you heard? The troops are being moved from the district . . . they're being sent somewhere a long way off.

OLGA. That's only a rumour.

IRENA. We'll be left quite alone then. . . . Olia!

OLGA. Well?

IRENA. Olia, darling, I do respect the Baron. . . . I think a lot of him, he's a very good man. . . . I'll marry him, Olia, I'll agree to marry him, if only we can go to Moscow! Let's go, please do let's go! There's nowhere in all the world like Moscow. Let's go, Olia! Let's go!

ACT FOUR

[*The old garden belonging to the Prozorovs' house. A river is seen at the end of a long avenue of fir-trees, and on the far bank of the river a forest. On the right of the stage there is a verandah with a table on which champagne bottles and glasses have been left. It is midday. From time to time people from the street pass through the garden to get to the river. Five or six soldiers march through quickly.*

CHEBUTYKIN, radiating a mood of benevolence which does not leave him throughout the act, is sitting in a chair in the garden. He is wearing his army cap and is holding a walking stick, as if ready to be called away at any moment. KOOLYGHIN, with a decoration round his neck and with his moustache shaved off, TOOZENBACH and IRENA are standing on the verandah saying good-bye to FEDOTIK and RODÉ, who are coming down the steps. Both officers are in marching uniform.]

TOOZENBACH [*embracing* FEDOTIK]. You're a good fellow, Fedotik; we've been good friends! [*Embraces* RODÉ.] Once more, then. . . . Good-bye, my dear friends!

IRENA. Au revoir!

FEDOTIK. It's not "au revoir." It's good-bye. We shall never meet again!

KOOLYGHIN. Who knows? [*Wipes his eyes, smiling.*] There! you've made me cry.

IRENA. We'll meet some time.

FEDOTIK. Perhaps in ten or fifteen years' time. But then we'll hardly know one another. . . . We shall just meet and say. "How are you?" coldly. . . . [*Takes a snapshot.*] Wait a moment. . . . Just one more, for the last time.

RODÉ [*embraces* TOOZENBACH]. We're not likely to meet again.

. . . [*Kisses* IRENA's *hand.*] Thank you for everything . . .
everything!

FEDOTIK [*annoyed*]. Do just wait a second!

TOOZENBACH. We'll meet again if we're fated to meet. Do write
to us. Be sure to write.

RODÉ [*glancing round the garden*]. Good-bye, trees! [*Shouts.*]
Heigh-ho! [*A pause.*] Good-bye, echo!

KOOLYGHIN. I wouldn't be surprised if you got married out
there, in Poland. . . . You'll get a Polish wife, and she'll put
her arms round you and say: Kohane![1] [*Laughs.*]

FEDOTIK [*glances at his watch*]. There's less than an hour to go.
Soliony is the only one from our battery who's going down
the river on the barge. All the others are marching with the
division. Three batteries are leaving to-day by road and
three more to-morrow—then the town will be quite peaceful.

TOOZENBACH. Yes, and dreadfully dull, too.

RODÉ. By the way, where's Maria Serghyeevna?

KOOLYGHIN. She's somewhere in the garden.

FEDOTIK. We must say good-bye to her.

RODÉ. Good-bye. I really must go, or I'll burst into tears.
[*Quickly embraces* TOOZENBACH *and* KOOLYGHIN, *kisses*
IRENA's *hand.*] Life's been very pleasant here. . . .

FEDOTIK [*to* KOOLYGHIN]. Here's something for a souvenir for
you—a note-book with a pencil. . . . We'll go down to the
river through here. [*They go off, glancing back.*]

RODÉ [*shouts*]. Heigh-ho!

KOOLYGHIN [*shouts*]. Good-bye!

[*At the back of the stage* FEDOTIK *and* RODÉ *meet* MASHA
and say good-bye to her; she goes off with them.]

IRENA. They've gone. . . . [*Sits down on the bottom step of the
verandah.*]

CHEBUTYKIN. They forgot to say good-bye to me.

IRENA. Well, what about you?

CHEBUTYKIN. That's true, I forgot, too. Never mind, I'll be

[1]A Polish word meaning "beloved".

seeing them again quite soon. I'll be leaving to-morrow. Yes . . . only one more day. And then, in a year's time I'll be retiring. I'll come back here and finish the rest of my life near you. There's just one more year to go and then I get my pension. . . . [*Puts a newspaper in his pocket and takes out another.*] I'll come back here and lead a reformed life. I'll be a nice, quiet, well-behaved little man.

RENA. Yes, it's really time you reformed, my dear friend. You ought to live a different sort of life, somehow.

HEBUTYKIN. Yes. . . . I think so, too. [*Sings quietly.*] Tarara-boom-di-ay. . . . I'm sitting on a tomb-di-ay. . . .

OOLYGHIN. Ivan Romanych is incorrigible! Incorrigible!

HEBUTYKIN. Yes, you ought to have taken me in hand. You'd have reformed me!

RENA. Fiodor's shaved his moustache off. I can't bear to look at him.

OOLYGHIN. Why not?

HEBUTYKIN. If I could just tell you what your face looks like now—but I daren't.

OOLYGHIN. Well! Such are the conventions of life! *Modus vivendi,* you know. The director shaved his moustache off, so I shaved mine off when they gave me an inspectorship. No one likes it, but personally I'm quite indifferent. I'm content. Whether I've got a moustache or not, it's all the same to me. [*Sits down.*]

NDREY [*passes across the back of the stage pushing a pram with a child asleep in it*].

RENA. Ivan Romanych, my dear friend, I'm awfully worried about something. You were out in the town garden last night—tell me what happened there?

HEBUTYKIN. What happened? Nothing. Just a trifling thing. [*Reads his paper.*] It doesn't matter anyway.

KOOLYGHIN. They say that Soliony and the Baron met in the town garden outside the theatre last night and . . .

OOZENBACH. Don't please! What's the good? . . . [*Waves his hand at him deprecatingly and goes into the house.*]

KOOLYGHIN. It was outside the theatre. . . . Soliony started

badgering the Baron, and he lost patience and said some
thing that offended him.

CHEBUTYKIN. I don't know anything about it. It's all nonsense

KOOLYGHIN. A school-master once wrote "nonsense" in Russia
over a pupil's essay, and the pupil puzzled over it, think
it was a Latin word. [*Laughs.*] Frightfully funny, you know
They say that Soliony's in love with Irena and that he go
to hate the Baron more and more. . . . Well, that's under
standable. Irena's a very nice girl. She's a bit like Masha
she tends to get wrapped up in her own thoughts. [*To* IRENA
But your disposition is more easy-going than Masha's. An
yet Masha has a very nice disposition, too. I love her, I lov
my Masha.

[*From the back of the stage comes a shout: "Heigh-ho!"*]

IRENA [*starts*]. Anything seems to startle me to-day. [*A pause.*
I've got everything ready, too. I'm sending my luggage of
after lunch. The Baron and I are going to get married to
morrow, and directly afterwards we're moving to the brick
works, and the day after to-morrow I'm starting work at th
school. So our new life will begin, God willing! When
was sitting for my teacher's diploma, I suddenly started cry
ing for sheer joy, with a sort of feeling of blessedness. . .
[*A pause.*] The carrier will be coming for my luggage in
minute. . . .

KOOLYGHIN. That's all very well, but somehow I can't feel tha
it's meant to be serious. All ideas and theories, but nothin
really serious. Anyway, I wish you luck from the bottom o
my heart.

CHEBUTYKIN [*moved*]. My dearest girl, my precious child
You've gone on so far ahead of me, I'll never catch you u
now. I've got left behind like a bird which has grown to
old and can't keep up with the rest of the flock. Fly away
my dears, fly away, and God be with you! [*A pause.*] It's
pity you've shaved your moustache off, Fiodor Illyich.

KOOLYGHIN. Don't keep on about it, please! [*Sighs.*] Well, th
soldiers will be leaving to-day, and everything will go bac

to what it was before. Anyway, whatever they say, Masha is a good, loyal wife. Yes, I love her dearly and I'm thankful for what God has given me. Fate treats people so differently. For instance, there's an excise clerk here called Kozyrev. He was at school with me and he was expelled in his fifth year because he just couldn't grasp the *ut consecutivum.* He's dreadfully hard up now, and in bad health, too, and whenever I meet him, I just say to him: 'Hullo, *ut consecutivum!'* "Yes," he replies, "that's just the trouble— *consecutivum"* . . . and he starts coughing. Whereas I—I've been lucky all my life. I'm happy, I've actually been awarded the order of Saint Stanislav, second class—and now I'm teaching the children the same old *ut consecutivum.* Of course, I'm clever, cleverer than plenty of other people, but happiness does not consist of merely being clever. . . .

[In the house someone plays "The Maiden's Prayer."]

IRENA. To-morrow night I shan't have to listen to the "Maiden's Prayer." I shan't have to meet Protopopov. . . . *[A pause.]* By the way, he's in the sitting-room. He's come again.

KOOLYGHIN. Hasn't our headmistress arrived yet?

IRENA. No, we've sent for her. If you only knew how difficult it is for me to live here by myself, without Olia! She lives at the school now; she's the headmistress and she's busy the whole day. And I'm here alone, bored, with nothing to do, and I hate the very room I live in. So I've just made up my mind—if I'm really not going to be able to live in Moscow, that's that. It's my fate, that's all. Nothing can be done about it. It's God's will, everything that happens, and that's the truth. Nikolai Lvovich proposed to me. . . . Well, I thought it over, and I made up my mind. He's such a nice man, it's really extraordinary how nice he is. . . . And then suddenly I felt as though my soul had grown wings, I felt more cheerful and so relieved somehow that I wanted to work again. Just to start work! . . . Only something happened yesterday, and now I feel as though something mysterious is hanging over me. . . .

CHEBUTYKIN. Nonsense!

NATASHA [*speaking through the window*]. Our headmistress!

KOOLYGHIN. Our headmistress has arrived! Let's go indoors.

[*Goes indoors with* IRENA.]

CHEBUTYKIN [*reads his paper and sings quietly to himself*]. Ta-rara-boom-di-ay. . . . I'm sitting on a tomb-di-ay. . . .

[MASHA *walks up to him;* ANDREY *passes across the back of the stage pushing the pram.*]

MASHA. You look very comfortable sitting here. . . .

CHEBUTYKIN. Well, why not? Anything happening?

MASHA [*sits down*]. No, nothing. [*A pause.*] Tell me something. Were you in love with my mother?

CHEBUTYKIN. Yes, very much in love.

MASHA. Did she love you?

CHEBUTYKIN [*after a pause*]. I can't remember now.

MASHA. Is my man here? Our cook Marfa always used to call her policeman "my man." Is he here?

CHEBUTYKIN. Not yet.

MASHA. When you have to take your happiness in snatches, in little bits, as I do, and then lose it, as I've lost it, you gradually get hardened and bad-tempered. [*Points at her breast.*] Something's boiling over inside me, here. [*Looking at* AN-DREY, *who again crosses the stage with the pram.*] There's Andrey, our dear brother. . . . All our hopes are gone. It's the same as when thousands of people haul a huge bell up into a tower. Untold labour and money is spent on it, and then suddenly it falls and gets smashed. Suddenly, without rhyme or reason. It was the same with Andrey. . . .

ANDREY. When are they going to settle down in the house? They're making such a row.

CHEBUTYKIN. They will soon. [*Looks at his watch.*] This is an old-fashioned watch: it strikes. . . . [*Winds his watch which then strikes.*] The first, second and fifth batteries will be leaving punctually at one o'clock. [*A pause.*] And I shall leave to-morrow.

ANDREY. For good?

CHEBUTYKIN. I don't know. I may return in about a year. Although, God knows . . . it's all the same. . . .

[*The sounds of a harp and a violin are heard.*]

ANDREY. The town will seem quite empty. Life will be snuffed out like a candle. [*A pause.*] Something happened yesterday outside the theatre; everybody's talking about it. I'm the only one that doesn't seem to know about it.

CHEBUTYKIN. It was nothing. A lot of nonsense. Soliony started badgering the Baron, or something. The Baron lost his temper and insulted him, and in the end Soliony had to challenge him to a duel. [*Looks at his watch.*] I think it's time to go. . . . At half-past twelve, in the forest over there, on the other side of the river. . . . Bang-bang! [*Laughs.*] Soliony imagines he's like Lermontov. He actually writes poems. But, joking apart, this is his third duel.

MASHA. Whose third duel?

CHEBUTYKIN. Soliony's.

MASHA. What about the Baron?

CHEBUTYKIN. Well, what about him? [*A pause.*]

MASHA. My thoughts are all in a muddle. . . . But what I mean to say is that they shouldn't be allowed to fight. He might wound the Baron or even kill him.

CHEBUTYKIN. The Baron's a good enough fellow, but what does it really matter if there's one Baron more or less in the world? Well, let it be! It's all the same. [*The shouts of "Ah-oo!" and "Heigh-ho!" are heard from beyond the garden.*] That's Skvortsov, the second, shouting from the boat. He can wait.

ANDREY. I think it's simply immoral to fight a duel, or even to be present at one as a doctor.

CHEBUTYKIN. That's only how it seems. . . . We don't exist, nothing exists, it only seems to us that we do. . . . And what difference does it make?

MASHA. Talk, talk, nothing but talk all day long! . . . [*Starts to go.*] Having to live in this awful climate with the snow threatening to fall at any moment, and then on the top of it having to listen to all this sort of talk. . . . [*Stops.*] I won't go into the house, I can't bear going in there. . . . Will you let me know when Vershinin comes? . . . [*Walks off along the avenue.*] Look, the birds are beginning to fly away already! [*Looks up.*] Swans or geese. . . . Dear birds, happy birds. . . . [*Goes off.*]

ANDREY. Our house will seem quite deserted. The officers will go, you'll go, my sister will get married, and I'll be left alone in the house.

CHEBUTYKIN. What about your wife?

[*Enter* FERAPONT *with some papers.*]

ANDREY. My wife is my wife. She's a good, decent sort of woman . . . she's really very kind, too, but there's something about her which pulls her down to the level of an animal . . . a sort of mean, blind, thick-skinned animal—anyway, not a human being. I'm telling you this as a friend, the only person I can talk openly to. I love Natasha, it's true. But at times she appears to me so utterly vulgar, that I feel quite bewildered by it, and then I can't understand why, for what reasons I love her—or, anyway, did love her.

CHEBUTYKIN [*gets up*]. Well, dear boy, I'm going away tomorrow and it may be we shall never see each other again. So I'll give you a bit of advice. Put on your hat, take a walking stick, and go away. . . . Go away, and don't ever look back. And the further you go, the better.

[SOLIONY *passes across the back of the stage accompanied by two officers. Seeing* CHEBUTYKIN, *he turns towards him, while the officers walk on.*]

SOLIONY. It's time, Doctor. Half past twelve already. [*Shakes hands with* ANDREY.]

CHEBUTYKIN. In a moment. Oh, I'm tired of you all. [*To* ANDREY.] Andriusha, if anyone asks for me, tell them I'll be back presently. [*Sighs.*] Oh-ho-ho!

SOLIONY. "He had no time to say 'Oh, oh!'"

Before that bear had struck him low." . . .

[*Walks off with him.*] What are you groaning about, old man?

CHEBUTYKIN. Oh, well!

SOLIONY. How do you feel?

CHEBUTYKIN [*crossly*]. Like a last year's bird's-nest.

SOLIONY. You needn't be so agitated about it, old boy. I shan't indulge in anything much, I'll just scorch his wings a little, like a woodcock's. [*Takes out a scent bottle and sprinkles scent over his hands.*] I've used up a whole bottle to-day, but my hands still smell. They smell like a corpse. [*A pause.*] Yes. . . . Do you remember that poem of Lermontov's?

"And he, rebellious, seeks a storm,
As if in storms there were tranquillity." . . .

CHEBUTYKIN. Yes.

"He had no time to say 'Oh, oh!'
Before that bear had struck him low."

[*Goes out with* SOLIONY.]

[*Shouts of "Heigh-ho!" "Ah-oo!" are heard. Enter* ANDREY *and* FERAPONT.]

FERAPONT. Will you sign these papers, please?

ANDREY [*with irritation*]. Leave me alone! Leave me alone, for Heaven's sake. [*Goes off with the pram.*]

FERAPONT. Well, what am I supposed to do with the papers then? They are meant to be signed, aren't they? [*Goes to back of stage.*]

[*Enter* IRENA *and* TOOZENBACH, *the latter wearing a straw hat.* KOOLYGHIN *crosses the stage, calling: "Ah-oo! Masha! Ah-oo!"*]

TOOZENBACH. I think he's the only person in the whole town who's glad that the army is leaving.

IRENA. That's quite understandable, really. [*A pause.*] The town will look quite empty.

TOOZENBACH. My dear, I'll be back in a moment.

IRENA. Where are you going?

TOOZENBACH. I must slip back to the town, and then . . . I want to see some of my colleagues off.

IRENA. It's not true. . . . Nikolai, why are you so absent-minded to-day? [*A pause.*] What happened outside the theatre last night?

TOOZENBACH [*with a movement of impatience*]. I'll be back in an hour. . . . I'll be back with you again. [*Kisses her hands.*] My treasure! . . . [*Gazes into her eyes.*] It's five years since I first began to love you, and still I can't get used to it, and you seem more beautiful every day. What wonderful, lovely hair! What marvellous eyes! I'll take you away to-morrow. We'll work, we'll be rich, my dreams will come to life again. And you'll be happy! But—there's only one "but," only one—you don't love me!

IRENA. I can't help that! I'll be your wife, I'll be loyal and obedient to you, but I can't love you. . . . What's to be done? [*Weeps.*] I've never loved anyone in my life. Oh, I've had such dreams about being in love! I've been dreaming about it for ever so long, day and night . . . but somehow my soul seems like an expensive piano which someone has locked up and the key's got lost. [*A pause.*] Your eyes are so restless.

TOOZENBACH. I was awake all night. Not that there's anything to be afraid of in my life, nothing threatening. . . . Only the thought of that lost key torments me and keeps me awake. Say something to me. . . . [*A pause.*] Say something!

IRENA. What? What am I to say? What?

TOOZENBACH. Anything.

IRENA. Don't, my dear, don't. . . . [*A pause.*]

TOOZENBACH. Such trifles, such silly little things sometimes become so important suddenly, for no apparent reason. You laugh at them, just as you always have done, you still regard them as trifles, and yet you suddenly find they're in control, and you haven't the power to stop them. But don't let us talk about all that! Really, I feel quite elated. I feel as if I was seeing those fir-trees and maples and birches for the first time in my life. They all seem to be looking at me with a sort of inquisitive look and waiting for something. What beautiful trees—and how beautiful, when you think of it, life ought to be with trees like these! [*Shouts of "Ah-oo! Heigh-ho" are heard.*] I must go, it's time. . . . Look at that dead tree, it's all dried-up, but it's still swaying in the wind along with the others. And in the same way, it seems to me that, if I die, I shall still have a share in life somehow or other. Goodbye, my dear. . . . [*Kisses her hands.*] Your papers, the ones you gave me, are on my desk, under the calendar.

IRENA. I'm coming with you.

TOOZENBACH [*alarmed*]. No, no! [*Goes off quickly, then stops in the avenue.*] Irena!

IRENA. What?

TOOZENBACH [*not knowing what to say*]. I didn't have any coffee this morning. Will you tell them to get some ready for me? [*Goes off quickly.*]

[IRENA *stands, lost in thought, then goes to the back of the stage and sits down on a swing. Enter* ANDREY *with the pram;* FERAPONT *appears.*]

FERAPONT. Andrey Serghyeech, the papers aren't mine, you know, they're the office papers. I didn't make them up.

ANDREY. Oh, where has all my past life gone to?—the time when I was young and gay and clever, when I used to have fine dreams and great thoughts, and the present and the future were bright with hope? Why do we become so dull and commonplace and uninteresting almost before we've begun to live? Why do we get lazy, indifferent, useless, unhappy? . . . This town's been in existence for two hundred years; a hundred thousand people live in it, but there's not one who's any different from all the others! There's never been a scholar or an artist or a saint in this place, never a single man sufficiently outstanding to make you feel passionately that you wanted to emulate him. People here do nothing but eat, drink and sleep. . . . Then they die and some more take their places, and they eat, drink and sleep, too,—and just to introduce a bit of variety into their lives, so as to avoid getting completely stupid with boredom, they indulge in their disgusting gossip and vodka and gambling and law-suits. The wives deceive their husbands, and the husbands lie to their wives, and pretend they don't see anything and don't hear anything. . . . And all this overwhelming vulgarity and pettiness crushes the children and puts out any spark they might have in them, so that they, too, become miserable, half-dead creatures, just like one another and just like their parents! . . . [*To* FERAPONT, *crossly.*] What do you want?

FERAPONT. What? Here are the papers to sign.

ANDREY. What a nuisance you are!

FERAPONT [*hands him the papers*]. The porter at the finance department told me just now . . . he said last winter they had two hundred degrees of frost in Petersburg.

ANDREY. I hate the life I live at present, but oh! the sense of elation when I think of the future! Then I feel so light-hearted, such a sense of release! I seem to see light ahead, light and freedom. I see myself free, and my children, too, —free from idleness, free from *kvass,* free from eternal meals of goose and cabbage, free from after-dinner naps, free from all this degrading parasitism! . . .

FERAPONT. They say two thousand people were frozen to death. They say everyone was scared stiff. It was either in Petersburg or in Moscow, I can't remember exactly.

ANDREY [*with sudden emotion, tenderly*]. My dear sisters, my dear good sisters! [*Tearfully.*] Masha, my dear sister! . . .

NATASHA [*through the window.*] Who's that talking so loudly there? Is that you, Andriusha? You'll wake Sofochka. *Il ne faut pas faire du bruit, la Sophie est dormie déjà. Vous êtes un ours.* [*Getting angry.*] If you want to talk, give the pram to someone else. Ferapont, take the pram from the master.

FERAPONT. Yes, Madam. [*Takes the pram.*]

ANDREY [*shamefacedly*]. I was talking quietly.

NATASHA [*in the window, caressing her small son*]. Bobik!

Naughty Bobik! Aren't you a naughty boy!

ANDREY [*glancing through the papers*]. All right, I'll go through them and sign them if they need it. You can take them back to the office later. [*Goes into the house, reading the papers.*]

[FERAPONT *wheels the pram into the garden.*]

NATASHA [*in the window*]. What's Mummy's name, Bobik? You darling! And who's that lady? Auntie Olia. Say: "Hullo, Auntie Olia."

[*Two street musicians, a man and a girl, enter and begin to play on a violin and a harp;* VERSHININ, OLGA *and* ANFISA *come out of the house and listen in silence for a few moments; then* IRENA *approaches them.*]

OLGA. Our garden's like a public road; everybody goes through it. Nanny, give something to the musicians.

ANFISA [*giving them money*]. Go along now, God bless you, good people! [*The musicians bow and go away.*] Poor, homeless folk! Whoever would go dragging round the streets playing tunes if he had enough to eat? [*To* IRENA.] How are you, Irenushka? [*Kisses her.*] Ah, my child, what a life I'm having! Such comfort! In a large flat at the school with Oliushka—and no rent to pay, either! The Lord's been kind to me in my old age. I've never had such a comfortable time in my life, old sinner that I am! A big flat, and no rent to pay, and a whole room to myself, with my own bed. All free. Sometimes when I wake up in the night I begin to think, and then— Oh, Lord! Oh, Holy Mother of God!— there's no one happier in the world than me!

VERSHININ [*glances at his watch*]. We shall be starting in a moment, Olga Serghyeevna. It's time I went. [*A pause.*] I wish you all the happiness in the world . . . everything. . . . Where's Maria Serghyeevna?

IRENA. She's somewhere in the garden. I'll go and look for her.

VERSHININ. That's kind of you. I really must hurry.

ANFISA. I'll come and help to look for her. [*Calls out.*] Ma-shenka, ah-oo! [*Goes with* IRENA *towards the far end of the garden.*] Ah-oo! Ah-oo!

VERSHININ. Everything comes to an end. Well, here we are—
and now it's going to be "good-bye." [*Looks at his watch.*]
The city gave us a sort of farewell lunch. There was champagne, and the mayor made a speech, and I ate and listened, but in spirit I was with you here. . . . [*Glances
round the garden.*] I've grown so . . . so accustomed to you.

OLGA. Shall we meet again some day, I wonder?

VERSHININ. Most likely not! [*A pause.*] My wife and the two
little girls will be staying on here for a month or two.
Please, if anything happens, if they need anything. . . .

OLGA. Yes, yes, of course. You needn't worry about that. [*A
pause.*] To-morrow there won't be a single officer or soldier
in the town. . . . All that will be just a memory, and, of
course, a new life will begin for us here. . . . [*A pause.*]
Nothing ever happens as we'd like it to. I didn't want to be
a headmistress, and yet now I am one. It means we shan't
be going to live in Moscow. . . .

VERSHININ. Well. . . . Thank you for everything. Forgive me if
ever I've done anything. . . . I've talked a lot too much,
far too much. . . . Forgive me for that, don't think too un-
kindly of me.

OLGA [*wipes her eyes*]. Now . . . why is Masha so long coming?

VERSHININ. What else can I tell you now it's time to say "good-
bye?" What shall I philosophize about now? . . . [*Laughs.*]
Yes, life is difficult. It seems quite hopeless for a lot of us,
just a kind of impasse. . . . And yet you must admit that it
is gradually getting easier and brighter, and it's clear that
the time isn't far off when the light will spread everywhere.
[*Looks at his watch.*] Time, it's time for me to go. . . . In the
old days the human race was always making war, its entire
existence was taken up with campaigns, advances, retreats,
victories. . . . But now all that's out of date, and in its place
there's a huge vacuum, clamouring to be filled. Humanity
is passionately seeking something to fill it with and, of
course, it will find something some day. Oh! If only it
would happen soon! [*A pause.*] If only we could educate the

industrious people and make the educated people industrious. . . . [*Looks at his watch.*] I really must go. . . .

OLGA. Here she comes!

[*Enter* MASHA.]

VERSHININ. I've come to say good-bye. . . .

[OLGA *walks off and stands a little to one side so as not to interfere with their leave-taking.*]

MASHA [*looking into his face*]. Good-bye! . . . [*A long kiss.*]
OLGA. That'll do, that'll do.
MASHA [*sobs loudly.*]
VERSHININ. Write to me. . . . Don't forget me! Let me go . . . it's time. Olga Serghyeevna, please take her away . . . I must go . . . I'm late already. . . . [*Deeply moved, kisses* OLGA's *hands, then embraces* MASHA *once again and goes out quickly.*]
OLGA. That'll do, Masha! Don't, my dear, don't. . . .

[*Enter* KOOLYGHIN.]

KOOLYGHIN [*embarrassed*]. Never mind, let her cry, let her. . . . My dear Masha, my dear, sweet Masha. . . . You're my wife, and I'm happy in spite of everything. . . . I'm not complaining, I've no reproach to make—not a single one. . . . Olga here is my witness. . . . We'll start our life over again in the same old way, and you won't hear a word from me . . . not a hint. . . .
MASHA [*suppressing her sobs.* "A green oak grows by a curving shore, And round that oak hangs a golden chain." . . . "A golden chain round that oak." . . . Oh, I'm going mad. . . . By a curving shore . . . a green oak. . . .
OLGA. Calm yourself, Masha, calm yourself. . . . Give her some water.
MASHA. I'm not crying any more. . . .
KOOLYGHIN. She's not crying any more . . . she's a good girl.

[*The hollow sound of a gun-shot is heard in the distance.*]

MASHA. "A green oak grows by a curving shore, And round that oak hangs a golden chain." ... A green cat ... a green oak ... I've got it all mixed up. ... [*Drinks water.*] My life's messed up. ... I don't want anything now. ... I'll calm down in a moment. ... it doesn't matter. ... What *is* "the curving shore"? Why does it keep coming into my head all the time? My thoughts are all mixed up.

[*Enter* IRENA.]

OLGA. Calm down, Masha. That's right ... good girl! ... Let's go indoors.

MASHA [*irritably*]. I'm not going in there! [*Sobs, but immediately checks herself.*] I don't go into that house now, and I'm not going to. ...

IRENA. Let's sit down together for a moment, and not talk about anything. I'm going away to-morrow, you know. ...

[*A pause.*]

KOOLYGHIN. Yesterday I took away a false beard and a moustache from a boy in the third form. I've got them here. [*Puts them on.*] Do I look like our German teacher? ... [*Laughs.*] I do, don't I? The boys are funny.

MASHA. It's true, you do look like that German of yours.

OLGA [*laughs.*]. Yes, he does.

[MASHA *cries.*]

IRENA. That's enough, Masha!

KOOLYGHIN. Very much like him, I think!

[*Enter* NATASHA.]

NATASHA [*to the maid*]. What? Oh, yes. Mr. Protopopov is going to keep an eye on Sofochka, and Andrey Serghyee-vich is going to take Bobik out in the pram. What a lot of work these children make! ... [*To* IRENA.] Irena, you're really leaving to-morrow? What a pity! Do stay just another week, won't you? [*Catching sight of* KOOLYGHIN, *shrieks; he laughs and takes off the false beard and moustache.*] Get

away with you! How you scared me! [*To* IRENA.] I've grown
so accustomed to you being here. . . . You mustn't think
it's going to be easy for me to be without you. I'll get Andrey and his old violin to move into your room: he can
saw away at it as much as he likes there. And then we'll
move Sofochka into his room. She's such a wonderful
child, really! Such a lovely little girl! This morning she
looked at me with such a sweet expression, and then she
said: "Ma-mma!"

KOOLYGHIN. It's quite true, she is a beautiful child.

NATASHA. So to-morrow I'll be alone here. [*Sighs.*] I'll have
this fire-tree avenue cut down first, then that maple tree
over there. It looks so awful in the evenings. . . . [*To* IRENA.]
My dear, that belt you're wearing doesn't suit you at all.
Not at all in good taste. You want something brighter to
go with that dress. . . . I'll tell them to put flowers all round
here, lots of flowers, so that we get plenty of scent from
them. . . . [*Sternly.*] Why is there a fork lying on this
seat? [*Going into the house, to the maid.*] Why is that fork
left on the seat there? [*Shouts.*] Don't answer me back!

KOOLYGHIN. There she goes again!

[*A band plays a military march off-stage; all listen.*]

OLGA. They're going.

[*Enter* CHEBUTYKIN.].

MASHA. The soldiers are going. Well. . . . Happy journey to
them! [*To her husband.*] We must go home. . . . Where's
my hat and cape? . . .

KOOLYGHIN. I took them indoors. I'll bring them at once.

OLGA. Yes, we can go home now. It's time.

CHEBUTYKIN. Olga Serghyeevna!

OLGA. What is it? [*A pause.*] What?

CHEBUTYKIN. Nothing. . . . I don't know quite how to tell
you. . . . [*Whispers into her ear.*]

OLGA [*frightened*]. It can't be true!

CHEBUTYKIN. Yes . . . a bad business. . . . I'm so tired . . .

quite worn out. . . . I don't want to say another word. . . .
[*With annoyance.*] Anyway, nothing matters! . . .

MASHA. What's happened?

OLGA. [*puts her arms round* IRENA]. What a dreadful day! . . . I
don't know how to tell you, dear. . . .

IRENA. What is it? Tell me quickly, what is it? For Heaven's
sake! . . . [*Cries.*]

CHEBUTYKIN. The Baron's just been killed in a duel.

IRENA [*cries quietly*]. I knew it, I knew it. . . .

CHEBUTYKIN [*goes to the back of the stage and sits down*].
I'm tired. . . . [*Takes a newspaper out of his pocket.*] Let
them cry for a bit. . . . [*Sings quietly to himself.*] Tarara-
boom-di-ay, I'm sitting on a tomb-di-ay. . . . What difference does it make? . . .

[*The three sisters stand huddled together.*]

MASHA. Oh, listen to that band! They're leaving us . . . one
of them's gone for good . . . for ever! We're left alone . . .
to start our lives all over again. We must go on living . . .
we must go on living. . . .

IRENA [*puts her head on* OLGA'S *breast*]. Some day people will
know why such things happen, and what the purpose of all
this suffering is. . . . Then there won't be any more riddles.
. . . Meanwhile we must go on living . . . and working. Yes,
we must just go on working! To-morrow I'll go away alone
and teach in a school somewhere; I'll give my life to
people who need it. . . . It's autumn now, winter will soon
be here, and the snow will cover everything . . . but I'll go
on working and working! . . .

OLGA [*puts her arms round both her sisters*]. How cheerfully
and jauntily that band's playing—really I feel as if I wanted
to live! Merciful God! The years will pass, and we shall
all be gone for good and quite forgotten. . . . Our faces
and our voices will be forgotten and people won't even
know that there were once three of us here. . . . But our suf-
ferings may mean happiness for the people who come after
us. . . . There'll be a time when peace and happiness reign

in the world, and then we shall be remembered kindly and blessed. No, my dear sisters, life isn't finished for us yet! We're going to live! The band is playing so cheerfully and joyfully—maybe, if we wait a little longer, we shall find out why we live, why we suffer.... Oh, if we only knew, if only we knew!

[*The music grows fainter and fainter.* KOOLYGHIN, *smiling happily, brings out the hat and the cape.* ANDREY *enters; he is pushing the pram with* BOBIK *sitting in it.*]

CHEBUTYKIN [*sings quietly to himself*]. Tarara-boom-di-ay.... I'm sitting on a tomb-di-ay.... [*Reads the paper.*] What does it matter? Nothing matters!

OLGA. If only we knew, if only we knew!...

THE MASTER BUILDER   [*1892*]

---

by Henrik Ibsen
[1828-1906]

CHARACTERS

HALVARD SOLNESS, *Master Builder.*

ALINE SOLNESS, *his wife.*

DOCTOR HERDAL, *physician.*

KNUT BROVIK, *formerly an architect, now in* SOLNESS'S *employment.*

RAGNAR BROVIK, *his son, draughtsman.*

KAIA FOSLI, *his niece, book-keeper.*

MISS HILDA WANGEL.

Some Ladies.

A Crowd in the street.
The action passes in and about SOLNESS'S *house.*

ACT ONE

_____

A plainly furnished work-room in the house of HALVARD SOL-
NESS. *Folding doors on the left lead out to the hall. On the
right is the door leading to the inner rooms of the house. At
the back is an open door into the draughtsmen's office. In
front, on the left, a desk with books, papers and writing materials. Further back than the folding-door, a stove. In the
right-hand corner, a sofa, a table and one or two chairs. On
the table a water-bottle and glass. A smaller table, with a
rocking-chair and arm-chair, in front on the right. Lighted
lamps, with shades, on the table in the draughtsmen's office,
on the table in the corner and on the desk.*

In the draughtsmen's office sit KNUT BROVIK *and his son* RAGNAR,
*occupied with plans and calculations. At the desk in the
outer office stands* KAIA FOSLI, *writing in the ledger.* KNUT
BROVIK *is a spare old man with white hair and beard. He
wears a rather threadbare but well-brushed black coat, spectacles and a somewhat discoloured white neckcloth.* RAG-
NAR BROVIK *is a well-dressed, light-haired man in his thirties,
with a slight stoop.* KAIA FOSLI *is a slightly built girl, a little
over twenty, carefully dressed and delicate-looking. She has
a green shade over her eyes.——All three go on working for
some time in silence.*

KNUT BROVIK [*rises suddenly, as if in distress, from the table;
breathes heavily and laboriously as he comes forward into*

the doorway]. No, I can't bear it much longer!

KAIA [*going up to him*]. You are feeling ill this evening, are you not, uncle?

BROVIK. Oh, I seem to get worse every day.

RAGNAR [*has risen and advances*]. You ought to go home, father. Try to get a little sleep——

BROVIK [*impatiently*]. Go to bed, I suppose? Would you have me stifled outright?

KAIA. Then take a little walk.

RAGNAR. Yes, do. I will come with you.

BROVIK [*with warmth*]. I will not go till he comes! I am determined to have it out this evening with—[*in a tone of suppressed bitterness*]—with him—with the chief.

KAIA [*anxiously*]. Oh no, uncle—do wait awhile before doing that.

RAGNAR. Yes, better wait, father!

BROVIK [*draws his breath laboriously*]. Ha—ha——! I haven't much time for waiting.

KAIA [*listening*]. Hush! I hear him on the stairs.

[*All three go back to their work. A short silence.*] [HALVARD SOLNESS *comes in through the hall door. He is a man no longer young, but healthy and vigorous, with close-cut curly hair, dark moustache and dark thick eyebrows. He wears a greyish-green buttoned jacket with an upstanding collar and broad lapels. On his head he wears a soft grey felt hat, and he has one or two light portfolios under his arm.*]

SOLNESS [*near the door, points towards the draughtsmen's office, and asks in a whisper:*] Are they gone?

KAIA [*softly, shaking her head*]. No.

[*She takes the shade off her eyes.* SOLNESS *crosses the room, throws his hat on a chair, places the portfolios on the table by the sofa and approaches the desk again.* KAIA *goes on writing without intermission, but seems nervous and uneasy.*]

SOLNESS [*aloud*]. What is that you are entering, Miss Fosli?

KAIA [*starts*]. Oh, it is only something that——

SOLNESS. Let me look at it, Miss Fosli. [*Bends over her, pretends to be looking into the ledger, and whispers:*] Kaia!

KAIA [*softly, still writing*]. Well?

SOLNESS. Why do you always take that shade off when I come?

KAIA [*as before*]. I look so ugly with it on.

SOLNESS [*smiling*]. Then you don't like to look ugly, Kaia?

KAIA [*half glancing up at him*]. Not for all the world. Not in your eyes.

SOLNESS [*stroking her hair gently*]. Poor, poor little Kaia——

KAIA [*bending her head*]. Hush—they can hear you.

[SOLNESS *strolls across the room to the right, turns and pauses at the door of the draughtsmen's office.*]

SOLNESS. Has any one been here for me?

RAGNAR [*rising*]. Yes, the young couple who want a villa built, out at Lövstrand.

SOLNESS [*growling*]. Oh, those two! They must wait. I am not quite clear about the plans yet.

RAGNAR [*advancing, with some hesitation*]. They were very anxious to have the drawings at once.

SOLNESS [*as before*]. Yes, of course—so they all are.

BROVIK [*looks up*]. They say they are longing so to get into a house of their own.

SOLNESS. Yes, yes—we know all that! And so they are content to take whatever is offered them. They get a—a roof over their heads—an address—but nothing to call a home. No thank you! In that case, let them apply to somebody else. Tell them that, the next time they call.

BROVIK [*pushes his glasses up on to his forehead and looks in astonishment at him*]. To somebody else? Are you prepared to give up the commission?

SOLNESS [*impatiently*]. Yes, yes, yes, devil take it! If that is to be the way of it——. Rather that, than build away at random. [*Vehemently.*] Besides, I know very little about these people as yet.

BROVIK. The people are safe enough. Ragnar knows them. He is a friend of the family. Perfectly safe people.

SOLNESS. Oh, safe—safe enough! That is not at all what I mean.
Good Lord—don't you understand me either? [*Angrily.*] I
won't have anything to do with these strangers. They may
apply to whom they please, so far as I am concerned.

BROVIK [*rising*]. Do you really mean that?

SOLNESS [*sulkily*]. Yes I do,—For once in a way.

[*He comes forward.*]

[BROVIK *exchanges a glance with* RAGNAR, *who makes a
warning gesture. Then* BROVIK *comes into the front room.*]

BROVIK. May I have a few words with you?

SOLNESS. Certainly.

BROVIK [*to* KAIA]. Just go in there for a moment, Kaia.

KAIA [*uneasily*]. Oh, but uncle——

BROVIK. Do as I say, child. And shut the door after you.

[KAIA *goes reluctantly into the draughtsmen's office, glances
anxiously and imploringly at* SOLNESS, *and shuts the door.*]

BROVIK [*lowering his voice a little*]. I don't want the poor children to know how ill I am.

SOLNESS. Yes, you have been looking very poorly of late.

BROVIK. It will soon be all over with me. My strength is ebbing—
from day to day.

SOLNESS. Won't you sit down?

BROVIK. Thanks—may I?

SOLNESS [*placing the arm-chair more conveniently*]. Here—
take this chair.—And now?

BROVIK [*has seated himself with difficulty*]. Well, you see, it's
about Ragnar. That is what weighs most upon me. What is
to become of him?

SOLNESS. Of course your son will stay with me as long as ever
he likes.

BROVIK. But that is just what he does not like. He feels that he
cannot stay here any longer.

SOLNESS. Why, I should say he was very well off here. But if
he wants more money, I should not mind——

BROVIK. No, no! It is not that. [*Impatiently.*] But sooner or later he, too, must have a chance of doing something on his own account.

SOLNESS [*without looking at him*]. Do you think that Ragnar has quite talent enough to stand alone?

BROVIK. No, that is just the heartbreaking part of it—I have begun to have my doubts about the boy. For you have never said so much as—as one encouraging word about him. And yet I cannot but think there must be something in him—he can't be without talent.

SOLNESS. Well, but he has learnt nothing—nothing thoroughly, I mean. Except, of course, to draw.

BROVIK [*looks at him with covert hatred and says hoarsely*]. You had learned little enough of the business when you were in my employment. But that did not prevent you from setting to work—[*breathing with difficulty*]—and pushing your way up and taking the wind out of my sails—mine, and so many other people's.

SOLNESS. Yes, you see—circumstances favoured me.

BROVIK. You are right there. Everything favoured you. But then how can you have the heart to let me go to my grave—without having seen what Ragnar is fit for? And of course I am anxious to see them married, too—before I go.

SOLNESS [*sharply*]. Is it she who wishes it?

BROVIK. Not Kaia so much as Ragnar—he talks about it every day. [*Appealingly.*] You must—you must help him to get some independent work now! I must see something that the lad has done. Do you hear?

SOLNESS [*peevishly*]. Hang it, man, you can't expect me to drag commissions down from the moon for him!

BROVIK. He has the chance of a capital commission at this very moment. A big bit of work.

SOLNESS [*uneasily, startled*]. Has he?

BROVIK. If you would give your consent.

SOLNESS. What sort of work do you mean?

BROVIK [*with some hesitation*]. He can have the building of that villa out at Lövstrand.

SOLNESS. That! Why, I am going to build that myself.

BROVIK. Oh, you don't much care about doing it.

SOLNESS [*flaring up*]. Don't care! I? Who dares to say that?

BROVIK. You said so yourself just now.

SOLNESS. Oh, never mind what I say.—Would they give Ragnar the building of that villa?

BROVIK. Yes. You see, he knows the family. And then—just for the fun of the thing—he has made drawings and estimates and so forth——

SOLNESS. Are they pleased with the drawings? The people who will have to live in the house?

BROVIK. Yes. If you would only look through them and approve of them.

SOLNESS. Then they would let Ragnar build their home for them?

BROVIK. They were immensely pleased with his idea. They thought it exceedingly original, they said.

SOLNESS. Oho! Original! Not the old-fashioned stuff that *I* am in the habit of turning out!

BROVIK. It seemed to them different.

SOLNESS [*with suppressed irritation*]. So it was to see Ragnar that they came here—whilst I was out!

BROVIK. They came to call upon you—and at the same time to ask whether you would mind retiring——

SOLNESS [*angrily*]. Retire? I?

BROVIK. In case you thought that Ragnar's drawings——

SOLNESS. I? Retire in favour of your son!

BROVIK. Retire from the agreement, they meant.

SOLNESS. Oh, it comes to the same thing. [*Laughs angrily.*] So that is it, is it? Halvard Solness is to see about retiring now! To make room for younger men! For the very youngest perhaps! He must make room! Room! Room!

BROVIK. Why, good heavens! there is surely room for more than one single man——

SOLNESS. Oh, there's not so very much room to spare either. But, be that as it may—I will never retire! I will never give way to anybody! Never of my own free will. Never in this world will I do that!

BROVIK [*rises with difficulty*]. Then I am to pass out of life without any certainty? Without a gleam of happiness? Without any faith or trust in Ragnar? Without having seen a single piece of work of his doing? Is that to be the way of it?

SOLNESS [*turns half aside and mutters*]. H'm—don't ask more just now.

BROVIK. I must have an answer to this one question. Am I to pass out of life in such utter poverty?

SOLNESS [*seems to struggle with himself; finally he says, in a low but firm voice:*] You must pass out of life as best you can.

BROVIK. Then be it so. [*He goes up the room.*]

SOLNESS [*following him, half in desperation*]. Don't you understand that I cannot help it? I am what I am, and I cannot change my nature!

BROVIK. No, no; I suppose you can't. [*Reels and supports himself against the sofa-table.*] May I have a glass of water?

SOLNESS. By all means. [*Fills a glass and hands it to him.*]

BROVIK. Thanks. [*Drinks and puts the glass down again.*]

[SOLNESS *goes up and opens the door of the draughtsmen's office.*]

SOLNESS. Ragnar—you must come and take your father home.

[RAGNAR *rises quickly. He and* KAIA *come into the workroom.*]

RAGNAR. What is the matter, father?

BROVIK. Give me your arm. Now let us go.

RAGNAR. Very well. You had better put your things on, too, Kaia.

SOLNESS. Miss Fosli must stay—just for a moment. There is a letter I want written.

BROVIK [*looks at* SOLNESS]. Good night. Sleep well—if you can.

SOLNESS. Good night.

[BROVIK *and* RAGNAR *go out by the hall door.* KAIA *goes to the desk.* SOLNESS *stands with bent head, to the right, by the armchair.*]

KAIA [*dubiously*]. Is there any letter——?

SOLNESS [*curtly*]. No, of course not. [*Looks sternly at her*]. Kaia!

KAIA [*anxiously, in a low voice*]. Yes!

SOLNESS [*points imperatively to a spot on the floor*]. Come here! At once!

KAIA [*hesitatingly*]. Yes.

SOLNESS [*as before*]. Nearer!

KAIA [*obeying*]. What do you want with me?

SOLNESS [*looks at her for a while*]. Is it you I have to thank for all this?

KAIA. No, no, don't think that!

SOLNESS. But confess now—you want to get married!

KAIA [*softly*]. Ragnar and I have been engaged for four or five years, and so——

SOLNESS. And so you think it time there were an end to it. Is not that so?

KAIA. Ragnar and Uncle say I must. So I suppose I shall have to give in.

SOLNESS [*more gently*]. Kaia, don't you really care a little bit for Ragnar, too?

KAIA. I cared very much for Ragnar once—before I came here to you.

SOLNESS. But you don't now? Not in the least?

KAIA [*passionately, clasping her hands and holding them out towards him*]. Oh, you know very well there is only one person I care for now! One, and one only, in all the world! I shall never care for any one else.

SOLNESS. Yes, you say that. And yet you go away from me—leave me alone here with everything on my hands.

KAIA. But could I not stay with you, even if Ragnar——?

SOLNESS [*repudiating the idea*]. No, no, that is quite impossible. If Ragnar leaves me and starts work on his own account, then of course he will need you himself.

KAIA [*wringing her hands*]. Oh, I feel as if I could not be separated from you! It's quite, quite impossible!

SOLNESS. Then be sure you get those foolish notions out of Ragnar's head. Marry him as much as you please—[*alters his tone*]. I mean—don't let him throw up his good situation with me. For then I can keep you, too, my dear Kaia.

KAIA. Oh yes, how lovely that would be, if it could only be managed!

SOLNESS [*clasps her head with his two hands and whispers*]. For I cannot get on without you, you see. I must have you with me every single day.

KAIA [*in nervous exaltation*]. My God! My God!

SOLNESS [*kisses her hair*]. Kaia—Kaia!

KAIA [*sinks down before him*]. Oh, how good you are to me! How unspeakably good you are!

SOLNESS [*vehemently*]. Get up! For goodness' sake get up! I think I hear some one!

[*He helps her to rise. She staggers over to the desk*].

[MRS. SOLNESS *enters by the door on the right. She looks thin and wasted with grief, but shows traces of bygone beauty. Blonde ringlets. Dressed with good taste, wholly in black. Speaks somewhat slowly and in a plaintive voice.*]

MRS. SOLNESS [*in the doorway*]. Halvard!

SOLNESS [*turns*]. Oh, are you there, my dear——?

MRS. SOLNESS [*with a glance at* KAIA]. I am afraid I am disturbing you.

SOLNESS. Not in the least. Miss Fosli has only a short letter to write.

MRS. SOLNESS. Yes, so I see.

SOLNESS. What do you want with me, Aline?

MRS. SOLNESS. I merely wanted to tell you that Dr. Herdal is in the drawing-room. Won't you come and see him, Halvard?

SOLNESS [*looks suspiciously at her*]. H'm—is the doctor so very anxious to talk to me?

MRS. SOLNESS. Well, not exactly anxious. He really came to see me; but he would like to say how-do-you-do to you at the same time.

SOLNESS [*laughs to himself*]. Yes, I daresay. Well, you must ask him to wait a little.

MRS. SOLNESS. Then you will come in presently?

SOLNESS. Perhaps I will. Presently, presently, dear. In a little while.

MRS. SOLNESS [*glancing again at* KAIA]. Well, now, don't forget, Halvard.   [*Withdraws and closes the door behind her*].

KAIA [*softly*]. Oh dear, oh dear—I am sure Mrs. Solness thinks ill of me in some way!

SOLNESS. Oh, not in the least. Not more than usual, at any rate. But all the same, you had better go now, Kaia.

KAIA. Yes, yes, now I must go.

SOLNESS [*severely*]. And mind you get that matter settled for me. Do you hear?

KAIA. Oh, if it only depended on me——

SOLNESS. I will have it settled, I say! And to-morrow too—not a day later!

KAIA [*terrified*]. If there's nothing else for it, I am quite willing to break off the engagement.

SOLNESS [*angrily*]. Break it off? Are you mad? Would you think of breaking it off?

KAIA [*distracted*]. Yes, if necessary. For I must—I must stay here with you! I can't leave you! That is utterly—utterly impossible!

SOLNESS [*with a sudden outburst*]. But deuce take it—how about Ragnar then! It's Ragnar that I——

KAIA [*looks at him with terrified eyes*]. It is chiefly on Ragnar's account, that—that you——

SOLNESS [*collecting himself*]. No, no, of course not! You don't understand me either. [*Gently and softly.*] Of course it is you I want to keep—you above everything, Kaia. But for that very reason, you must prevent Ragnar, too, from throwing up his situation. There, there,—now go home.

KAIA. Yes, yes—good-night, then.

SOLNESS. Good-night. [*As she is going.*] Oh, stop a moment! Are Ragnar's drawings in there?

KAIA. I did not see him take them with him.

SOLNESS. Then just go and find them for me. I might perhaps glance over them, after all.

KAIA [*happy*]. Oh yes, please do!

SOLNESS. For your sake, Kaia dear. Now, let me have them at once, please.

[KAIA *hurries into the draughtsmen's office, searches anxiously in the table-drawer, finds a portfolio and brings it with her.*]

KAIA. Here are all the drawings.

SOLNESS. Good. Put them down there on the table.

KAIA [*putting down the portfolio*]. Good-night, then. [*Beseechingly.*] And please, please think kindly of me.

SOLNESS. Oh, that I always do. Good-night, my dear little Kaia. [*Glances to the right.*] Go, go now!

[MRS. SOLNESS *and* DR. HERDAL *enter by the door on the right. He is a stoutish, elderly man, with a round, good-humoured face, clean shaven, with thin, light hair, and gold spectacles.*]

MRS. SOLNESS [*still in the doorway*]. Halvard, I cannot keep the doctor any longer.

SOLNESS. Well then, come in here.

MRS. SOLNESS [*to* KAIA *who is turning down the desk lamp*]. Have you finished the letter already, Miss Fosli?

KAIA [*in confusion*]. The letter——?

SOLNESS. Yes, it was quite a short one.

MRS. SOLNESS. It must have been very short.

SOLNESS. You may go now, Miss Fosli. And please come in good time to-morrow morning.

KAIA. I will be sure to. Good-night, Mrs. Solness.

[*She goes out by the hall door.*]

MRS. SOLNESS. She must be quite an acquisition to you, Halvard, this Miss Fosli.

SOLNESS. Yes, indeed. She is useful in all sorts of ways.

MRS. SOLNESS. So it seems.

DR. HERDAL. Is she good at book-keeping too?

SOLNESS. Well—of course she has had a good deal of practice
during these two years. And then she is so nice and willing
to do whatever one asks of her.

MRS. SOLNESS. Yes, that must be very delightful——

SOLNESS. It is. Especially when one is not too much accustomed to that sort of thing.

MRS. SOLNESS [*in a tone of gentle remonstrance*]. Can you say
that, Halvard?

SOLNESS. Oh, no, no, my dear Aline; I beg your pardon.

MRS. SOLNESS. There's no occasion.—Well then, doctor, you
will come back later on and have a cup of tea with us?

DR. HERDAL. I have only that one patient to see and then I'll
come back.

MRS. SOLNESS. Thank you.

[*She goes out by the door on the right.*]

SOLNESS. Are you in a hurry, doctor?

DR. HERDAL. No, not at all.

SOLNESS. May I have a little chat with you?

DR. HERDAL. With the greatest of pleasure.

SOLNESS. Then let us sit down. [*He motions the doctor to take
the rocking-chair and sits down himself in the arm-chair.
Looks searchingly at him.*] Tell me—did you notice anything odd about Aline?

DR. HERDAL. Do you mean just now, when she was here?

SOLNESS. Yes, in her manner to me. Did you notice anything?

DR. HERDAL [*smiling*]. Well, I admit—one couldn't well avoid
noticing that your wife—h'm——

SOLNESS. Well?

DR. HERDAL. ——that your wife is not particularly fond of this
Miss Fosli.

SOLNESS. Is that all? I have noticed that myself.

DR. HERDAL. And I must say I am scarcely surprised at it.

SOLNESS. At what?

DR. HERDAL. That she should not exactly approve of your seeing so much of another woman, all day and every day.

SOLNESS. No, no, I suppose you are right there—and Aline too. But it's impossible to make any change.

DR. HERDAL. Could you not engage a clerk?

SOLNESS. The first man that came to hand? No, thank you— that would never do for me.

DR. HERDAL. But now, if your wife——? Suppose, with her delicate health, all this tries her too much?

SOLNESS. Even then—I might almost say—it can make no difference. I must keep Kaia Fosli. No one else could fill her place.

DR. HERDAL. No one else?

SOLNESS [curtly]. No, no one.

DR. HERDAL [drawing his chair closer]. Now listen to me, my dear Mr. Solness. May I ask you a question, quite between ourselves?

SOLNESS. By all means.

DR. HERDAL. Women, you see—in certain matters, they have a deucedly keen intuition——

SOLNESS. They have, indeed. There is not the least doubt of that. But——?

DR. HERDAL. Well, tell me now—if your wife can't endure this Kaia Fosli——?

SOLNESS. Well, what then?

DR. HERDAL. ——may she not have just—just the least little bit of reason for this instinctive dislike?

SOLNESS [looks at him and rises]. Oho!

DR. HERDAL. Now don't be offended—but hasn't she?

SOLNESS [with curt decision]. No.

DR. HERDAL. No reason of any sort?

SOLNESS. No other reason than her own suspicious nature.

DR. HERDAL. I know you have known a good many women in your time.

SOLNESS. Yes, I have.

DR. HERDAL. And have been a good deal taken with some of them, too.

SOLNESS. Oh, yes, I don't deny it.

DR. HERDAL. But as regards Miss Fosli, then? There is nothing of that sort in the case?

SOLNESS. No, nothing at all—on my side.

DR. HERDAL. But on her side.

SOLNESS. I don't think you have any right to ask that question, doctor.

DR. HERDAL. Well, you know, we were discussing your wife's intuition.

SOLNESS. So we were. And for that matter—[*lowers his voice*] —Aline's intuition, as you call it—in a certain sense, it has not been so far astray.

DR. HERDAL. Aha! there we have it!

SOLNESS [*sits down*]. Doctor Herdal—I am going to tell you a strange story—if you care to listen to it.

DR. HERDAL. I like listening to strange stories.

SOLNESS. Very well then. I daresay you recollect that I took Knut Brovik and his son into my employment—after the old man's business had gone to the dogs.

DR. HERDAL. Yes, so I have understood.

SOLNESS. You see, they really are clever fellows, these two. Each of them has talent in his own way. But then the son took it into his head to get engaged; and the next thing, of course, was that he wanted to get married—and begin to build on his own account. That is the way with all these young people.

DR. HERDAL [*laughing*]. Yes, they have a bad habit of wanting to marry.

SOLNESS. Just so. But of course that did not suit my plans; for I needed Ragnar myself—and the old man, too. He is exceedingly good at calculating bearing-strains and cubic contents—and all that sort of devilry, you know.

DR. HERDAL. Oh, yes, no doubt that's indispensable.

SOLNESS. Yes, it is. But Ragnar was absolutely bent on setting to work for himself. He would hear of nothing else.

DR. HERDAL. But he has stayed with you all the same.

SOLNESS. Yes, I'll tell you how that came about. One day this girl, Kaia Fosli, came to see them on some errand or other.

She had never been here before. And when I saw how utterly infatuated they were with each other, the thought occurred to me: if I could only get her into the office here, then perhaps Ragnar, too, would stay where he is.

DR. HERDAL. That was not at all a bad idea.

SOLNESS. Yes, but at the time I did not breathe a word of what was in my mind. I merely stood and looked at her—and kept on wishing intently that I could have her here. Then I talked to her a little, in a friendly way—about one thing and another. And then she went away.

DR. HERDAL. Well?

SOLNESS. Well, then, next day, pretty late in the evening, when old Brovik and Ragnar had gone home, she came here again and behaved as if I had made an arrangement with her.

DR. HERDAL. An arrangement? What about?

SOLNESS. About the very thing my mind had been fixed on. But I hadn't said one single word about it.

DR. HERDAL. That was most extraordinary.

SOLNESS. Yes, was it not? And now she wanted to know what she was to do here—whether she could begin the very next morning, and so forth.

DR. HERDAL. Don't you think she did it in order to be with her sweetheart?

SOLNESS. That was what occurred to me at first. But no, that was not it. She seemed to drift quite away from him—when once she had come here to me.

DR. HERDAL. She drifted over to you, then?

SOLNESS. Yes, entirely. If I happen to look at her when her back is turned, I can tell that she feels it. She quivers and trembles the moment I come near her. What do you think of that?

DR. HERDAL. H'm—that's not very hard to explain.

SOLNESS. Well, but what about the other thing? That she believed I had said to her what I had only wished and willed —silently—inwardly—to myself? What do you say to that? Can you explain that, Dr. Herdal?

DR. HERDAL. No, I won't undertake to do that.

SOLNESS. I felt sure you would not; and so I have never cared to talk about it till now. But it's a cursed nuisance to me in the long run, you understand. Here I have to go on day after day pretending——. And it's a shame to treat her so, too, poor girl. [*Vehemently.*] But I cannot do anything else. For if she runs away from me—then Ragnar will be off too.

DR. HERDAL. And you have not told your wife the rights of the story?

SOLNESS. No.

DR. HERDAL. Then why on earth don't you?

SOLNESS [*looks fixedly at him, and says in a low voice:*] Because I seem to find a sort of—of salutary self-torture in allowing Aline to do me an injustice.

DR. HERDAL [*shakes his head*]. I don't in the least understand what you mean.

SOLNESS. Well, you see—it is like paying off a little bit of a huge, immeasurable debt——

DR. HERDAL. To your wife?

SOLNESS. Yes; and that always helps to relieve one's mind a little. One can breathe more freely for a while, you understand.

DR. HERDAL. No, goodness knows, I don't understand at all——

SOLNESS [*breaking off, rises again*]. Well, well, well—then we won't talk any more about it. [*He saunters across the room, returns and stops beside the table. Looks at the doctor with a sly smile.*] I suppose you think you have drawn me out nicely now, doctor?

DR. HERDAL [*with some irritation*]. Drawn you out? Again I have not the faintest notion what you mean, Mr. Solness.

SOLNESS. Oh come, out with it; I have seen it quite clearly, you know.

DR. HERDAL. What have you seen?

SOLNESS [*in a low voice, slowly*]. That you have been quietly keeping an eye upon me.

DR. HERDAL. That *I* have! And why in all the world should I do that?

SOLNESS. Because you think that I—— [*Passionately.*] Well,

devil take it—you think the same of me as Aline does.

DR. HERDAL. And what does she think of you?

SOLNESS [*having recovered his self-control*]. She has begun to think that I am——that I am——ill.

DR. HERDAL. Ill! You! She has never hinted such a thing to me. Why, what can she think is the matter with you?

SOLNESS [*leans over the back of the chair and whispers*]. Aline has made up her mind that I am mad. That is what she thinks.

DR. HERDAL [*rising*]. Why, my dear good fellow——!

SOLNESS. Yes, on my soul she does! I tell you it is so. And she has got you to think the same! Oh, I can assure you, doctor, I see it in your face as clearly as possible. You don't take me in so easily, I can tell you.

DR. HERDAL [*looks at him in amazement*]. Never, Mr. Solness— never has such a thought entered my mind.

SOLNESS [*with an incredulous smile*]. Really? Has it not?

DR. HERDAL. No, never! Nor your wife's mind either, I am convinced. I could almost swear to that.

SOLNESS. Well, I wouldn't advise you to. For, in a certain sense, you see, perhaps—perhaps she is not so far wrong in thinking something of the kind.

DR. HERDAL. Come now, I really must say——

SOLNESS [*interrupting with a sweep of his hand*]. Well, well, my dear doctor—don't let us discuss this any further. We had better agree to differ. [*Changes to a tone of quiet amusement.*] But look here now, doctor—h'm——

DR. HERDAL. Well?

SOLNESS. Since you don't believe that I am—ill—and crazy, and mad, and so forth——

DR. HERDAL. What then?

SOLNESS. Then I daresay you fancy that I am an extremely happy man.

DR. HERDAL. Is that mere fancy?

SOLNESS [*laughs*]. No, no—of course not! Heaven forbid! Only think—to be Solness the master builder! Halvard Solness! What could be more delightful?

DR. HERDAL. Yes, I must say it seems to me you have had the luck on your side to an astounding degree.

SOLNESS [suppresses a gloomy smile]. So I have, I can't complain on that score.

DR. HERDAL. First of all that grim old robbers' castle was burnt down for you. And that was certainly a great piece of luck.

SOLNESS [seriously]. It was the home of Aline's family. Remember that.

DR. HERDAL. Yes, it must have been a great grief to her.

SOLNESS. She has not got over it to this day—not in all these twelve or thirteen years.

DR. HERDAL. Ah, but what followed must have been the worst blow for her.

SOLNESS. The one thing with the other.

DR. HERDAL. But you—yourself—you rose upon the ruins. You began as a poor boy from a country village—and now you are at the head of your profession. Ah, yes, Mr. Solness, you have undoubtedly had the luck on your side.

SOLNESS [looking at him with embarrassment]. Yes, but that is just what makes me so horribly afraid.

DR. HERDAL. Afraid? Because you have the luck on your side!

SOLNESS. It terrifies me—terrifies me every hour of the day. For sooner or later the luck must turn, you see.

DR. HERDAL. Oh nonsense! What should make the luck turn?

SOLNESS [with firm assurance]. The younger generation.

DR. HERDAL. Pooh! The younger generation! You are not laid on the shelf yet, I should hope. Oh no—your position here is probably firmer now than it has ever been.

SOLNESS. The luck will turn. I know it—I feel the day approaching. Some one or other will take it into his head to say: Give me a chance! And then all the rest will come clamouring after him, and shake their fists at me and shout: Make room—make room—make room! Yes, just you see, doctor—presently the younger generation will come knock at my door——

DR. HERDAL [laughing]. Well, and what if they do?

SOLNESS. What if they do? Then there's an end of Halvard

Solness.

[*There is a knock at the door on the left.*]

SOLNESS [*starts*]. What's that? Did you not hear something?

DR. HERDAL. Some one is knocking at the door.

SOLNESS [*loudly*]. Come in.

[HILDA WANGEL *enters by the hall door. She is of middle height, supple and delicately built. Somewhat sunburnt. Dressed in a tourist costume, with skirt caught up for walking, a sailor's collar open at the throat and a small sailor hat on her head. Knapsack on back, plaid in strap, and alpenstock.*]

HILDA [*goes straight up to* SOLNESS, *her eyes sparkling with happiness*]. Good evening!

SOLNESS [*looks doubtfully at her*]. Good evening——

HILDA [*laughs*]. I almost believe you don't recognise me!

SOLNESS. No——I must admit that——just for the moment——

DR. HERDAL [*approaching*]. But I recognise you, my dear young lady——

HILDA [*pleased*]. Oh, is it you that——

DR. HERDAL. Of course it is. [*To* SOLNESS.] We met at one of the mountain stations this summer. [*To* HILDA.] What became of the other ladies?

HILDA. Oh, they went westward.

DR. HERDAL. They didn't much like all the fun we used to have in the evenings.

HILDA. No, I believe they didn't.

DR. HERDAL [*holds up his finger at her*]. And I am afraid it can't be denied that you flirted a little with us.

HILDA. Well that was better fun than to sit there knitting stockings with all those old women.

DR. HERDAL [*laughs*]. There I entirely agree with you.

SOLNESS. Have you come to town this evening?

HILDA. Yes, I have just arrived.

DR. HERDAL. Quite alone, Miss Wangel?

HILDA. Oh, yes!

SOLNESS. Wangel? Is your name Wangel?

HILDA [*looks in amused surprise at him*]. Yes, of course it is.

SOLNESS. Then you must be a daughter of the district doctor up at Lysanger?

HILDA [*as before*]. Yes, who else's daughter should I be?

SOLNESS. Oh, then I suppose we met up there, that summer when I was building a tower on the old church.

HILDA [*more seriously*]. Yes, of course it was then we met.

SOLNESS. Well, that is a long time ago.

HILDA [*looks hard at him*]. It is exactly ten years.

SOLNESS. You must have been a mere child then, I should think.

HILDA [*carelessly*]. Well, I was twelve or thirteen.

DR. HERDAL. Is this the first time you have ever been up to town, Miss Wangel?

HILDA. Yes, it is indeed.

SOLNESS. And don't you know any one here?

HILDA. Nobody but you. And of course, your wife.

SOLNESS. So you know her, too?

HILDA. Only a little. We spent a few days together at the sanitorium.

SOLNESS. Ah, up there?

HILDA. She said I might come and pay her a visit if ever I came up to town. [*Smiles.*] Not that that was necessary.

SOLNESS. Odd that she should never have mentioned it.

[HILDA *puts her stick down by the stove, takes off the knapsack and lays it and the plaid on the sofa.* DR. HERDAL *offers to help her.* SOLNESS *stands and gazes at her.*]

HILDA [*going towards him*]. Well, now I must ask you to let me stay the night here.

SOLNESS. I am sure there will be no difficulty about that.

HILDA. For I have no other clothes than those I stand in, except a change of linen in my knapsack. And that has to go to the wash, for it's very dirty.

SOLNESS. Oh, yes, that can be managed. Now I'll just let my wife know——

DR. HERDAL. Meanwhile I will go and see my patient.

SOLNESS. Yes, do; and come again later on.

DR. HERDAL [*playfully, with a glance at* HILDA]. Oh, that I will, you may be very certain! [*Laughs.*] So your prediction has come true, Mr. Solness!

SOLNESS. How so?

DR. HERDAL. The younger generation did come knocking at your door.

SOLNESS [*cheerfully*]. Yes, but in a very different way from what I meant.

DR. HERDAL. Very different, yes. That's undeniable.

[*He goes out by the hall door.* SOLNESS *opens the door on the right and speaks into the side room.*]

SOLNESS. Aline! Will you come in here, please. Here is a friend of yours—Miss Wangel.

MRS. SOLNESS [*appears in the doorway*]. Who did you say it is? [*Sees* HILDA.] Oh, is it you, Miss Wangel? [*Goes up to her and offers her hand.*] So you have come to town after all.

SOLNESS. Miss Wangel has this moment arrived: and she would like to stay the night here.

MRS. SOLNESS. Here with us? Oh yes, certainly.

SOLNESS. Till she can get her things a little in order, you know.

MRS. SOLNESS. I will do the best I can for you. It's no more than my duty. I suppose your trunk is coming on later?

HILDA. I have no trunk.

MRS. SOLNESS. Well, it will be all right, I daresay. In the meantime, you must excuse my leaving you here with my husband, until I can get a room made a little comfortable for you.

SOLNESS. Can we not give her one of the nurseries? They are all ready as it is.

MRS. SOLNESS. Oh, yes. There we have room and to spare [*To* HILDA.] Sit down now, and rest a little.

[*She goes out to the right.*]

[HILDA, *with her hands behind her back, strolls about the*

room and looks at various objects. SOLNESS *stands in front, beside the table, also with his hands behind his back, and follows her with his eyes.*]

HILDA [*stops and looks at him*]. Have you several nurseries?

SOLNESS. There are three nurseries in the house.

HILDA. That's a lot. Then I suppose you have a great many children?

SOLNESS. No. We have no child. But now you can be the child here, for the time being.

HILDA. For to-night, yes. I shall not cry. I mean to sleep as sound as a stone.

SOLNESS. Yes, you must be very tired, I should think.

HILDA. Oh, no! But all the same—— It's so delicious to lie and dream.

SOLNESS. Do you dream much of nights?

HILDA. Oh, yes! Almost always.

SOLNESS. What do you dream about most?

HILDA. I shan't tell you to-night. Another time, perhaps.

[*She again strolls about the room, stops at the desk and turns over the books and papers a little.*]

SOLNESS [*approaching*]. Are you searching for anything?

HILDA. No, I am merely looking at all these things. [*Turns.*] Perhaps I mustn't?

SOLNESS. Oh, by all means.

HILDA. Is it you that writes in this great ledger?

SOLNESS. No, it's my book-keeper.

HILDA. Is it a woman?

SOLNESS [*smiles*]. Yes.

HILDA. One you employ here, in your office?

SOLNESS. Yes.

HILDA. Is she married?

SOLNESS. No, she is single.

HILDA. Oh, indeed!

SOLNESS. But I believe she is soon going to be married.

HILDA. That's a good thing for her.

SOLNESS. But not such a good thing for me. For then I shall have nobody to help me.

HILDA. Can't you get hold of some one else who will do just as well?

SOLNESS. Perhaps you would stay here and write in the ledger?

HILDA [*measures him with a glance*]. Yes, I daresay! No, thank you—nothing of that sort for me.

[*She again strolls across the room and sits down in the rocking-chair.* SOLNESS, *too, goes to the table.*]

HILDA [*continuing*]. For there must surely be plenty of other things to be done here. [*Looks smiling at him.*] Don't you think so, too?

SOLNESS. Of course. First of all, I suppose, you want to make a round of the shops and get yourself up in the height of fashion.

HILDA [*amused*]. No, I think I shall let that alone!

SOLNESS. Indeed.

HILDA. For you must know I have run through all my money.

SOLNESS [*laughs*]. Neither trunk nor money, then.

HILDA. Neither one nor the other. But never mind—it doesn't matter now.

SOLNESS. Come now, I like you for that.

HILDA. Only for that?

SOLNESS For that among other things. [*Sits in the armchair.*] Is your father alive still?

HILDA. Yes, father's alive.

SOLNESS. Perhaps you are thinking of studying here?

HILDA. No, that hadn't occurred to me.

SOLNESS. But I suppose you will be staying for some time?

HILDA. That must depend upon circumstances.

[*She sits awhile rocking herself and looking at him, half seriously, half with a suppressed smile. Then she takes off her hat and puts it on the table in front of her.*]

HILDA. Mr. Solness!

SOLNESS. Well?

HILDA. Have you a very bad memory?

SOLNESS. A bad memory? No, not that I am aware of.

HILDA. Then have you nothing to say to me about what happened up there?

SOLNESS [*in momentary surprise*]. Up at Lysanger? [*Indifferently.*] Why, it was nothing much to talk about, it seems to me.

HILDA [*looks reproachfully at him*]. How can you sit there and say such things?

SOLNESS. Well, then, you talk to me about it.

HILDA. When the tower was finished, we had grand doings in the town.

SOLNESS. Yes, I shall not easily forget that day.

HILDA [*smiles*]. Will you not? That comes well from you.

SOLNESS. Comes well?

HILDA. There was music in the churchyard—and many, many hundreds of people. We school-girls were dressed in white; and we all carried flags.

SOLNESS. Ah yes, those flags—I can tell you I remember them!

HILDA. Then you climbed right up the scaffolding, straight to the very top; and you had a great wreath with you; and you hung that wreath right away up on the weather-vane.

SOLNESS [*curtly interrupting*]. I always did that in those days. It was an old custom.

HILDA. It was so wonderfully thrilling to stand below and look up at you. Fancy, if he should fall over! He—the master builder himself!

SOLNESS [*as if to divert her from the subject*]. Yes, yes, yes that might very well have happened, too. For one of those white-frocked little devils,—she went on in such a way, and screamed up at me so——

HILDA [*sparkling with pleasure*]. "Hurrah for Master Builder Solness!" Yes!

SOLNESS. ——and waved and flourished with her flag, so that I—so that it almost made me giddy to look at it.

HILDA [*in a lower voice, seriously*]. That little devil—that was *I*.

SOLNESS [*fixes his eyes steadily upon her*]. I am sure of that now.

It must have been you.

HILDA [*lively again*]. Oh, it was so gloriously thrilling! I could not have believed there was a builder in the whole world that could build such a tremendously high tower. And then, that you yourself should stand at the very top of it, as large as life! And that you should not be the least bit dizzy! It was that above everything that made one—made one dizzy to think of.

SOLNESS. How could you be so certain that I was not——?

HILDA [*scouting the idea*]. No indeed! Oh, no! I knew that instinctively. For if you had been, you could never have stood up there and sung.

SOLNESS [*looks at her in astonishment*]. Sung? Did I sing?

HILDA. Yes, I should think you did.

SOLNESS [*shakes his head*]. I have never sung a note in my life.

HILDA. Yes indeed, you sang then. It sounded like harps in the air.

SOLNESS [*thoughtfully*]. This is very strange—all this.

HILDA [*is silent awhile, looks at him and says in a low voice:*] But then,—it was after that—and the real thing happened.

SOLNESS. The real thing?

HILDA [*sparkling with vivacity*]. Yes, I surely don't need to remind you of that?

SOLNESS. Oh, yes, do remind me a little of that, too.

HILDA. Don't you remember that a great dinner was given in your honour at the Club?

SOLNESS. Yes, to be sure. It must have been the same afternoon, for I left the place next morning.

HILDA. And from the Club you were invited to come round to our house to supper.

SOLNESS. Quite right, Miss Wangel. It is wonderful how all these trifles have impressed themselves on your mind.

HILDA. Trifles! I like that! Perhaps it was a trifle, too, that I was alone in the room when you came in?

SOLNESS. Were you alone?

HILDA [*without answering him*]. You didn't call me a little devil then?

SOLNESS. No, I suppose I did not.

HILDA. You said I was lovely in my white dress, and that I looked like a little princess.

SOLNESS. I have no doubt you did, Miss Wangel.—And besides —I was feeling so buoyant and free that day——

HILDA. And then you said that when I grew up I should be your princess.

SOLNESS [*laughing a little*]. Dear, dear—did I say that, too?

HILDA. Yes, you did. And when I asked how long I should have to wait, you said that you would come again in ten years— like a troll and carry me off—to Spain or some such place. And you promised you would buy me a kingdom there.

SOLNESS [*as before*]. Yes, after a good dinner one doesn't haggle about the halfpence. But did I really say all that?

HILDA [*laughs to herself*]. Yes. And you told me, too, what the kingdom was to be called.

SOLNESS. Well, what was it?

HILDA. It was to be called the kingdom of Orangia,* you said.

SOLNESS. Well, that was an appetising name.

HILDA. No, I didn't like it a bit; for it seemed as though you wanted to make a game of me.

SOLNESS. I am sure that cannot have been my intention.

HILDA. No, I should hope not—considering what you did next——

SOLNESS. What in the world did I do next?

HILDA. Well, that's the finishing touch, if you have forgotten that, too. I should have thought no one could help remembering such a thing as that.

SOLNESS. Yes, yes, just give me a hint, and then perhaps—— Well——

HILDA [*looks fixedly at him*]. You came and kissed me, Mr. Solness.

SOLNESS [*open-mouthed, rising from his chair*]. *I* did!

HILDA. Yes, indeed you did. You took me in both your arms, and bent my head back and kissed me—many times.

SOLNESS. Now really, my dear Miss Wangel——!

* In the original "Appelsinia," "appelsin" meaning "orange."

HILDA [*rises*]. You surely cannot mean to deny it?

SOLNESS. Yes, I do. I deny it altogether!

HILDA [*looks scornfully at him*]. Oh, indeed!

[*She turns and goes slowly close up to the stove, where she remains standing motionless, her face averted from him. her hands behind her back. Short pause.*]

SOLNESS [*goes cautiously up behind her*]. Miss Wangel——!

HILDA [*is silent and does not move*].

SOLNESS. Don't stand there like a statue. You must have dreamt all this. [*Lays his hand on her arm.*] Now just listen——

HILDA [*makes an impatient movement with her arm*].

SOLNESS [*as a thought flashes upon him*]. Or——! Wait a moment! There is something under all this, you may depend!

HILDA [*does not move*].

SOLNESS [*in a low voice, but with emphasis*]. I must have thought all that. I must have wished it—have willed it—have longed to do it. And then——. May not that be the explanation?

HILDA [*is still silent*].

SOLNESS [*impatiently*]. Oh very well, deuce take it all—then I did it, I suppose.

HILDA [*turns her head a little, but without looking at him*]. Then you admit it now?

SOLNESS. Yes—whatever you like.

HILDA. You came and put your arms around me?

SOLNESS. Oh, yes!

HILDA. And bent my head back?

SOLNESS. Very far back.

HILDA. And kissed me?

SOLNESS. Yes, I did.

HILDA. Many times?

SOLNESS. As many as ever you like.

HILDA [*turns quickly towards him and has once more the sparkling expression of gladness in her eyes*]. Well, you see, I got it out of you at last!

SOLNESS [*with a slight smile*]. Yes—just think of my forgetting such a thing as that.

HILDA [*again a little sulky, retreats from him*]. Oh, you have kissed so many people in your time, I suppose.

SOLNESS. No, you mustn't think that of me. [HILDA *seats herself in the arm-chair.* SOLNESS *stands and leans against the rocking-chair. Looks observantly at her.*] Miss Wangel!

HILDA. Yes!

SOLNESS. How was it now? What came of all this—between us two?

HILDA. Why, nothing more came of it. You know that quite well. For then the other guests came in, and then—bah!

SOLNESS. Quite so! The others came in. To think of my forgetting that, too!

HILDA. Oh, you haven't really forgotten anything: you are only a little ashamed of it all. I am sure one doesn't forget things of that kind.

SOLNESS. No, one would suppose not.

HILDA [*lively again, looks at him*]. Perhaps you have even forgotten what day it was?

SOLNESS. What day——?

HILDA. Yes, on what day did you hang the wreath on the tower? Well? Tell me at once!

SOLNESS. H'm—I confess I have forgotten the particular day. I only knew it was ten years ago. Sometime in the autumn.

HILDA [*nods her head slowly several times*]. It was ten years ago —on the 19th of September.

SOLNESS. Yes, it must have been about that time. Fancy your remembering that, too! [*Stops.*] But wait a moment——! Yes—it's the 19th of September to-day.

HILDA. Yes, it is; and the ten years are gone. And you didn't come—as you promised me.

SOLNESS. Promised you? Threatened, I suppose you mean?

HILDA. I don't think there was any sort of threat in that.

SOLNESS. Well then, a little bit of fun.

HILDA. Was that all you wanted? To make fun of me?

SOLNESS. Well, or to have a little joke with you. Upon my soul, I don't recollect. But it must have been something of that kind; for you were a mere child then.

HILDA. Oh, perhaps I wasn't quite such a child either. Not such a mere chit as you imagine.

SOLNESS [looks searchingly at her]. Did you really and seriously expect me to come again?

HILDA [conceals a half-teasing smile]. Yes, indeed; I did expect that of you.

SOLNESS. That I should come back to your home and take you away with me?

HILDA. Just like a troll—yes.

SOLNESS. And make a princess of you?

HILDA. That's what you promised.

SOLNESS. And give you a kingdom as well?

HILDA [looks up at the ceiling]. Why not? Of course it need not have been an actual, every-day sort of kingdom.

SOLNESS. But something else just as good?

HILDA. Yes, at least as good. [Looks at him a moment.] I thought, if you could build the highest church-towers in the world, you could surely manage to raise a kingdom of one sort or another as well.

SOLNESS [shakes his head]. I can't quite make you out, Miss Wangel.

HILDA. Can you not? To me it seems all so simple.

SOLNESS. No, I can't make up my mind whether you mean all you say, or are simply having a joke with me.

HILDA [smiles]. Making fun of you, perhaps? I, too?

SOLNESS. Yes, exactly. Making fun—of both of us. [Looks at her.] Is it long since you found out that I was married?

HILDA. I have known it all along. Why do you ask me that?

SOLNESS [lightly]. Oh, well, it just occurred to me. [Looks earnestly at her and says in a low voice.] What have you come for?

HILDA. I want my kingdom. The time is up.

SOLNESS [laughs involuntarily]. What a girl you are!

HILDA [gaily]. Out with my kingdom, Mr. Solness! [Raps with her fingers.] The kingdom on the table!

SOLNESS [pushing the rocking-chair nearer and sitting down].

Now, seriously speaking—what have you come for? What do you really want to do here?

HILDA. Oh, first of all, I want to go around and look at all the things that you have built.

SOLNESS. That will give you plenty of exercise.

HILDA. Yes, I know you have built a tremendous lot.

SOLNESS. I have indeed—especially of late years.

HILDA. Many church-towers among the rest? Immensely high ones?

SOLNESS. No. I build no more church-towers now. Nor churches either.

HILDA. What do you build, then?

SOLNESS. Homes for human beings.

HILDA [*reflectively*]. Couldn't you build a little—a little bit of a church-tower over these homes as well?

SOLNESS [*starting*]. What do you mean by that?

HILDA. I mean—something that points—points up into the free air. With the vane at a dizzy height.

SOLNESS [*pondering a little*]. Strange that you should say that —for that is just what I am most anxious to do.

HILDA [*impatiently*]. Why don't you do it, then?

SOLNESS [*shakes his head*]. No, the people will not have it.

HILDA. Fancy their not wanting it!

SOLNESS [*more lightly*]. But now I am building a new home for myself—just opposite here.

HILDA. For yourself?

SOLNESS. Yes. It is almost finished. And on that there is a tower.

HILDA. A high tower?

SOLNESS. Yes.

HILDA. Very high?

SOLNESS. No doubt people will say it is too high—too high for a dwelling-house.

HILDA. I'll go out and look at that tower the first thing to-morrow morning.

SOLNESS [*sits resting his cheek on his hand and gazes at her*]. Tell me, Miss Wangel—what is your name? Your Christian name, I mean?

HILDA. Why, Hilda, of course.

SOLNESS [*as before*]. Hilda? Indeed?

HILDA. Don't you remember that? You called me Hilda yourself—that day when you misbehaved.

SOLNESS. Did I really?

HILDA. But then you said "little Hilda"; and I didn't like that.

SOLNESS. Oh, you didn't like that, Miss Hilda?

HILDA. No, not at such a time as that. But—"Princess Hilda"—
that will sound very well, I think.

SOLNESS. Very well indeed. Princess Hilda of—of—what was
to be the name of the kingdom?

HILDA. Pooh! I won't have anything to do with that stupid
kingdom. I have set my heart upon quite a different one!

SOLNESS [*has leaned back in the chair, still gazing at her*]. Isn't
it strange——? The more I think of it now, the more it
seems to me as though I had gone about all these years tor-
turing myself with—h'm——

HILDA. With what?

SOLNESS. With the effort to recover something—some experience, which I seemed to have forgotten. But I never had the
least inkling of what it could be.

HILDA. You should have tied a knot in your pockethandker-
chief, Mr. Solness.

SOLNESS. In that case, I should simply have had to go racking
my brains to discover what the knot could mean.

HILDA. Oh, yes, I suppose there are trolls of that kind in the
world, too.

SOLNESS [*rises slowly*]. What a good thing it is that you have
come to me now.

HILDA [*looks deeply into his eyes*]. Is it a good thing?

SOLNESS. For I have been so lonely here. I have been gazing so
helplessly at it all. [*In a lower voice.*] I must tell you—I have
begun to be so afraid—so terribly afraid of the younger
generation.

HILDA [*with a little snort of contempt*]. Pooh—is the younger
generation a thing to be afraid of?

SOLNESS. It is indeed. And that is why I have locked and barred myself in. [*Mysteriously.*] I tell you the younger generation will one day come and thunder at my door! They will break in upon me!

HILDA. Then I should say you ought to go out and open the door to the younger generation.

SOLNESS. Open the door?

HILDA. Yes. Let them come in to you on friendly terms, as it were.

SOLNESS. No, no, no! The younger generation—it means retribution, you see. It comes, as if under a new banner, heralding the turn of fortune.

HILDA [*rises, looks at him and says with a quivering twitch of her lips*]. Can I be of any use to you, Mr. Solness?

SOLNESS. Yes, you can indeed! For you, too, come—under a new banner, it seems to me. Youth marshalled against youth——!

[DR. HERDAL *comes in by the hall-door.*]

DR. HERDAL. What—you and Miss Wangel here still?

SOLNESS. Yes. We have had no end of things to talk about.

HILDA. Both old and new.

DR. HERDAL. Have you really?

HILDA. Oh, it has been the greatest fun. For Mr. Solness—he has such a miraculous memory. All the least little details he remembers instantly.

[MRS. SOLNESS *enters by the door on the right.*]

MRS. SOLNESS. Well, Miss Wangel, your room is quite ready for you now.

HILDA. Oh, how kind you are to me!

SOLNESS [*to* MRS. SOLNESS]. The nursery?

MRS. SOLNESS. Yes, the middle one. But first let us go in to supper.

SOLNESS [*nods to* HILDA]. Hilda shall sleep in the nursery, she shall.

MRS. SOLNESS [*looks at him*]. Hilda?

SOLNESS. Yes, Miss Wangel's name is Hilda. I knew her when she was a child.

MRS. SOLNESS. Did you really, Halvard? Well, shall we go? Supper is on the table.

[*She takes* DR. HERDAL'S *arm and goes out with him to the right.* HILDA *has meanwhile been collecting her travelling things.*]

HILDA [*softly and rapidly to* SOLNESS]. Is it true, what you said? Can I be of use to you?

SOLNESS [*takes the things from her*]. You are the very being I have needed most.

HILDA [*looks at him with happy, wondering eyes and clasps her hands*]. But then, great heavens——!

SOLNESS [*eagerly*]. What——?

HILDA. Then I have my kingdom!

SOLNESS [*involuntarily*]. Hilda——!

HILDA [*again with the quivering twitch of her lips*]. Almost—I was going to say.

[*She goes out to the right,* SOLNESS *follows her.*]

ACT TWO

A prettily furnished small drawing-room in SOLNESS's *house. In the back, a glass door leading out to the verandah and garden. The right-hand corner is cut off transversely by a large bay-window, in which are flower-stands. The left-hand corner is similarly cut off by a transverse wall, in which is a small door papered like the wall. On each side, an ordinary door. In front, on the right, a console table with a large mirror over it. Well-filled stands of plants and flowers. In front, on the left, a sofa with a table and chairs. Further back, a bookcase. Well forward in the room, before the bay window, a small table and some chairs. It is early in the day.*
SOLNESS *sits by the little table with* RAGNAR BROVIK's *portfolio open in front of him. He is turning the drawings over and closely examining some of them.* MRS. SOLNESS *moves about noiselessly with a small watering-pot, attending to her flowers. She is dressed in black as before. Her hat, cloak and parasol lie on a chair near the mirror. Unobserved by her,* SOLNESS *now and again follows her with his eyes. Neither of them speaks.*

KAIA FOSLI *enters quietly by the door on the left.*

SOLNESS [*turns his head, and says in an off-hand tone of indifference*]. Well, is that you?

KAIA. I merely wished to let you know that I have come.

SOLNESS. Yes, yes, that's all right. Hasn't Ragnar come, too?

KAIA. No, not yet. He had to wait a little while to see the doctor. But he is coming presently to hear——

SOLNESS. How is the old man to-day?

KAIA. Not well. He begs you to excuse him; he is obliged to keep his bed to-day.

SOLNESS. Why, of course; by all means let him rest. But now, get to work.

KAIA. Yes. [*Pauses at the door*.] Do you wish to speak to Ragnar when he comes?

SOLNESS. No—I don't know that I have anything particular to say to him.

[KAIA *goes out again to the left.* SOLNESS *remains seated, turning over the drawings.*]

MRS. SOLNESS [*over beside the plants*]. I wonder if he isn't going to die now, as well?

SOLNESS [*looks up to her*]. As well as who?

MRS. SOLNESS [*without answering*]. Yes, yes—depend upon it, Halvard, old Brovik is going to die, too. You'll see that he will.

SOLNESS. My dear Aline, ought you not to go out for a little walk?

MRS. SOLNESS Yes, I suppose I ought to.

[*She continues to attend to the flowers.*]

SOLNESS [*bending over the drawings*]. Is she still asleep?

MRS. SOLNESS [*looking at him*]. Is it Miss Wangel you are sitting there thinking about?

SOLNESS [*indifferently*]. I just happened to recollect her.

MRS. SOLNESS. Miss Wangel was up long ago.

SOLNESS. Oh, was she?

MRS. SOLNESS. When I went in to see her, she was busy putting her things in order.

[*She goes in front of the mirror and slowly begins to put on her hat.*]

SOLNESS [*after a short pause*]. So we have found a use for one of our nurseries after all, Aline.

MRS. SOLNESS. Yes, we have.

SOLNESS. That seems to me better than to have them all standing empty.

MRS. SOLNESS. That emptiness is dreadful; you are right there.

SOLNESS [*closes the portfolio, rises and approaches her*]. You will find that we shall get on far better after this, Aline.

Things will be more comfortable. Life will be easier—especially for you.

MRS. SOLNESS [*looks at him*]. After this?

SOLNESS. Yes, believe me, Aline——

MRS. SOLNESS. Do you mean—because she has come here?

SOLNESS [*checking himself*]. I mean, of course—when once we have moved into the new house.

MRS. SOLNESS [*takes her cloak*]. Ah, do you think so, Halvard? Will it be better then?

SOLNESS. I can't think otherwise. And surely you think so, too?

MRS. SOLNESS. I think nothing at all about the new house.

SOLNESS [*cast down*]. It's hard for me to hear you say that; for you know it is mainly for your sake that I have built it.

[*He offers to help her on with her cloak.*]

MRS. SOLNESS [*evades him*]. The fact is, you do far too much for my sake.

SOLNESS [*with certain vehemence*]. No, no, you really mustn't say that, Aline! I cannot bear to hear you say such things!

MRS. SOLNESS. Very well, then I won't say it, Halvard.

SOLNESS. But I stick to what *I* said. You'll see that things will be easier for you in the new place.

MRS. SOLNESS. O heavens—easier for me——!

SOLNESS [*eagerly*]. Yes, indeed they will! You may be quite sure of that! For you see—there will be so very, very much there that will remind you of your own home——

MRS. SOLNESS. The home that used to be father's and mother's—and that was burnt to the ground——

SOLNESS [*in a low voice*]. Yes, yes, my poor Aline. That was a terrible blow for you.

MRS. SOLNESS [*breaking out in lamentation*]. You may build as much as ever you like, Halvard—you can never build up again a real home for me!

SOLNESS [*crosses the room*]. Well, in heaven's name, let us talk no more about it, then.

MRS. SOLNESS. Oh, yes, Halvard, I understand you very well. You are so anxious to spare me—and to find excuses for me, too—as much as ever you can.

SOLNESS [*with astonishment in his eyes*]. *You!* Is it you—yourself, that you are talking about, Aline?

MRS. SOLNESS. Yes, who else should it be but myself?

SOLNESS [*involuntarily to himself*]. That, too!

MRS. SOLNESS. As for the old house, I wouldn't mind so much about that. When once misfortune was in the air—why——

SOLNESS. Ah, you are right there. Misfortune will have its way —as the saying goes.

MRS. SOLNESS. But it's what came of the fire—the dreadful thing that followed——! That is the thing! That, that, that!

SOLNESS [*vehemently*]. Don't think about that, Aline!

MRS. SOLNESS. Ah, that is exactly what I cannot help thinking about. And now, at last, I must speak about it, too; for I don't seem able to bear it any longer. And then never to be able to forgive myself——

SOLNESS [*exclaiming*]. Yourself——!

MRS. SOLNESS. Yes, for I had duties on both sides—both towards you and towards the little ones. I ought to have hardened myself—not to have let the horror take such hold upon me—nor the grief for the burning of my old home. [*Wrings her hands.*] Oh, Halvard, if I had only had the strength!

SOLNESS [*softly, much moved, comes closer*]. Aline—you must promise me never to think these thoughts any more.— Promise me that, dear!

MRS. SOLNESS. Oh, promise, promise! One can promise anything.

SOLNESS [*clenches his hands and crosses the room*]. Oh, but this is hopeless, hopeless! Never a ray of sunlight! Not so much as a gleam of brightness to light up our home!

MRS. SOLNESS. This is no home, Halvard.

SOLNESS. Oh no, you may well say that. [*Gloomily.*] And God knows whether you are not right in saying that it will be no better for us in the new house, either.

MRS. SOLNESS. It will never be any better. Just as empty—just as desolate—there as here.

SOLNESS [*vehemently*]. Why in all the world have we built it then? Can you tell me that?

MRS. SOLNESS. No; you must answer that question for yourself.

SOLNESS [*glances suspiciously at her*]. What do you mean by that, Aline?

MRS. SOLNESS. What do I mean?

SOLNESS. Yes, in the devil's name! You said it so strangely— as if you had hidden some meaning in it.

MRS. SOLNESS. No, indeed, I assure you——

SOLNESS [*comes closer*]. Oh, come now—I know what I know. I have both my eyes and my ears about me, Aline—you may depend upon that!

MRS. SOLNESS. Why, what are you talking about? What is it?

SOLNESS [*places himself in front of her*]. Do you mean to say you don't find a kind of lurking, hidden meaning in the most innocent word I happen to say?

MRS. SOLNESS. *I*, do you say? *I* do that?

SOLNESS [*laughs*]. Ho-ho-ho! It's natural enough, Aline! When you have a sick man on your hands——

MRS. SOLNESS [*anxiously*]. Sick? Are you ill, Halvard?

SOLNESS [*violently*]. A half-mad man then! A crazy man! Call me what you will.

MRS. SOLNESS [*feels blindly for a chair and sits down*]. Halvard —for God's sake——

SOLNESS. But you are wrong, both you and the doctor. I am not in the state you imagine.

[*He walks up and down the room.* MRS. SOLNESS *follows him anxiously with her eyes. Finally he goes up to her.*]

SOLNESS [*calmly*]. In reality there is nothing whatever the matter with me.

MRS. SOLNESS. No, there isn't, is there? But then what is it that troubles you so?

SOLNESS. Why this, that I often feel ready to sink under this terrible burden of debt——

MRS. SOLNESS. Debt, do you say? But you owe no one anything, Halvard!

SOLNESS [*softly, with emotion*]. I owe a boundless debt to you —to you—to you, Aline.

MRS. SOLNESS [*rises slowly*]. What is behind all this? You may just as well tell me at once.

SOLNESS. But there is nothing behind it; I have never done you any wrong—not wittingly and wilfully, at any rate. And yet —and yet it seems as though a crushing debt rested upon me and weighed me down.

MRS. SOLNESS. A debt to me?

SOLNESS. Chiefly to you.

MRS. SOLNESS. Then you are—ill after all, Halvard.

SOLNESS [*gloomily*]. I suppose I must be—or not far from it. [*Looks towards the door to the right, which is opened at this moment.*] Ah! now it grows lighter.

[HILDA WANGEL *comes in. She has made some alteration in her dress and let down her skirt.*]

HILDA. Good morning, Mr. Solness!

SOLNESS [*nods*]. Slept well?

HILDA. Quite deliciously! Like a child in a cradle. Oh—I lay and stretched myself like—like a princess!

SOLNESS [*smiles a little*]. You were thoroughly comfortable then?

HILDA. I should think so.

SOLNESS. And no doubt you dreamed, too.

HILDA. Yes, I did. But that was horrid.

SOLNESS. Was it?

HILDA. Yes, for I dreamed I was falling over a frightfully high, sheer precipice. Do you never have that kind of dream?

SOLNESS. Oh yes—now and then——

HILDA. It's tremendously thrilling—when you fall and fall——

SOLNESS. It seems to make one's blood run cold.

HILDA. Do you draw your legs up under you while you are falling?

SOLNESS. Yes, as high as ever I can.

HILDA. So do I.

MRS. SOLNESS [*takes her parasol*]. I must go into town now,

Halvard. [*To* HILDA.] And I'll try to get one or two things
that you may require.

HILDA [*making a motion to throw her arms round her neck*].
Oh, you dear, sweet Mrs. Solness! You are really much too
kind to me! Frightfully kind——

MRS. SOLNESS [*deprecatingly, freeing herself*]. Oh, not at all.
It's only my duty, so I am very glad to do it.

HILDA [*offended, pouts*]. But really, I think I am quite fit to be
seen in the streets—now that I've put my dress to rights. Or
do you think I am not?

MRS. SOLNESS. To tell the truth, I think people would stare at
you a little.

HILDA [*contemptuously*]. Pooh! Is that all? That only amuses
me.

SOLNESS [*with suppressed ill-humour*]. Yes, but people might
take it into their heads that you were mad, too, you see.

HILDA. Mad? Are there so many mad people here in town, then?

SOLNESS [*points to his own forehead*]. Here you see one, at all
events.

HILDA. You—Mr. Solness!

MRS. SOLNESS. Oh, don't talk like that, my dear Halvard!

SOLNESS. Have you not noticed that yet?

HILDA. No, I certainly have not. [*Reflects and laughs a little.*]
And yet—perhaps in one single thing.

SOLNESS. Ah, do you hear that, Aline?

MRS. SOLNESS. What is that one single thing, Miss Wangel?

HILDA. No, I won't say.

SOLNESS. Oh, yes, do!

HILDA. No, thank you—I am not so mad as that.

MRS. SOLNESS. When you and Miss Wangel are alone, I daresay
she will tell you, Halvard.

SOLNESS. Ah—you think she will?

MRS. SOLNESS. Oh, yes, certainly. For you have known her so
well in the past. Ever since she was a child—you tell me.

[*She goes out by the door on the left.*]

HILDA [*after a little while*]. Does your wife dislike me very much?

SOLNESS. Did you think you noticed anything of the kind?

HILDA. Did you not notice it yourself?

SOLNESS [*evasively*]. Aline has become exceedingly shy with strangers of late years.

HILDA. Has she really?

SOLNESS. But if only you could get to know her thoroughly——! Ah! she is so good—so kind—so excellent a creature——

HILDA [*impatiently*]. But if she is all that—what made her say that about her duty?

SOLNESS. Her duty?

HILDA. She said that she would go out and buy something for me, because it was her duty. Oh, I can't bear that ugly, horrid word!

SOLNESS. Why not?

HILDA. It sounds so cold and sharp and stinging. Duty—duty— duty. Don't you think so, too? Doesn't it seem to sting you?

SOLNESS. H'm—haven't thought much about it.

HILDA. Yes, it does. And if she is so good—as you say she is— why should she talk in that way?

SOLNESS. But, good Lord, what would you have had her say, then?

HILDA. She might have said she would do it because she had taken a tremendous fancy to me. She might have said something like that—something really warm and cordial, you understand.

SOLNESS [*looks at her*]. Is that how you would like to have it?

HILDA. Yes, precisely. [*She wanders about the room, stops at the bookcase and looks at the books.*] What a lot of books you have.

SOLNESS. Yes, I have got together a good many.

HILDA. Do you read them all, too?

SOLNESS. I used to try to. Do you read much?

HILDA. No, never! I have given it up. For it all seems so irrelevant.

SOLNESS. That is just my feeling.

[HILDA *wanders about a little, stops at the small table, opens the portfolio and turns over the contents.*]

HILDA. Are all these drawings yours?

SOLNESS. No, they are drawn by a young man whom I employ to help me.

HILDA. Some one you have taught?

SOLNESS. Oh, yes, no doubt he has learnt something from one, too.

HILDA [*sits down*]. Then I suppose he is very clever. [*Looks at a drawing.*] Isn't he?

SOLNESS. Oh, he might be worse. For my purpose——

HILDA. Oh, yes—I'm sure he is frightfully clever.

SOLNESS. Do you think you can see that in the drawings?

HILDA. Pooh—these scrawlings! But if he has been learning from you——

SOLNESS. Oh, so far as that goes—there are plenty of people that have learnt from me and have come to little enough for all that.

HILDA [*looks at him and shakes her head*]. No, I can't for the life of me understand how you can be so stupid.

SOLNESS. Stupid? Do you think I am so very stupid?

HILDA. Yes, I do indeed. If you are content to go about here teaching all these people——

SOLNESS [*with a slight start*]. Well, and why not?

HILDA [*rises, half serious, half laughing*]. No indeed, Mr. Solness! What can be the good of that? No one but you should be allowed to build. You should stand quite alone—do it all yourself. Now you know it.

SOLNESS [*involuntarily*]. Hilda——!

HILDA. Well!

SOLNESS. How in the world did that come into your head?

HILDA. Do you think I am so very far wrong, then?

SOLNESS. No, that's not what I mean. But now I'll tell you something.

HILDA. Well?

SOLNESS. I keep on—incessantly—in silence and alone—brooding on that very thought.

HILDA. Yes, that seems to me perfectly natural.

SOLNESS [*looks somewhat searchingly at her*]. Perhaps you have noticed it already?

HILDA. No, indeed I haven't.

SOLNESS. But just now—when you said you thought I was— off my balance? In one thing, you said——

HILDA. Oh, I was thinking of something quite different.

SOLNESS. What was it?

HILDA. I am not going to tell you.

SOLNESS [*crosses the room*]. Well, well—as you please. [*Stops at the bow-window.*] Come here, and I will show you something.

HILDA [*approaching*]. What is it?

SOLNESS. Do you see—over there in the garden——?

HILDA. Yes.

SOLNESS [*points*]. Right above the great quarry——?

HILDA. That new house, you mean?

SOLNESS. The one that is being built, yes. Almost finished.

HILDA. It seems to have a very high tower.

SOLNESS. The scaffolding is still up.

HILDA. Is that your new house?

SOLNESS. Yes.

HILDA. The house you are soon going to move into?

SOLNESS. Yes.

HILDA [*looks at him*]. Are there nurseries in that house, too?

SOLNESS. Three, as there are here.

HILDA. And no child.

SOLNESS. And there never will be one.

HILDA [*with a half-smile*]. Well, isn't it just as I said——?

SOLNESS. That——?

HILDA. That you are a little—a little mad after all.

SOLNESS. Was that what you were thinking of?

HILDA. Yes, of all the empty nurseries I slept in.

SOLNESS [*lowers his voice*]. We have had children—Aline and I.

HILDA [*looks eagerly at him*]. Have you——?

SOLNESS. Two little boys. They were of the same age.

HILDA. Twins, then.

SOLNESS. Yes, twins. It's eleven or twelve years ago now.

HILDA [*cautiously*]. And so both of them——? You have lost both the twins, then?

SOLNESS [*with quiet emotion*]. We kept them only about three weeks. Or scarcely so much. [*Bursts forth.*] Oh, Hilda, I can't tell you what a good thing it is for me that you have come! For now at last I have some one I can talk to!

HILDA. Can you not talk to—her, too?

SOLNESS. Not about this. Not as I want to talk and must talk. [*Gloomily.*] And not about so many other things, either.

HILDA [*in a subdued voice*]. Was that all you meant when you said you needed me?

SOLNESS. That was mainly what I meant—at all events, yesterday. For to-day I am not so sure——[*Breaking off.*] Come here and let us sit down, Hilda. Sit there on the sofa—so that you can look into the garden. [HILDA *seats herself in the corner of the sofa.* SOLNESS *brings a chair closer.*] Should you like to hear about it?

HILDA. Yes, I shall love to sit and listen to you.

SOLNESS [*sits down*]. Then I will tell you all about it.

HILDA. Now I can see both the garden and you, Mr. Solness. So now, tell away! Begin!

SOLNESS [*points towards the bow-window*]. Out there on the rising ground—where you see the new house——

HILDA. Yes?

SOLNESS. Aline and I lived there in the first years of our married life. There was an old house up there that had belonged to her mother; and we inherited it, and the whole of the great garden with it.

HILDA. Was there a tower on that house, too?

SOLNESS. No, nothing of the kind. From the outside it looked like a great, dark, ugly wooden box; but all the same, it was snug and comfortable enough inside.

HILDA. Then did you pull down the ramshackle old place?

SOLNESS. No, it burnt down.

HILDA. The whole of it?

SOLNESS. Yes.

HILDA. Was that a great misfortune for you?

SOLNESS. That depends on how you look at it. As a builder, the fire was the making of me——

HILDA. Well, but——?

SOLNESS. It was just after the birth of the two little boys——

HILDA. The poor little twins, yes.

SOLNESS. They came healthy and bonny into the world. And they were growing too—you could see the difference from day to day.

HILDA. Little children do grow quickly at first.

SOLNESS. It was the prettiest sight in the world to see Aline lying with the two of them in her arms.—But then came the night of the fire——

HILDA [*excitedly*]. What happened? Do tell me! Was any one burnt?

SOLNESS. No, not that. Every one got safe and sound out of the house——

HILDA. Well, and what then——?

SOLNESS. The fright had shaken Aline terribly. The alarm—the escape—the break-neck hurry—and then the ice-cold night air—for they had to be carried out just as they lay—both she and the little ones.

HILDA. Was it too much for them?

SOLNESS. Oh no, they stood it well enough. But Aline fell into a fever, and it affected her milk. She would insist on nursing them herself; because it was her duty, she said. And both our little boys, they—[*Clenching his hands.*]—they—oh!

HILDA. They did not get over that?

SOLNESS. No, that they did not get over. That was how we lost them.

HILDA. It must have been terribly hard for you.

SOLNESS. Hard enough for me; but ten times harder for Aline. [*Clenching his hands in suppressed fury.*] Oh, that such things should be allowed to happen here in the world! [*Shortly and firmly.*] From the day I lost them, I had no heart for building churches.

HILDA. Did you not like the church-tower in our town?

SOLNESS. I didn't like it. I know how free and happy I felt when the tower was finished.

HILDA. *I* know that, too.

SOLNESS. And now I shall never—never build anything of that sort again! Neither churches nor church-towers.

HILDA [*nods slowly*]. Nothing but houses for people to live in.

SOLNESS. Homes for human beings, Hilda.

HILDA. But homes with high towers and pinnacles upon them.

SOLNESS. If possible. [*Adopts a lighter tone.*] But, as I said before, that fire was the making of me—as a builder, I mean.

HILDA. Why don't you call yourself an architect, like the others?

SOLNESS. I have not been systematically enough taught for that. Most of what I know, I have found out for myself.

HILDA. But you succeeded all the same.

SOLNESS. Yes, thanks to the fire. I laid out almost the whole of the garden in villa lots; and there I was able to build after my own heart. So I came to the front with a rush.

HILDA [*looks keenly at him*]. You must surely be a very happy man, as matters stand with you.

SOLNESS [*gloomily*]. Happy? Do you say that, too—like all the rest of them?

HILDA. Yes, I should say you must be. If you could only cease thinking about the two little children——

SOLNESS [*slowly*]. The two little children—they are not so easy to forget, Hilda.

HILDA [*somewhat uncertainly*]. Do you still feel their loss so much—after all these years?

SOLNESS [*looks fixedly at her, without replying*]. A happy man you said——

HILDA. Well, now, are you not happy—in other respects?

SOLNESS [*continues to look at her*]. When I told you all this about the fire—h'm——

HILDA. Well?

SOLNESS. Was there not one special thought that you—that you seized upon?

HILDA [*reflects in vain*]. No. What thought should that be?

SOLNESS [*with subdued emphasis*]. It was simply and solely by

that fire that I was enabled to build homes for human beings. Cosy, comfortable, bright homes, where father and
mother and the whole troop of children can live in safety
and gladness, feeling what a happy thing it is to be alive in
the world—and most of all to belong to each other—in great
things and in small.

HILDA [*ardently*]. Well, and is it not a great happiness for you
to be able to build such beautiful homes?

OLNESS. The price, Hilda! The terrible price I had to pay for
the opportunity!

HILDA. But can you never get over that?

OLNESS. No. That I might build homes for others, I had to
forego—to forego for all time—the home that might have
been my own. I mean a home for a troop of children—and
for father and mother, too.

HILDA [*cautiously*]. But need you have done that? For all time,
you say?

OLNESS [*nods slowly*]. That was the price of this happiness that
people talk about. [*Breathes heavily.*] This happiness—h'm
—this happiness was not to be bought any cheaper, Hilda.

HILDA [*as before*]. But may it not come right even yet?

OLNESS. Never in this world—never. That is another consequence of the fire—and of Aline's illness afterwards.

HILDA [*looks at him with an indefinable expression*]. And yet
you build all these nurseries?

OLNESS [*seriously*]. Have you never noticed, Hilda, how the
impossible—how it seems to beckon and cry aloud to one?

HILDA [*reflecting*]. The impossible? [*With animation.*] Yes, indeed! Is that how you feel too?

OLNESS. Yes, I do.

HILDA. There must be—a little of the troll in you, too.

OLNESS. Why of the troll?

HILDA. What would you call it, then?

OLNESS [*rises*]. Well, well, perhaps you are right. [*Vehemently.*] But how can I help turning into a troll, when this is
how it always goes with me in everything—in everything!

HILDA. How do you mean?

SOLNESS [*speaking low, with inward emotion*]. Mark what I say
to you, Hilda. All that I have succeeded in doing, building,
creating—all the beauty, security, cheerful comfort—ay,
and magnificence, too—[*Clenches his hands.*] Oh, is it not
terrible even to think of——!

HILDA. What is so terrible?

SOLNESS. That all this I have to make up for, to pay for—not
in money, but in human happiness. And not with my own
happiness only, but with other people's, too. Yes, yes, do
you see that, Hilda? That is the price which my position as
an artist has cost me—and others. And every single day I
have to look on while the price is paid for me anew. Over
again, and over again—and over again for ever!

HILDA [*rises and looks steadily at him*]. Now I can see that you
are thinking of—of her.

SOLNESS. Yes, mainly of Aline. For Aline—she, too, had her
vocation in life, just as much as I had mine. [*His voice
quivers.*] But her vocation has had to be stunted, and
crushed and shattered—in order that mine might force its
way to—to a sort of great victory. For you must know that
Aline—she, too, had a talent for building.

HILDA. She! For building?

SOLNESS [*shakes his head*]. Not houses and towers, and spires—
not such things as I work away at——

HILDA. Well, but what then?

SOLNESS [*softly, with emotion*]. For building up the souls of
little children, Hilda. For building up children's souls in
perfect balance, and in noble and beautiful forms. For en-
abling them to soar up into erect and full-grown human
souls. That was Aline's talent. And there it all lies now——
unused and unusable for ever—of no earthly service to any
one—just like the ruins left by a fire.

HILDA. Yes, but even if this were so——?

SOLNESS. It is so! It is so! I know it!

HILDA. Well, but in any case it is not your fault.

SOLNESS [*fixes his eyes on her and nods slowly*]. Ah, that is the
great, terrible question. That is the doubt that is gnawing me

—night and day.

HILDA. That?

SOLNESS. Yes. Suppose the fault was mine—in a certain sense.

HILDA. Your fault! The fire!

SOLNESS. All of it; the whole thing. And yet, perhaps—I may not have had anything to do with it.

HILDA [*looks at him with a troubled expression*]. Oh, Mr. Solness—if you can talk like that, I am afraid you must be— ill, after all.

SOLNESS. H'm—I don't think I shall ever be of quite sound mind on that point.

[RAGNAR BROVIK *cautiously opens the little door in the left-hand corner.* HILDA *comes forward.*]

RAGNAR [*when he sees* HILDA]. Oh. I beg pardon, Mr. Solness—

[*He makes a movement to withdraw.*]

SOLNESS. No, no, don't go. Let us get it over.

RAGNAR. Oh, yes—if only we could.

SOLNESS. I hear your father is no better?

RAGNAR. Father is fast growing weaker—and therefore I beg and implore you to write a few kind words for me on one of the plans! Something for father to read before he——

SOLNESS [*vehemently*]. I won't hear anything more about those drawings of yours!

RAGNAR. Have you looked at them?

SOLNESS. Yes—I have.

RAGNAR. And they are good for nothing? And *I* am good for nothing, too?

SOLNESS [*evasively*]. Stay here with me, Ragnar. You shall have everything your own way. And then you can marry Kaia and live at your ease—and happily, too, who knows? Only don't think of building on your own account.

RAGNAR. Well, well, then I must go home and tell father what you say—I promised I would.—Is this what I am to tell father—before he dies?

SOLNESS [*with a groan*]. Oh tell him—tell him what you will, for me. Best to say nothing at all to him! [*With a sudden outburst.*] I cannot do anything else, Ragnar!

RAGNAR. May I have the drawings to take with me?

SOLNESS. Yes, take them—take them by all means They are lying there on the table.

RAGNAR [*goes to the table*]. Thanks.

HILDA [*puts her hand on the portfolio*]. No, no; leave them here.

SOLNESS. Why?

HILDA. Because I want to look at them, too.

SOLNESS. But you have been—— [*To* RAGNAR.] Well, leave them here, then.

RAGNAR. Very well.

SOLNESS And go home at once to your father.

RAGNAR. Yes. I suppose I must.

SOLNESS [*as if in desperation*]. Ragnar—you must not ask me to do what is beyond my power! Do you hear, Ragnar? You must not!

RAGNAR. No, no. I beg your pardon——

[*He bows and goes out by the corner door.* HILDA *goes over and sits down on a chair near the mirror.*]

HILDA [*looks angrily at* SOLNESS]. That was a very ugly thing to do.

SOLNESS. Do you think so, too?

HILDA. Yes, it was horrible ugly—and hard and bad and cruel as well.

SOLNESS. Oh, you don't understand my position.

HILDA. No matter——. I say you ought not to be like that.

SOLNESS. You said yourself, only just now, that no one but *I* ought to be allowed to build.

HILDA. *I* may say such things—but you must not.

SOLNESS. I most of all, surely, who have paid so dear for my position.

HILDA. Oh yes—with what you call domestic comfort—and that sort of thing.

SOLNESS. And with my peace of soul into the bargain.

HILDA [*rising*]. Peace of soul! [*With feeling.*] Yes, yes, you are right in that! Poor Mr. Solness—you fancy that——

SOLNESS [*with a quiet, chuckling laugh*]. Just sit down again, Hilda, and I'll tell you something funny.

HILDA [*sits down; with intent interest*]. Well?

SOLNESS. It sounds such a ludicrous thing; for, you see, the whole story turns upon nothing but a crack in a chimney.

HILDA. No more than that?

SOLNESS. No, not to begin with.

[*He moves a chair nearer to* HILDA *and sits down.*]

HILDA [*impatiently, taps on her knee*]. Well, now for the crack in the chimney!

SOLNESS. I had noticed the split in the flue long, long before the fire. Every time I went up into the attic, I looked to see if it was still here.

HILDA. And it was?

SOLNESS. Yes; for no one else knew about it.

HILDA. And you said nothing?

SOLNESS. Nothing.

HILDA. And did not think of repairing the flue either?

SOLNESS. Oh, yes, I thought about it—but never got any further. Every time I intended to set to work, it seemed just as if a hand held me back. Not to-day, I thought—to-morrow; and nothing ever came of it.

HILDA. But why did you keep putting it off like that?

SOLNESS. Because I was revolving something in my mind. [*Slowly, and in a low voice.*] Through that little black crack in the chimney, I might, perhaps, force my way upwards—as a builder.

HILDA [*looking straight in front of her*]. That must have been thrilling.

SOLNESS. Almost irresistible—quite irresistible. For at that time it appeared to me a perfectly simple and straight-forward matter. I would have had it happen in the wintertime

—a little before midday. I was to be out driving Aline in the sleigh. The servants at home would have made huge fires in the stoves.

HILDA. For, of course, it was to be bitterly cold that day?

SOLNESS. Rather biting, yes—and they would want Aline to find it thoroughly snug and warm when she came home.

HILDA. I suppose she is very chilly by nature?

SOLNESS. She is. And as we drove home, we were to see the smoke.

HILDA. Only the smoke?

SOLNESS. The smoke first. But when we came up to the garden gate, the whole of the old timber-box was to be a rolling mass of flames.—That is how I wanted it to be, you see.

HILDA. Oh why, why could it not have happened so!

SOLNESS. You may well say that, Hilda.

HILDA. Well, but now listen, Mr. Solness. Are you perfectly certain that the fire was caused by that little crack in the chimney?

SOLNESS. No, on the contrary—I am perfectly certain that the crack in the chimney had nothing whatever to do with the fire.

HILDA. What?

SOLNESS. It has been clearly ascertained that the fire broke out in a clothes-cupboard—in a totally different part of the house.

HILDA. Then what is all this nonsense you are talking about the crack in the chimney?

SOLNESS. May I go on talking to you a little, Hilda?

HILDA. Yes, if you'll only talk sensibly——

SOLNESS. I will try. [*He moves his chair nearer.*]

HILDA. Out with it, then, Mr. Solness.

SOLNESS [*confidentially*]. Don't you agree with me, Hilda, that there exist special, chosen people who have been endowed with the power and faculty of desiring a thing, craving for a thing, willing a thing—so persistently and so—so inexorably—that at last it has to happen? Don't you believe that?

HILDA [*with an indefinable expression in her eyes*]. If that is so, we shall see, one of these days, whether *I* am one of the chosen.

SOLNESS. It is not one's self that can do such great things. Oh, no,—the helpers and the servers—they must do their part, too, if it is to be of any good. But they never come of themselves. One has to call upon them very persistently—inwardly, you understand.

HILDA. What are these helpers and servers?

SOLNESS. Oh, we can talk about that some other time. For the present, let us keep to this business of the fire.

HILDA. Don't you think that fire would have happened all the same—even without your wishing for it?

SOLNESS. If the house had been old Knut Brovik's, it would never have burnt down so conveniently for him. I am sure of that; for he does not know how to call for the helpers— no, nor for the servers, either. [*Rises in unrest.*] So you see, Hilda—it is my fault, after all, that the lives of the two little boys had to be sacrificed. And do you think it is not my fault, too, that Aline has never been the woman she should and might have been—and that she most longed to be?

HILDA. Yes, but if it is all the work of those helpers and servers——?

SOLNESS. Who called for the helpers and servers? It was I! And they came and obeyed my will. [*In increasing excitement.*] That is what people call having the luck on your side; but I must tell you what this sort of luck feels like! It feels like a great raw place here on my breast. And the helpers and servers keep on flaying pieces of skin off other people in order to close my sore!—But still the sore is not healed— never, never! Oh, if you knew how it can sometimes gnaw and burn.

HILDA [*looks attentively at him*]. You are ill, Mr. Solness. Very ill, I almost think.

SOLNESS. Say mad; for that is what you mean.

HILDA. No, I don't think there is much amiss with your intellect.

SOLNESS. With what then? Out with it!

HILDA. I wonder whether you were not sent into the world with a sickly conscience.

SOLNESS. A sickly conscience? What devilry is that?

HILDA. I mean that your conscience is feeble—too delicately built, as it were—hasn't strength to take a grip of things—to lift and bear what is heavy.

SOLNESS [*growls*]. H'm! May I ask, then, what sort of conscience one ought to have?

HILDA. I should like your conscience to be—to be thoroughly robust.

SOLNESS. Indeed? Robust, eh? Is your own conscience robust, may I ask?

HILDA. Yes, I think it is. I have never noticed that it wasn't.

SOLNESS. It has not been put very severely to the test, I should think.

HILDA [*with a quivering of the lips*]. Oh, it was no such simple matter to leave father—I am so awfully fond of him.

SOLNESS. Dear me! for a month or two——

HILDA. I think I shall never go home again.

SOLNESS. Never? Then why did you leave him?

HILDA [*half-seriously, half-banteringly*]. Have you forgotten that the ten years are up?

SOLNESS. Oh nonsense. Was anything wrong at home? Eh?

HILDA [*quite seriously*]. It was this impulse within me that urged and goaded me to come—and lured and drew me on, as well.

SOLNESS [*eagerly*]. There we have it! There we have it, Hilda! There is a troll in you, too, as in me. For it's the troll in one, you see—it is that that calls to the powers outside us. And then you must give in—whether you will or no.

HILDA. I almost think you are right, Mr. Solness.

SOLNESS [*walks about the room*]. Oh, there are devils innumerable abroad in the world, Hilda, that one never sees!

HILDA. Devils, too?

SOLNESS [*stops*]. Good devils and bad devils; light-haired devils and black-haired devils. If only you could always tell whether it is the light or dark ones that have got hold of you! [*Paces about.*] Ho-ho! Then it would be simple enough.

HILDA [*follows him with her eyes*]. Or if one had a really vigorous, radiantly healthy conscience——so that one dared to do what one would.

SOLNESS [*stops beside the console table*]. I believe, now, that most people are just as puny creatures as I am in that respect.

HILDA. I shouldn't wonder.

SOLNESS [*leaning against the table*]. In the sagas—— Have you read any of the old sagas?

HILDA. Oh, yes! When I used to read books, I——

SOLNESS. In the sagas you read about vikings, who sailed to foreign lands, and plundered and burned and killed men——

HILDA. And carried off women——

SOLNESS. ——and kept them in captivity——

HILDA. ——took them home in their ships——

SOLNESS. ——and behaved to them like—like the very worst of trolls.

HILDA [*looks straight before her, with a half-veiled look*]. I think that must have been thrilling.

SOLNESS [*with a short, deep laugh*]. To carry off women.

HILDA. To be carried off.

SOLNESS [*looks at her a moment.*] Oh, indeed.

HILDA [*as if breaking the thread of the conversation*]. But what made you speak of these vikings, Mr. Solness?

SOLNESS. Why, those fellows must have had robust consciences, if you like! When they got home again, they could eat, and drink and be as happy as children. And the women, too! They often would not leave them on any account. Can you understand that, Hilda?

HILDA. Those women I can understand exceedingly well.

SOLNESS. Oho! Perhaps you could do the same yourself?

HILDA. Why not?

SOLNESS. Live—of your own free will—with a ruffian like that?

HILDA. If it was a ruffian I had come to love——

SOLNESS. Could you come to love a man like that?

HILDA. Good heavens, you know very well one can't choose
whom one is going to love.

SOLNESS [*looks meditatively at her*]. Oh, no, I suppose it is the
troll within one that's responsible for that.

HILDA [*half-laughing*]. And all those blessed devils, that you
know so well—both the light-haired and the dark-haired
ones.

SOLNESS [*quietly and warmly*]. Then I hope with all my heart
that the devils will choose carefully for you, Hilda.

HILDA. For me they have chosen already—once and for all.

SOLNESS [*looks earnestly at her*]. Hilda—you are like a wild
bird of the woods.

HILDA. Far from it. I don't hide myself away under the bushes.

SOLNESS. No, no. There is rather something of the bird of prey
in you.

HILDA. That is nearer it—perhaps. [*Very earnestly.*] And why
not a bird of prey? Why should not *I* go a-hunting—I, as
well as the rest. Carry off the prey I want—if only I can
get my claws into it and do with it as I will.

SOLNESS. Hilda—do you know what you are?

HILDA. Yes, I suppose I am a strange sort of bird.

SOLNESS. No. You are like a dawning day. When I look at
you—I seem to be looking towards the sunrise.

HILDA. Tell me, Mr. Solness—are you certain that you have
never called me to you? Inwardly, you know?

SOLNESS [*softly and slowly*]. I almost think I must have.

HILDA. What did you want with me?

SOLNESS. You are the younger generation, Hilda.

HILDA [*smiles*]. That younger generation that you are so afraid
of?

SOLNESS [*nods slowly*]. And which, in my heart, I yearn towards so deeply.

[HILDA *rises, goes to the little table and fetches* RAGNAR BRO-
VIK's *portfolio.*]

HILDA [*holds out the portfolio to him*]. We were talking of
these drawings——

SOLNESS [*shortly, waving them away*]. Put those things away! I have seen enough of them.

HILDA. Yes, but you have to write your approval on them.

SOLNESS. Write my approval on them? Never!

HILDA. But the poor old man is lying at death's door! Can't you give him and his son this pleasure before they are parted? And perhaps he might get the commission to carry them out, too.

SOLNESS. Yes, that is just what he would get. He has made sure of that—has my fine gentleman!

HILDA. Then, good heavens—if that is so—can't you tell the least little bit of a lie for once in a way?

SOLNESS. A lie? [*Raging.*] Hilda—take those devil's drawings out of my sight!

HILDA [*draws the portfolio a little nearer to herself*]. Well, well, well—don't bite me.—You talk of trolls—but I think you go on like a troll yourself. [*Looks around.*] Where do you keep your pen and ink?

SOLNESS. There is nothing of the sort in here.

HILDA [*goes towards the door*]. But in the office where that young lady is——

SOLNESS. Stay where you are, Hilda!—I ought to tell a lie, you say. Oh, yes, for the sake of his old father I might well do that—for in my time I have crushed him, trodden him under foot——

HILDA. Him, too?

SOLNESS. I needed room for myself. But this Ragnar—he must on no account be allowed to come to the front.

HILDA. Poor fellow, there is surely no fear of that. If he has nothing in him——

SOLNESS [*comes closer, looks at her and whispers*]. If Ragnar Brovik gets his chance, he will strike me to the earth. Crush me—as I crushed his father.

HILDA. Crush you? Has he the ability for that?

SOLNESS. Yes, you may depend upon it he has the ability! He is the younger generation that stands ready to knock at my door—to make an end of Halvard Solness.

HILDA [*looks at him with quiet reproach*]. And yet you would bar him out. Fie, Mr. Solness!

SOLNESS. The fight I have been fighting has cost heart's blood enough.—And I am afraid, too, that the helpers and servers will not obey me any longer.

HILDA. Then you must go ahead without them. There is nothing else for it.

SOLNESS. It is hopeless, Hilda. The luck is bound to turn. A little sooner or a little later. Retribution is inexorable.

HILDA [*in distress, putting her hands over her ears*]. Don't talk like that! Do you want to kill me? To take from me what is more than my life?

SOLNESS. And what is that?

HILDA. The longing to see you great. To see you, with a wreath in your hand, high, high up upon a church-tower. [*Calm again.*] Come, out with your pencil now. You must have a pencil about you?

SOLNESS [*takes out his pocket-book*]. I have one here.

HILDA [*lays the portfolio on the sofa-table*]. Very well. Now let us two sit down here, Mr. Solness. [SOLNESS *seats himself at the table.* HILDA *stands behind him, leaning over the back of the chair.*] And now we will write on the drawings. We must write very, very nicely and cordially—for this horrid Ruar—or whatever his name is.

SOLNESS [*writes a few words, turns his head and looks at her*]. Tell me one thing, Hilda.

HILDA. Yes!

SOLNESS. If you have been waiting for me all these ten years——

HILDA. What then?

SOLNESS. Why have you never written to me? Then I could have answered you.

HILDA [*hastily*]. No, no, no! That was just what I did not want.

SOLNESS. Why not?

HILDA. I was afraid the whole thing might fall to pieces.—But we were going to write on the drawings, Mr. Solness.

SOLNESS. So we were.

HILDA [*bends forward and looks over his shoulder while he*

writes]. Mind now, kindly and cordially! Oh how I hate—
how I hate this Ruald——

SOLNESS [*writing*]. Have you never really cared for any one,
Hilda?

HILDA [*harshly*]. What do you say?

SOLNESS. Have you never cared for any one?

HILDA. For any one else, I suppose you mean?

SOLNESS [*looks up at her*]. For any one else, yes. Have you
never? In all these ten years? Never?

HILDA. Oh, yes, now and then. When I was perfectly furious
with you for not coming.

SOLNESS. Then you did take an interest in other people, too?

HILDA. A little bit—for a week or so. Good heavens, Mr. Solness, you surely know how such things come about.

SOLNESS. Hilda—what is it you have come for?

HILDA. Don't waste time talking. The poor old man might go
and die in the meantime.

SOLNESS. Answer me, Hilda. What do you want of me?

HILDA. I want my kingdom.

SOLNESS. H'm——

[*He gives a rapid glance towards the door on the left and
then goes on writing on the drawings. At the same moment* MRS. SOLNESS *enters; she has some packages in her
hand.*]

MRS. SOLNESS. Here are a few things I have got for you, Miss
Wangel. The large parcels will be sent later on.

HILDA. Oh, how very, very kind of you!

MRS. SOLNESS. Only my simple duty. Nothing more than that.

SOLNESS [*reading over what he has written*]. Aline!

MRS. SOLNESS. Yes?

SOLNESS. Did you notice whether the—the book-keeper was
out there?

MRS. SOLNESS. Yes, of course, she was out there.

SOLNESS [*puts the drawings in the portfolio*]. H'm——

MRS. SOLNESS. She was standing at the desk, as she always is—
when *I* go through the room.

SOLNESS [*rises*]. Then I'll give this to her and tell her that——

HILDA [*takes the portfolio from him*]. Oh, no, let me have the pleasure of doing that! [*Goes to the door, but turns.*] What is her name?

SOLNESS. Her name is Miss Fosli.

HILDA. Pooh, that sounds too cold! Her Christian name, I mean?

SOLNESS. Kaia—I believe.

HILDA [*opens the door and calls out*]. Kaia, come in here! Make haste! Mr. Solness wants to speak to you.

[KAIA FOSLI *appears at the door.*]

KAIA [*looking at him in alarm*]. Here I am——?

HILDA [*handing her the portfolio*]. See here, Kaia! You can take this home; Mr. Solness has written on them now.

KAIA. Oh, at last!

SOLNESS. Give them to the old man as soon as you can.

KAIA. I will go straight home with them.

SOLNESS. Yes, do. Now Ragnar will have a chance of building for himself.

KAIA. Oh, may he come and thank you for all——?

SOLNESS [*harshly*]. I won't have any thanks! Tell him that from me.

KAIA. Yes, I will——

SOLNESS. And tell him at the same time that henceforward I do not require his services—nor yours either.

KAIA [*softly and quiveringly*]. Not mine either?

SOLNESS. You will have other things to think of now and to attend to; and that is a very good thing for you. Well, go home with the drawings now, Miss Fosli. At once! Do you hear?

KAIA [*as before*]. Yes, Mr. Solness.

[*She goes out.*]

MRS. SOLNESS. Heavens! what deceitful eyes she has.

SOLNESS. She? That poor little creature?

MRS. SOLNESS. Oh—I can see what I can see, Halvard.——Are you really dismissing them?

SOLNESS. Yes.

MRS. SOLNESS. Her as well?

SOLNESS. Was not that what you wished?

MRS. SOLNESS. But how can you get on without her——? Oh, well, no doubt you have some one else in reserve, Halvard.

HILDA [playfully]. Well, I for one am not the person to stand at that desk.

SOLNESS. Never mind, never mind—it will be all right, Aline. Now all you have to do is to think about moving into our new home—as quickly as you can. This evening we will hang up the wreath—[Turns to Hilda.]—right on the very pinnacle of the tower. What do you say to that, Miss Hilda?

HILDA [looks at him with sparkling eyes]. It will be splendid to see you so high up once more.

SOLNESS. Me!

MRS. SOLNESS. For heaven's sake, Miss Wangel, don't imagine such a thing! My husband!—when he always gets so dizzy!

HILDA. He get dizzy! No, I know quite well he does not!

MRS. SOLNESS. Oh, yes, indeed he does.

HILDA. But I have seen him with my own eyes right up at the top of a high church-tower!

MRS. SOLNESS. Yes, I hear people talk of that; but it is utterly impossible——

SOLNESS [vehemently]. Impossible—impossible, yes! But there I stood all the same!

MRS. SOLNESS. Oh, how can you say so, Halvard? Why, you can't even bear to go out on the second-story balcony here. You have always been like that.

SOLNESS. You may perhaps see something different this evening.

MRS. SOLNESS [in alarm]. No, no, no! Please God I shall never see that. I will write at once to the doctor—and I am sure he won't let you do it.

SOLNESS. Why, Aline——!

MRS. SOLNESS. Oh, you know you're ill, Halvard. This proves it! Oh God—Oh God!

[*She goes hastily out to the right.*]

HILDA [*looks intently at him*]. Is it so, or is it not?

SOLNESS. That I turn dizzy?

HILDA. That my master builder dares not—cannot—climb as high as he builds?

SOLNESS. Is that the way you look at it?

HILDA. Yes.

SOLNESS. I believe there is scarcely a corner in me that is safe from you.

HILDA [*looks towards the bow-window*]. Up there, then. Right up there——

SOLNESS [*approaches her*]. You might have the topmost room in the tower, Hilda—there you might live like a princess.

HILDA [*indefinably, between earnest and jest*]. Yes, that is what you promised me.

SOLNESS. Did I really?

HILDA. Fie, Mr. Solness! You said I should be a princess, and that you would give me a kingdom. And then you went and ——Well!

SOLNESS [*cautiously*]. Are you quite certain that this is not a dream—a fancy, that has fixed itself in your mind?

HILDA [*sharply*]. Do you mean that you did not do it?

SOLNESS. I scarcely know myself. [*More softly.*] But now I know so much for certain, that I——

HILDA. That you——? Say it at once!

SOLNESS. —that I ought to have done it.

HILDA [*exclaims with animation*]. Don't tell me you can ever be dizzy!

SOLNESS. This evening, then, we will hang up the wreath— Princess Hilda.

HILDA [*with a bitter curve of the lips*]. Over your new home, yes.

SOLNESS. Over the new house, which will never be a home for me.

[*He goes out through the garden door.*]

HILDA [*looks straight in front of her with a far-away expression and whispers to herself. The only words audible are*] —frightfully thrilling——

ACT THREE

The large, broad verandah of SOLNESS's *dwelling-house. Part of the house, with outer door leading to the verandah, is seen to the left. A railing along the verandah to the right. At the back, from the end of the verandah, a flight of steps leads down to the garden below. Tall old trees in the garden spread their branches over the verandah and towards the house. Far to the right, in among the trees, a glimpse is caught of the lower part of the new villa, with scaffolding round so much as is seen of the tower. In the background the garden is bounded by an old wooden fence. Outside the fence, a street with low, tumble-down cottages.*

Evening sky with sun-lit clouds.

On the verandah, a garden bench stands along the wall of the house, and in front of the bench a long table. On the other side of the table, an arm-chair and some stools. All the furniture is of wicker-work.

MRS. SOLNESS, *wrapped in a large white crape shawl, sits resting in the arm-chair and gazes over to the right. Shortly after,* HILDA WANGEL *comes up the flight of steps from the garden. She is dressed as in the last act and wears her hat. She has in her bodice a little nosegay of small common flowers.*

MRS. SOLNESS [*turning her head a little*]. Have you been round the garden, Miss Wangel?

HILDA. Yes, I have been taking a look at it.

MRS. SOLNESS. And found some flowers, too, I see.

HILDA. Yes, indeed! There are such heaps of them in among the bushes.

MRS. SOLNESS. Are there really? Still? You see I scarcely ever go there.

HILDA [*closer*]. What! Don't you take a run down into the garden every day, then?

MRS. SOLNESS [*with a faint smile*]. I don't "run" anywhere, nowadays.

HILDA. Well, but do you not go down now and then to look at all the lovely things there?

MRS. SOLNESS. It has all become so strange to me. I am almost afraid to see it again.

HILDA. Your own garden!

MRS. SOLNESS. I don't feel that it is mine any longer.

HILDA. What do you mean——?

MRS. SOLNESS. No, no, it is not—not—not as it was in my mother's and father's time. They have taken away so much —so much of the garden, Miss Wangel. Fancy—they have parcelled it out—and built houses for strangers—people that I don't know. And they can sit and look in upon me from their windows.

HILDA [*with a bright expression*]. Mrs. Solness!

MRS. SOLNESS. Yes!

HILDA. May I stay here with you a little?

MRS. SOLNESS. Yes, by all means, if you care to.

[HILDA *moves a stool close to the arm-chair and sits down.*]

HILDA. Ah—here one can sit and sun oneself like a cat.

MRS. SOLNESS [*lays her hand softly on* HILDA's *neck*]. It is nice of you to be willing to sit with me. I thought you wanted to go in to my husband.

HILDA. What should I want with him?

MRS. SOLNESS. To help him, I thought.

HILDA. No, thank you. And besides, he is not in. He is over there with the workmen. But he looked so fierce that I did not care to talk to him.

MRS. SOLNESS. He is so kind and gentle in reality.

HILDA. He!

MRS. SOLNESS. You do not really know him yet, Miss Wangel.

HILDA [*looks affectionately at her*]. Are you pleased at the thought of moving over to the new house?

MRS. SOLNESS. I ought to be pleased; for it is what Halvard

wants——

HILDA. Oh, not just on that account, surely.

MRS. SOLNESS. Yes, yes, Miss Wangel; for it is only my duty to submit myself to him. But very often it is dreadfully difficult to force one's mind to obedience.

HILDA. Yes, that must be difficult indeed.

MRS. SOLNESS. I can tell you it is—when one has so many faults as I have——

HILDA. When one has gone through so much trouble as you have——

MRS. SOLNESS. How do you know about that?

HILDA. Your husband told me.

MRS. SOLNESS. To me he very seldom mentions these things. ——Yes, I can tell you I have gone through more than enough trouble in my life, Miss Wangel.

HILDA [looks sympathetically at her and nods slowly]. Poor Mrs. Solness. First of all there was the fire——

MRS. SOLNESS [with a sigh]. Yes, everything that was mine was burnt.

HILDA. And then came what was worse.

MRS. SOLNESS [looking inquiringly at her]. Worse?

HILDA. The worst of all.

MRS. SOLNESS. What do you mean?

HILDA [softly]. You lost the two little boys.

MRS. SOLNESS. Oh, yes, the boys. But, you see, that was a thing apart. That was a dispensation of Providence; and in such things one can only bow in submission—yes, and be thankful, too.

HILDA. Then you are so?

MRS. SOLNESS. Not always, I am sorry to say. I know well enough that it is my duty—but all the same I cannot.

HILDA. No, no, I think that is only natural.

MRS. SOLNESS. And often and often I have to remind myself that it was a righteous punishment for me——

HILDA. Why?

MRS. SOLNESS. Because I had not fortitude enough in misfortune.

HILDA. But I don't see that——

MRS. SOLNESS. Oh, no, no, Miss Wangel—do not talk to me any more about the two little boys. We ought to feel nothing but joy in thinking of them; for they are so happy—so happy now. No, it is the small losses in life that cut one to the heart—the loss of all that other people look upon as almost nothing.

HILDA [lays her arms on MRS. SOLNESS's knees and looks up at her affectionately]. Dear Mrs. Solness—tell me what things you mean!

MRS. SOLNESS. As I say, only little things. All the old portraits were burnt on the walls. And all the old silk dresses were burnt, that had belonged to the family for generations and generations. And all mother's and grandmother's lace—that was burnt, too. And only think—the jewels, too! [Sadly.] And then all the dolls.

HILDA. The dolls?

MRS. SOLNESS [choking with tears]. I had nine lovely dolls.

HILDA. And they were burnt, too?

MRS. SOLNESS. All of them. Oh, it was hard—so hard for me.

HILDA. Had you put by all these dolls, then? Ever since you were little?

MRS. SOLNESS. I had not put them by. The dolls and I had gone on living together.

HILDA. After you were grown up?

MRS. SOLNESS. Yes, long after that.

HILDA. After you were married, too?

MRS. SOLNESS. Oh, yes, indeed. So long as he did not see it——. But they were all burnt up, poor things. No one thought of saving them. Oh, it is so miserable to think of. You mustn't laugh at me, Miss Wangel.

HILDA. I am not laughing in the least.

MRS. SOLNESS. For you see, in a certain sense, there was life in them, too. I carried them under my heart—like little unborn children.

[DR. HERDAL, with his hat in his hand, comes out through the *door and observes* MRS. SOLNESS *and* HILDA.]

DR. HERDAL. Well, Mrs. Solness, so you are sitting out here catching cold?

MRS. SOLNESS. I find it so pleasant and warm here to-day.

DR. HERDAL. Yes, yes. But is there anything going on here? I got a note from you.

MRS. SOLNESS [*rises*]. Yes, there is something I must talk to you about.

DR. HERDAL. Very well; then perhaps we had better go in. [*To* HILDA]. Still in your mountaineering dress, Miss Wangel?

HILDA [*gaily, rising*]. Yes—in full uniform! But to-day I am not going climbing and breaking my neck. We two will stop quietly below and look on, doctor.

DR. HERDAL. What are we to look on at?

MRS. SOLNESS [*softly, in alarm, to* HILDA]. Hush, hush—for God's sake! He is coming. Try to get that idea out of his head. And let us be friends, Miss Wangel. Don't you think we can?

HILDA [*throws her arms impetuously round* MRS. SOLNESS'S *neck*]. Oh, if we only could!

MRS. SOLNESS [*gently disengages herself*]. There, there, there! There he comes, doctor. Let me have a word with you.

DR. HERDAL. Is it about him?

MRS. SOLNESS. Yes, to be sure it's about him. Do come in.

[*She and the doctor enter the house. Next moment* SOLNESS *comes up from the garden by the flight of steps. A serious look comes over* HILDA's *face.*]

SOLNESS [*glances at the house-door, which is closed cautiously from within*]. Have you noticed, Hilda, that as soon as I come she goes?

HILDA. I have noticed that as soon as you come, you make her go.

SOLNESS. Perhaps so. But I cannot help it. [*Looks observantly at her*]. Are you cold, Hilda? I think you look cold.

HILDA. I have just come up out of a tomb.

SOLNESS. What do you mean by that?

HILDA. That I have got chilled through and through, Mr. Solness.

SOLNESS [*slowly*]. I believe I understand——

HILDA. What brings you up here just now?

SOLNESS. I caught sight of you from over there.

HILDA. But then you must have seen her too?

SOLNESS. I knew she would go at once if I came.

HILDA. Is it very painful for you that she should avoid you in this way?

SOLNESS. In one sense, it's a relief as well.

HILDA. Not to have her before your eyes?

SOLNESS. Yes.

HILDA. Not to be always seeing how heavily the loss of the little boys weighs upon her?

SOLNESS. Yes. Chiefly that.

[HILDA *drifts across the verandah with her hands behind her back, stops at the railing and looks out over the garden.*]

SOLNESS [*after a short pause*]. Did you have a long talk with her?

[HILDA *stands motionless and does not answer.*]

SOLNESS. Had you a long talk, I asked?

[HILDA *is silent as before.*]

SOLNESS. What was she talking about, Hilda?

[HILDA *continues silent.*]

SOLNESS. Poor Aline! I suppose it was about the little boys.

HILDA [*a nervous shudder runs through her; then she nods hurriedly once or twice*].

SOLNESS. She will never get over it—never in this world. [*Approaches her.*] Now you are standing there again like a statue; just as you stood last night.

HILDA [*turns and looks at him, with great serious eyes*]. I am going away.

SOLNESS [*sharply*]. Going away!

HILDA. Yes.

SOLNESS. But I won't allow you to!

HILDA. What am I to do here now?

SOLNESS. Simply to be here, Hilda!

HILDA [*measures him with a look*]. Oh, thank you. You know it wouldn't end there.

SOLNESS [*heedlessly*]. So much the better!

HILDA [*vehemently*]. I cannot do any harm to one whom I know! I can't take away anything that belongs to her.

SOLNESS. Who wants you to do that?

HILDA [*continuing*]. A stranger, yes! for that is quite a different thing! A person I have never set eyes on. But one that I have come into close contact with——! Oh, no! Oh, no! Ugh!

SOLNESS. Yes, but I never proposed you should.

HILDA. Oh, Mr. Solness, you know quite well what the end of it would be. And that is why I am going away.

SOLNESS. And what is to become of me when you are gone? What shall I have to live for then?—— After that?

HILDA [*with the indefinable look in her eyes*]. It is surely not so hard for you. You have your duties to her. Live for those duties.

SOLNESS. Too late. These powers—these—these——

HILDA. —devils!

SOLNESS. Yes, these devils! And the troll within me as well— they have drawn all the life-blood out of her. [*Laughs in desperation.*] They did it for my happiness! Yes, yes! [*Sadly.*] And now she is dead—for my sake. And I am chained alive to a dead woman. [*In wild anguish.*] I—I who cannot live without joy in life!

[HILDA *moves round the table and seats herself on the bench, with her elbows on the table, and her head supported by her hands.*]

HILDA [*sits and looks at him awhile*]. What will you build next?

SOLNESS [*shakes his head*]. I don't believe I shall build much more.

HILDA. Not those cosy, happy homes for mother and father, and for the troop of children?

SOLNESS. I wonder whether there will be any use for such homes in the coming time.

HILDA. Poor Mr. Solness! And you have gone all these ten years—and staked your whole life—on that alone.

SOLNESS. Yes, you may well say so, Hilda.

HILDA [with an outburst]. Oh, it all seems to me so foolish—so foolish!

SOLNESS. All what?

HILDA. Not to be able to grasp at your own happiness—at your own life! Merely because some one you know happens to stand in the way!

SOLNESS. One whom you have no right to set aside.

HILDA. I wonder whether one really has not the right! And yet, and yet——. Oh, if one could only sleep the whole thing away!

[She lays her arms flat on the table, rests the left side of her head on her hands and shuts her eyes.]

SOLNESS [turns the arm-chair and sits down at the table]. Had you a cosy, happy home—up there with your father, Hilda?

HILDA [without stirring, answers as if half asleep]. I had only a cage.

SOLNESS. And you are determined not to go back to it?

HILDA [as before]. The wild bird never wants to go into the cage.

SOLNESS. Rather range through the free air——

HILDA [still as before]. The bird of prey loves to range——

SOLNESS [lets his eyes rest on her]. If only one had the viking-spirit in life——

HILDA [in her usual voice; opens her eyes but does not move]. And the other thing? Say what that was!

SOLNESS. A robust conscience.

[HILDA sits erect on the bench, with animation. Her eyes have once more the sparkling expression of gladness.]

HILDA [*nods to him*]. I know what you are going to build next!

SOLNESS. Then you know more than I do, Hilda.

HILDA. Yes, builders are such stupid people.

SOLNESS. What is it to be then?

HILDA [*nods again*]. The castle.

SOLNESS. What castle?

HILDA. My castle, of course.

SOLNESS. Do you want a castle now?

HILDA. Don't you owe me a kingdom, I should like to know?

SOLNESS. You say I do.

HILDA. Well—you admit you owe me this kingdom. And you
can't have a kingdom without a royal castle, I should think!

SOLNESS [*more and more animated*]. Yes, they usually go together.

HILDA. Good! Then build it for me! This moment!

SOLNESS [*laughing*]. Must you have that on the instant, too?

HILDA. Yes, to be sure! For the ten years are up now, and I
am not going to wait any longer. So—out with the castle,
Mr. Solness!

SOLNESS. It's no light matter to owe you anything, Hilda.

HILDA. You should have thought of that before. It is too late
now. So—[*tapping the table*]—the castle on the table! It
is my castle! I will have it at once!

SOLNESS [*more seriously, leans over towards her, with his arms
on the table*]. What sort of castle have you imagined, Hilda?

[*Her expression becomes more and more veiled. She seems
gazing inwards at herself.*]

HILDA [*slowly*]. My castle shall stand on a height—on a very
great height—with a clear outlook on all sides, so that I
can see far—far around.

SOLNESS. And no doubt it is to have a high tower!

HILDA. A tremendously high tower. And at the very top of the
tower there shall be a balcony. And I will stand out upon
it——

SOLNESS [*involuntarily clutches at his forehead*]. How can you
like to stand at such a dizzy height——?

HILDA. Yes, I will, right up there will I stand and look down on the other people—on those that are building churches, and homes for mother and father and the troop of children. And you may come up and look on at it, too.

SOLNESS [*in a low tone*]. Is the builder to be allowed to come up beside the princess?

HILDA. If the builder will.

SOLNESS [*more softly*]. Then I think the builder will come.

HILDA [*nods*]. The builder—he will come.

SOLNESS. But he will never be able to build any more. Poor builder!

HILDA [*animated*]. Oh yes, he will! We two will set to work together. And then we will build the loveliest—the very loveliest—thing in all the world.

SOLNESS [*intently*]. Hilda—tell me what that is!

HILDA [*looks smilingly at him, shakes her head a little, pouts and speaks as if to a child*]. Builders—they are such very—very stupid people.

SOLNESS. Yes, no doubt they are stupid. But now tell me what it is—the loveliest thing in the world—that we two are to build together?

HILDA [*is silent a little while, then says with an indefinable expression in her eyes*]. Castles in the air.

SOLNESS. Castles in the air?

HILDA [*nods*]. Castles in the air, yes! Do you know what sort of thing a castle in the air is?

SOLNESS. It is the loveliest thing in the world, you say.

HILDA [*rises with vehemence and makes a gesture of repulsion with her hand*]. Yes, to be sure it is! Castles in the air—they are so easy to take refuge in. And so easy to build, too—[*looks scornfully at him*]—especially for the builders who have a—a dizzy conscience.

SOLNESS [*rises*]. After this day we two will build together, Hilda.

HILDA [*with a half-dubious smile*]. A real castle in the air?

SOLNESS. Yes. One with a firm foundation under it.

[RAGNAR BROVIK *comes out from the house. He is carrying a large, green wreath with flowers and silk ribbons.*]

HILDA [*with an outburst of pleasure*]. The wreath! Oh, that will be glorious!

SOLNESS [*in surprise*]. Have you brought the wreath, Ragnar?

RAGNAR. I promised the foreman I would.

SOLNESS [*relieved*]. Ah, then I suppose your father is better?

RAGNAR. No.

SOLNESS. Was he not cheered by what I wrote?

RAGNAR. It came too late.

SOLNESS. Too late!

RAGNAR. When she came with it he was unconscious. He had had a stroke.

SOLNESS. Why, then, you must go home to him! You must attend to your father!

RAGNAR. He does not need me any more.

SOLNESS. But surely you ought to be with him.

RAGNAR. She is sitting by his bed.

SOLNESS [*rather uncertainly*]. Kaia?

RAGNAR [*looking darkly at him*]. Yes—Kaia.

SOLNESS. Go home, Ragnar—both to him and to her. Give me the wreath.

RAGNAR [*suppresses a mocking smile*]. You don't mean that you yourself——?

SOLNESS. I will take it down to them myself. [*Takes the wreath from him.*] And now you go home; we don't require you to-day.

RAGNAR. I know you do not require me any more; but to-day I shall remain.

SOLNESS. Well, remain then, since you are bent upon it.

HILDA [*at the railing*]. Mr. Solness, I will stand here and look on at you.

SOLNESS. At me!

HILDA. It will be fearfully thrilling.

SOLNESS [*in a low tone*]. We will talk about that presently, Hilda.

[*He goes down the flight of steps with the wreath and away through the garden.*]

HILDA [*looks after him, then turns to* RAGNAR]. I think you might at least have thanked him.

RAGNAR. Thanked him? Ought I to have thanked him?

HILDA. Yes, of course you ought!

RAGNAR. I think it is rather you I ought to thank.

HILDA. How can you say such a thing?

RAGNAR [*without answering her*]. But I advise you to take care, Miss Wangel! For you don't know him rightly yet.

HILDA [*ardently*]. Oh, no one knows him as I do!

RAGNAR [*laughs in exasperation*]. Thank him, when he has held me down year after year! When he made father disbelieve in me—made me disbelieve in myself! And all merely that he might——!

HILDA [*as if divining something*]. That he might——? Tell me at once!

RAGNAR. That he might keep her with him.

HILDA [*with a start towards him*]. The girl at the desk.

RAGNAR. Yes.

HILDA [*threateningly, clenching her hands*]. That is not true! You are telling falsehoods about him!

RAGNAR. I would not believe it either until to-day—when she said so herself.

HILDA [*as if beside herself*]. What did she say? I will know! At once! at once!

RAGNAR. She said that he had taken possession of her mind—her whole mind—centred all her thoughts upon himself alone. She says that she can never leave him—that she will remain here, where he is——

HILDA [*with flashing eyes*]. She will not be allowed to!

RAGNAR [*as if feeling his way*]. Who will not allow her?

HILDA [*rapidly*]. He will not either!

RAGNAR. Oh no—I understand the whole thing now. After this, she would merely be—in the way.

HILDA. You understand nothing—since you can talk like that!

No, *I* will tell you why he kept hold of her.

RAGNAR. Well then, why?

HILDA. In order to keep hold of you.

RAGNAR. Has he told you so?

HILDA. No, but it is so. It must be so. [*Wildly.*] I will— I will have it so!

RAGNAR. And at the very moment when you came—he let her go.

HILDA. It was you—you that he let go. What do you suppose he cares about strange women like her?

RAGNAR [*reflects*]. Is it possible that all this time he has been afraid of me?

HILDA. He afraid! I would not be so conceited if I were you.

RAGNAR. Oh, he must have seen long ago that I had something in me, too. Besides—cowardly—that is just what he is, you see.

HILDA. He! Oh, yes, I am likely to believe that!

RAGNAR. In a certain sense he is cowardly—he, the great master builder. He is not afraid of robbing others of their life's happiness—as he has done both for my father and for me. But when it comes to climbing up a paltry bit of scaffolding —he will do anything rather than that.

HILDA. Oh, you should just have seen him high, high up—at the dizzy height where I once saw him.

RAGNAR. Did you see that?

HILDA. Yes, indeed I did. How free and great he looked as he stood and fastened the wreath to the church-vane!

RAGNAR. I know that he ventured that, once in his life—one solitary time. It is a legend among us younger men. But no power on earth would induce him to do it again.

HILDA. To-day he will do it again!

RAGNAR [*scornfully*]. Yes, I daresay!

HILDA. We shall see it!

RAGNAR. That neither you nor I will see.

HILDA [*with uncontrollable vehemence*]. I will see it! I will and must see it!

RAGNAR. But he will not do it. He simply dare not do it. For you see he cannot get over this infirmity—master builder though he be.

[MRS. SOLNESS *comes from the house on to the verandah.*]

MRS. SOLNESS [*looks around*]. Is he not here? Where has he gone to?

RAGNAR. Mr. Solness is down with the men.

HILDA. He took the wreath with him.

MRS. SOLNESS [*terrified*]. Took the wreath with him! Oh, God! oh, God! Brovik—you must go down to him! Get him to come back here!

RAGNAR. Shall I say you want to speak to him, Mrs. Solness?

MRS. SOLNESS. Oh, yes, do!—No, no—don't say that *I* want anything! You can say that somebody is here, and that he must come at once.

RAGNAR. Good. I will do so, Mrs. Solness.

[*He goes down the flight of steps and away through the garden.*]

MRS. SOLNESS. Oh, Miss Wangel, you can't think how anxious I feel about him.

HILDA. Is there anything in this to be so terribly frightened about?

MRS. SOLNESS. Oh, yes; surely you can understand. Just think, if he were really to do it! If he should take it into his head to climb up the scaffolding!

HILDA [*eagerly*]. Do you think he will?

MRS. SOLNESS. Oh, one can never tell what he might take into his head. I am afraid there is nothing he mightn't think of doing.

HILDA. Aha! Perhaps you too think that he is—well——?

MRS. SOLNESS. Oh, I don't know what to think about him now. The doctor has been telling me all sorts of things; and putting it all together with several things I have heard him say——

[DR. HERDAL *looks out, at the door.*]

DR. HERDAL. Is he not coming soon?

MRS. SOLNESS. Yes, I think so. I have sent for him at any rate.

DR. HERDAL [*advancing*]. I am afraid you will have to go in, my dear lady——

MRS. SOLNESS. Oh, no! Oh, no! I shall stay out here and wait for Halvard.

DR. HERDAL. But some ladies have just come to call on you——

MRS. SOLNESS. Good heavens, that too! And just at this moment!

DR. HERDAL. They say they positively must see the ceremony.

MRS. SOLNESS. Well, well, I suppose I must go to them after all. It is my duty.

HILDA. Can't you ask the ladies to go away?

MRS. SOLNESS. No, that would never do. Now that they are here, it is my duty to see them. But do you stay out here in the meantime—and receive him when he comes.

DR. HERDAL. And try to occupy his attention as long as possible——

MRS. SOLNESS. Yes, do, dear Miss Wangel. Keep a firm hold of him as ever you can.

HILDA. Would it not be best for you to do that?

MRS. SOLNESS. Yes! God knows that is my duty. But when one has duties in so many .directions——

DR. HERDAL [*looks towards the garden*]. There he is coming.

MRS. SOLNESS. And I have to go in!

DR. HERDAL [*to* HILDA]. Don't say anything about my being here.

HILDA. Oh, no! I daresay I shall find something else to talk to Mr. Solness about.

MRS. SOLNESS. And be sure you keep firm hold of him. I believe you can do it best.

[MRS. SOLNESS *and* DR. HERDAL *go into the house.* HILDA

remains standing on the verandah. SOLNESS *comes from the garden, up the flight of steps.*]

SOLNESS. Somebody wants me, I hear.

HILDA. Yes; it is I, Mr. Solness.

SOLNESS. Oh, is it you, Hilda? I was afraid it might be Aline or the Doctor.

HILDA. You are very easily frightened, it seems!

SOLNESS. Do you think so?

HILDA. Yes; people say that you are afraid to climb about— on the scaffoldings, you know.

SOLNESS. Well, that is quite a special thing.

HILDA. Then it is true that you are afraid to do it?

SOLNESS. Yes, I am.

HILDA. Afraid of falling down and killing yourself?

SOLNESS. No, not of that.

HILDA. Of what, then?

SOLNESS. I am afraid of retribution, Hilda.

HILDA. Of retribution? [*Shakes her head.*] I don't understand that.

SOLNESS. Sit down and I will tell you something.

HILDA. Yes, do! At once!

[*She sits on a stool by the railing and looks expectantly at him.*]

SOLNESS [*throws his hat on the table*]. You know that I began by building churches.

HILDA [*nods*]. I know that well.

SOLNESS. For, you see, I came as a boy from a pious home in the country; and so it seemed to me that this church-building was the noblest task I could set myself.

HILDA. Yes, yes.

SOLNESS. And I venture to say that I built those poor little churches with such honest and warm and heartfelt devotion that—that——

HILDA. That——? Well?

SOLNESS. Well, that I think that he ought to have been pleased with me.

HILDA. He? What he?

SOLNESS. He who was to have the churches, of course! He to whose honour and glory they were dedicated.

HILDA. Oh, indeed! But are you certain, then, that—that he was not—pleased with you?

SOLNESS [*scornfully*]. He pleased with me! How can you talk so, Hilda? He who gave the troll in me leave to lord it just as it pleased. He who bade them be at hand to serve me, both day and night—all these—all these——

HILDA. Devils——

SOLNESS. Yes, of both kinds. Oh, no, he made me feel clearly enough that he was not pleased with me. [*Mysteriously.*] You see, that was really the reason why he made the old house burn down.

HILDA. Was that why?

SOLNESS. Yes, don't you understand? He wanted to give me the chance of becoming an accomplished master in my own sphere—so that I might build all the more glorious churches for him. At first I did not understand what he was driving at; but all of a sudden it flashed upon me.

HILDA. When was that?

SOLNESS. It was when I was building the church-tower up at Lysanger.

HILDA. I thought so.

SOLNESS. For you see, Hilda—up there, amidst those new surroundings, I used to go about musing and pondering within myself. Then I saw plainly why he had taken my little children from me. It was that I should have nothing else to attach myself to. No such thing as love and happiness, you understand. I was to be only a master builder—nothing else. And all my life long I was to go on building for him. [*Laughs.*] But I can tell you nothing came of that.

HILDA. What did you do, then?

SOLNESS. First of all, I searched and tried my own heart——

HILDA. And then?

SOLNESS. Then I did the impossible—I no less than he.

HILDA. The impossible?

SOLNESS. I had never before been able to climb up to a great, free height. But that day I did it.

HILDA [*leaping up*]. Yes, yes, you did!

SOLNESS. And when I stood there, high over everything, and was hanging the wreath over the vane, I said to him: Hear me now, thou Mighty One! From this day forward I will be a free builder—I, too, in my sphere—just as thou in thine. I will never more build churches for thee—only homes for human beings.

HILDA [*with great sparkling eyes*]. That was the song that I heard through the air!

SOLNESS. But afterwards his turn came.

HILDA. What do you mean by that?

SOLNESS [*looks despondently at her*]. Building homes for human beings—is not worth a rap, Hilda.

HILDA. Do you say that now?

SOLNESS. Yes, for now I see it. Men have no use for these homes of theirs—to be happy in. And I should not have had any use for such a home, if I had had one. [*With a quiet, bitter laugh.*] See, that is the upshot of the whole affair, however far back I look. Nothing really built; nor anything sacrificed for the chance of building. Nothing, nothing! the whole is nothing.

HILDA. Then you will never build anything more?

SOLNESS [*with animation*]. On the contrary, I am just going to begin!

HILDA. What, then? What will you build? Tell me at once!

SOLNESS. I believe there is only one possible dwelling-place for human happiness—and that is what I am going to build now.

HILDA [*looks fixedly at him*]. Mr. Solness—you mean our castle?

SOLNESS. The castles in the air—yes.

HILDA. I am afraid you would turn dizzy before we got half-way up.

SOLNESS. Not if I can mount hand in hand with you, Hilda.

HILDA [*with an expression of suppressed resentment*]. Only with me? Will there be no others of the party?

SOLNESS. Who else should there be?

HILDA. Oh—that girl—that Kaia at the desk. Poor thing—
don't you want to take her with you, too?

SOLNESS. Oho! Was it about her that Aline was talking to you?

HILDA. Is it so—or is it not?

SOLNESS [*vehemently*]. I will not answer such a question. You
must believe in me, wholly and entirely!

HILDA. All these ten years I have believed in you so utterly—
so utterly.

SOLNESS. You must go on believing in me!

HILDA. Then let me see you stand free and high up!

SOLNESS [*sadly*]. Oh Hilda—it is not every day that I can do
that.

HILDA [*passionately*]. I will have you do it! I will have it! [*Imploringly*.] Just once more Solness! Do the impossible once
again!

SOLNESS [*stands and looks deep into her eyes*]. If I try it, Hilda,
I will stand up there and talk to him as I did that time before.

HILDA [*in rising excitement*]. What will you say to him?

SOLNESS. I will say to him: Hear me, Mighty Lord—thou may'st
judge me as seems best to thee. But hereafter I will build
nothing but the loveliest thing in the world——

HILDA [*carried away*]. Yes—yes—yes!

SOLNESS. —build it together with a princess, whom I love——

HILDA. Yes, tell him that! Tell him that!

SOLNESS. Yes. And then I will say to him: Now I shall go down
and throw my arms round her and kiss her——

HILDA. —many times! Say that!

SOLNESS. —many, many times, I will say.

HILDA. And then——?

SOLNESS. Then I will wave my hat—and come down to the
earth—and do as I said to him.

HILDA [*with outstretched arms*]. Now I see you again as I did
when there was song in the air.

SOLNESS [*looks at her with his head bowed*]. How have you become what you are, Hilda?

HILDA. How have you made me what I am?

SOLNESS [*shortly and firmly*]. The princess shall have her castle.

HILDA [*jubilant, clapping her hands*]. Oh, Mr. Solness——! My lovely, lovely castle. Our castle in the air!

SOLNESS. On a firm foundation.

[*In the street a crowd of people has assembled, vaguely seen through the trees. Music of wind-instruments is heard far away behind the new house.*]

[MRS. SOLNESS, *with a fur collar round her neck,* DOCTOR HERDAL *with her white shawl. on his arm, and some ladies, come out on the verandah.* RAGNAR BROVIK *comes at the same time up from the garden.*]

MRS. SOLNESS [*to* RAGNAR]. Are we to have music, too?

RAGNAR. Yes. It's the band of the Mason's Union. [*To* SOLNESS.] The foreman asked me to tell you that he is ready now to go up with the wreath.

SOLNESS [*takes his hat*]. Good. I will go down to him myself.

MRS. SOLNESS [*anxiously*]. What have you to do down there, Halvard?

SOLNESS [*curtly*]. I must be down below with the men.

MRS. SOLNESS. Yes, down below—only down below.

SOLNESS. That is where I always stand—on everyday occasions.

[*He goes down the flight of steps and away through the garden.*]

MRS. SOLNESS [*calls after him over the railing*]. But do beg the man to be careful when he goes up? Promise me that, Halvard!

DR. HERDAL [*to* MRS. SOLNESS]. Don't you see that I was right? He has given up all thought of that folly.

MRS. SOLNESS. Oh, what a relief! Twice workmen have fallen, and each time they were killed on the spot. [*Turns to* HILDA.] Thank you, Miss Wangel, for having kept such a firm hold upon him. I should never have been able to manage him.

DR. HERDAL [*playfully*]. Yes, yes, Miss Wangel, you know how to keep firm hold on a man, when you give your mind to it.

[MRS. SOLNESS *and* DR. HERDAL *go up to the ladies, who are standing nearer to the steps and looking over the garden.* HILDA *remains standing beside the railing in the foreground.* RAGNAR *goes up to her.*]

RAGNAR [*with suppressed laughter, half whispering*]. Miss Wangel—do you see all those young fellows down in the street?

HILDA. Yes.

RAGNAR. They are my fellow-students, come to look at the master.

HILDA. What do they want to look at him for?

RAGNAR. They want to see how he daren't climb to the top of his own house.

HILDA. Oh, that is what those boys want, is it?

RAGNAR [*spitefully and scornfully*]. He has kept us down so long—now we are going to see him keep quietly down below himself.

HILDA. You will not see that—not this time.

RAGNAR [*smiles*]. Indeed! Then where shall we see him?

HILDA. High—high up by the vane! That is where you will see him!

RAGNAR [*laughs*]. Him! Oh, yes, I daresay!

HILDA. His will is to reach the top—so at the top you shall see him.

RAGNAR. His will, yes; that I can easily believe. But he simply cannot do it. His head would swim round, long, long before he got half-way. He would have to crawl down again on his hands and knees.

DR. HERDAL [*points across*]. Look! There goes the foreman up the ladders.

MRS. SOLNESS. And of course he has the wreath to carry, too. Oh, I do hope he will be careful!

RAGNAR [*stares incredulously and shouts*]. Why, but it's——

HILDA [*breaking out in jubilation*]. It is the master builder himself!

MRS. SOLNESS [*screams with terror*]. Yes, it is Halvard! Oh, my great God——! Halvard! Halvard!

DR. HERDAL. Hush! Don't shout to him!

MRS. SOLNESS [*half beside herself*]. I must go to him! I must get him to come down again!

DR. HERDAL [*holds her*]. Don't move, any of you! Not a sound!

HILDA [*immovable, follows* SOLNESS *with her eyes*]. He climbs and climbs. Higher and higher! Higher and higher! Look! Just look!

RAGNAR [*breathless*]. He must turn now. He can't possibly help it.

HILDA. He climbs and climbs. He will soon be at the top now.

MRS. SOLNESS. Oh, I shall die of terror. I cannot bear to see it.

DR. HERDAL. Then don't look up at him.

HILDA. There he is standing on the topmost planks. Right at the top!

DR. HERDAL. Nobody must move! Do you hear?

HILDA [*exulting, with quiet intensity*]. At last! At last! Now I see him great and free again!

RAGNAR [*almost voiceless*]. But this is im——

HILDA. So I have seen him all through these ten years. How secure he stands! Frightfully thrilling all the same. Look at him! Now he is hanging the wreath round the vane.

RAGNAR. I feel as if I were looking at something utterly impossible.

HILDA. Yes, it is the impossible that he is doing now! [*With the indefinable expression in her eyes.*] Can you see any one else up there with him?

RAGNAR. There is no one else.

HILDA. Yes, there is one he is striving with.

RAGNAR. You are mistaken.

HILDA. Then do you hear no song in the air, either?

RAGNAR. It must be the wind in the tree-tops.

HILDA. *I* hear a song—a mighty song! [*Shouts in wild jubila-
tion and glee.*] Look, look! Now he is waving his hat! He is
waving it to us down here! Oh, wave, wave back to him.
For now it is finished! [*Snatches the white shawl from the
Doctor, waves it and shouts up to* SOLNESS.] Hurrah for
Master Builder Solness!

DR. HERDAL. Stop! Stop! For God's sake——!

[*The ladies on the verandah wave their pockethandker-
chiefs and the shouts of "Hurrah" are taken up in the street
below. Then they are suddenly silenced, and the crowd
bursts out into a shriek of horror. A human body, with
planks and fragments of wood, is vaguely perceived crash-
ing down behind the trees.*]

MRS. SOLNESS AND THE LADIES [*at the same time*]. He is falling!
He is falling!

[MRS. SOLNESS *totters, falls backwards, swooning, and is
caught, amid cries and confusion, by the ladies. The crowd
in the street breaks down the fence and storms into the garden. At the same time* DR. HERDAL, *too, rushes down thither.
A short pause.*]

HILDA [*stares fixedly upwards and says, as if petrified*]. My
Master Builder.

RAGNAR [*supports himself, trembling, against the railing*]. He
must be dashed to pieces—killed on the spot.

ONE OF THE LADIES [*whilst* MRS. SOLNESS *is carried into the
house*]. Run down for the doctor——

RAGNAR. I can't stir a foot——

ANOTHER LADY. Then call to some one!

RAGNAR [*tries to call out*]. How is it? Is he alive?

A VOICE [*below in the garden*]. Mr. Solness is dead!

OTHER VOICES [*nearer*]. The head is all crushed.—— He fell
right into the quarry.

HILDA [*turns to* RAGNAR *and says quietly*]. I can't see him up
there now.

RAGNAR. This is terrible. So, after all, he could not do it.

HILDA [*as if in quiet spell-bound triumph*]. But he mounted right to the top. And I heard harps in the air. [*Waves her shawl in the air, and shrieks with wild intensity.*] My—my Master Builder!

MRS. WARREN'S PROFESSION   [*1898*]

---

by George Bernard Shaw
[1856-1950]

CHARACTERS

MRS. KITTY WARREN, *"a genial and fairly presentable old black-guard of a woman"*

VIVIE WARREN, *her daughter*

FRANK GARDNER, *friend and suitor of Vivie*

THE REVEREND SAMUEL GARDNER, *his father*

MR. PRAED, *friend of Mrs. Warren*

SIR GEORGE CROFTS, *friend of Mrs. Warren*

ACT ONE

[*Summer afternoon in a cottage garden on the eastern slope of a hill a little south of Haslemere in Surrey. Looking up the hill, the cottage is seen in the left hand corner of the garden, with its thatched roof and porch, and a large latticed window to the left of the porch. A paling completely shuts in the garden, except for a gate on the right. The common rises uphill beyond the paling to the sky line. Some folded canvas garden chairs are leaning against the side bench in the porch. A lady's bicycle is propped against the wall, under the window. A little to the right of the porch a hammock is slung from two posts. A big canvas umbrella, stuck in the ground, keeps the sun off the hammock, in which a young lady lies reading and making notes, her head towards the cottage and her feet towards the gate. In front of the hammock, and within reach of her hand, is a common kitchen chair, with a pile of serious-looking books and a supply of writing paper on it.*

A gentleman walking on the common comes into sight from behind the cottage. He is hardly past middle age, with something of the artist about him, unconventionally but carefully dressed, and clean-shaven except for a moustache, with an eager susceptible face and very amiable and considerate manners. He has silky black hair, with waves of grey and white in it. His eyebrows are white, his moustache black. He seems not certain of his way. He looks over the palings; takes stock of the place; and sees the young lady.]

THE GENTLEMAN [*taking off his hat*]. I beg your pardon. Can you direct me to Hindview—Mrs. Alison's?

THE YOUNG LADY [*glancing up from her book*]. This is Mrs. Alison's. [*She resumes her work.*]

THE GENTLEMAN. Indeed! Perhaps—may I ask are you Miss Vivie Warren?

THE YOUNG LADY [*sharply, as she turns on her elbow to get a good look at him*]. Yes.

THE GENTLEMAN [*daunted and conciliatory*]. I'm afraid I appear intrusive. My name is Praed. [*Vivie at once throws her books upon the chair, and gets out of the hammock.*] Oh, pray don't let me disturb you.

VIVIE [*striding to the gate and opening it for him*]. Come in, Mr. Praed. [*He comes in.*] Glad to see you. [*She proffers her hand and takes his with a resolute and hearty grip. She is an attractive specimen of the sensible, able, highly-educated young middle-class Englishwoman. Age 22. Prompt, strong, confident, self-possessed. Plain business-like dress, but not dowdy. She wears a chatelaine at her belt, with a fountain pen and a paper knife among its pendants.*]

PRAED. Very kind of you indeed, Miss Warren. [*She shuts the gate with a vigorous slam. He passes in to the middle of the garden, exercising his fingers, which are slightly numbed by her greeting.*] Has your mother arrived?

VIVIE [*quickly, evidently scenting aggression*]. Is she coming?

PRAED [*surprised*]. Didn't you expect us?

VIVIE. No.

PRAED. Now, goodness me, I hope I've not mistaken the day. That would be just like me, you know. Your mother arranged that she was to come down from London and that I was to come over from Horsham to be introduced to you.

VIVIE [*not at all pleased*]. Did she? H'm! My mother has rather a trick of taking me by surprise—to see how I behave myself when she's away, I suppose. I fancy I shall take my mother very much by surprise one of these days, if she makes arrangements that concern me without consulting me beforehand. She hasn't come.

PRAED [*embarrassed*]. I'm really very sorry.

VIVIE [*throwing off her displeasure*]. It's not your fault, Mr. Praed, is it? And I'm very glad you've come. You are the only one of my mother's friends I have ever asked her to bring to see me.

PRAED [*relieved and delighted*]. Oh, now this is really very good of you, Miss Warren!

VIVIE. Will you come indoors; or would you rather sit out here and talk?

PRAED. It will be nicer out here, don't you think?

VIVIE. Then I'll go and get you a chair. [*She goes to the porch for a garden chair.*]

PRAED [*following her*]. Oh, pray, pray! Allow me. [*He lays hands on the chair.*]

VIVIE [*letting him take it*]. Take care of your fingers: they're rather dodgy things, those chairs. [*She goes across to the chair with the books on it; pitches them into the hammock; and brings the chair forward with one swing.*]

PRAED [*who has just unfolded his chair*]. Oh, now do let me take that hard chair. I like hard chairs.

VIVIE. So do I. Sit down, Mr. Praed. [*This invitation she gives with genial peremptoriness, his anxiety to please her clearly striking her as a sign of weakness of character on his part. But he does not immediately obey.*]

PRAED. By the way, though, hadn't we better go to the station to meet your mother?

VIVIE [*coolly*]. Why? She knows the way.

PRAED [*disconcerted*]. Er—I suppose she does. [*He sits down.*]

VIVIE. Do you know, you are just like what I expected. I hope you are disposed to be friends with me.

PRAED [*again beaming*]. Thank you, my dear Miss Warren: thank you. Dear me! I'm so glad your mother hasn't spoilt you!

VIVIE. How?

PRAED. Well, in making you too conventional. You know, my dear Miss Warren, I am a born anarchist. I hate authority. It spoils the relations between parent and child: even between mother and daughter. Now I was always afraid that your mother would strain her authority to make you very conventional. It's such a relief to find that she hasn't.

VIVIE. Oh! have I been behaving unconventionally?

PRAED. Oh no: oh dear no. At least not conventionally unconventionally, you understand. [*She nods and sit down. He goes on, with a cordial outburst.*] But it was so charming of you to say that you were disposed to be friends with me! You modern young ladies are splendid: perfectly splendid!

VIVIE [*dubiously*]. Eh? [*Watching him with dawning disappointment as to the quality of his brains and character.*]

PRAED. When I was your age, young men and women were afraid of each other: there was no good fellowship. Nothing real. Only gallantry copied out of novels, and as vulgar and affected as it could be. Maidenly reserve! gentlemanly chivalry! always saying no when you meant yes! simple purgatory for shy and sincere souls.

VIVIE. Yes, I imagine there must have been a frightful waste of time. Especially women's time.

PRAED. Oh, waste of life, waste of everything. But things are improving. Do you know, I have been in a positive state of excitement about meeting you ever since your magnificent achievements at Cambridge: a thing unheard of in my day. It was perfectly splendid, your tieing with the third wrangler. Just the right place, you know. The first wrangler is always a dreamy, morbid fellow, in whom the thing is pushed to the length of a disease.

VIVIE. It doesn't pay. I wouldn't do it again for the same money.

PRAED [*aghast*]. The same money!

VIVIE. I did it for £50.

PRAED. Fifty pounds!

VIVIE. Yes. Fifty pounds. Perhaps you don't know how it was. Mrs. Latham, my tutor at Newnham, told my mother that I could distinguish myself in the mathematical tripos if I went in for it in earnest. The papers were full just then of Phillipa Summers beating the senior wrangler. You remember about it, of course.

PRAED [*shakes his head energetically*] *!!!*

VIVIE. Well anyhow she did; and nothing would please my mother but that I should do the same thing. I said flatly it was not worth my while to face the grind since I was not going in for teaching; but I offered to try for fourth wrangler or thereabouts for £50. She closed with me at that, after a little grumbling; and I was better than my bargain. But I wouldn't do it again for that. £200 would have been nearer the mark.

PRAED [*much damped*]. Lord bless me! That's a very practical way of looking at it.

VIVIE. Did you expect to find me an unpractical person?

PRAED. But surely it's practical to consider not only the work these honors cost, but also the culture they bring.

VIVIE. Culture! My dear Mr. Praed: do you know what the mathematical tripos means? It means grind, grind, grind for six to eight hours a day at mathematics, and nothing but mathematics. I'm supposed to know something about science; but I know nothing except the mathematics it involves. I can make calculations for engineers, electricians, insurance companies, and so on; but I know next to nothing about engineering or electricity or insurance. I don't even know arithmetic well. Outside mathematics, lawn-tennis, eating, sleeping, cycling, and walking, I'm a more ignorant barbarian than any woman could possibly be who hadn't gone in for the tripos.

PRAED [*revolted*]. What a monstrous, wicked, rascally system! I know it! I felt at once that it meant destroying all that makes womanhood beautiful.

VIVIE. I don't object to it on that score in the least. I shall turn it to very good account, I assure you.

PRAED. Pooh! In what way?

VIVIE. I shall set up in chambers in the City, and work at actu-

arial calculations and conveyancing. Under cover of that I
shall do some law, with one eye on the Stock Exchange all
the time. I've come down here by myself to read law: not
for a holiday, as my mother imagines. I hate holidays.

PRAED. You make my blood run cold. Are you to have no romance, no beauty in your life?

VIVIE. I don't care for either, I assure you.

PRAED. You can't mean that.

VIVIE. Oh yes I do. I like working and getting paid for it. When
I'm tired of working, I like a comfortable chair, a cigar, a
little whisky, and a novel with a good detective story in it.

PRAED [rising in a frenzy of repudiation]. I don't believe it. I'm
an artist; and I can't believe it: I refuse to believe it. It's only
that you haven't discovered yet what a wonderful world art
can open up to you.

VIVIE. Yes I have. Last May I spent six weeks in London with
Honoria Fraser. Mamma thought we were doing a round
of sightseeing together; but I was really at Honoria's chambers in Chancery Lane every day, working away at actuarial
calculations for her, and helping her as well as a greenhorn
could. In the evenings we smoked and talked, and never
dreamt of going out except for exercise. And I never enjoyed myself more in my life. I cleared all my expenses,
and got initiated into the business without a fee into the
bargain.

PRAED. But bless my heart and soul, Miss Warren, do you call
that discovering art?

VIVIE. Wait a bit. That wasn't the beginning. I went up to town
on an invitation from some artistic people in Fitzjohn's
Avenue: one of the girls was a Newnham chum. They took
me to the National Gallery—

PRAED [approving]. Ah!!. [He sits down, much relieved.]

VIVIE [continuing].—to the Opera—

PRAED [still more pleased]. Good!

VIVIE.—and to a concert where the band played all the evening: Beethoven and Wagner and so on. I wouldn't go
through that experience again for anything you could offer

me. I held out for civility's sake until the third day; and then I said, plump out, that I couldn't stand any more of it, and went off to Chancery Lane. Now you know the sort of perfectly splendid modern young lady I am. How do you think I shall get on with my mother?

PRAED [*startled*]. Well, I hope—er—

VIVIE. It's not so much what you hope as what you believe, that I want to know.

PRAED. Well, frankly, I am afraid your mother will be a little disappointed. Not from any shortcoming on your part, you know: I don't mean that. But you are so different from her ideal.

VIVIE. Her what?

PRAED. Her ideal.

VIVIE. Do you mean her ideal of ME?

PRAED. Yes.

VIVIE. What on earth is it like?

PRAED. Well, you must have observed, Miss Warren, that people who are dissatisfied with their own bringing-up generally think that the world would be all right if everybody were to be brought up quite differently. Now your mother's life has been—er—I suppose you know—

VIVIE. Don't suppose anything, Mr. Praed. I hardly know my mother. Since I was a child I have lived in England, at school or college, or with people paid to take charge of me. I have been boarded out all my life. My mother has lived in Brussels or Vienna and never let me go to her. I only see her when she visits England for a few days. I don't complain: it's been very pleasant; for people have been very good to me; and there has always been plenty of money to make things smooth. But don't imagine I know anything about my mother. I know far less than you do.

PRAED [*very ill at ease*]. In that case—[*He stops, quite at a loss. Then, with a forced attempt at gaiety.*] But what nonsense we are talking! Of course you and your mother will get on capitally. [*He rises, and looks abroad at the view.*] What a charming little place you have here!

VIVIE [*unmoved*]. Rather a violent change of subject, Mr. Praed.
Why won't my mother's life bear being talked about?

PRAED. Oh, you really mustn't say that. Isn't it natural that I
should have a certain delicacy in talking to my old friend's
daughter about her behind her back? You and she will have
plenty of opportunity of talking about it when she comes.

VIVIE. No: she won't talk about it either. [*Rising.*] However, I
daresay you have good reasons for telling me nothing. Only,
mind this, Mr. Praed. I expect there will be a battle royal
when my mother hears of my Chancery Lane project.

PRAED [*ruefully*]. I'm afraid there will.

VIVIE. Well, I shall win, because I want nothing but my fare to
London to start there to-morrow earning my own living by
devilling for Honoria. Besides, I have no mysteries to keep
up; and it seems she has. I shall use that advantage over her
if necessary.

PRAED [*greatly shocked*]. Oh no! No, pray. You'd not do such
a thing.

VIVIE. Then tell me why not.

PRAED. I really cannot. I appeal to your good feeling. [*She smiles
at his sentimentality.*] Besides, you may be too bold. Your
mother is not to be trifled with when she's angry.

VIVIE. You can't frighten me, Mr. Praed. In that month at
Chancery Lane I had opportunities of taking the measure of
one or two women very like my mother. You may back me
to win. But if I hit harder in my ignorance than I need, remember that it is you who refuse to enlighten me. Now, let
us drop the subject. [*She takes her chair and replaces it near
the hammock with the same vigorous swing as before.*]

PRAED [*taking a desperate resolution*]. One word, Miss Warren.
I had better tell you. It's very difficult; but—

[MRS. WARREN *and* SIR GEORGE CROFTS *arrive at the gate.*
MRS. WARREN *is between 40 and 50, formerly pretty, show-
ily dressed in a brilliant hat and a gay blouse fitting tightly
over her bust and flanked by fashionable sleeves. Rather
spoilt and domineering, and decidedly vulgar, but, on the*

whole, a genial and fairly presentable old blackguard of a woman.]

[CROFTS *is a tall powerfully-built man of about 50, fashionably dressed in the style of a young man. Nasal voice, reedier than might be expected from his strong frame. Clean-shaven bulldog jaws, large flat ears, and thick neck: gentlemanly combination of the most brutal types of city man, sporting man, and man about town.*]

VIVIE. Here they are. [*Coming to them as they enter the garden.*] How do, mater? Mr. Praed's been here this half hour, waiting for you.

MRS. WARREN. Well, if you've been waiting, Praddy, it's your own fault: I thought you'd have had the gumption to know I was coming by the 3:10 train. Vivie: put your hat on, dear: you'll get sunburnt. Oh, I forgot to introduce you. Sir George Crofts: my little Vivie.

[CROFTS *advances to* VIVIE *with his most courtly manner. She nods, but makes no motion to shake hands.*]

CROFTS. May I shake hands with a young lady whom I have known by reputation very long as the daughter of one of my oldest friends?

VIVIE [*who has been looking him up and down sharply*]. If you like. [*She takes his tenderly proffered hand and gives it a squeeze that makes him open his eyes; then turns away, and says to her mother:*] Will you come in, or shall I get a couple more chairs? [*She goes into the porch for the chairs.*]

MRS. WARREN. Well, George, what do you think of her?

CROFTS [*ruefully*]. She has a powerful fist. Did you shake hands with her, Praed?

PRAED. Yes: it will pass off presently.

CROFTS. I hope so. [VIVIE *reappears with two more chairs. He hurries to her assistance.*] Allow me.

MRS. WARREN [*patronizingly*]. Let Sir George help you with the chairs, dear.

VIVIE [*pitching them into his arms*]. Here you are. [*She dusts her hands and turns to* MRS. WARREN.] You'd like some tea, wouldn't you?

MRS. WARREN [*sitting in* PRAED'S *chair and fanning herself*]. I'm dying for a drop to drink.

VIVIE. I'll see about it. [*She goes into the cottage.*]

[SIR GEORGE *has by this time managed to unfold a chair and plants it beside* MRS. WARREN, *on her left. He throws the other on the grass and sits down, looking dejected and rather foolish, with the handle of his stick in his mouth.* PRAED, *still very uneasy, fidgets about the garden on their right.*]

MRS. WARREN [*to* PRAED, *looking at* CROFTS]. Just look at him, Praddy: he looks cheerful, don't he? He's been worrying my life out these three years to have that little girl of mine shewn to him; and now that I've done it, he's quite out of countenance. [*Briskly.*] Come! sit up, George; and take your stick out of your mouth. [CROFTS *sulkily obeys.*]

PRAED. I think, you know——if you don't mind my saying so—— that we had better get out of the habit of thinking of her as a little girl. You see she has really distinguished herself; and I'm not sure, from what I have seen of her, that she is not older than any of us.

MRS. WARREN [*greatly amused*]. Only listen to him, George! Older than any of us! Well, she has been stuffing you nicely with her importance.

PRAED. But young people are particularly sensitive about being treated in that way.

MRS. WARREN. Yes; and young people have to get all that nonsense taken out of them, and a good deal more besides. Don't you interfere, Praddy: I know how to treat my own child as well as you do. [PRAED, *with a grave shake of his head, walks up the garden with his hands behind his back.* MRS. WARREN *pretends to laugh, but looks after him with perceptible concern. Then she whispers to* CROFTS.] What's the matter with him? What does he take it like that for?

CROFTS [*morosely*]. You're afraid of Praed.

MRS. WARREN. What! Me! Afraid of dear old Praddy! Why, a

fly wouldn't be afraid of him.

CROFTS. You're afraid of him.

MRS. WARREN [*angry*]. I'll trouble you to mind your own business, and not try any of your sulks on me. I'm not afraid of you, anyhow. If you can't make yourself agreeable, you'd better go home. [*She gets up, and, turning her back on him, finds herself face to face with* PRAED.] Come, Praddy, I know it was only your tender-heartedness. You're afraid I'll bully her.

PRAED. My dear Kitty: you think I'm offended. Don't imagine that: pray don't. But you know I often notice things that escape you; and though you never take my advice, you sometimes admit afterwards that you ought to have taken it.

MRS. WARREN. Well, what do you notice now?

PRAED. Only that Vivie is a grown woman. Pray, Kitty, treat her with every respect.

MRS. WARREN [*with genuine amazement*]. Respect! Treat my own daughter with respect! What next, pray!

VIVIE [*appearing at the cottage door and calling to* MRS. WARREN]. Mother: will you come to my room before tea?

MRS. WARREN. Yes, dearie. [*She laughs indulgently at* PRAED'S *gravity, and pats him on the cheek as she passes him on her way to the porch.*] Don't be cross, Praddy. [*She follows* VIVIE *into the cottage.*]

CROFTS [*furtively*]. I say, Praed.

PRAED. Yes.

CROFTS. I want to ask you a rather particular question.

PRAED. Certainly. [*He takes* MRS. WARREN'S *chair and sits close to* CROFTS.]

CROFTS. That's right: they might hear us from the window. Look here: did Kitty ever tell you who that girl's father is?

PRAED. Never.

CROFTS. Have you any suspicion of who it might be?

PRAED. None.

CROFTS [*not believing him*]. I know, of course, that you perhaps might feel bound not to tell if she had said anything to you. But it's very awkward to be uncertain about it now that we shall be meeting the girl every day. We don't exactly know how we ought to feel towards her.

PRAED. What difference can that make? We take her on her own merits. What does it matter who her father was?

CROFTS [*suspiciously*]. Then you know who he was?

PRAED [*with a touch of temper*]. I said no just now. Did you not hear me?

CROFTS. Look here, Praed. I ask you as a particular favor. If you do know [*Movement of protest from* PRAED.]—I only say, if you know, you might at least set my mind at rest about her. The fact is, I feel attracted.

PRAED [*sternly*]. What do you mean?

CROFTS. Oh, don't be alarmed: it's quite an innocent feeling. That's what puzzles me about it. Why, for all I know, *I* might be her father.

PRAED. You! Impossible!

CROFTS [*catching him up cunningly*]. You know for certain that I'm not?

PRAED. I know nothing about it, I tell you, any more than you. But really, Crofts—oh no, it's out of the question. There's not the least resemblance.

CROFTS. As to that, there's no resemblance between her and her mother that I can see. I suppose she's not your daughter, is she?

PRAED [*rising indignantly*]. Really, Crofts—!

CROFTS. No offence, Praed. Quite allowable as between two men of the world.

PRAED [*recovering himself with an effort and speaking gently and gravely*]. Now listen to me, my dear Crofts. [*He sits down again.*] I have nothing to do with that side of Mrs. Warren's life, and never had. She has never spoken to me about it; and of course I have never spoken to her about it. Your delicacy will tell you that a handsome woman needs some friends who are not—well, not on that footing with her. The effect of her own beauty would become a torment to her if she could not escape from it occasionally. You are probably on much more confidential terms with Kitty than

I am. Surely you can ask her the question yourself.

CROFTS. I have asked her, often enough. But she's so determined to keep the child all to herself that she would deny that it ever had a father if she could. [*Rising.*] I'm thoroughly uncomfortable about it, Praed.

PRAED [*rising also*]. Well, as you are, at all events, old enough to be her father, I don't mind agreeing that we both regard Miss Vivie in a parental way, as a young girl whom we are bound to protect and help. What do you say?

CROFTS [*aggressively*]. I'm no older than you, if you come to that.

PRAED. Yes you are, my dear fellow: you were born old. I was born a boy: I've never been able to feel the assurance of a grown-up man in my life. [*He folds his chair and carries it to the porch.*]

MRS. WARREN [*calling from within the cottage*]. Prad-dee! George! Tea-ea-ea-ea!

CROFTS [*hastily*]. She's calling us. [*He hurries in.*]

[*PRAED shakes his head bodingly, and is following* CROFTS *when he is hailed by a young gentleman who has just appeared on the common, and is making for the gate. He is pleasant, pretty, smartly dressed, cleverly good-for-nothing, not long turned 20, with a charming voice and agreeably disrespectful manners. He carries a light sporting magazine rifle.*]

THE YOUNG GENTLEMAN. Hallo! Praed!

PRAED. Why, Frank Gardner! [*FRANK comes in and shakes hands cordially.*] What on earth are you doing here?

FRANK. Staying with my father.

PRAED. The Roman father?

FRANK. He's rector here. I'm living with my people this autumn for the sake of economy. Things came to a crisis in July: the Roman father had to pay my debts. He's stony broke in consequence; and so am I. What are you up to in these parts? Do you know the people here?

PRAED. Yes: I'm spending the day with a Miss Warren.

FRANK [*enthusiastically*]. What! Do you know Vivie? Isn't she a jolly girl? I'm teaching her to shoot with this [*putting down the rifle*]. I'm so glad she knows you: you're just the sort of fellow she ought to know. [*He smiles, and raises the charming voice almost to a singing tone as he exclaims:*] It's ever so jolly to find you here, Praed.

PRAED. I'm an old friend of her mother. Mrs. Warren brought me over to make her daughter's acquaintance.

FRANK. The mother! Is she here?

PRAED. Yes: inside, at tea.

MRS. WARREN [*calling from within*]. Prad-dee-ee-ee-eee! The tea-cake'll be cold.

PRAED [*calling*]. Yes, Mrs. Warren. In a moment. I've just met a friend here.

MRS. WARREN. A what?

PRAED [*louder*]. A friend.

MRS. WARREN. Bring him in.

PRAED. All right. [*To* FRANK.] Will you accept the invitation?

FRANK [*incredulous, but immensely amused*]. Is that Vivie's mother?

PRAED. Yes.

FRANK. By Jove! What a lark! Do you think she'll like me?

PRAED. I've no doubt you'll make yourself popular, as usual. Come in and try [*moving towards the house*].

FRANK. Stop a bit. [*Seriously.*] I want to take you into my confidence.

PRAED. Pray don't. It's only some fresh folly, like the barmaid at Redhill.

FRANK. It's ever so much more serious than that. You say you've only just met Vivie for the first time?

PRAED. Yes.

FRANK [*rhapsodically*]. Then you can have no idea what a girl she is. Such character! Such sense! And her cleverness! Oh, my eye, Praed, but I can tell you she is clever! And—need I add?—she loves me.

CROFTS [*putting his head out of the window*]. I say, Praed: what are you about? Do come along. [*He disappears.*]

FRANK. Hallo! Sort of chap that would take a prize at a dog
show, ain't he? Who's he?

PRAED. Sir George Crofts, an old friend of Mrs. Warren's. I
think we had better come in.

[*On their way to the porch they are interrupted by a call
from the gate. Turning, they see an elderly clergyman looking over it.*]

THE CLERGYMAN [*calling*]. Frank!

FRANK. Hallo! [*To* PRAED.] The Roman father. [*To the clergyman.*] Yes, gov'nor: all right: presently. [*To* PRAED.] Look
here, Praed: you'd better go in to tea. I'll join you directly.

PRAED. Very good. [*He goes into the cottage.*]

[*The clergyman remains outside the gate, with his hands on
the top of it. The* REV. SAMUEL GARDNER, *a beneficed clergyman of the Established Church, is over 50. Externally he is
pretentious, booming, noisy, important. Really he is that
obsolescent social phenomenon the fool of the family
dumped on the Church by his father the patron, clamor-
ously asserting himself as father and clergyman without
being able to command the respect in either capacity.*]

REV. S. Well, sir. Who are your friends here, if I may ask?

FRANK. Oh, it's all right, gov'nor! Come in.

REV. S. No, sir; not until I know whose garden I am entering.

FRANK. It's all right. It's Miss Warren's.

REV. S. I have not seen her at church since she came.

FRANK. Of course not: she's a third wrangler. Ever so intellectual. Took a higher degree than you did; so why should
she go to hear you preach?

REV. S. Don't be disrespectful, sir.

FRANK. Oh, it don't matter: nobody hears us. Come in. [*He
opens the gate, unceremoniously pulling his father with it
into the garden.*] I want to introduce you to her. Do you
remember the advice you gave me last July, gov'nor?

REV. S. [*severely*]. Yes. I advised you to conquer your idleness
and flippancy, and to work your way into an honorable pro-

fession and live on it and not upon me.

FRANK. No: that's what you thought afterwards. What you actually said was that since I had neither brains nor money, I'd better turn my good looks to account by marrying somebody with both. Well, look here. Miss Warren has brains: you can't deny that.

REV. S. Brains are not everything.

FRANK. No, of course not: there's the money—

REV. S. [*interrupting him austerely*]. I was not thinking of money, sir. I was speaking of higher things. Social position, for instance.

FRANK. I don't care a rap about that.

REV. S. But I do, sir.

FRANK. Well, nobody wants you to marry her. Anyhow, she has what amounts to a high Cambridge degree; and she seems to have as much money as she wants.

REV. S. [*sinking into a feeble vein of humor*]. I greatly doubt whether she has as much money as you will want.

FRANK. Oh, come: I haven't been so very extravagant. I live ever so quietly; I don't drink; I don't bet much; and I never go regularly on the razzle-dazzle as you did when you were my age.

REV. S. [*booming hollowly*]. Silence, sir.

FRANK. Well, you told me yourself, when I was making ever such an ass of myself about the barmaid at Redhill, that you once offered a woman £50 for the letters you wrote to her when—

REV. S. [*terrified*]. Sh-sh-sh, Frank, for Heaven's sake! [*He looks round apprehensively. Seeing no one within earshot he plucks up courage to boom again, but more subduedly.*] You are taking an ungentlemanly advantage of what I confided to you for your own good, to save you from an error you would have repented all your life long. Take warning by your father's follies, sir; and don't make them an excuse for your own.

FRANK. Did you ever hear the story of the Duke of Wellington and his letters?

REV. S. No, sir; and I don't want to hear it.

FRANK. The old Iron Duke didn't throw away £50: not he. He just wrote: "Dear Jenny: publish and be damned! Yours affectionately, Wellington." That's what you should have done.

REV. S. [*piteously*]. Frank, my boy: when I wrote those letters I put myself into that woman's power. When I told you about them I put myself, to some extent, I am sorry to say, in your power. She refused my money with these words, which I shall never forget. "Knowledge is power" she said; "and I never sell power." That's more than twenty years ago; and she has never made use of her power or caused me a moment's uneasiness. You are behaving worse to me than she did, Frank.

FRANK. Oh yes I dare say! Did you ever preach at her the way you preach at me every day?

REV. S. [*wounded almost to tears*]. I leave you, sir. You are incorrigible. [*He turns towards the gate.*]

FRANK [*utterly unmoved*]. Tell them I shan't be home to tea, will you, gov'nor, like a good fellow? [*He moves towards the cottage door and is met by* PRAED *and* VIVIE *coming out.*]

VIVIE [*to* FRANK]. Is that your father, Frank? I do so want to meet him.

FRANK. Certainly. [*Calling after his father:*] Gov'nor. You're wanted. [*The parson turns at the gate, fumbling nervously at his hat.* PRAED *crosses the garden to the opposite side, beaming in anticipation of civilities.*] My father: Miss Warren.

VIVIE [*going to the clergyman and shaking his hand*]. Very glad to see you here, Mr. Gardner. [*Calling to the cottage:*] Mother: come along: you're wanted.

[MRS. WARREN *appears on the threshold, and is immediately transfixed, recognizing the clergyman.*]

VIVIE [*continuing*]. Let me introduce—

MRS. WARREN [*swooping on the* REVEREND SAMUEL]. Why, it's Sam Gardner, gone into the Church! Well, I never! Don't

you know us, Sam? This is George Crofts, as large as life
and twice as natural. Don't you remember me?

REV. S. [*very red*]. I really—er—

MRS. WARREN. Of course you do. Why, I have a whole album
of your letters still: I came across them only the other day.

REV. S. [*miserably confused*]. Miss Vavasour, I believe.

MRS. WARREN [*correcting him quickly in a loud whisper*]. Tch!
Nonsense! Mrs. Warren: don't you see my daughter there?

ACT TWO

[*Inside the cottage after nightfall. Looking eastward from within instead of westward from without, the latticed window, with its curtains drawn, is now seen in the middle of the front wall of the cottage, with the porch door to the left of it. In the left-hand side wall is the door leading to the kitchen. Farther back against the same wall is a dresser with a candle and matches on it, and Frank's rifle standing beside them, with the barrel resting in the plate-rack. In the centre a table stands with a lighted lamp on it.* VIVIE'S *books and writing materials are on a table to the right of the window, against the wall. The fireplace is on the right, with a settle: there is no fire. Two of the chairs are set right and left of the table.*

The cottage door opens, shewing a fine starlit night without; and MRS. WARREN, *her shoulders wrapped in a shawl borrowed from* VIVIE, *enters, followed by* FRANK, *who throws his cap on the window seat. She has had enough of walking, and gives a gasp of relief as she unpins her hat; takes it off; sticks the pin through the crown; and puts it on the table.*]

MRS. WARREN. O Lord! I don't know which is the worst of the country, the walking or the sitting at home with nothing to do. I could do with a whisky and soda now very well, if only they had such a thing in this place.

FRANK. Perhaps Vivie's got some.

MRS. WARREN. Nonsense! What would a young girl like her be doing with such things! Never mind: it don't matter. I wonder how she passes her time here! I'd a good deal rather be in Vienna.

FRANK. Let me take you there. [*He helps her to take off her shawl, gallantly giving her shoulders a very perceptible squeeze as he does so.*]

MRS. WARREN. Ah! would you? I'm beginning to think you're a chip of the old block.

FRANK. Like the gov'nor, eh? [*He hangs the shawl on the nearest chair, and sits down.*]

MRS. WARREN. Never you mind. What do you know about such things? You're only a boy. [*She goes to the hearth, to be farther from temptation.*]

FRANK. Do come to Vienna with me? It'd be ever such larks.

MRS. WARREN. No, thank you. Vienna is no place for you—at least not until you're a little older. [*She nods at him to emphasize this piece of advice. He makes a mock-piteous face, belied by his laughing eyes. She looks at him; then comes back to him.*] Now, look here, little boy [*taking his face in her hands and turning it up to her*]: I know you through and through by your likeness to your father, better than you know yourself. Don't you go taking any silly ideas into your head about me. Do you hear?

FRANK [*gallantly wooing her with his voice*]. Can't help it, my dear Mrs. Warren: it runs in the family.

[*She pretends to box his ears; then looks at the pretty laughing upturned face for a moment, tempted. At last she kisses him, and immediately turns away, out of patience with herself.*]

MRS. WARREN. There! I shouldn't have done that. I am wicked. Never you mind, my dear: it's only a motherly kiss. Go and make love to Vivie.

FRANK. So I have.

MRS. WARREN [*turning on him with a sharp note of alarm in her voice*]. What!

FRANK. Vivie and I are ever such chums.

MRS. WARREN. What do you mean? Now see here: I won't have any young scamp tampering with my little girl. Do you hear? I won't have it.

FRANK. [*quite unabashed*]. My dear Mrs. Warren: don't you be
alarmed. My intentions are honorable: ever so honorable;
and your little girl is jolly well able to take care of herself.
She don't need looking after half so much as her mother.
She ain't so handsome, you know.

MRS. WARREN [*taken aback by his assurance*]. Well, you have
got a nice healthy two inches thick of cheek all over you. I
don't know where you got it. Not from your father, anyhow.

CROFTS [*in the garden*]. The gipsies, I suppose?

REV. S. [*replying*]. The broomsquires are far worse.

MRS. WARREN [*to* FRANK]. S-sh! Remember! you've had your
warning.

[CROFTS *and the* REVEREND SAMUEL *come in from the garden, the clergyman continuing his conversation as he enters.*]

REV. S. The perjury at the Winchester assizes is deplorable.

MRS. WARREN. Well? what became of you two? And where's
Praddy and Vivie?

CROFTS [*putting his hat on the settle and his stick in the chimney corner*]. They went up the hill. We went to the village. I
wanted a drink. [*He sits down on the settle, putting his legs
up along the seat.*]

MRS. WARREN. Well, she oughtn't to go off like that without
telling me. [*To* FRANK.] Get your father a chair, Frank:
where are your manners? [*Frank springs up and gracefully
offers his father his chair; then takes another from the wall
and sits down at the table, in the middle, with his father on
his right and* MRS. WARREN *on his left.*] George: Where are
you going to stay to-night? You can't stay here. And what's
Praddy going to do?

CROFTS. Gardner'll put me up.

MRS. WARREN. Oh, no doubt you've taken care of yourself! But
what about Praddy?

CROFTS. Don't know. I suppose he can sleep at the inn.

MRS. WARREN. Haven't you room for him, Sam?

REV. S. Well—er—you see, as rector here, I am not free to do as

I like. Er—what is Mr. Praed's social position?

MRS. WARREN. Oh, he's all right: he's an architect. What an old stick-in-the-mud you are, Sam!

FRANK. Yes, it's all right, gov'nor. He built that place down in Wales for the Duke. Caernarvon Castle they call it. You must have heard of it. [*He winks with lightning smartness at* MRS. WARREN, *and regards his father blandly.*]

REV. S. Oh, in that case, of course we shall only be too happy. I suppose he knows the Duke personally.

FRANK. Oh, ever so intimately! We can stick him in Georgina's old room.

MRS. WARREN. Well, that's settled. Now if those two would only come in and let us have supper. They've no right to stay out after dark like this.

CROFTS [*aggressively*]. What harm are they doing you?

MRS. WARREN. Well, harm or not, I don't like it.

FRANK. Better not wait for them, Mrs. Warren. Praed will stay out as long as possible. He has never known before what it is to stray over the heath on a summer night with my Vivie.

CROFTS [*sitting up in some consternation*]. I say, you know! Come!

REV. S. [*rising, startled out of his professional manner into real force and sincerity*]. Frank, once for all, it's out of the question. Mrs. Warren will tell you that it's not to be thought of.

CROFTS. Of course not.

FRANK [*with enchanting placidity*]. Is that so, Mrs. Warren?

MRS. WARREN [*reflectively*]. Well, Sam, I don't know. If the girl wants to get married, no good can come of keeping her unmarried.

REV. S. [*astounded*]. But married to him!—your daughter to my son! Only think: it's impossible.

CROFTS. Of course it's impossible. Don't be a fool, Kitty.

MRS. WARREN [*nettled*]. Why not? Isn't my daughter good enough for your son?

REV. S. But surely, my dear Mrs. Warren, you know the reasons—

MRS. WARREN [*defiantly*]. I know no reasons. If you know any, you can tell them to the lad, or to the girl, or to your congregation, if you like.

REV. S. [*collapsing helplessly into his chair*]. You know very well that I couldn't tell anyone the reasons. But my boy will believe me when I tell him there are reasons.

FRANK. Quite right, Dad: he will. But has your boy's conduct ever been influenced by your reasons?

CROFTS. You can't marry her; and that's all about it. [*He gets up and stands on the hearth, with his back to the fireplace, frowning determinedly.*]

MRS. WARREN [*turning on him sharply*]. What have you got to do with it, pray?

FRANK [*with his prettiest lyrical cadence*]. Precisely what I was going to ask, myself, in my own graceful fashion.

CROFTS [*to* MRS. WARREN]. I suppose you don't want to marry the girl to a man younger than herself and without either a profession or twopence to keep her on. Ask Sam, if you don't believe me. [*To the parson.*] How much more money are you going to give him?

REV. S. Not another penny. He has had his patrimony; and he spent the last of it in July. [MRS. WARREN's *face falls.*]

CROFTS [*watching her*]. There! I told you. [*He resumes his place on the settle and puts up his legs on the seat again, as if the matter were finally disposed of.*]

FRANK [*plaintively*]. This is ever so mercenary. Do you suppose Miss Warren's going to marry for money? If we love one another—

MRS. WARREN. Thank you. Your love's a pretty cheap commodity, my lad. If you have no means of keeping a wife, that settles it: you can't have Vivie.

FRANK [*much amused*]. What do you say, gov'nor, eh?

REV. S. I agree with Mrs. Warren.

FRANK. And good old Crofts has already expressed his opinion.

CROFTS [*turning angrily on his elbow*]. Look here: I want none of your cheek.

FRANK [*pointedly*]. I'm ever so sorry to surprise you, Crofts;
but you allowed yourself the liberty of speaking to me
like a father a moment ago. One father is enough, thank
you.

CROFTS [*contemptuously*]. Yah! [*He turns away again.*]

FRANK [*rising*]. Mrs. Warren: I cannot give my Vivie up, even
for your sake.

MRS. WARREN [*muttering*]. Young scamp!

FRANK [*continuing*]. And as you no doubt intend to hold out
other prospects to her, I shall lose no time in placing my
case before her. [*They stare at him; and he begins to declaim
gracefully.*]

> He either fears his fate too much,
> Or his deserts are small,
> That dares not put it to the touch
> To gain or lose it all.

[*The cottage door opens whilst he is reciting; and* VIVIE *and*
PRAED *come in. He breaks off.* PRAED *puts his hat on the
dresser. There is an immediate improvement in the company's behavior.* CROFTS *takes down his legs from the settle
and pulls himself together as* PRAED *joins him at the fireplace.*
MRS. WARREN *loses her ease of manner and takes refuge
in querulousness.*]

MRS. WARREN. Wherever have you been, Vivie?

VIVIE [*taking off her hat and throwing it carelessly on the table*].
On the hill.

MRS. WARREN. Well, you shouldn't go off like that without
letting me know. How could I tell what had become of you?
And night coming on too!

VIVIE [*going to the door of the kitchen and opening it, ignoring
her mother*]. Now, about supper? [*All rise except* MRS. WAR-
REN.] We shall be rather crowded in here, I'm afraid.

MRS. WARREN. Did you hear what I said, Vivie?

VIVIE [*quietly*]. Yes, mother. [*Reverting to the supper difficulty.*] How many are we? [*Counting:*] One, two, three, four,

five, six. Well, two will have to wait until the rest are done: Mrs. Alison has only plates and knives for four.

PRAED. Oh, it doesn't matter about me. I—

VIVIE. You have had a long walk and are hungry, Mr. Praed: you shall have your supper at once. I can wait myself. I want one person to wait with me. Frank: are you hungry?

FRANK. Not the least in the world. Completely off my peck, in fact.

MRS. WARREN [*to* CROFTS]. Neither are you, George. You can wait.

CROFTS. Oh, hang it, I've eaten nothing since tea-time. Can't Sam do it?

FRANK. Would you starve my poor father?

REV. S. [*testily*]. Allow me to speak for myself, sir. I am perfectly willing to wait.

VIVIE [*decisively*]. There's no need. Only two are wanted. [*She opens the door of the kitchen.*] Will you take my mother in, Mr. Gardner. [*The parson takes* MRS. WARREN; *and they pass into the kitchen.* PRAED *and* CROFTS *follow. All except* PRAED *clearly disapprove of the arrangement, but do not know how to resist it.* VIVIE *stands at the door looking in at them.*] Can you squeeze past to that corner, Mr. Praed: it's rather a tight fit. Take care of your coat against the white-wash: that's right. Now, are you all comfortable?

PRAED [*within*]. Quite, thank you.

MRS. WARREN [*within*]. Leave the door open, dearie. [VIVIE *frowns; but* FRANK *checks her with a gesture, and steals to the cottage door, which he softly sets wide open.*] Oh Lor, what a draught! You'd better shut it, dear.

[VIVIE *shuts it with a slam, and then, noting with disgust that her mother's hat and shawl are lying about, takes them tidily to the window seat, whilst* FRANK *noiselessly shuts the cottage door.*]

FRANK [*exulting*]. Aha! Got rid of 'em. Well, Vivvums: what do you think of my governor?

VIVIE [*preoccupied and serious*]. I've hardly spoken to him. He doesn't strike me as being a particularly able person.

FRANK. Well, you know, the old man is not altogether such a fool as he looks. You see, he was shoved into the Church rather; and in trying to live up to it he makes a much bigger ass of himself than he really is. I don't dislike him as much as you might expect. He means well. How do you think you'll get on with him?

VIVIE [*rather grimly*]. I don't think my future life will be much concerned with him, or with any of that old circle of my mother's, except perhaps Praed. [*She sits down on the settle.*] What do you think of my mother?

FRANK. Really and truly?

VIVIE. Yes, really and truly.

FRANK. Well, she's ever so jolly. But she's rather a caution, isn't she? And Crofts! Oh, my eye, Crofts! [*He sits beside her.*]

VIVIE. What a lot, Frank!

FRANK. What a crew!

VIVIE [*with intense contempt for them*]. If I thought that *I* was like that—that I was going to be a waster, shifting along from one meal to another with no purpose, and no character, and no grit in me, I'd open an artery and bleed to death without one moment's hesitation.

FRANK. Oh no, you wouldn't. Why should they take any grind when they can afford not to? I wish I had their luck. No: what I object to is their form. It isn't the thing: it's slovenly, ever so slovenly.

VIVIE. Do you think your form will be any better when you're as old as Crofts, if you don't work?

FRANK. Of course I do. Ever so much better. Vivvums mustn't lecture: her little boy's incorrigible. [*He attempts to take her face caressingly in his hands.*]

VIVIE [*striking his hands down sharply*]. Off with you: Vivvums is not in a humor for petting her little boy this evening. [*She rises and comes forward to the other side of the room.*]

FRANK [*following her*]. How unkind!

VIVIE [*stamping at him*]. Be serious. I'm serious.

FRANK. Good. Let us talk learnedly. Miss Warren: do you
    know that all the most advanced thinkers are agreed that
    half the diseases of modern civilization are due to starva-
    tion of the affections in the young. Now, I—

VIVIE [*cutting him short*]. You are very tiresome. [*She opens
    the inner door.*] Have you room for Frank there? He's com-
    plaining of starvation.

MRS. WARREN [*within*]. Of course there is. [*Clatter of knives and
    glasses as she moves the things on the table.*] Here! there's
    room now beside me. Come along, Mr. Frank.

FRANK. Her little boy will be ever so even with his Vivvums
    for this. [*He passes into the kitchen.*]

MRS. WARREN [*within*]. Here, Vivie: come on you too, child.
    You must be famished. [*She enters, followed by* CROFTS,
    who holds the door open for VIVIE *with marked deference.
    She goes out without looking at him; and he shuts the door
    after her.*] Why, George, you can't be done: you've eaten
    nothing. Is there anything wrong with you?

CROFTS. Oh, all I wanted was a drink. [*He thrusts his hands in
    his pockets, and begins prowling about the room, restless
    and sulky.*]

MRS. WARREN. Well, I like enough to eat. But a little of that
    cold beef and cheese and lettuce goes a long way. [*With
    a sigh of only half repletion she sits down lazily on the
    settle.*]

CROFTS. What do you go encouraging that young pup for?

MRS. WARREN [*on the alert at once*]. Now see here, George:
    what are you up to about that girl? I've been watching your
    way of looking at her. Remember: I know you and what
    your looks mean.

CROFTS. There's no harm in looking at her, is there?

MRS. WARREN. I'd put you out and pack you back to London
    pretty soon if I saw any of your nonsense. My girl's little
    finger is more to me than your whole body and soul. [CROFTS

receives this with a sneering grin. MRS. WARREN, *flushing a
little at her failure to impose on him in the character of a
theatrically devoted mother, adds in a lower key.*] Make
your mind easy: the young pup has no more chance than
you have.

CROFTS. Mayn't a man take an interest in a girl?

MRS. WARREN. Not a man like you.

CROFTS. How old is she?

MRS. WARREN. Never you mind how old she is.

CROFTS. Why do you make such a secret of it?

MRS. WARREN. Because I choose.

CROFTS. Well, I'm not fifty yet; and my property is as good as
ever it was—

MRS. WARREN [*interrupting him*]. Yes; because you're as stingy
as you're vicious.

CROFTS [*continuing*]. And a baronet isn't to be picked up every
day. No other man in my position would put up with you
for a mother-in-law. Why shouldn't she marry me?

MRS. WARREN. You!

CROFTS. We three could live together quite comfortably. I'd
die before her and leave her a bouncing widow with plenty
of money. Why not? It's been growing in my mind all the
time I've been walking with that fool inside there.

MRS. WARREN [*revolted*]. Yes: it's the sort of thing that would
grow in your mind.

[*He halts in his prowling; and the two look at one another,
she steadfastly, with a sort of awe behind her contemptuous disgust: he stealthily, with a carnal gleam in his eye and
a loose grin.*]

CROFTS [*suddenly becoming anxious and urgent as he sees no
sign of sympathy in her*]. Look here, Kitty: you're a sensible
woman: you needn't put on any moral airs. I'll ask no more
questions; and you need answer none. I'll settle the whole
property on her; and if you want a cheque for yourself on
the wedding day, you can name any figure you like—in

reason.

MRS. WARREN. So it's come to that with you, George, like all the other worn-out old creatures!

CROFTS [*savagely*]. Damn you!

[*Before she can retort the door of the kitchen is opened; and the voices of the others are heard returning.* CROFTS, *unable to recover his presence of mind, hurries out of the cottage. The clergyman appears at the kitchen door.*]

REV. S. [*looking round*]. Where is Sir George?

MRS. WARREN. Gone out to have a pipe. [*The clergyman takes his hat from the table, and joins* MRS. WARREN *at the fireside. Meanwhile* VIVIE *comes in, followed by* FRANK, *who collapses into the nearest chair with an air of extreme exhaustion.* MRS. WARREN *looks round at* VIVIE *and says, with her affectation of maternal patronage even more forced than usual.*] Well, dearie: have you had a good supper?

VIVIE. You know what Mrs. Alison's suppers are. [*She turns to* FRANK *and pets him.*] Poor Frank! was all the beef gone? did it get nothing but bread and cheese and ginger beer? [*Seriously, as if she had done quite enough trifling for one evening.*] Her butter is really awful. I must get some down from the stores.

FRANK. Do, in Heaven's name!

[VIVIE *goes to the writing-table and makes a memorandum to order the butter.* PRAED *comes in from the kitchen, putting up his handkerchief, which he has been using as a napkin.*]

REV. S. Frank, my boy: it is time for us to be thinking of home. Your mother does not know yet that we have visitors.

PRAED. I'm afraid we're giving trouble.

FRANK [*rising*]. Not the least in the world: my mother will be delighted to see you. She's a genuinely intellectual artistic woman; and she sees nobody here from one year's end to

another except the gov'nor; so you can imagine how jolly
dull it pans out for her. [*To his father.*] You're not intellectual or artistic: are you, pater? So take Praed home at once;
and I'll stay here and entertain Mrs. Warren. You'll pick up
Crofts in the garden. He'll be excellent company for the
bull-pup.

PRAED [*taking his hat from the dresser, and coming close to*
FRANK]. Come with us, Frank. Mrs. Warren has not seen Miss
Vivie for a long time; and we have prevented them from
having a moment together yet.

FRANK [*quite softened, and looking at* PRAED *with romantic ad-*
miration]. Of course. I forgot. Ever so thanks for remind-
ing me. Perfect gentleman, Praddy. Always were. My ideal
through life. [*He rises to go, but pauses a moment between*
the two older men, and puts his hand on PRAED'S *shoulder.*]
Ah, if you had only been my father instead of this un-
worthy old man! [*He puts his other hand on his father's*
shoulder.]

REV. S. [*blustering*]. Silence, sir, silence: you are profane.

MRS. WARREN [*laughing heartily*]. You should keep him in better
order, Sam. Good-night. Here: take George his hat and
stick with my compliments.

REV. S. [*taking them*]. Good-night. [*They shake hands. As he*
passes VIVIE *he shakes hands with her also and bids her*
good-night. Then, in booming command, to FRANK.] Come
along, sir, at once. [*He goes out.*]

MRS. WARREN. Byebye, Praddy.

PRAED. Byebye, Kitty.

[*They shake hands affectionately and go out together, she*
accompanying him to the garden gate.]

FRANK [*to* VIVIE]. Kissums?

VIVIE [*fiercely*]. No. I hate you. [*She takes a couple of books*
and some paper from the writing-table, and sits down with
them at the middle table, at the end next the fireplace.]

FRANK [*grimacing*]. Sorry. [*He goes for his cap and rifle.* MRS.

WARREN *returns. He takes her hand.*] Good-night, dear Mrs.
Warren. [*He kisses her hand. She snatches it away, her lips
tightening, and looks more than half disposed to box his
ears. He laughs mischievously and runs off, clapping-to the
door behind him.*]

MRS. WARREN [*resigning herself to an evening of boredom now
that the men are gone*]. Did you ever in your life hear anyone rattle on so? Isn't he a tease? [*She sits at the table.*] Now
that I think of it, dearie, don't you go encouraging him. I'm
sure he's a regular good-for-nothing.

VIVIE [*rising to fetch more books*]. I'm afraid so. Poor Frank!
I shall have to get rid of him; but I shall feel sorry for him,
though he's not worth it. That man Crofts does not seem
to me to be good for much either: is he? [*She throws the
books on the table rather roughly.*]

MRS. WARREN [*galled by* VIVIE'S *indifference*]. What do you
know of men, child, to talk that way about them? You'll
have to make up your mind to see a good deal of Sir George
Crofts, as he's a friend of mine.

VIVIE [*quite unmoved*]. Why? [*She sits down and opens a book.*]
Do you expect that we shall be much together? You and I,
I mean?

MRS. WARREN [*staring at her*]. Of course: until you're married.
You're not going back to college again.

VIVIE. Do you think my way of life would suit you? I doubt it.

MRS. WARREN. Your way of life! What do you mean?

VIVIE [*cutting a page of her book with the paper knife on her
chatelaine*]. Has it really never occurred to you, mother, that
I have a way of life like other people?

MRS. WARREN. What nonsense is this you're trying to talk? Do
you want to shew your independence, now that you're a
great little person at school? Don't be a fool, child.

VIVIE [*indulgently*]. That's all you have to say on the subject,
is it, mother?

MRS. WARREN [*puzzled, then angry*]. Don't you keep on asking
me questions like that. [*Violently.*] Hold your tongue. [VIVIE
works on, losing no time, and saying nothing.] You and

your way of life, indeed! What next? [*She looks at* VIVIE *again. No reply.*] Your way of life will be what I please, so it will. [*Another pause.*] I've been noticing these airs in you ever since you got that tripos or whatever you call it. If you think I'm going to put up with them you're mistaken; and the sooner you find it out, the better. [*Muttering.*] All I have to say on the subject, indeed! [*Again raising her voice angrily.*] Do you know who you're speaking to, Miss?

VIVIE [*looking across at her without raising her head from her book*]. No. Who are you? What are you?

MRS. WARREN [*rising breathlessly*]. You young imp!

VIVIE. Everybody knows my reputation, my social standing, and the profession I intend to pursue. I know nothing about you. What is that way of life which you invite me to share with you and Sir George Crofts, pray?

MRS. WARREN. Take care. I shall do something I'll be sorry for after, and you too.

VIVIE [*putting aside her books with cool decision*]. Well, let us drop the subject until you are better able to face it. [*Looking critically at her mother.*] You want some good walks and a little lawn tennis to set you up. You are shockingly out of condition: you were not able to manage twenty yards uphill today without stopping to pant; and your wrists are mere rolls of fat. Look at mine. [*She holds out her wrists.*]

MRS. WARREN [*after looking at her helplessly, begins to whimper*]. Vivie—

VIVIE [*springing up sharply*]. Now pray don't begin to cry. Anything but that. I really cannot stand whimpering. I will go out of the room if you do.

MRS. WARREN [*piteously*]. Oh, my darling, how can you be so hard on me? Have I no rights over you as your mother?

VIVIE. Are you my mother?

MRS. WARREN [*appalled*]. Am I your mother! Oh, Vivie!

VIVIE. Then where are our relatives? my father? our family friends? You claim the rights of a mother: the right to call me fool and child; to speak to me as no woman in authority over me at college dare speak to me; to dictate my way of life; and to force on me the acquaintance of a brute whom anyone can see to be the most vicious sort of London man about town. Before I give myself the trouble to resist such claims, I may as well find out whether they have any real existence.

MRS. WARREN [*distracted, throwing herself on her knees*]. Oh no, no. Stop, stop. I am your mother: I swear it. Oh, you can't mean to turn on me—my own child! it's not natural. You believe me, don't you? Say you believe me.

VIVIE. Who was my father?

MRS. WARREN. You don't know what you're asking. I can't tell you.

VIVIE [*determinedly*]. Oh yes you can, if you like. I have a right to know; and you know very well that I have that right. You can refuse to tell me, if you please; but if you do, you will see the last of me tomorrow morning.

MRS. WARREN. Oh, it's too horrible to hear you talk like that. You wouldn't—you couldn't leave me.

VIVIE [*ruthlessly*]. Yes, without a moment's hesitation, if you trifle with me about this. [*Shivering with disgust.*] How can I feel sure that I may not have the contaminated blood of that brutal waster in my veins?

MRS. WARREN. No, no. On my oath it's not he, nor any of the rest that you have ever met. I'm certain of that, at least.

[VIVIE's *eyes fasten sternly on her mother as the significance of this flashes on her.*]

VIVIE [*slowly*]. You are certain of that, at least. Ah! You mean that that is all you are certain of. [*Thoughtfully.*] I see. [MRS. WARREN *buries her face in her hands.*] Don't do that, mother: you know you don't feel it a bit. [MRS. WARREN *takes down her hands and looks up deplorably at* VIVIE, *who takes out her watch and says:*] Well, that is enough for tonight. At what hour would you like breakfast? Is half-past eight too early for you?

MRS. WARREN [*wildly*]. My God, what sort of woman are you?

VIVIE [*coolly*]. The sort the world is mostly made of, I should hope. Otherwise I don't understand how it gets its business done. Come [*taking her mother by the wrist, and pulling her up pretty resolutely*]: pull yourself together. That's right.

MRS. WARREN [*querulously*]. You're very rough with me, Vivie.

VIVIE. Nonsense. What about bed? It's past ten.

MRS. WARREN [*passionately*]. What's the use of my going to bed? Do you think I could sleep?

VIVIE. Why not? I shall.

MRS. WARREN. You! you've no heart. [*She suddenly breaks out vehemently in her natural tongue—the dialect of a woman of the people—with all her affectations of maternal authority and conventional manners gone, and an overwhelming inspiration of true conviction and scorn in her.*] Oh, I won't bear it: I won't put up with the injustice of it. What right have you to set yourself up above me like this? You boast of what you are to me—to me, who gave you the chance of being what you are. What chance had I? Shame on you for a bad daughter and a stuck-up prude!

VIVIE [*sitting down with a shrug, no longer confident; for her replies, which have sounded sensible and strong to her so far, now begin to ring rather woodenly and even priggishly against the new tone of her mother*]. Don't think for a moment I set myself above you in any way. You attacked me with the conventional authority of a mother: I defended myself with the conventional superiority of a respectable woman. Frankly, I am not going to stand any of your nonsense; and when you drop it I shall not expect you to stand any of mine. I shall always respect your right to your own opinions and your own way of life.

MRS. WARREN. My own opinions and my own way of life! Listen to her talking! Do you think I was brought up like you? able to pick and choose my own way of life? Do you think I did what I did because I liked it, or thought it right, or wouldn't rather have gone to college and been a lady if I'd had the chance?

VIVIE. Everybody has some choice, mother. The poorest girl alive may not be able to choose between being Queen of England or Principal of Newnham; but she can choose between ragpicking and flowerselling, according to her taste. People are always blaming their circumstances for what they are. I don't believe in circumstances. The people who get on in this world are the people who get up and look for the circumstances they want, and, if they can't find them, make them.

MRS. WARREN. Oh, it's easy to talk, very easy, isn't it? Here I would you like to know what my circumstances were?

VIVIE. Yes: you had better tell me. Won't you sit down?

MRS. WARREN. Oh, I'll sit down: don't you be afraid. [*She plants her chair farther forward with brazen energy, and sits down.* VIVIE *is impressed in spite of herself.*] D'you know what your gran'mother was?

VIVIE. No.

MRS. WARREN. No you don't. I do. She called herself a widow and had a fried-fish shop down by the Mint, and kept herself and four daughters out of it. Two of us were sisters: that was me and Liz; and we were both good-looking and well made. I suppose our father was a well-fed man: mother pretended he was a gentleman; but I don't know. The other two were only half sisters: undersized, ugly, starved looking, hard working, honest poor creatures: Liz and I would have half-murdered them if mother hadn't half-murdered us to keep our hands off them. They were the respectable ones. Well, what did they get by their respectability? I'll tell you. One of them worked in a whitelead factory twelve hours a day for nine shillings a week until she died of lead poisoning. She only expected to get her hands a little paralyzed; but she died. The other was always held up to us as a model because she married a Government laborer in the Deptford victualling yard, and kept his room and the three children neat and tidy on eighteen shillings a week—until he took to drink. That was worth being respectable for, wasn't it?

VIVIE [*now thoughtfully attentive*]. Did you and your sister think so?

MRS. WARREN. Liz didn't, I can tell you: she had more spirit. We both went to a church school—that was part of the ladylike airs we gave ourselves to be superior to the children that knew nothing and went nowhere—and we stayed there until Liz went out one night and never came back. I know the schoolmistress thought I'd soon follow her example; for the clergyman was always warning me that Lizzie'd end by jumping off Waterloo Bridge. Poor fool: that was all he knew about it! But I was more afraid of the whitelead factory than I was of the river; and so would you have been in my place. That clergyman got me a situation as scullery maid in a temperance restaurant where they sent out for anything you liked. Then I was waitress; and then I went to the bar at Waterloo station: fourteen hours a day serving drinks and washing glasses for four shillings a week and my board. That was considered a great promotion for me. Well, one cold, wretched night, when I was so tired I could hardly keep myself awake, who should come up for a half of Scotch but Lizzie, in a long fur cloak, elegant and comfortable, with a lot of sovereigns in her purse.

VIVIE [*grimly*]. My aunt Lizzie!

MRS. WARREN. Yes; and a very good aunt to have, too. She's living down at Winchester now, close to the cathedral, one of the most respectable ladies there. Chaperones girls at the county ball, if you please. No river for Liz, thank you! You remind me of Liz a little: she was a first-rate business woman—saved money from the beginning—never let herself look too like what she was—never lost her head or threw away a chance. When she saw I'd grown up good-looking she said to me across the bar "What are you doing there, you little fool? wearing out your health and your appearance for other people's profit!" Liz was saving money then to take a house for herself in Brussels; and she thought we two could save faster than one. So she lent me some money and gave me a start; and I saved steadily and first paid her back, and then went into business with her as her partner. Why shouldn't I have done it? The house in Brussels was real high class: a much better place for a woman to be in than the factory where Anne Jane got poisoned. None of our girls were ever treated as I was treated in the scullery of that temperance place, or at the Waterloo bar, or at home. Would you have had me stay in them and become a worn out old drudge before I was forty?

VIVIE [*intensely interested by this time*]. No; but why did you choose that business? Saving money and good management will succeed in any business.

MRS. WARREN. Yes, saving money. But where can a woman get the money to save in any other business? Could you save out of four shillings a week and keep yourself dressed as well? Not you. Of course, if you're a plain woman and can't earn anything more; or if you have a turn for music, or the stage, or newspaper-writing: that's different. But neither Liz nor I had any turn for such things: all we had was our appearance and our turn for pleasing men. Do you think we were such fools as to let other people trade in our good looks by employing us as shopgirls, or barmaids, or waitresses, when we could trade in them ourselves and get all the profits instead of starvation wages? Not likely.

VIVIE. You were certainly quite justified—from the business point of view.

MRS. WARREN. Yes; or any other point of view. What is any respectable girl brought up to do but to catch some rich man's fancy and get the benefit of his money by marrying him?—as if a marriage ceremony could make any difference in the right or wrong of the thing! Oh, the hypocrisy of the world makes me sick! Liz and I had to work and save and calculate just like other people; elseways we should be as poor as any good-for-nothing drunken waster of a woman that thinks her luck will last for ever. [*With great energy.*] I despise such people: they've no character; and if there's a thing I hate in a woman, it's want of character.

VIVIE. Come now, mother: frankly! Isn't it part of what you call character in a woman that she should greatly dislike such a way of making money?

MRS. WARREN. Why, of course. Everybody dislikes having to work and make money; but they have to do it all the same. I'm sure I've often pitied a poor girl, tired out and in low spirits, having to try to please some man that she doesn't care two straws for—some half-drunken fool that thinks he's making himself agreeable when he's teasing and worrying and disgusting a woman so that hardly any money could pay her for putting up with it. But she has to bear with disagreeables and take the rough with the smooth, just like a nurse in a hospital or anyone else. It's not work that any woman would do for pleasure, goodness knows; though to hear the pious people talk you would suppose it was a bed of roses.

VIVIE. Still, you consider it worth while. It pays.

MRS. WARREN. Of course it's worth while to a poor girl, if she can resist temptation and is good-looking and well conducted and sensible. It's far better than any other employment open to her. I always thought that oughtn't to be. It can't be right, Vivie, that there shouldn't be better opportunities for women. I stick to that: it's wrong. But it's so, right or wrong; and a girl must make the best of it. But of course it's not worth while for a lady. If you took to it you'd be a fool; but I should have been a fool if I'd taken to anything else.

VIVIE [*more and more deeply moved*]. Mother: suppose we were both as poor as you were in those wretched old days, are you quite sure that you wouldn't advise me to try the Waterloo bar, or marry a laborer, or even go into the factory?

MRS. WARREN [*indignantly*]. Of course not. What sort of mother do you take me for! How could you keep your self-respect in such starvation and slavery? And what's a woman worth? what's life worth? without self-respect! Why am I independent and able to give my daughter a first-rate education, when other women that had just as good opportunities are

in the gutter? Because I always knew how to respect myself
and control myself. Why is Liz looked up to in a cathedral
town? The same reason. Where would we be now if we'd
minded the clergyman's foolishness? Scrubbing floors for
one and sixpence a day and nothing to look forward to but
the workhouse infirmary. Don't you be led astray by people
who don't know the world, my girl. The only way for a
woman to provide for herself decently is for her to be good
to some man that can afford to be good to her. If she's in
his own station of life, let her make him marry her; but if
she's far beneath him she can't expect it: why should she?
it wouldn't be for her own happiness. Ask any lady in London society that has daughters; and she'll tell you the same,
except that I tell you straight and she'll tell you crooked.
That's all the difference.

VIVIE [*fascinated, gazing at her*]. My dear mother: you are a
wonderful woman: you are stronger than all England. And
are you really and truly not one wee bit doubtful—or—
or—ashamed?

MRS. WARREN. Well, of course, dearie, it's only good manners
to be ashamed of it: it's expected from a woman. Women
have to pretend to feel a great deal that they don't feel. Liz
used to be angry with me for plumping out the truth about
it. She used to say that when every woman could learn
enough from what was going on in the world before her
eyes, there was no need to talk about it to her. But then Liz
was such a perfect lady! She had the true instinct of it;
while I was always a bit of vulgarian. I used to be so pleased
when you sent me your photos to see that you were growing
up like Liz: you've just her ladylike, determined way. But I
can't stand saying one thing when everyone knows I mean
another. What's the use in such hypocrisy? If people arrange the world that way for women, there's no good pretending it's arranged the other way. No: I never was a bit
ashamed really. I consider I had a right to be proud of how
we managed everything so respectably, and never had a
word against us, and how the girls were so well taken care

of. Some of them did very well: one of them married an
ambassador. But of course now I daren't talk about such
things: whatever would they think of us! [*She yawns.*] Oh
dear! I do believe I'm getting sleepy after all. [*She stretches
herself lazily, thoroughly relieved by her explosion, and
placidly ready for her night's rest.*]

VIVIE. I believe it is I who will not be able to sleep now. [*She
goes to the dresser and lights the candle. Then she extin-
guishes the lamp, darkening the room a good deal.*] Better
let in some fresh air before locking up. [*She opens the cottage door, and finds that it is broad moonlight.*] What a
beautiful night! Look! [*She draws aside the curtains of the
window. The landscape is seen bathed in the radiance of
the harvest moon rising over Blackdown.*]

MRS. WARREN [*with a perfunctory glance at the scene*]. Yes,
dear; but take care you don't catch your death of cold
from the night air.

VIVIE [*contemptuously*]. Nonsense.

MRS. WARREN [*querulously*]. Oh yes: everything I say is nonsense, according to you.

VIVIE [*turning to her quickly*]. No: really that is not so, mother.
You have got completely the better of me tonight, though
I intended it to be the other way. Let us be good friends
now.

MRS. WARREN [*shaking her head a little ruefully*]. So it has
been the other way. But I suppose I must give in to it. I
always got the worst of it from Liz; and now I suppose it'll
be the same with you.

VIVIE. Well, never mind. Come: good-night, dear old mother.

[*She takes her mother in her arms.*]

MRS. WARREN [*fondly*]. I brought you up well, didn't I, dearie?

VIVIE. You did.

MRS. WARREN. And you'll be good to your poor old mother for
it, won't you?

VIVIE. I will, dear. [*Kissing her.*] Good-night.

MRS. WARREN [*with unction*]. Blessings on my own dearie darling! a mother's blessing!

[*She embraces her daughter protectingly, instinctively looking upward for divine sanction.*]

ACT THREE

[*In the Rectory garden next morning, with the sun shining from a cloudless sky. The garden wall has a five-barred wooden gate, wide enough to admit a carriage, in the middle. Beside the gate hangs a bell on a coiled spring, communicating with a pull outside. The carriage drive comes down the middle of the garden and then swerves to its left, where it ends in a little gravelled circus opposite the Rectory porch. Beyond the gate is seen the dusty high road, parallel with the wall, bounded on the farther side by a strip of turf and an unfenced pine wood. On the lawn, between the house and the drive, is a clipped yew tree, with a garden bench in its shade. On the opposite side the garden is shut in by a box hedge; and there is a sundial on the turf, with an iron chair near it. A little path leads off through the box hedge, behind the sundial.*

FRANK, seated on the chair near the sundial, on which he has placed the morning papers, is reading The Standard. His father comes from the house, red-eyed and shivery, and meets Frank's eye with misgiving.]

FRANK [*looking at his watch*]. Half-past eleven. Nice hour for a rector to come down to breakfast!

REV. s. Don't mock, Frank; Don't mock. I am a little—er—[*Shivering.*]—

FRANK. Off color?

REV. s. [*repudiating the expression*]. No, sir: unwell this morning. Where's your mother?

FRANK. Don't be alarmed: she's not here. Gone to town by the 11:13 with Bessie. She left several messages for you. Do you feel equal to receiving them now, or shall I wait til you've breakfasted?

REV. S. I have breakfasted, sir. I am surprised at your mother going to town when we have people staying with us. They'll think it very strange.

FRANK. Possibly she has considered that. At all events, if Crofts is going to stay here, and you are going to sit up every night with him until four, recalling the incidents of your fiery youth, it is clearly my mother's duty, as a prudent housekeeper, to go up to the stores and order a barrel of whiskey and a few hundred siphons.

REV. S. I did not observe that Sir George drank excessively.

FRANK. You were not in a condition to, gov'nor.

REV. S. Do you mean to say that *I*—?

FRANK [*calmly*]. I never saw a beneficed clergyman less sober. The anecdotes you told about your past career were so awful that I really don't think Praed would have passed the night under your roof if it hadn't been for the way my mother and he took to one another.

REV. S. Nonsense, sir. I am Sir George Crofts' host. I must talk to him about something; and he has only one subject. Where is Mr. Praed now?

FRANK. He is driving my mother and Bessie to the station.

REV. S. Is Crofts up yet?

FRANK. Oh, long ago. He hasn't turned a hair: he's in much better practice than you. Has kept it up ever since, probably. He's taken himself off somewhere to smoke.

[*Frank resumes his paper. The parson turns disconsolately towards the gate; then comes back irresolutely.*]

REV. S. Er—Frank.

FRANK. Yes.

REV. S. Do you think the Warrens will expect to be asked here after yesterday afternoon?

FRANK. They've been asked already.

REV. S. [*appalled*]. What!!!

FRANK. Crofts informed us at breakfast that you told him to bring Mrs. Warren and Vivie over here to-day, and to invite them to make this house their home. My mother then found she must go to town by the 11:13 train.

REV. S. [*with despairing vehemence*]. I never gave any such invitation. I never thought of such a thing.

FRANK [*compassionately*]. How do you know, gov'nor, what you
said and thought last night?

PRAED [*coming in through the hedge*]. Good morning.

REV. S. Good morning. I must apologize for not having met you
at breakfast. I have a touch of—of—

FRANK. Clergyman's sore throat, Praed. Fortunately not
chronic.

PRAED [*changing the subject*]. Well, I must say your house is
in a charming spot here. Really most charming.

REV. S. Yes: it is indeed. Frank will take you for a walk, Mr.
Praed, if you like. I'll ask you to excuse me: I must take
the opportunity to write my sermon while Mrs. Gardner is
away and you are all amusing yourselves. You won't mind,
will you?

PRAED. Certainly not. Don't stand on the slightest ceremony
with me.

REV. S. Thank you. I'll—er—er—[*He stammers his way to the
porch and vanishes into the house.*]

PRAED. Curious thing it must be writing a sermon every week.

FRANK. Ever so curious, if he did it. He buys 'em. He's gone
for some soda water.

PRAED. My dear boy: I wish you would be more respectful to
your father. You know you can be so nice when you like.

FRANK. My dear Praddy: you forget that I have to live with the
governor. When two people live together—it don't matter
whether they're father and son or husband and wife or
brother and sister—they can't keep up the polite humbug
that's so easy for ten minutes on an afternoon call. Now
the governor, who unites to many admirable domestic qualities the irresoluteness of a sheep and the pompousness and
aggressiveness of a jackass—

PRAED. No, pray, pray, my dear Frank, remember! He is your
father.

FRANK. I give him due credit for that. [*Rising and flinging down *his paper.*] But just imagine his telling Crofts to bring the Warrens over here! He must have been ever so drunk. You know, my dear Praddy, my mother wouldn't stand Mrs. Warren for a moment. Vivie mustn't come here until she's gone back to town.

PRAED. But your mother doesn't know anything about Mrs. Warren, does she? [*He picks up the paper and sits down to read it.*]

FRANK. I don't know. Her journey to town looks as if she did. Not that my mother would mind in the ordinary way: she has stuck like a brick to lots of women who had got into trouble. But they were all nice women. That's what makes the real difference. Mrs. Warren, no doubt, has her merits; but she's ever so rowdy; and my mother simply wouldn't put up with her. So—hallo! [*This exclamation is provoked by the reappearance of the clergyman, who comes out of the house in haste and dismay.*]

REV. S. Frank: Mrs. Warren and her daughter are coming across the heath with Crofts: I saw them from the study windows. What am I to say about your mother?

FRANK. Stick on your hat and go out and say how delighted you are to see them; and that Frank's in the garden; and that mother and Bessie have been called to the bedside of a sick relative, and were ever so sorry they couldn't stop; and that you hope Mrs. Warren slept well; and—and—say any blessed thing except the truth, and leave the rest to Providence.

REV. S. But how are we to get rid of them afterwards?

FRANK. There's no time to think of that now. Here! [*He bounds into the house.*]

REV. S. He's so impetuous. I don't know what to do with him, Mr. Praed.

FRANK [*returning with a clerical felt hat, which he claps on his father's head*]. Now: off with you. [*Rushing him through the gate.*] Praed and I'll wait here, to give the thing an unpremeditated air. [*The clergyman, dazed but obedient, hurries off.*]

FRANK. We must get the old girl back to town somehow, Praed. Come! Honestly, dear Praddy, do you like seeing them together?

PRAED. Oh, why not?

FRANK [*his teeth on edge*]. Don't it make your flesh creep ever so little? that wicked old devil, up to every villainy under the sun, I'll swear, and Vivie—ugh!

PRAED. Hush, pray. They're coming.

[*The clergyman and* CROFTS *are seen coming along the road, followed by* MRS. WARREN *and* VIVIE *walking affectionately together.*]

FRANK. Look: she actually has her arm round the old woman's waist. It's her right arm: she began it. She's gone sentimental, by God! Ugh! ugh! Now do you feel the creeps? [*The clergyman opens the gate; and* MRS. WARREN *and* VIVIE *pass him and stand in the middle of the garden looking at the house.* FRANK, *in an ecstasy of dissimulation, turns gaily to* MRS. WARREN, *exclaiming:*] Ever so delighted to see you, Mrs. Warren. This quiet old rectory garden becomes you perfectly.

MRS. WARREN. Well, I never! Did you hear that, George? He says I look well in a quiet old rectory garden.

REV. S. [*still holding the gate for* CROFTS, *who loafs through it, heavily bored*]. You look well everywhere, Mrs. Warren.

FRANK. Bravo, gov'nor! Now look here: let's have a treat before lunch. First let's see the church. Everyone has to do that. It's a regular old thirteenth century church, you know: the gov'nor's ever so fond of it, because he got up a restoration fund and had it completely rebuilt six years ago. Praed will be able to shew its points.

PRAED [*rising*]. Certainly, if the restoration has left any to shew.

REV. S. [*mooning hospitably at them*]. I shall be pleased, I'm sure, if Sir George and Mrs. Warren really care about it.

MRS. WARREN. Oh, come along and get it over.

CROFTS [*turning back towards the gate*]. I've no objection.

REV. S. Not that way. We go through the fields, if you don't mind. Round here. [*He leads the way by the little path through the box hedge.*]

CROFTS. Oh, all right. [*He goes with the parson.*]

[PRAED *follows with* MRS. WARREN. VIVIE *does not stir: she watches them until they have gone, with all the lines of purpose in her face marking it strongly.*]

FRANK. Ain't you coming?

VIVIE. No. I want to give you a warning, Frank. You were making fun of my mother just now when you said that about the rectory garden. That is barred in future. Please treat my mother with as much respect as you treat your own.

FRANK. My dear Viv: she wouldn't appreciate it: the two cases require different treatment. But what on earth has happened to you? Last night we were perfectly agreed as to your mother and her set. This morning I find you attitudinizing sentimentally with your arm round your parent's waist.

VIVIE [*flushing*]. Attitudinizing!

FRANK. That was how it struck me. First time I ever saw you do a second-rate thing.

VIVIE [*controlling herself*]. Yes, Frank: there has been a change; but I don't think it a change for the worse. Yesterday I was a little prig.

FRANK. And today?

VIVIE [*wincing; then looking at him steadily*]. Today I know my mother better than you do.

FRANK. Heaven forbid!

VIVIE. What do you mean?

FRANK. Viv: there's a freemasonry among thoroughly immoral people that you know nothing of. You've too much character. That's the bond between your mother and me: that's why I know her better than you'll ever know her.

VIVIE. You are wrong: you know nothing about her. If you knew the circumstances against which my mother had to struggle—

FRANK [*adroitly finishing the sentence for her*]. I should know why she is what she is, shouldn't I? What difference would that make? Circumstances or no circumstances, Viv, you won't be able to stand your mother.

VIVIE [*very angry*] Why not?

FRANK. Because she's an old wretch, Viv. If you ever put your arm round her waist in my presence again, I'll shoot myself there and then as a protest against an exhibition which revolts me.

VIVIE. Must I choose between dropping your acquaintance and dropping my mother's?

FRANK [*gracefully*]. That would put the old lady at ever such a disadvantage. No, Viv: your infatuated little boy will have to stick to you in any case. But he's all the more anxious that you shouldn't make mistakes. It's no use, Viv: your mother's impossible. She may be a good sort; but she's a bad lot, a very bad lot.

VIVIE [*hotly*]. Frank—! [*He stands his ground. She turns away and sits down on the bench under the yew tree, struggling to recover her self-command. Then she says:*] Is she to be deserted by all the world because she's what you call a bad lot? Has she no right to live?

FRANK. No fear of that, Viv: she won't ever be deserted. [*He sits on the bench beside her.*]

VIVIE. But I am to desert her, I suppose.

FRANK [*babyishly, lulling her and making love to her with his voice*]. Mustn't go live with her. Little family group of mother and daughter wouldn't be a success. Spoil our little group.

VIVIE [*falling under the spell*]. What little group?

FRANK. The babes in the wood: Vivie and little Frank [*He nestles against her like a weary child.*] Let's go and get covered up with leaves.

VIVIE [*rhythmically, rocking him like a nurse*]. Fast asleep, hand in hand, under the trees.

FRANK. The wise little girl with her silly little boy.

VIVIE. The dear little boy with his dowdy little girl.

FRANK. Ever so peaceful, and relieved from the imbecility of the little boy's father and the questionableness of the little girl's—

VIVIE [*smothering the word against her breast*]. Sh-sh-sh-sh! little girl wants to forget all about her mother. [*They are silent for some moments, rocking one another. Then* VIVIE *wakes up with a shock, exclaiming.*] What a pair of fools we are! Come: sit up. Gracious! your hair. [*She smooths it.*] I wonder do all grown up people play in that childish way when nobody is looking. I never did it when I was a child.

FRANK. Neither did I. You are my first playmate. [*He catches her hand to kiss it, but checks himself to look round first. Very unexpectedly, he see* CROFTS *emerging from the box hedge.*] Oh damn!

VIVIE. Why damn, dear?

FRANK [*whispering*]. Sh! Here's this brute Crofts. [*He sits farther away from her with an unconcerned air.*]

CROFTS. Could I have a few words with you, Miss Vivie?

VIVIE. Certainly.

CROFTS [*to Frank*]. You'll excuse me, Gardner. They're waiting for you in the church, if you don't mind.

FRANK [*rising*]. Anything to oblige you, Crofts—except church. If you should happen to want me, Vivvums, ring the gate bell. [*He goes into the house with unruffled suavity.*]

CROFTS [*watching him with a crafty air as he disappears, and speaking to* VIVIE *with an assumption of being on privileged terms with her*]. Pleasant young fellow that, Miss Vivie. Pity he has no money, isn't it?

VIVIE. Do you think so?

CROFTS. Well, what's he to do? No profession. No property. What's he good for?

VIVIE. I realize his disadvantages, Sir George.

CROFTS [*a little taken aback at being so precisely interpreted*]. Oh, it's not that. But while we're in this world we're in it; and money's money. [VIVIE *does not answer.*] Nice day, isn't it?

VIVIE [*with scarcely veiled contempt for this effort at conversation*]. Very.

CROFTS [*with brutal good humor, as if he liked her pluck*]. Well, that's not what I came to say. [*Sitting down beside her.*] Now listen, Miss Vivie. I'm quite aware that I'm not a young lady's man.

VIVIE. Indeed, Sir George?

CROFTS. No; and to tell you the honest truth I don't want to be either. But when I say a thing I mean it; when I feel a sentiment I feel it in earnest; and what I value I pay hard money for. That's the sort of man I am.

VIVIE. It does you great credit, I'm sure.

CROFTS. Oh, I don't mean to praise myself. I have my faults, Heaven knows: no man is more sensible of that than I am. I know I'm not perfect: that's one of the advantages of being a middle-aged man; for I'm not a young man, and I know it. But my code is a simple one, and, I think, a good one. Honor between man and man; fidelity between man and woman; and no cant about this religion or that religion, but an honest belief that things are making for good on the whole.

VIVIE [*with biting irony*]. "A power, not ourselves, that makes for righteousness," eh?

CROFTS [*taking her seriously*]. Oh certainly. Not ourselves, of course. You understand what I mean. Well, now as to practical matters. You may have an idea that I've flung my money about; but I haven't: I'm richer today than when I first came into the property. I've used my knowledge of the world to invest my money in ways that other men have overlooked; and whatever else I may be, I'm a safe man from the money point of view.

VIVIE. It's very kind of you to tell me all this.

CROFTS. Oh well, come, Miss Vivie: you needn't pretend you don't see what I'm driving at. I want to settle down with a Lady Crofts. I suppose you think me very blunt, eh?

VIVIE. Not at all: I am much obliged to you for being so definite and business-like. I quite appreciate the offer: the money, the position, Lady Crofts, and so on. But I think I will say no, if you don't mind. I'd rather not. [*She rises,*

*and strolls across to the sundial to get out of his immediate
neighborhood.*]

CROFTS [*not at all discouraged, and taking advantage of the
additional room left him on the seat to spread himself comfortably, as if a few preliminary refusals were part of the
inevitable routine of courtship*]. I'm in no hurry. It was only
just to let you know in case young Gardner should try to
trap you. Leave the question open.

VIVIE [*sharply*]. My no is final. I won't go back from it.

[CROFTS *is not impressed. He grins; leans forward with his
elbows on his knees to prod with his stick at some unfor-
tunate insect in the grass; and looks cunningly at her. She
turns away impatiently.*]

CROFTS. I'm a good deal older than you. Twenty-five years:
quarter of a century. I shan't live for ever; and I'll take care
that you shall be well off when I'm gone.

VIVIE. I am proof against even that inducement, Sir George.
Don't you think you'd better take your answer? There is not
the slightest chance of my altering it.

CROFTS [*rising, after a final slash at a daisy, and coming nearer
to her*]. Well, no matter. I could tell you some things that
would change your mind fast enough; but I won't, because
I'd rather win you by honest affection. I was a good friend
to your mother: ask her whether I wasn't. She'd never have
made the money that paid for your education if it hadn't
been for my advice and help, not to mention the money
I advanced her. There are not many men would have stood
by her as I have. I put not less than £40,000 into it, from
first to last.

VIVIE [*staring at him*]. Do you mean to say you were my
mother's business partner?

CROFTS. Yes. Now just think of all the trouble and the explana-
tions it would save if we were to keep the whole thing in
the family, so to speak. Ask your mother whether she'd
like to have to explain all her affairs to a perfect stranger.

VIVIE. I see no difficulty, since I understand that the business is wound up, and the money invested.

CROFTS [*stopping short, amazed*]. Wound up! Wind up a business that's paying 35 per cent in the worst years! Not likely. Who told you that?

VIVIE [*her color quite gone*]. Do you mean that it is still—? [*She stops abruptly, and puts her hand on the sundial to support herself. Then she gets quickly to the iron chair and sits down.*] What business are you talking about?

CROFTS. Well, the fact is it's not what would be considered exactly a high-class business in my set—the county set, you know—our set it will be if you think better of my offer. Not that there's any mystery about it: don't think that. Of course you know by your mother's being in it that it's perfectly straight and honest. I've known her for many years; and I can say of her that she'd cut off her hands sooner than touch anything that was not what it ought to be. I'll tell you all about it if you like. I don't know whether you've found in travelling how hard it is to find a really comfortable private hotel.

VIVIE [*sickened, averting her face*]. Yes: go on.

CROFTS. Well, that's all it is. Your mother has a genius for managing such things. We've got two in Brussels, one in Ostend, one in Vienna, and two in Budapest. Of course there are others besides ourselves in it; but we hold most of the capital; and your mother's indispensable as managing director. You've noticed, I daresay, that she travels a good deal. But you see you can't mention such things in society. Once let out the word hotel and everybody says you keep a public-house. You wouldn't like people to say that of your mother, would you? That's why we're so reserved about it. By the way, you'll keep it to yourself, won't you? Since it's been a secret so long, it had better remain so.

VIVIE. And this is the business you invite me to join you in?

CROFTS. Oh no. My wife shan't be troubled with business. You'll not be in it more than you've always been.

VIVIE. *I* always been! What do you mean?

CROFTS. Only that you've always lived on it. It paid for your education and the dress you have on your back. Don't turn up your nose at business, Miss Vivie: where would your Newnhams and Girtons be without it?

VIVIE [*rising, almost beside herself*]. Take care. I know what this business is.

CROFTS [*starting, with a suppressed oath*]. Who told you?

VIVIE. Your partner. My mother

CROFTS [*black with rage*]. The old—

VIVIE. Just so.

[*He swallows the epithet and stands for a moment swearing and raging foully to himself. But he knows that his cue is to be sympathetic. He takes refuge in generous indignation.*]

CROFTS. She ought to have had more consideration for you. *I'd* never have told you.

VIVIE. I think you would probably have told me when we were married: it would have been a convenient weapon to break me in with.

CROFTS [*quite sincerely*]. I never intended that. On my word as a gentleman I didn't.

[VIVIE *wonders at him. Her sense of the irony of his protest cools and braces her. She replies with contemptuous self-possession.*]

VIVIE. It does not matter. I suppose you understand that when we leave here today our acquaintance ceases.

CROFTS. Why? Is it for helping your mother?

VIVIE. My mother was a very poor woman who had no reasonable choice but to do as she did. You were a rich gentleman; and you did the same for the sake of 35 per cent. You are a pretty common sort of scoundrel, I think. That is my opinion of you.

CROFTS [*after a stare: not at all displeased, and much more at his ease on these frank terms than on their former ceremonious ones*]. Ha! ha! ha! ha! Go it, little missie, go it: it doesn't hurt me and it amuses you. Why the devil shouldn't

I invest my money that way? I take the interest on my capital like other people: I hope you don't think I dirty my own hands with the work. Come! you wouldn't refuse the acquaintance of my mother's cousin the Duke of Belgravia because some of the rents he gets are earned in queer ways. You wouldn't cut the Archbishop of Canterbury, I suppose, because the Ecclesiastical Commissioners have a few publicans and sinners among their tenants. Do you remember your Crofts scholarship at Newnham? Well, that was founded by my brother the M.P. He gets his 22 per cent out of a factory with 600 girls in it, and not one of them getting wages enough to live on. How d'ye suppose they manage when they have no family to fall back on? Ask your mother. And do you expect me to turn my back on 35 per cent when all the rest are pocketing what they can, like sensible men? No such fool! If you're going to pick and choose your acquaintances on moral principles, you'd better clear out of this country, unless you want to cut yourself out of all decent society.

VIVIE [*conscience stricken*]. You might go on to point out that I myself never asked where the money I spent came from. I believe I am just as bad as you.

CROFTS [*greatly reassured*]. Of course you are; and a very good thing too! What harm does it do after all? [*Rallying her jocularly.*] So you don't think me such a scoundrel now you come to think it over. Eh?

VIVIE. I have shared profits with you; and I admitted you just now to the familiarity of knowing what I think of you.

CROFTS [*with serious friendliness*]. To be sure you did. You won't find me a bad sort: I don't go in for being superfine intellectually; but I've plenty of honest human feeling; and the old Crofts breed comes out in a sort of instinctive hatred of anything low, in which I'm sure you'll sympathize with me. Believe me, Miss Vivie, the world isn't such a bad place as the croakers make out. As long as you don't fly openly in the face of society, society doesn't ask any inconvenient questions; and it makes precious short work of the cads who do. There are no secrets better kept than the secrets everybody guesses. In the class of people I can introduce you to, no lady or gentleman would so far forget themselves as to discuss my business affairs or your mother's. No man can offer you a safer position.

VIVIE [*studying him curiously*]. I suppose you really think you're getting on famously with me.

CROFTS. Well, I hope I may flatter myself that you think better of me than you did at first.

VIVIE [*quietly*]. I hardly find you worth thinking about at all now. When I think of the society that tolerates you, and the laws that protect you! when I think of how helpless nine out of ten young girls would be in the hands of you and my mother! the unmentionable woman and her capitalist bully—

CROFTS [*livid*]. Damn you!

VIVIE. You need not. I feel among the damned already.

[*She raises the latch of the gate to open it and go out. He follows her and puts his hand heavily on the top bar to prevent its opening.*]

CROFTS [*panting with fury*]. Do you think I'll put up with this from you, you young devil?

VIVIE [*unmoved*]. Be quiet. Some one will answer the bell.

[*Without flinching a step she strikes the bell with the back of her hand. It clangs harshly; and he starts back involuntarily. Almost immediately FRANK appears at the porch with his rifle.*]

FRANK [*with cheerful politeness*]. Will you have the rifle, Viv; or shall I operate?

VIVIE. Frank: have you been listening?

FRANK [*coming down into the garden*]. Only for the bell, I assure you; so that you shouldn't have to wait. I think I shewed great insight into your character, Crofts.

CROFTS. For two pins I'd take that gun from you and break it across your head.

FRANK [*stalking him cautiously*]. Pray don't. I'm ever so careless in handling firearms. Sure to be a fatal accident, with
a reprimand from the coroner's jury for my negligence.

VIVIE. Put the rifle away, Frank: it's quite unnecessary.

FRANK. Quite right, Viv. Much more sportsmanlike to catch
him in a trap. [CROFTS, *understanding the insult, makes a
threatening movement*.] Crofts: there are fifteen cartridges in
the magazine here; and I am a dead shot at the present distance and at an object of your size.

CROFTS. Oh, you needn't be afraid. I'm not going to touch you.

FRANK. Ever so magnanimous of you under the circumstances!
Thank you.

CROFTS. I'll just tell you this before I go. It may interest you,
since you're so fond of one another. Allow me, Mister
Frank, to introduce you to your half-sister, the eldest daughter of the Reverend Samuel Gardner. Miss Vivie: your
half-brother. Good morning. [*He goes out through the
gate and along the road.*]

FRANK [*after a pause of stupefaction, raising the rifle*]. You'll
testify before the coroner that it's an accident, Viv. [*He
takes aim at the retreating figure of* CROFTS. VIVIE *seizes the
muzzle and pulls it round against her breast.*]

VIVIE. Fire now. You may.

FRANK [*dropping his end of the rifle hastily*]. Stop! take care.
[*She lets it go. It falls on the turf.*] Oh, you've given your
little boy such a turn. Suppose it had gone off! ugh! [*He sinks
on the garden seat, overcome.*]

VIVIE. Suppose it had: do you think it would not have been a
relief to have some sharp physical pain tearing through me?

FRANK [*coaxingly*]. Take it ever so easy, dear Viv. Remember:
even if the rifle scared that fellow into telling the truth
for the first time in his life, that only makes us the babes
in the wood in earnest. [*He holds out his arms to her.*] Come
and be covered up with leaves again.

VIVIE [*with a cry of disgust*]. Ah, not that, not that. You make
all my flesh creep.

FRANK. Why, what's the matter?

VIVIE. Goodbye. [*She makes for the gate.*]

FRANK [*jumping up*]. Hallo! Stop! Viv! Viv! [*She turns in the gateway.*] Where are you going to? Where shall we find you?

VIVIE. At Honoria Fraser's chambers, 67 Chancery Lane, for the rest of my life. [*She goes off quickly in the opposite direction to that taken by* CROFTS.]

FRANK. But I say—wait—dash it! [*He runs after her.*]

ACT FOUR

[*Honoria Fraser's chambers in Chancery Lane. An office at the top of New Stone Buildings, with a plate-glass window, distempered walls, electric light, and a patent stove. Saturday afternoon. The chimneys of Lincoln's Inn and the western sky beyond are seen through the window. There is a double writing table in the middle of the room, with a cigar box, ash pans, and a portable electric reading lamp almost snowed up in heaps of papers and books. This table has knee holes and chairs right and left and is very untidy. The clerk's desk, closed and tidy, with its high stool, is against the wall, near a door communicating with the inner rooms. In the opposite wall is the door leading to the public corridor. Its upper panel is of opaque glass, lettered in black on the outside,* FRASER AND WARREN. *A baize screen hides the corner between this door and the window.*

FRANK, *in a fashionable light-colored coaching suit, with his stick, gloves, and white hat in his hands, is pacing up and down the office. Somebody tries the door with a key.*]

FRANK [*calling*]. Come in. It's not locked.

[VIVIE *comes in, in her hat and jacket. She stops and stares at him.*]

VIVIE [*sternly*]. What are you doing here?
FRANK. Waiting to see you. I've been here for hours. Is this the way you attend to your business? [*He puts his hat and stick on the table, and perches himself with a vault on the clerk's stool, looking at her with every appearance of being in a specially restless, teasing, flippant mood.*]

VIVIE. I've been away exactly twenty minutes for a cup of tea. [*She takes off her hat and jacket and hangs them up behind the screen.*] How did you get in?

FRANK. The staff had not left when I arrived. He's gone to play cricket on Primrose Hill. Why don't you employ a woman, and give your sex a chance?

VIVIE. What have you come for?

FRANK [*springing off the stool and coming close to her*]. Viv: let's go and enjoy the Saturday half-holiday somewhere, like the staff. What do you say to Richmond, and then a music hall, and a jolly supper?

VIVIE. Can't afford it. I shall put in another six hours work before I go to bed.

FRANK. Can't afford it, can't we? Aha! Look here. [*He takes out a handful of sovereigns and makes them chink.*] Gold, Viv: gold!

VIVIE. Where did you get it?

FRANK. Gambling, Viv: Gambling. Poker.

VIVIE. Pah! It's meaner than stealing it. No: I'm not coming.

[*She sits down to work at the table, with her back to the glass door, and begins turning over the papers.*]

FRANK [*remonstrating piteously*]. But, my dear Viv, I want to talk to you ever so seriously.

VIVIE. Very well: sit down in Honoria's chair and talk here. I like ten minutes chat after tea. [*He murmurs.*] No use groaning: I'm inexorable. [*He takes the opposite seat disconsolately.*] Pass that cigar box, will you?

FRANK [*pushing the cigar box across*]. Nasty womanly habit. Nice men don't do it any longer.

VIVIE. Yes: they object to the smell in the office; and we've had to take to cigarets. See! [*She opens the box and takes out a cigaret, which she lights. She offers him one; but he shakes his head with a wry face. She settles herself comfortably in her chair, smoking.*] Go ahead.

FRANK. Well, I want to know what you've done—what arrangements you've made.

VIVIE. Everything was settled twenty minutes after I arrived here. Honoria has found the business too much for her this year; and she was on the point of sending for me and proposing a partnership when I walked in and told her I hadn't a farthing in the world. So I installed myself and packed her off for a fortnight's holiday. What happened at Haslemere when I left?

FRANK. Nothing at all. I said you'd gone to town on particular business.

VIVIE. Well?

FRANK. Well, either they were too flabbergasted to say anything, or else Crofts had prepared your mother. Anyhow, she didn't say anything; and Crofts didn't say anything; and Praddy only stared. After tea they got up and went; and I've not seen them since.

VIVIE [nodding placidly with one eye on a wreath of smoke]. That's all right.

FRANK [looking round disparagingly]. Do you intend to stick in this confounded place?

VIVIE [blowing the wreath decisively away, and sitting straight up]. Yes. These two days have given me back all my strength and self-possession. I will never take a holiday again as long as I live.

FRANK [with a very wry face]. Mps! You look quite happy. And as hard as nails.

VIVIE [grimly]. Well for me that I am!

FRANK [rising]. Look here, Viv: we must have an explanation. We parted the other day under a complete misunderstanding. [He sits on the table, close to her.]

VIVIE [putting away the cigaret]. Well: clear it up.

FRANK. You remember what Crofts said?

VIVIE. Yes.

FRANK. That revelation was supposed to bring about a complete change in the nature of our feeling for one another. It placed us on the footing of brother and sister.

VIVIE. Yes.

FRANK. Have you ever had a brother?

VIVIE. No.

FRANK. Then you don't know what being brother and sister feels like? Now I have lots of sisters; and the fraternal feeling is quite familiar to me. I assure you my feeling for you is not the least in the world like it. The girls will go their way; I will go mine; and we shan't care if we never see one another again. That's brother and sister. But as to you, I can't be easy if I have to pass a week without seeing you. That's not brother and sister. It's exactly what I felt an hour before Crofts made his revelation. In short, dear Viv, it's love's young dream.

VIVIE [*bitingly*]. The same feeling, Frank, that brought your father to my mother's feet. Is that it?

FRANK [*so revolted that he slips off the table for a moment*]. I very strongly object, Viv, to have my feelings compared to any which the Reverend Samuel is capable of harboring; and I object still more to a comparison of you to your mother. [*Resuming his perch.*] Besides, I don't believe the story. I have taxed my father with it, and obtained from him what I consider tantamount to a denial.

VIVIE. What did he say?

FRANK. He said he was sure there must be some mistake.

VIVIE. Do you believe him?

FRANK. I am prepared to take his word as against Crofts'.

VIVIE. Does it make any difference? I mean in your imagination or conscience; for of course it makes no real difference.

FRANK [*shaking his head*]. None whatever to me.

VIVIE. Nor to me.

FRANK [*staring*]. But this is ever so surprising! [*He goes back to his chair.*] I thought our whole relations were altered in your imagination and conscience, as you put it, the moment those words were out of that brute's muzzle.

VIVIE. No: it was not that. I didn't believe him. I only wish I could.

FRANK. Eh?

VIVIE. I think brother and sister would be a very suitable relation for us.

FRANK. You really mean that?

VIVIE. Yes. It's the only relation I care for, even if we could afford any other. I mean that.

FRANK [*raising his eyebrows like one on whom a new light has dawned, and rising with quite an effusion of chivalrous sentiment*]. My dear Viv: why didn't you say so before? I am ever so sorry for persecuting you. I understand, of course.

VIVIE [*puzzled*]. Understand what?

FRANK. Oh, I'm not a fool in the ordinary sense: only in the Scriptural sense of doing all the things the wise man declared to be folly, after trying them himself on the most extensive scale. I see I am no longer Vivvum's little boy. Don't be alarmed: I shall never call you Vivvums again— at least unless you get tired of your new little boy, whoever he may be.

VIVIE. My new little boy!

FRANK [*with conviction*]. Must be a new little boy. Always happens that way. No other way, in fact.

VIVIE. None that you know of, fortunately for you.

[*Someone knocks at the door.*]

FRANK. My curse upon yon caller, whoe'er he be!

VIVIE. It's Praed. He's going to Italy and wants to say goodbye. I asked him to call this afternoon. Go and let him in.

FRANK. We can continue our conversation after his departure for Italy. I'll stay him out. [*He goes to the door and opens it.*] How are you, Praddy? Delighted to see you. Come in.

[PRAED, *dressed for travelling, comes in, in high spirits.*]

PRAED. How do you do, Miss Warren? [*She presses his hand cordially, though a certain sentimentality in his high spirits jars on her.*] I start in an hour for Holborn Viaduct. I wish I could persuade you to try Italy.

VIVIE. What for?

PRAED. Why, to saturate yourself with beauty and romance, of course.

[VIVIE, *with a shudder, turns her chair to the table, as if the work waiting for her there were a support to her.* PRAED *sits opposite to her.* FRANK *places a chair near* VIVIE, *and drops lazily and carelessly into it, talking at her over his shoulder.*]

FRANK. No use, Praddy. Viv is a little Philistine. She is indifferent to my romance, and insensible to my beauty.

VIVIE. Mr. Praed: once for all, there is no beauty and no romance in life for me. Life is what it is; and I am prepared to take it as it is.

PRAED [*enthusiastically*]. You will not say that if you come with me to Verona and on to Venice. You will cry with delight at living in such a beautiful world.

FRANK. This is most eloquent, Praddy. Keep it up.

PRAED. Oh, I assure you *I* have cried—I shall cry again, I hope —at fifty! At your age, Miss Warren, you would not need to go so far as Verona. Your spirits would absolutely fly up at the mere sight of Ostend. You would be charmed with the gaiety, the vivacity, the happy air of Brussels.

VIVIE [*springing up with an exclamation of loathing*]. Agh!

PRAED [*rising*]. What's the matter?

FRANK [*rising*]. Hallo, Viv!

VIVIE [*to* PRAED, *with deep reproach*]. Can you find no better example of your beauty and romance than Brussels to talk to me about?

PRAED [*puzzled*]. Of course it's very different from Verona. I don't suggest for a moment that—

VIVIE [*bitterly*]. Probably the beauty and romance come to much the same in both places.

PRAED [*completely sobered and much concerned*]. My dear Miss Warren: I—[*looking enquiringly at* FRANK]. Is anything the matter?

FRANK. She thinks your enthusiasm frivolous, Praddy. She's had ever such a serious call.

VIVIE [*sharply*]. Hold your tongue, Frank. Don't be silly.

FRANK [*sitting down*]. Do you call this good manners, Praed?

PRAED [*anxious and considerate*]. Shall I take him away, Miss

Warren? I feel sure we have disturbed you at your work.

VIVIE. Sit down: I'm not ready to go back to work yet. [PRAED *sits*.] You both think I have an attack of nerves. Not a bit of it. But there are two subjects I want dropped, if you don't mind. One of them [*To* FRANK] is love's young dream in any shape or form: the other [*To* PRAED] is the romance and beauty of life, especially Ostend and the gaiety of Brussels. You are welcome to any illusions you may have left on these subjects: I have none. If we three are to remain friends, I must be treated as a woman of business, permanently single [*To* FRANK] and permanently unromantic [*To* PRAED].

FRANK. I also shall remain permanently single until you change your mind. Praddy: change the subject. Be eloquent about something else.

PRAED [*diffidently*]. I'm afraid there's nothing else in the world that I can talk about. The Gospel of Art is the only one I can preach. I know Miss Warren is a great devotee of the Gospel of Getting On; but we can't discuss that without hurting your feelings, Frank, since you are determined not to get on.

FRANK. Oh, don't mind my feelings. Give me some improving advice by all means: it does me ever so much good. Have another try to make a successful man of me, Viv. Come: let's have it all: energy, thrift, foresight, self-respect, character. Don't you hate people who have no character, Viv?

VIVIE [*wincing*]. Oh, stop, stop: let us have no more of that horrible cant. Mr. Praed: if there are really only those two gospels in the world, we had better all kill ourselves; for the same taint is in both, through and through.

FRANK [*looking critically at her*]. There is a touch of poetry about you today, Viv, which has hitherto been lacking.

PRAED [*remonstrating*]. My dear Frank: aren't you a little unsympathetic?

VIVIE [*merciless to herself*]. No: it's good for me. It keeps me from being sentimental.

FRANK [*bantering her*]. Checks your strong natural propensity that way, don't it?

VIVIE [*almost hysterically*]. Oh yes: go on: don't spare me. I was sentimental for one moment in my life—beautifully sentimental—by moonlight; and now—

FRANK [*quickly*]. I say, Viv: take care. Don't give yourself away.

VIVIE. Oh, do you think Mr. Praed does not know all about my mother? [*Turning on* PRAED.] You had better have told me that morning, Mr. Praed. You are very old fashioned in your delicacies, after all.

PRAED. Surely it is you who are a little old fashioned in your prejudices, Miss Warren. I feel bound to tell you, speaking as an artist, and believing that the most intimate human relationships are far beyond and above the scope of the law, that though I know that your mother is an unmarried woman, I do not respect her the less on that account. I respect her more.

FRANK [*airily*]. Hear! hear!

VIVIE [*staring at him*]. Is that all you know?

PRAED. Certainly that is all.

VIVIE. Then you neither of you know anything. Your guesses are innocence itself compared to the truth.

PRAED [*rising, startled and indignant, and preserving his politeness with an effort*]. I hope not. [*More emphatically.*] I hope not, Miss Warren.

FRANK [*whistles*]. Whew!

VIVIE. You are not making it easy for me to tell you, Mr. Praed.

PRAED [*his chivalry drooping before their conviction*]. If there is anything worse—that is, anything else—are you sure you are right to tell us, Miss Warren?

VIVIE. I am sure that if I had the courage I should spend the rest of my life in telling everybody—stamping and branding it into them until they all felt their part in its abomination as I feel mine. There is nothing I despise more than the wicked convention that protects these things by forbidding a woman to mention them. And yet I can't tell you. The two infamous words that describe what my mother is are ring-

ing in my ears and struggling on my tongue; but I can't
utter them: the shame of them is too horrible for me. [*She
buries her face in her hands. The two men, astonished, stare
at one another and then at her. She raises her head again
desperately and snatches a sheet of paper and a pen.*] Here:
let me draft you a prospectus.

FRANK. Oh, she's mad. Do you hear, Viv? mad. Come! pull
yourself together.

VIVIE. You shall see. [*She writes.*] "Paid up capital: not less
than £40,000 standing in the name of Sir George Crofts,
Baronet, the chief shareholder. Premises at Brussels, Ostend, Vienna and Budapest. Managing director: Mrs. Warren"; and now don't let us forget her qualifications: the
two words. [*She writes the words and pushes the paper to
them.*] There! Oh no: don't read it: don't! [*She snatches
it back and tears it to pieces; then seizes her head in her
hands and hides her face on the table.*]

[FRANK, *who has watched the writing over her shoulder,
and opened his eyes very widely at it, takes a card from
his pocket; scribbles the two words on it; and silently
hands it to* PRAED, *who reads it with amazement, and hides
it hastily in his pocket.*]

FRANK [*whispering tenderly*]. Viv, dear: that's all right. I read
what you wrote: so did Praddy. We understand. And we
remain, as this leaves us at present, yours ever so devot-
edly.

PRAED. We do indeed, Miss Warren. I declare you are the
most splendidly courageous woman I ever met.

[*This sentimental compliment braces* VIVIE. *She throws it
away from her with an impatient shake, and forces herself to stand up, though not without some support from
the table.*]

FRANK. Don't stir, Viv, if you don't want to. Take it easy.

VIVIE. Thank you. You can always depend on me for two
things: not to cry and not to faint. [*She moves a few steps*

towards the door of the inner room, and stops close to PREAD *to say:*] I shall need much more courage than that when I tell my mother that we have come to the parting of the ways. Now I must go into the next room for a moment to make myself neat again, if you don't mind.

PRAED. Shall we go away?

VIVIE. No: I'll be back presently. Only for a moment. [*She goes into the other room,* PRAED *opening the door for her.*]

PRAED. What an amazing revelation! I'm extremely disappointed in Crofts: I am indeed.

FRANK. I'm not in the least. I feel he's perfectly accounted for at last. But what a facer for me, Praddy! I can't marry her now.

PRAED [*sternly*]. Frank! [*The two look at one another,* FRANK *unruffled,* PRAED *deeply indignant.*] Let me tell you, Gardner, that if you desert her now you will behave very despicably.

FRANK. Good old Praddy! Ever chivalrous! But you mistake: it's not the moral aspect of the case: it's the money aspect. I really can't bring myself to touch the old woman's money now.

PRAED. And was that what you were going to marry on?

FRANK. What else? *I* haven't any money, nor the smallest turn for making it. If I married Viv now she would have to support me; and I should cost her more than I am worth.

PRAED. But surely a clever bright fellow like you can make something by your own brains.

FRANK. Oh yes, a little. [*He takes out his money again.*] I made all that yesterday in an hour and a half. But I made it in a highly speculative business. No, dear Praddy: even if Bessie and Georgina marry millionaires and the governor dies after cutting them off with a shilling, I shall have only four hundred a year. And he won't die until he's three score and ten: he hasn't originality enough. I shall be on short allowance for the next twenty years. No short allowance for Viv, if I can help it. I withdraw gracefully and leave the field to the gilded youth of England. So that's settled. I shan't worry her about it: I'll just send her a little note after we're gone. She'll understand.

PRAED [*grasping his hand*]. Good fellow, Frank! I heartily beg your pardon. But must you never see her again?

FRANK. Never see her again! Hang it all, be reasonable. I shall come along as often as possible, and be her brother. I can not understand the absurd consequences you romantic people expect from the most ordinary transactions. [*A knock at the door.*] I wonder who this is. Would you mind opening the do.. ? If it's a client it will look more respectable than if I appeared.

PRAED. Certainly. [*He goes to the door and opens it.* FRANK *sits down in* VIVIE'S *chair to scribble a note.*] My dear Kitty: come in: come in.

[MRS. WARREN *comes in, looking apprehensively round for* VIVIE. *She has done her best to make herself matronly and dignified. The brilliant hat is replaced by a sober bonnet, and the gay blouse covered by a costly black silk mantle. She is pitiably anxious and ill at ease: evidently panic-stricken.*]

MRS. WARREN [*to* FRANK]. What! You're here, are you?

FRANK [*turning in his chair from his writing, but not rising*]. Here, and charmed to see you. You come like a breath of spring.

MRS. WARREN. Oh, get out with your nonsense. [*In a low voice.*] Where's Vivie?

[FRANK *points expressively to the door of the inner room, but says nothing.*]

MRS. WARREN [*sitting down suddenly and almost beginning to cry*]. Praddy: won't she see me, don't you think?

PRAED. My dear Kitty: don't distress yourself. Why should she not?

MRS. WARREN. Oh, you never can see why not: you're too innocent. Mr. Frank: did she say anything to you?

FRANK [*folding his note*]. She must see you, if [*very expressively*] you wait till she comes in.

MRS. WARREN [*frightened*]. Why shouldn't I wait?

[FRANK *looks quizzically at her; puts his note carefully on the ink-bottle, so that* VIVIE *cannot fail to find it when next she dips her pen; then rises and devotes his attention entirely to her.*]

FRANK. My dear Mrs. Warren: suppose you were a sparrow—ever so tiny and pretty a sparrow hopping in the roadway—and you saw a steam roller coming in your direction, would you wait for it?

MRS. WARREN. Oh, don't bother me with your sparrows. What did she run away from Haslemere like that for?

FRANK. I'm afraid she'll tell you if you rashly await her return.

MRS. WARREN. Do you want me to go away?

FRANK. No: I always want you to stay. But I advise you to go away.

MRS. WARREN. What! And never see her again!

FRANK. Precisely.

MRS. WARREN [*crying again*]. Praddy: don't let him be cruel to me. [*She hastily checks her tears and wipes her eyes.*] She'll be so angry if she sees I've been crying.

FRANK [*with a touch of real compassion in his airy tenderness*]. You know that Praddy is the soul of kindness, Mrs. Warren. Praddy: what do you say? Go or stay?

PRAED [*to* MRS. WARREN]. I really should be very sorry to cause you unnecessary pain; but I think perhaps you had better not wait. The fact is—[VIVIE *is heard at the inner door.*]

FRANK. Sh! Too late. She's coming.

MRS. WARREN. Don't tell her I was crying. [VIVIE *comes in. She stops gravely on seeing* MRS. WARREN, *who greets her with hysterical cheerfulness.*] Well, dearie. So here you are at last.

VIVIE. I am glad you have come: I want to speak to you. You

said you were going, Frank, I think.

FRANK. Yes. Will you come with me, Mrs. Warren? What do you say to a trip to Richmond, and the theatre in the evening? There is safety in Richmond. No steam roller there.

VIVIE. Nonsense, Frank. My mother will stay here.

MRS. WARREN [*scared*]. I don't know: perhaps I'd better go. We're disturbing you at your work.

VIVIE [*with quiet decision*]. Mr. Praed: please take Frank away. Sit down, mother. [MRS. WARREN *obeys helplessly.*]

PRAED. Come, Frank. Goodbye, Miss Vivie.

VIVIE [*shaking hands*]. Goodbye. A pleasant trip.

PRAED. Thank you: thank you. I hope so.

FRANK [*to* MRS. WARREN]. Goodbye: you'd ever so much better have taken my advice. [*He shakes hands with her. Then airily to* VIVIE.] Byebye, Viv.

VIVIE. Goodbye. [*He goes out gaily without shaking hands with her.*]

PRAED [*sadly*]. Goodbye, Kitty.

MRS. WARREN [*snivelling*].—oobye!

[PRAED *goes.* VIVIE, *composed and extremely grave, sits down in* HONORIA'S *chair, and waits for her mother to speak.* MRS. WARREN, *dreading a pause, loses no time in beginning.*]

MRS. WARREN. Well, Vivie, what did you go away like that for without saying a word to me? How could you do such a thing! And what have you done to poor George? I wanted him to come with me; but he shuffled out of it. I could see that he was quite afraid of you. Only fancy: he wanted me not to come. As if [*trembling*] I should be afraid of you, dearie. [VIVIE'S *gravity deepens.*] But of course I told him it was all settled and comfortable between us, and that we were on the best of terms. [*She breaks down.*] Vivie: what's the meaning of this? [*She produces a commercial envelope, and fumbles at the enclosure with trembling fingers.*] I got it from the bank this morning.

VIVIE. It is my month's allowance. They sent it to me as usual the other day. I simply sent it back to be placed to your credit, and asked them to send you the lodgment receipt. In future I shall support myself.

MRS. WARREN [*not daring to understand*]. Wasn't it enough? Why didn't you tell me? [*With a cunning gleam in her eye.*] I'll double it: I was intending to double it. Only let me know how much you want.

VIVIE. You know very well that that has nothing to do with it. From this time I go my own way in my own business and among my own friends. And you will go yours. [*She rises.*] Goodbye.

MRS. WARREN [*rising, appalled*]. Goodbye?

VIVIE. Yes: goodbye. Come: don't let us make a useless scene: you understand perfectly well. Sir George Crofts has told me the whole business.

MRS. WARREN [*angrily*]. Silly old— [*She swallows an epithet, and turns white at the narrowness of her escape from uttering it.*]

VIVIE. Just so.

MRS. WARREN. He ought to have his tongue cut out. But I thought it was ended: you said you didn't mind.

VIVIE [*steadfastly*]. Excuse me: I do mind.

MRS. WARREN. But I explained—

VIVIE. You explained how it came about. You did not tell me that it is still going on. [*She sits.*]

[MRS. WARREN, *silenced for a moment, looks forlornly at* VIVIE, *who waits, secretly hoping that the combat is over. But the cunning expression comes back into* MRS. WARREN'S *face; and she bends across the table, sly and urgent, half whispering.*]

MRS. WARREN. Vivie: do you know how rich I am?

VIVIE. I have no doubt you are very rich.

MRS. WARREN. But you don't know all that that means, you're too young. It means a new dress every day; it means theatres and balls every night; it means having the pick of all the gentlemen in Europe at your feet; it means a lovely house and plenty of servants; it means the choicest of eating and drinking; it means everything you like, everything you want, everything you can think of. And what are you here? A mere drudge, toiling and moiling early and late for your bare living and two cheap dresses a year. Think over it. [*Soothingly.*] You're shocked, I know. I can enter into your feelings; and I think they do you credit; but trust me, nobody will blame you: you may take my word for that. I know what young girls are; and I know you'll think better of it when you've turned it over in your mind.

VIVIE. So that's how it's done, is it? You must have said all that to many a woman, mother, to have it so pat.

MRS. WARREN [*passionately*]. What harm am I asking you to do? [VIVIE *turns away contemptuously.* MRS. WARREN *continues desperately.*] Vivie: listen to me: you don't understand: you've been taught wrong on purpose: you don't know what the world is really like.

VIVIE [*arrested*]. Taught wrong on purpose! What do you mean?

MRS. WARREN. I mean that you're throwing away all your chances for nothing. You think that people are what they pretend to be: that the way you were taught at school and college to think right and proper is the way things really are. But it's not: it's all only a pretence, to keep the cowardly slavish common run of people quiet. Do you want to find that out, like other women, at forty, when you've thrown yourself away and lost your chances; or won't you take it in good time now from your own mother, that loves you and swears to you that it's truth: gospel truth? [*Urgently.*] Vivie: the big people, the clever people, the managing people, all know it. They do as I do, and think what I think. I know plenty of them. I know them to speak to, to introduce you to, to make friends of for you. I don't mean anything wrong: that's what you don't understand: your head is full of ignorant ideas about me. What do the people that taught you know about life or about people like me? When did they ever meet me, or speak to me, or let anyone tell them about me? the fools! Would they ever have done anything for you if I hadn't paid them? Haven't I told you that I want you to be respectable? Haven't I brought you up to be respectable? And how can you keep it up without my money and my influence and Lizzie's friends? Can't you see that you're cutting your own throat as well as breaking my heart in turning your back on me?

VIVIE. I recognise the Crofts' philosophy of life, mother. I heard it all from him that day at the Gardners'.

MRS. WARREN. You think I want to force that played-out old sot on you! I don't, Vivie: on my oath I don't.

VIVIE. It would not matter if you did: you would not succeed. [MRS. WARREN *winces, deeply hurt by the implied indifference towards her affectionate intention.* VIVIE, *neither understanding this nor concerning herself about it, goes on calmly.*] Mother: you don't at all know the sort of person I am. I don't object to Crofts more than to any other coarsely built man of his class. To tell you the truth, I rather admire him for being strongminded enough to enjoy himself in his own way and make plenty of money instead of living the usual shooting, hunting, dining-out, tailoring, loafing life of his set merely because all the rest do it. And I'm perfectly aware that if I'd been in the same circumstances as my aunt Liz, I'd have done exactly what she did. I don't think I'm more prejudiced or straitlaced than you: I think I'm less. I'm certain I'm less sentimental. I know very well that fashionable morality i all a pretence, and that if I took your money and devoted the rest of my life to spending it fashionably, I might be as worthless and vicious as the silliest woman could possibly want to be without having a word said to me about it. But I don't want to be worthless. I shouldn't enjoy trotting about the park to advertise my dressmaker and carriage builder, or being bored at the opera to shew off a shopwindowful of diamonds.

MRS. WARREN [*bewildered*]. But—

VIVIE. Wait a moment: I've not done. Tell me why you continue your business now that you are independent of it. Your sister, you told me, has left all that behind her. Why don't you do the same?

MRS. WARREN. Oh, it's all very easy for Liz: she likes good society, and has the air of being a lady. Imagine me in a cathedral town! Why, the very rooks in the trees would find me out even if I could stand the dullness of it. I must have work and excitement, or I should go melancholy mad. And what else is there for me to do? The life suits me: I'm fit for it and not for anything else. If I didn't do it somebody else would; so I don't do any real harm by it. And then it brings in money; and I like making money. No: it's no use: I can't give it up—not for anybody. But what need you know about it? I'll never mention it. I'll keep Crofts away. I'll not trouble you much: you see I have to be constantly running about from one place to another. You'll be quit of me altogether when I die.

VIVIE. No: I am my mother's daughter. I am like you: I must have work, and must make more money than I spend. But my work is not your work, and my way not your way. We must part. It will not make much difference to us: instead of meeting one another for perhaps a few months in twenty years, we shall never meet: that's all.

MRS. WARREN [*her voice stifled in tears*]. Vivie: I meant to have been more with you: I did indeed.

VIVIE. It's no use, mother: I am not to be changed by a few cheap tears and entreaties any more than you are, I daresay.

MRS. WARREN [*wildly*]. Oh, you call a mother's tears cheap.

VIVIE. They cost you nothing; and you ask me to give you the peace and quietness of my whole life in exchange for them. What use would my company be to you if you could get it? What have we two in common that could make either of us happy together?

MRS. WARREN [*lapsing recklessly into her dialect*]. We're

mother and daughter. I want my daughter. I've a right to you. Who is to care for me when I'm old? Plenty of girls have taken to me like daughters and cried at leaving me; but I let them all go because I had you to look forward to. I kept myself lonely for you. You've no right to turn on me now and refuse to do your duty as a daughter.

VIVIE [*jarred and antagonized by the echo of the slums in her mother's voice*]. My duty as a daughter! I thought we should come to that presently. Now once for all, mother, you want a daughter and Frank wants a wife. I don't want a mother; and I don't want a husband. I have spared neither Frank nor myself in sending him about his business. Do you think I will spare you?

MRS. WARREN [*violently*]. Oh, I know the sort you are: no mercy for yourself or anyone else. *I* know. My experience has done that for me anyhow: I can tell the pious, canting, hard, selfish woman when I meet her. Well, keep yourself to yourself: *I* don't want you. But listen to this. Do you know what I would do with you if you were a baby again? aye, as sure as there's a Heaven above us.

VIVIE. Strangle me, perhaps.

MRS. WARREN. No: I'd bring you up to be a real daughter to me, and not what you are now, with your pride and your prejudices and the college education you stole from me: yes, stole: deny it if you can: what was it but stealing? I'd bring you up in my own house, I would.

VIVIE [*quietly*]. In one of your own houses.

MRS. WARREN [*screaming*]. Listen to her! listen to how she spits on her mother's grey hairs! Oh, may you live to have your own daughter tear and trample on you as you have trampled on me. And you will: you will. No woman ever had luck with a mother's curse on her.

VIVIE. I wish you wouldn't rant, mother. It only hardens me. Come: I suppose I am the only young woman you ever had in your power that you did good to. Don't spoil it all now.

MRS. WARREN. Yes, Heaven forgive me, it's true; and you are

the only one that ever turned on me. Oh, the injustice of
it! the injustice! the injustice! I always wanted to be a good
woman. I tried honest work; and I was slave-driven until
I cursed the day I ever heard of honest work. I was a good
mother; and because I made my daughter a good woman
she turns me out as if I was a leper. Oh, if I only had my
life to live over again! I'd talk to that lying clergyman in
the school. From this time forth, so help me Heaven in my
last hour, I'll do wrong and nothing but wrong. And I'll
prosper on it.

VIVIE. Yes: it's better to choose your line and go through with
it. If I had been you, mother, I might have done as you
did; but I should not have lived one life and believed in
another. You are a conventional woman at heart. That
is why I am bidding you goodbye now. I am right, am
I not?

MRS. WARREN [*taken aback*]. Right to throw away all my
money!

VIVIE. No: right to get rid of you? I should be a fool not to?
Isn't that so?

MRS. WARREN [*sulkily*]. Oh well, yes, if you come to that, I
suppose you are. But Lord help the world if everybody
took to doing the right thing! And now I'd better go than
stay where I'm not wanted. [*She turns to the door.*]

VIVIE [*kindly*]. Won't you shake hands?

MRS. WARREN [*after looking at her fiercely for a moment
with a savage impulse to strike her*]. No, thank you. Good-
bye.

VIVIE [*matter-of-factly*]. Goodbye. [MRS. WARREN *goes out,
slamming the door behind her. The strain on* VIVIE'S *face
relaxes; her grave expression breaks up into one of joyous
content; her breath goes out in a half sob, half laugh of
intense relief. She goes buoyantly to her place at the writing-table; pushes the electric lamp out of the way; pulls
over a great sheaf of papers; and is in the act of dipping
her pen in the ink when she find's* FRANK'S *note. She opens
it unconcernedly and reads it quickly, giving a little laugh*

at some quaint turn of expression in it.] And goodbye, Frank. [*She tears the note up and tosses the pieces into the wastepaper basket without a second thought. Then she goes at her work with a plunge, and soon becomes absorbed in its figures.*]

RED ROSES FOR ME   *[1942]*

---

by Sean O'Casey
[1880-   ]

"You may break, you may shatter the vase, if you will,
But the scent of the roses will hang round it still."

To Dr. J. D. Cummins, in memory of the grand chats
around his surgery fire

My thanks to Brigid Edwards for setting down the airs to
the songs

CHARACTERS

MRS. BREYDON

AYAMONN BREYDON, *her son*

EEADA ⎫

DYMPNA ⎬ *Mrs. Breydon's neighbours in the house*

FINNOOLA ⎭

SHEILA MOORNEEN, *Ayamonn's sweetheart*

BRENNAN O' THE MOOR, *Owner of a few oul' houses*

A SINGER, *A young man with a good voice*

ROORY O'BALACAUN, *A zealous Irish Irelander*

MULLCANNY, *A mocker of sacred things*

REV. E. CLINTON, *Rector of St. Burnupus*

SAMUEL, *Sexton to the church*

INSPECTOR FINGLAS, *Of the Mounted Police, and the Rector's churchwarden*

1ST MAN ⎫

2ND MAN ⎬ *Neighbours in the next house to Breydons'*

3RD MAN ⎭

DOWZARD ⎫

FOSTER ⎬ *Members of St. Burnupus' Select Vestry*

A LAMPLIGHTER

1ST RAILWAYMAN

2ND RAILWAYMAN

SCENES

I.—Two-roomed home of the Breydons.

II.—The same.

III.—A Dublin street, beside a bridge over the river Liffey.

IV.—Part of the grounds around the Protestant Church of St. Burnupus. In this Act the curtain is lowered for a few minutes to denote the passing of a few hours.

TIME.—A little while ago.

ACT ONE

SCENE: *The front one of two rather dilapidated rooms in a poor working-class locality. The walls, whitewashed, are dwindling into a rusty yellowish tinge. The main door, leading to the hall, is at the back, a little towards the right. The fireplace is in the right-hand wall, and a brilliant fire is burning in the large, old-fashioned grate. In the centre of the room is an old ebony-hued table on which stands a one-wick oil-lamp, its chimney a little smoky from the bad oil in the reservoir. Some books lie on the table, some paper, coloured chalks, a pen, and a small bottle of ink. In the left wall, up towards the back, is the door leading to the second room. Below this door is a horsehair sofa showing signs of old age. On it, to the head, is a neatly folded bundle of sheets and blankets, showing that it is used as a bed during the night. To the left of the main door at back is a large basket used by actors when on tour. On the other side of this door is an ordinary kitchen dresser on which some of the crockery is on the ledge, for the upper shelf is filled with a row of books, by the look of them second-hand. Over the basket, on the wall, is tacked a childlike, brightly-coloured pastel of what is meant to be a copy of one of Fra Angelico's angels blowing a curved and golden trumpet; and beside it is a small coloured reproduction of Constable's "Cornfield". In the same wall, towards the back, is a large, tall window, nearly reaching the ceiling, and, when one is in front of it, the top of a railway signal, with transverse arms, showing green and red lights, can be seen. Under this window, on a roughly made bench, stand three biscuit tins. In the first grows a geranium, in the second, musk, and in the third, a fuchsia. The disks of the geranium are extremely large and glowing; the tubular blooms of the golden musk, broad, gay, and rich; and the purple bells of the fuchsia, surrounded by their long white waxy sepals, seem to be as big as arum lilies. These crimson, gold, and purple flowers give a regal tint to the poor room. Occasionally in the distance can be heard the whistle of an engine, followed by its strenuous puffing as it pulls at a heavy rake of goods wagons. A chair or two stand about the room.*

It is towards the evening of a mid-spring day, and the hour would make it dusk, but it is darker than that, for the sky is cloudy and rain is falling heavily over the city.

AYAMONN *and his mother are in the room when the scene shows itself. He is tall, well built, twenty-two or so, with deep brown eyes, fair hair, rather bushy, but tidily kept, and his face would remind an interested observer of a rather handsome, firm-minded, thoughtful, and good-humoured bulldog. His mother is coming up to fifty, her face brownish, dark eyes with a fine glint in them, and she bears on her cheeks and brow the marks of struggle and hard work. She is dressed in a black jacket, fitting close, marred by several patches, done very neatly, dark-blue skirt, a little faded, and rather heavily-soled boots. At the moment this is all covered with a rich blue velvet cloak, broidered with silver lace, and she is sitting on a kitchen chair covered with a dark-red ragged cloth.*

AYAMONN *wears a bright green silk doublet over which is a crimson velvet armless cloak bordered with white fur. The back part of the cloak is padded so as to form a big hump between his shoulders. Across his chest is a dark-green baldric from which hangs a scabbard. A cross-hilted sword is in his hand. On his head he has a black felt hat with narrow turned-up rims. A black band goes round the hat, and a crimson feather sticks up from it. His legs are in heavy, black, working corduroy trousers, and he wears heavy hobnailed boots. She and he are in an intently listening attitude.*

MRS. BREYDON [*whispering over to* AYAMONN]. She's gone; wanted to borra something else, I suppose. They're feverish with borrowing in this blessed house!

AYAMONN. Damn her for a troublesome fool! Where's this I was when the knock came?

MRS. BREYDON. I was just goin' to say

> Ay, an' for much more slaughter after this,
> O God! forgive my sins, and pardon thee!

AYAMONN [*looking at the floor*]. Oh yes! [*He recites*]—

> What, will th' aspiring blood of Lancaster
> Sink to the ground? I thought it would have
> mounted.

[*He holds the sword aloft, and stares at it.*]

> See how my sword weeps for the poor king's
> death!
> O, may such purple tears be always shed
> For those that wish the downfall of our house!
> If any spark of life be yet remaining,
> [*He stabs at the floor.*] Down, down to hell; and
> say I sent thee thither!

[*A knuckle-knock is heard at the door.* AYAMONN *and* MRS. BREYDON *stiffen into a silent listening attitude. A fine bari-tone voice, husky with age, is heard speaking outside.*]

VOICE. Is anyone in or out or what? [*Louder raps are given as* AYAMONN *steals over, and places his back to the door.*] Eh, in there—is there anyone movin', or is the oul' shack empty?

MRS. BREYDON [*in a whisper*]. Oul' Brennan on the Moor. He was here before, today. He's got his rent for his oul' houses, an' he wants to be told again that the Bank of Ireland's a safe place to put it.

AYAMONN [*warningly*]. Ssshush!

VOICE. No answer, eh? An' me afther seein' a light in th' win-dow. Maybe they are out. For their own sakes, I hope they are; for it's hardly an honourable thing to gainsay a neigh-bour's knock.

[*The sound of feet shuffling away is heard outside, and*

then there is silence for a few moments.]

MRS. BREYDON. He's gone. He's always a bit lively the day he gets his rents. How a man, with his money, can go on livin' in two rooms in a house an' sthreet only a narrow way betther than this, I don't know. What was he but an oul' painter an' paperhanger, starvin' to save, an' usin' his cunnin' to buy up a few oul' houses, give them a lick o' paint, and charge the highest rent for th' inconvenience of livin' in them!

AYAMONN. I wish he'd keep himself and his throubles far away from me now. I've higher things to think of and greater things to do than to be attached to the agony of an old fool for ever afraid a fistful of money'll be snatched away from him. Still, he isn't a miser, for he gives kids toys at Christmas, and never puts less than half a crown on the plate in church on Sundays.

MRS. BREYDON. So well he may!

AYAMONN. What was he sayin' when he was here before?

MRS. BREYDON. Oh, th' usual question of askin' me what I thought about the Bank of Ireland; mutterin' about somebody not payin' the rent; and that his birthday's due tomorrow.

AYAMONN [*looking at the chair*]. I'll have to get a loan of a chair with arms on, and someway to make them golden to do the thing proper in the Temperance Hall; and I'll paint for the back of it, on thin cardboard, a cunning design of the House of Lancaster, the red rose, so that it'll look like a kingly seat.

MRS. BREYDON. Th' killin' o' th' king be th' Duke o' Gloster should go down well, an' th' whole thing should look sumptuous.

AYAMONN. So it will. It's only that they're afraid of Shakespeare out of all that's been said of him. They think he's beyond them, while all the time he's part of the kingdom of heaven in the nature of everyman. Before I'm done, I'll have him drinking in th' pubs with them!

MRS. BREYDON. I don't know that he'll go well with a Minstrel Show.

AYAMONN. He'll have to go well. If only King Henry doesn't rant too much, saw the air with his hands, and tear his passion to tatthers. The old fool saw someone do it that way, and thinks it must be right. [*With a sigh.*] I daren't attempt to recite my part now, for Oul' Brennan on the Moor's waitin' and listenin' somewhere down below; so I'll just get it off by heart. How old does he say he'll be tomorrow?

MRS. BREYDON. Only seventy-six, he says, an' feelin' as if he was lookin' forward to his twenty-first birthday.

AYAMONN. Well, he won't have long to wait.

MRS. BREYDON [*slyly*]. He was muttherin', too, about some air or other on the oul' piano he has at home.

AYAMONN [*springing up from where he has been sitting*]. It's one o' mine he's put an air to! [*He rushes from the room and returns in a few moments.*] He's not there; gone home, I suppose. [*Irritably.*] I wish you's told me that at first.

MRS. BREYDON. I'd thry to rest a little Ayamonn, before you go to work. You're overdoing it. Less than two hours' sleep today, and a long night's work before you. Sketchin', readin', makin' songs, an' learnin' Shakespeare: if you had a piano, you'd be thryin' to learn music. Why don't you stick at one thing, an' leave the others alone?

AYAMONN. They are all lovely, and my life needs them all.

MRS. BREYDON. I managed to get on well enough without them. [*A pause. She goes over to the window, and tenderly touches the fuchsia.*] There's this sorryful sthrike, too, about to come down on top of us.

AYAMONN [*sitting in the red-covered chair and reading Shakespeare—quietly and confidently*]. There'll be no strike. The bosses won't fight. They'll grant the extra shilling a week demanded.

MRS. BREYDON [*now fingering the musk*]. I thought this Minstrel Show was being run to gather funds together?

AYAMONN [*impatiently*]. So it is, so it is; but only in case the strike may have to take place. I haven't much to do with it, anyway. I'm with the men, spoke at a meeting in favour of the demand, and that's all.

MRS. BREYDON. You'll undhermine your health with all you're doin', tearin' away what's left of your time be runnin' afther—— [*She checks herself, and becomes silent.*]

AYAMONN [*lowing his book to his lap—angrily*]. Go on—finish what you started to say: runnin' afther who?

MRS. BREYDON. Nobody, nobody.

AYAMONN. Runnin' afther Sheila Moorneen—that's what was in your mind to say, wasn't it?

MRS. BREYDON. If it was aself; is there a new law out that a body's not to think her own thoughts?

AYAMONN [*sharply*]. What have you got against the girl?

MRS. BREYDON. Nothing. As a girl, I'd say she's a fine coloured silken shawl among a crowd of cotton ones. A girl I'd say could step away from the shadowy hedges where others slink along, tiltin' her head as she takes the centre of the road for the entherprisin' light o' day to show her off to everyone. Still—— [*She stops speaking again.*]

AYAMONN. Ay, but still what? You've a maddenin' way of never finishing some of your sentences.

MRS. BREYDON [*braving it out*]. She's a Roman Catholic; steeped in it, too, the way she'd never forgive a one for venturin' to test the Pope's pronouncement.

AYAMONN. And who wants to test the Pope's pronouncement? Life and all her vital changes'll go on testing everything, even to the Pope's pronouncement. D'ye think I've laboured as I have, and am labourin' now, to furnish myself with some of the greatness of the mighty minds of the past, just to sink down into passive acceptance of the Pope's pronouncement? Let the girl believe what she may, reverence what she can: it's her own use of her own mind. That she is fair to look upon, charming to talk with, and a dear companion, is well and away enough for me, were she even a believer in Mumbo Jumbo, and had a totem pole in her front garden

MRS. BREYDON. There's worse still than that in it.

AYAMONN. Worse, is there? An' what may that be?

MRS. BREYDON. She's th' child of a sergeant in the Royal Irish Constabulary, isn't she?

AYAMONN. Well, she can't help it, can she?

MRS. BREYDON. I know that; but many have murmured again' a son of mine goin' with the child of a man crouchin' close to their enemy.

AYAMONN. Everything, it seems, is against her, save herself. I like herself, and not her faith; I want herself, and not her father.

MRS. BREYDON. The bigger half of Ireland would say that a man's way with a maid must be regulated by his faith an' hers, an' the other half by the way her father makes his livin'.

AYAMONN. And let the whole world join them! Fair she is, and her little ear's open to hear all that I thry to say, so, were she the child of darkness aself, I'd catch her hand and lead her out and show her off to all men.

MRS. BREYDON. She wouldn't be a lot to look at afther she'd wended her way through poverty with you for a year an' a day.

AYAMONN. She gives no honour to gold; neither does her warm heart pine for silks and satins from China and Japan, or the spicy isles of Easthern Asia. A sober black shawl on her shoulders, a simple petticoat, and naked feet would fail to find her craving finer things that envious women love.

MRS. BREYDON. Ah, go on with you, Ayamonn, for a kingly fool. I'm tellin' you th' hearts of all proper girls glow with the dhream of fine things; an' I'm tellin' you, too, that the sword jinglin' on th' hip of Inspector Finglas, the red plume hangin' from his menacin' helmet, an' th' frosty silver sparklin' on his uniform, are a dazzle o' light between her tantalised eyes an' whatever she may happen to see in you.

AYAMONN. Tell me something else to add to my hope.

MRS. BREYDON. Go on readin', an' don't bother to listen to your mother.

AYAMONN [*going over and gently putting his hands on her*

shoulders]. I do listen, but I am drifting away from you, Mother, a dim shape now, in a gold canoe, dipping over a far horizon.

MRS. BREYDON [*with a catch in her voice*]. I did an' dared a lot for you, Ayamonn, my son, in my time, when jeerin' death hurried your father off to Heaven.

AYAMONN. It's I who know that well: when it was dark, you always carried the sun in your hand for me; when you suffered me to starve rather than thrive toward death in an Institution, you gave me life to play with as a richer child is given a coloured ball. [*He gently lifts up her face by putting a hand under her chin.*] The face, the dear face that once was smooth is wrinkled now; the eyes, brown still, that once were bright, have now been dimmed by a sthrained stare into the future; the sturdy back that stood so straight, is bending. A well-tried leaf, bronzed with beauty, waiting for a far-off winter wind to shake it from the tree.

MRS. BREYDON [*gently removing his hand from her chin*]. I have a tight hold still. My back can still bear many a heavy burden; and my eyes, dimmer now than once they were, can still see far enough. Well, I betther take this fancy robe off me, lest it give me gorgeous notions.

[*She takes off her robe, and leaves it carefully folded on the basket, then goes over and arranges the fire.* AYAMONN *looks thoughtfully out of the window, then takes off cloak, sword, and hat, leaving them carefully on the basket.*]

AYAMONN [*musingly*]. He'll hardly come tonight in this rain. If he does, I'll get him to read the King's part, and do mine over again.

MRS. BREYDON. Who's to come tonight?

AYAMONN. Mullcanny: he's searching Dublin for a book he wants to give me; and, if he got it, he was to bring it to-night—*The Riddle of the Universe.*

MRS. BREYDON. That's another one I wouldn't see too much of, for he has the whole neighbourhood up in arms against his reckless disregard of God, an' his mockery of everything solemn, set down as sacred.

AYAMONN. Oh, Tim is all right. The people are sensible enough to take all he says in good part; and a black flame stands out in a brightly-coloured world.

MRS. BREYDON. You don't know them, if you say that; he'll meet with a mishap, some day, if he doesn't keep his mouth shut.

AYAMONN. Nonsense.

[*She has quietly slipped a shawl around her, and is moving to the door so silently as to seem to want to prevent* AYAMONN *from noticing her movements, when the door opens and* EEADA, DYMPNA, FINNOOLA, *and several men, appear there. The three women come a little way into the room; the men stay around the door. All their faces are stiff and mask-like, holding tight an expression of dumb resignation; and are traversed with seams of poverty and a hard life. The face of* EEADA *is that of an old woman; that of* DYMPNA, *one coming up to middle age; and that of* FINNOOLA, *one of a young girl. Each shows the difference of age by more or less furrows, but each has the same expressionless stare out on life.*]

[DYMPNA *is carrying a statue of the Blessed Virgin, more than two feet high, in her arms. The figure was once a glory of purest white, sparkling blue, and luscious gilding; but the colours have faded, the gilt is gone, save for a spot or two of dull gold still lingering on the crown. She is wearing a crown that, instead of being domed, is castellated like a city's tower, resembling those of Dublin; and the pale face of the the Virgin is sadly soiled by the grime of the house. The men are dressed in drab brown, the women in a chill grey, each suit or dress having a patch of faded blue, red, green, or purple somewhere about them.*]

EEADA [*to* MRS. BREYDON]. Could you spare a pinch or two of your Hudson's soap, Mrs. Breydon, dear, to give the Blessed

Virgin a bit of a wash? [*To all in general.*] Though I've often said it's th' washin' that's done away with the bonnie blue of th' robe an' th' braver gold of its bordhers an' th' most o' th' royalty outa th' crown. Little Ursula below's savin' up her odd pennies to bring Her where She'll find a new blue robe, an' where they'll make the royalty of th' gilt glow again; though whenever she's a shillin' up, it's needed for food an' firin'; but we never yet found Our Lady of Eblana averse to sellin' Her crown an' Her blue robe to provide for Her people's need. [MRS. BREYDON *gives her half a packet of soap powder. Gratefully.*] Thank you, ma'am, an' though y'are of a different persuasion, Our Blessed Lady of Eblana's poor'll bless you an' your fine son for this little tribute to Her honour and circumspect appearance before the world.

THE REST [*murmuring*]. Ay will She, an' that's a sure thing.

[*They open a way for* EEADA *to pass out, with* DYMPNA *carrying the statue, following in a kind of a simple procession.* MRS. BREYDON *is moving slowly after them.*]

AYAMONN [*who has noticed her under his eyes*]. You're not going out again, surely—on a night like this, too?

MRS. BREYDON. Not really; only down the road to Mrs. Cashmore's. She's not too well; I promised I'd dhrop in, and see to a hot dhrink or something for her before she wandhered off to sleep.

AYAMONN [*irritably*]. You think more of other homes than you do of your own! Every night for the past week you've been going out on one silly mission or another like an imitation sisther of charity.

MRS. BREYDON. I couldn't sit quiet knowin' the poor woman needed me. I'd hear her voice all through the night complainin' I never came to give her a hot dhrink, settle her bed soft, an' make her safe for th' lonely hours of th' slow-movin' night.

AYAMONN. A lot they'd do for you if you happened to need help from them.

MRS. BREYDON. Ah, we don't know. A body shouldn't think of that, for such a belief would dismay an' dismantle everything done outside of our own advantage. No harm to use an idle hour to help another in need.

AYAMONN. An' wear yourself out in the process?

MRS. BREYDON [*with a sigh*]. I'll wear out, anyway, sometime, an' a tired ould body can, at least, go to its long rest without any excuse.

[*As she opens the door to go out,* SHEILA *appears on the threshold. She is a girl of about twenty-three, fairly tall, a fine figure, carrying herself with a sturdiness never ceasing to be graceful. She has large, sympathetic brown eyes, that dim, now and again, with a cloud of timidity. Her mouth is rather large, but sweetly made; her hair is brown and long, though now it is gathered up into a thick coil that rests on the nape of her neck. She is dressed in a tailor-made suit of rich brown tweed, golden-brown blouse, and a bright-blue hat. These are now covered with a fawn-coloured mackintosh, darkened with heavy rain, and a hastily folded umbrella is dripping on to the floor. She comes in shyly, evidently conscious of* MRS. BREYDON'S *presence; but fighting her timidity with a breezy and jovial demeanour.* MRS. BREYDON *tries, but can't keep a little stiffness out of her greeting.*]

SHEILA. Oh! good evening, Mrs. Breydon. What a night! I'm nearly blown to bits; and the rain—oh, the wind and the weather!

MRS. BREYDON. You must be perished. Take off your mac, and come over to the fire. Get Ayamonn to make you a cup o' tea, and bring you back to life again.

SHEILA. No, really; I'm burning—the battle with the wind and the rain has made me warm and lively.

AYAMONN. Hey ho, the wind and the rain, for the rain it raineth every day. Sit down and take the weight off your legs.

SHEILA. Not worth while, for I can't stop long. [*To* MRS. BREY-
DON.] Going out on a night like this, Mrs. Breydon?

AYAMONN [*hastily*]. She has to go: got an urgent call from a
poor sick neighbour.

SHEILA [*hesitatingly*]. What is it? Could . . . could I do it for
you?

AYAMONN [*decidedly*]. No, no, you couldn't. The woman knows
my mother. It's only to see her safe and warm in bed for
the night; Mother won't be long.

MRS. BREYDON. Good night, Miss Sheila; perhaps you'll be here
when I come back.

SHEILA. I don't think so. I must go almost at once.

MRS. BREYDON. Well, good night, then.

[*She goes out, and* AYAMONN *goes over to* SHEILA, *kisses her,
and helps her off with the mac.*]

SHEILA. You shouldn't let your mother go out on a night like
this—she's no longer a young woman.

AYAMONN. I don't like to interfere with her need to give help
to a neighbour. She likes it, and it does her good.

SHEILA. But the rain's coming down in sheets, and she's got but
a thin shawl round her shoulders.

AYAMONN [*impatiently*]. Oh, she hasn't very far to go. Let's
think of greater things than the pouring rain and an old
woman on her way to smooth pillows on a sick bed. Look!
—[*he feels her skirt*]—the hem's wringing. Better dry it
at the fire. Turn round and I'll unfasten it for you.

SHEILA [*forcing his hand away*]. It's nothing—you are thinking now of your own pleasure.

AYAMONN [*brightly*]. And so in that way thinking of yours too,
I hope. I never expected you today, and so the pleasure's
doubled.

SHEILA. You weren't so eager to see me when I was knocking
at the door a while ago.

AYAMONN. You! But it was Old Brennan on the Moor that was
there.

SHEILA. Before him, I was there. He hammered at the door

too.

AYAMONN [*angry with himself*]. And I thinking the rapping was that of a pestering neighbour! I might have guessed it wasn't, it was so gentle.

SHEILA. After trying to slip in unnoticed, there I was left with the whole house knowing I was at the door, and when I ran down, I heard them yelling that the stylish-dressed pusher was trying to get into Breydon's again! A nice time I'll have with my people when they hear it.

AYAMONN. I was doing my Shakespeare part, and didn't want disturbance, so there I was, standing stiff and breathless like a heron in a pond, keeping my dear one away from me! [*Going over and taking her in his arms.*] Well, it's all over now, and here you are in my arms, safe and sure and lovely.

SHEILA [*struggling away from him*]. No, it's not all over; and don't press me so hard; don't ruffle me tonight, for I feel a little tired.

AYAMONN [*peevishly*]. Tired again? Well, so am I, more than a little tired; but never too tired to put a sparkle into a welcome for a loved one.

SHEILA. Oh, Ayamonn, I do want you to be serious for one night.

AYAMONN. Very well, very well, Sheila. [*He moves away from her, and stands at the other side of the fire.*] Let us plan, then, of how we can spin joy into every moment of tomorrow's day.

SHEILA. That's why I hurried here to see you—I can't be with you tomorrow. [*There is a long pause.*]

AYAMONN. Why can't you be with me tomorrow?

SHEILA. The Daughters of St. Frigid begin a retreat tomorrow, to give the Saint a warm devotion and Mother insists I go.

AYAMONN. And I insist that you go with me. Is the Saint Frigid more to you than the sinner Ayamonn? Would you rather go to the meeting than come to see me? [*A pause.*] Would you, would you, Sheila?

SHEILA [*in a hesitant whisper*]. God forgive me, I'd rather come
  to see you.

AYAMONN. Come then; God will be sure to forgive you.

SHEILA. I daren't. My mother would be at me for ever if I failed
  to go. I've told you how she hates me to be near you. She
  chatters red-lined warnings and black-bordered appeals into
  my ears night and day, and when they dwindle for lack of
  breath, my father shakes them out of their drowsiness and
  sends them dancing round more lively still, dressed richly
  up in deadly black and gleaming scarlet.

AYAMONN. Sheila, Sheila, on the one day of the month when
  I'm free, you must be with me. I wouldn't go to a workers'
  meeting so that I might be with you.

SHEILA. There's another thing, Ayamonn—the threatened strike.
  Oh, why do you meddle with those sort of things!

AYAMONN. Oh, never mind that, now. Refuse to let yourself
  be like a timid little girl safely ensconced in a clear space
  in a thicket of thorns—safe from a scratch if she doesn't
  stir, but unable to get to the green grass or the open road
  unless she risks the tears the thorns can give.

SHEILA. Oh, Ayamonn, for my sake, if you love me, do try to
  be serious.

AYAMONN [*a little wildly*]. Oh, Sheila, our time is not yet come
  to be serious in the way of our elders. Soon enough to
  browse with wisdom when Time's grey finger puts a warning
  speck on the crimson rose of youth. Let no damned frosty
  prayer chill the sunny sighs that dread the joy of love.

SHEILA [*wildly*]. I won't listen, Ayamonn, I won't listen! We
  must look well ahead on the road to the future. You lead
  your life through too many paths instead of treading the one
  way of making it possible for us to live together.

AYAMONN. We live together now; live in the light of the burning bush. I tell you life is not one thing, but many things, a
  wide branching flame, grand and good to see and feel,
  dazzling to the eye of no-one loving it. I am not one to
  carry fear about with me as a priest carries the Host. Let
  the timid tiptoe through the way where the paler blossoms

grow; my feet shall be where the redder roses grow, though they bear long thorns, sharp and piercing, thick among them!

SHEILA [*rising from the chair—vehemently*]. I'll listen no more; I'll go. You want to make me a spark in a mere illusion. I'll go!

AYAMONN. Rather a spark from the althar of God, me girl; a spark that flames on a new path for a bubbling moment of life, or burns a song into the heart of a poet.

SHEILA. I came here as a last chance to talk things quiet with you, but you won't let me; so I'll go. [*As he seizes her in his arms.*] Let me go! [*Pleadingly.*] Please, Ayamonn, let me go!

AYAMONN. I tell you it is a gay sight for God to see joy shine for a moment on the faces of His much-troubled children. Oh, Sheila, Sheila, to be afraid of love is to be afraid for ever, for it is but the careless murmur of the rushy brook transfigured to a torrent.

SHEILA [*fearfully*]. Oh, don't bring God's name into this, for it will mean trouble to the pair of us. And your love for me lasts only while I'm here. When I'm gone, you think more of your poor painting, your poor oul' Ireland, your songs, and your workers' union than you think of Sheila.

AYAMONN. You're part of them all, in them all, and through them all; joyous, graceful, and a dearer vision; a bonnie rose, delectable and red. [*He draws her to him, presses her hard, lifts her on to his lap, and kisses her.*] Sheila, darling, you couldn't set aside the joy that makes the moon a golden berry in a hidden tree. You cannot close your ear to the sweet sound of the silver bell that strikes but once and never strikes again!

[*The door opens, and the head of* BRENNAN ON THE MOOR *looks into the room. It is a bald one, the dome highly polished; the face is wrinkled a lot, but the eyes are bright and peering. A long white beard gives him a far-away likeness to St. Jerome. He is dressed in a shabby-genteel way, and wears a long rain-soaked mackintosh. A faded bowler hat is on his head.*]

BRENNAN. Oh, dear, dear, dear me!

[*He comes into the room showing that his back is well bent, though he still has a sturdy look about him. A strap around his body holds a melodeon on his back.* SHEILA *and* AYAMONN *separate; he rises to meet the old man, while she stares, embarrassed, into the fire.*]

AYAMONN. Now what th' hell do you want?

BRENNAN [*taking no notice of* AYAMONN'S *remark—taking off his hat in a sweeping bow*]. Ah, me two sweet, snowy-breasted Dublin doves! Me woe it is to come ramblin' in through marjoram moments scentin' the serious hilarity of a genuine courtin' couple. I'm askin' now what's the dear one's name, if that isn't thresspassin' on others who are in a firmer condition of friendship? Though, be rights, it's a fair an' showy nosegay I should be throwin' through a shyly opened window into the adorable lady's lap.

SHEILA [*shyly*]. Me name is Sheila.

BRENNAN. Sheila is it? Ay, an' a Sheila are you? Ay, an' a suitable one too, for there's a gentle nature in the two soft sounds, an' a silver note in the echo, describin' grandly the pretty slendher lass me two ould eyes are now beholdin'.

AYAMONN [*going over and catching him by an arm to guide him out*]. I can't see you now, old friend, for the pair of us are heavily harnessed to a question that must be answered before either of us is a day older.

BRENNAN. Sure I know. An' isn't it only natural, too, that young people should have questions to ask and answers to give to the dewy problems that get in th' way of their dancin' feet?

AYAMONN [*impatiently*]. Come again, old friend, when time has halted us for an hour of rest.

BRENNAN. It isn't me, I'm sayin', that would be dense enough
to circumvent your longin' to be deep down in the silent consequence of regardin' each other without let or hindrance.
[*He goes towards* SHEILA, *eagerly, pulling* AYAMONN *after
him.*] It's easy seen, sweet lady, that you're well within the
compass of your young man's knowledge, an' unaware of
nothin', so I may speak as man to lady, so with cunnin'
confidence, tell me what you think of the Bank of Ireland?

AYAMONN. Oh, for goodness' sake, old man, Sheila's no intherest
in the Bank of Ireland. She cares nothing for money, or
for anything money can buy.

BRENNAN [*staring at* AYAMONN *for a moment as if he had received a shock*]. Eh? Ara, don't be talkin' nonsense, man!
Who is it daren't think of what money can buy? [*He crosses
to the door in a trot on his toes, opens it, looks out, and
closes it softly again. Then he tiptoes back to* SHEILA, *bends
down towards her, hands on knees, and whispers hoarsely.*]
I've just a little consideration of stocks and bonds nestin' in
the Bank of Ireland, at four per cent—just enough to guard
a poor man from ill, eh? Safe an' sound there, isn't it, eh?
[*To* AYAMONN.] Now, let the fair one speak out on her own.
[*Twisting his head back to Sheila.*] Safe there as if St. Peter
himself had the key of where the bonds are stationed, eh?

SHEILA. I'm sure they must be, sir.

BRENNAN [*with chuckling emphasis*]. Yehess! Aren't you the
sensible young lady; sure I knew you'd say that, without
fear or favour. [*Turning towards* AYAMONN.] What do you
say? You're a man, now, of tellin' judgement.

AYAMONN. Oh, the State would have to totther before you'd
lose a coin.

BRENNAN [*gleefully*]. Go bang, absolutely bang! Eh?

AYAMONN. Go bang!

BRENNAN. Bang! [*To* SHEILA.] Hear that, now, for a man
climbin' up to scholarship? Yehess! Stony walls, steely doors,
locks an' keys, bolts an' bars, an' all th' bonds warm an'
dhry, an' shinin' safe behind them.

SHEILA. Safe behind them.

BRENNAN [*gleefully*]. Ay, so. An' none of it sthrollin into Peter's Pence. [*Chuckling.*] Wouldn't the Pope be mad if he knew what he was missin'! Safe an' sound. [*To* AYAMONN]. You think so, too, eh?

AYAMONN. Yes, yes.

BRENNAN [*soberly*]. Ay, of course you do. [*To* SHEILA—*indicating* AYAMONN.] A good breed, me sweet an' fair one, brought up proper to see things in their right light.

AYAMONN [*catching him impatiently by the arm*]. And now, old friend, we have to get you to go.

BRENNAN. Eh?

AYAMONN. To go; Sheila and I have things to talk about.

BRENNAN [*suddenly*]. An' what about the song, then?

AYAMONN. Song?

BRENNAN. Th' one for the Show. Isn't that what brought me up? At long last, afther hard sthrainin', me an' Sammy have got the tune down in tested clefs, crotchets, an' quavers, fair set down to be sung be anyone in thrue time. An' Sammy's below, in his gay suit for the Show, waitin' to be called up to let yous hear th' song sung as only Sammy can sing it.

AYAMONN. Bring him up, bring him up—why in hell didn't you tell me all this before?

BRENNAN [*stormily*]. Wasn't I thryin' all the time an' you wouldn't let a man get a word in edgeways. [*Gesturing towards* SHEILA.] He'll jib at singin' in front of her. [*He whispers hoarsely towards* SHEILA.] He's as shy as a kid in his first pair o' pants, dear lady.

AYAMONN [*impatiently pushing him out of the room*]. Oh, go on, go on, man, and bring him up. [BRENNAN *goes out.*]

SHEILA [*earnestly.*] Wait till I'm gone, Ayamonn; I can't stop long, and I want to talk to you so much.

AYAMONN [*a little excited*]. Oh, you must hear the song, Sheila; they've been working to get the air down for a week, and it won't take a minute.

SHEILA [*angrily*]. I've waited too long already! Aren't you more interested in what I want to say than to be listening to some vain fool singing a song?

AYAMONN [*a little taken aback*]. Oh, Sheila, what's wrong with you tonight? The young carpenter who'll sing it, so far from being vain, is as shy as a field-mouse, and you'll see, when he starts to sing, he'll edge his face away from us. You do want to hear it, Sheila, don't you?

SHEILA [*appealingly*]. Let it wait over, Ayamonn; I can come to hear it some other time. I do want to say something, very serious, to you about our future meetings.

AYAMONN [*hastily*]. All right then; I'll hurry them off the minute the song's sung. Here they are, so sit down, do, just for one minute more.

[*But she goes towards the door, and reaches it just as OLD BRENNAN returns shoving in before him a young man of twenty-three, shy, and loth to come in. He is tall, but his face is pale and mask-like in its expression of resignation to the world and all around him. Even when he shows he's shy, the mask-like features do not alter. He is dressed in a white cut-away coat, shaped like a tailed evening dress, black waistcoat over a rather soiled shirt-front, frilled, and green trousers. He carries a sheet of manuscript music in his hand. BRENNAN unslings his melodeon from his back, fusses the young SINGER forward; bumping against SHEILA, who has moved toward the door, he pushes her back with a shove of his backside; and puts AYAMONN to the other end of the room with a push on the shoulder.*]

BRENNAN [*as he pushes SHEILA*]. Outa th' way, there! Stem your eagerness for a second, will yous? All in good time. Give the man a chance to get himself easy. [*As he pushes AYAMONN.*] Farther back, there, farther back! Give th' performer a chance to dispose himself. Isn't he a swell, wha'? The centre group's to be dhressed the same way, while th' corner men'll be in reverse colours—green coats, black trousers, an' white vest, see? Th' whole assembly'll look

famous. Benjamin's lendin' all the set o' twelve suits for
five bob, 'cause o' th' reason we're runnin' th' Show for.
[*To* SHEILA—*in a hoarse whisper.*] You stare at the fire
as if he wasn't here. He's extravagant in shyness, an'
sinks away into confusion at the stare of an eye—understand?

[*She slowly, and a little sullenly, sits down to stare into the
fire. The door is opened, and in comes* ROORY O'BALACAUN
*with a small roll of Irish Magazines under an arm. He
is a stout middle-aged man, dressed in rough homespun
coat, cap, and knee-breeches, wearing over all a trench
coat.*]

ROORY. Here y'are, Ayamonn, me son, avic's th' Irish magazines I got me friend to pinch for you. [*He looks at the*
SINGER.] Hello, what kind of a circus is it's goin' on here?

AYAMONN. Mr. Brennan Moore here's organising the singers
for the Minsthrel Show to help get funds in case we have
to go on sthrike, Roory.

ROORY. I'm one o' th' men meself, but I don't stand for a foreign Minsthrel Show bein' held, an' the Sword of Light
gettin' lifted up in th' land. We want no coon or Kaffir industry in our country.

BRENNAN [*indignantly*]. Doesn't matter what you stand for
before you came here, you'll sit down now. Thry to regard
yourself as a civilised member of the community, man, an'
hold your peace for th' present. [*To the* SINGER.] Now, Sam,
me son o' gold, excavate the shyness out of your system an' sing as if you were performin' before a Royal Command!

ROORY [*with a growl*]. There's no royal commands wanted
here.

BRENNAN [*with a gesture of disgusted annoyance*]. Will you
for goodness' sake not be be puttin' th' singer out? I used
the term only as an allegory, man.

ROORY. Allegory man, or allegory woman, there's goin' to be

no royal inthrusions where the Sword o' Light is shinin'.

AYAMONN. Aw, for Christ's sake, Roory, let's hear the song!

BRENNAN [*to the* SINGER, *who has been coughing shyly and turning sideways from his audience*]. Now, Sam, remember you're not in your working clothes, an' are a different man, entirely. Chin up and chest out. [*He gives a note or two on the melodeon.*] Now!

SINGER [*singing*].

> A sober black shawl hides her body entirely,
> Touch'd by th' sun and th' salt spray of the
>   sea;
> But down in th' darkness a slim hand, so
>   lovely,
> Carries a rich bunch of red roses for me.

[*He turns away a little more from his audience and coughs shyly.*]

BRENNAN [*enthusiastically*]. Sam, you're excellin' yourself! On again, me oul' son!

SINGER [*singing*].

> Her petticoat's simple, her feet are but bare,
> An' all that she has is but neat an' scantie;
> But stars in th' deeps of her eyes are exclaiming
> I carry a rich bunch of red roses for thee!

BRENNAN [*after giving a few curling notes on the melodeon*]. A second Count McCormack in th' makin'! An' whenever he sung Mother Mo Chree, wasn't there a fewroory in Heaven with the rush that was made to lean over an' hear his singin' it!

[*While* BRENNAN *has been speaking, the door has opened, and* MULLCANNY *now stands there gaping into the room. He is young, lusty, and restless. He is wearing fine tweeds that don't fit too well; and his tweed cap is set rakishly on his head. He, too, wears a mackintosh.*]

MULLCANNY. Is this a home-sweet-away-from-home hippodrome, or what?

BRENNAN [*clicking his tongue in annoyance*].Dtchdtchdtch!

MULLCANNY. An' did I hear someone pratin' about Heaven, an' I coming in? [*To* BRENNAN—*tapping him on the shoulder.*] Haven't you heard, old man, that God is dead?

BRENNAN. Well, keep your grand discovery to yourself for a minute or two more, please. [*To the* SINGER.] Now, Sam, apologisin' for th' other's rudeness, the last verse, please.

SINGER [*singing*].

> No arrogant gem sits enthron'd on her forehead,
> Or swings from a white ear for all men to see;
> But jewel'd desire in a bosom, most pearly,
> Carries a rich bunch of red roses for me!

BRENNAN [*after another curl of notes on the melodeon*]. Well, fair damsel and gentlemen all, what do you think of the song and the singer?

AYAMONN. The song was good, and the singer was splendid.

MULLCANNY. What I heard of it wasn't bad.

SINGER [*shyly*]. I'm glad I pleased yous all.

ROORY [*dubiously*]. D'ye not think th' song is a trifle indecent?

MULLCANNY [*mockingly*]. Indecent! And what may your eminence's specification of indecency be? [*Angrily.*] Are you catalogued, too, with the Catholic Young Men going about with noses long as a snipe's bill, sthripping the gayest rose of its petals in search of a beetle, and sniffing a taint in the freshest breeze blowing in from the sea?

BRENNAN [*warningly*]. Lady present, lady present, boys!

ROORY. It ill becomes a thrue Gael to stand unruffled when either song or story thries to introduce colour to the sabler nature of yearnin's in untuthored minds.

BRENNAN [*more loudly*]. Lady present, boys!

SHEILA [*rising out of the chair and going towards the door*]. The lady's going now, thank you all for the entertainment. [*To* AYAMONN]. I won't stay any longer to disturb the important dispute of your friends.

AYAMONN [*going over to her*]. Don't be foolish, Sheila, dear; but if you must go, you must. We'll see each other again tomorrow evening.

SHEILA [*firmly*]. No, not tomorrow, nor the next night either.

AYAMONN [*while* BRENNAN *plays softly on the melodeon to hide embarrassment*]. When then?

SHEILA. I can't tell. I'll write. Never maybe. [*Bitterly.*] I warned you this night might be the last chance of a talk for some time, and you didn't try to make use of it!

AYAMONN [*catching her arm*]. I made as much use of it as you'd let me. Tomorrow night, in the old place, near the bridge, the bridge of vision where we first saw Aengus and his coloured birds of passion passing.

SHEILA [*wildly*]. I can't; I won't, so there—oh, let me go!

[*She breaks away from him, runs out, and a silence falls on the room for a few moments.*]

ROORY [*breaking the silence*]. Women is strange things! Elegant animals, not knowin' their own minds a minute.

BRENNAN [*consolingly*]. She'll come back, she'll come back.

AYAMONN [*trying to appear unconcerned*]. Aw, to hell with her!

SINGER [*faintly*]. Can I go now?

BRENNAN. Wait, an' I'll be with you in a second.

MULLCANNY [*to* AYAMONN]. I just dropped in to say, Ayamonn, that I'll be getting Haeckel's *Riddle of the Universe* tomorrow, afther long searching, and I'll let you have it the minute it comes into my hand.

[*The door is suddenly flung wide open, and* EEADA, *followed by* DYMPNA *and* FINNOOLA, *with others, mingled with men behind them, rushes into the room in a very excited state. She comes forward, with her two companions a little behind, while the rest group themselves by the door.*]

EEADA [*distractedly*]. It's gone she is, an' left us lonesome; vanished she is like a fairy mist of an early summer mornin';

stolen she is be some pagan Protestan' hand, envious of
the love we had for our sweet Lady of Eblana's poor!

AYAMONN. Nonsense; no Protestant hand touched her. Where
was she?

DYMPNA. Safe in her niche in th' hall she was, afther her
washin' lookin' down on the comin's an' goin's of her strug-
glin' children: an' then we missed her, an' th' niche was
empty!

THE REST [in chorus]. An' dear knows that woe'll fall on our
poor house now.

BRENNAN. An' a good job, too. [Passionately]. Inflamin' yourselves with idols that have eyes an' see not; ears, an' hear
not; an' have hands that handle not; like th' chosen people
settin' moon-images an' sun-images, cuttin' away the thrue
and homely connection between the Christian an' his God!
Here, let me and me singer out of this unholy place!

[He pushes his way through the people, followed by the
SINGER, and goes out.]

EEADA [nodding her head, to AYAMONN]. All bark, but no bite!
We know him of old: a decent oul' blatherer. Sure, doesn't
he often buy violets and snowdhrops, even, for little Ursula,
below, tellin' her she mustn't put them before a graven
image, knowin' full well that that was th' first thing she'd
hurry home to do. An' she's breakin' her young heart below, now, because her dear Lady has left her. [Suspiciously.]
If oul' Brennan had a hand in her removal, woe betide
him.

MULLCANNY [mocking]. Couldn't you all do betther than wast-
ing your time making gods afther your own ignorant images?

AYAMONN [silencing him with a gesture]. That's enough, Pau-
dhrig. [To EEADA.] Tell little Ursula not to worry. Her
Lady'll come back. If your Lady of Eblana hasn't returned
by tonight, I'll surrender my sleep afther my night's work
to search for her, and bring her back safe to her niche in
the hall. No one in this house touched Her.

EEADA. An' you'll see She'll pay you back for your kindness, Ayamonn—[*Looking at* MULLCANNY.]—though it's little surprised I'd be if, of her own accord, She came down indignant, an' slipped off from us, hearin' the horrid talk that's allowed to float around this house lately.

MULLCANNY [*mocking*]. Afraid of me, She was. Well, Ayamonn, I've some lessons to get ready, so I'll be off. I'll bring you the book tomorrow. [*To the crowd—mocking.*] I hope the poor Lady of Eblana's poor'll find her way home again.

[*He goes out through a surly-faced crowd.*]

AYAMONN [*to* EEADA]. Don't mind Mullcanny. Good night, now; and don't worry about your dear statue. If She doesn't come back, we'll find another as bright and good to take her place.

EEADA [*growling*]. The fella that's gone'll have a rough end, jeerin' things sacred to our feelin'. For his own sake, I hope th' B. Virgin'll come to live with us all again.

[*They all go out, and* AYAMONN *is left alone with* ROORY. AYAMONN *takes off his doublet, folds it up, and puts it back in the basket. He goes into the other room and comes back with oilskin coat and thigh-high leggings. He puts the leggings on over his trousers.*]

AYAMONN [*putting on the leggings*]. Th' shunting-yard'll be a nice place to be tonight. D'ye hear it? [*He listens to the falling rain, now heavier than ever.*]

ROORY. Fallin' fast. That Mullcanny'll get into throuble yet.

AYAMONN. Not he. He's really a good fellow. Gave up his job rather than his beliefs—more'n many would do.

ROORY. An' how does he manage now?

AYAMONN. Hammering knowledge into deluded minds wishing to be civil servants, bank clerks, an' constables who hope to take the last sacraments as sergeants in the Royal Irish Constabulary or the Metropolitan Police.

ROORY. By God, he's his work cut out for him with the last lot!

[*The door is again opened and* EEADA *sticks her head into the room.*]

EEADA. Your mother's just sent word that the woman she's mindin's bad, an' she'll have to stay th' night. I'm just runnin' round meself to make your mother a cup o' tea.

AYAMONN [*irritably*]. Dtch dtch—she'll knock herself up before she's done! When I lock up, I'll leave the key with you for her, Eeada. [*He lights a shunter's lantern and puts out the lamp.*]

EEADA. Right y'are. [*She goes.*]

ROORY. What kid was it sketched th' angel on th' wall?

AYAMONN. Oh, I did that. I'd give anything to be a painter.

ROORY. What, like Oul' Brennan on th' Moor?

AYAMONN. No, no; like Angelico or Constable.

ROORY [*indifferently*]. Never heard of them.

AYAMONN [*musingly*]. To throw a whole world in colour on a canvas though it be but a man's fine face, a woman's shape asthride of a cushioned couch, or a three-bordered house on a hill, done with a glory; even delaying God, busy forgin' a new world, to stay awhile an' look upon their loveliness.

ROORY. Aw, Ayamonn, Ayamonn, man, put out your hand an' see if you're awake! [*He fiddles with the books on the table.*] What oul' book are you readin' now?

AYAMONN [*dressed now in oilskin leggings and coat, with an oilskin sou'wester on his head, comes over to look at the book in* ROORY'S *hand, and shines the lantern on it*]. Oh, that's Ruskin's *Crown of Wild Olives*—a grand book—I'll lend it to you.

ROORY. What for? What would I be doin' with it? I've no time to waste on books. Ruskin. Curious name; not Irish, is it?

AYAMONN. No, a Scotsman who wrote splendidly about a lot of things. Listen to this, spoken before a gathering of business men about to build an Exchange in their town.

ROORY. Aw, Ayamonn—an Exchange! What have we got to do with an Exchange?

AYAMONN [*impatiently*]. Listen a second, man! Ruskin, speakin'
to the business men, says: "Your ideal of life is a pleasant
and undulating world, with iron and coal everywhere beneath it. On each pleasant bank of this world is to be a
beautiful mansion; stables, and coach-houses; a park and
hot-houses; carriage-drives and shrubberies; and here are to
live the votaries of the Goddess of Getting-On—the English
gentleman——"

ROORY [*interrupting*]. There you are, you see, Ayamonn—th'
English gentleman!

AYAMONN. Wait a second—Irish or English—a gentleman's
th' same.

ROORY. 'Tisn't. I'm tellin' you it's different. What's in this Ruskin
of yours but another oul' cod with a gift of the gab? Right
enough for th' English, pinin' afther little things, ever
rakin' cindhers for th' glint o' gold. We're different—we
have th' light.

AYAMONN. You mean th' Catholic Faith?

ROORY [*impatiently*]. No, no; that's there, too; I mean th' light
of freedom; th' tall white candle tipped with its golden
spear of flame. The light we thought we'd lost; but it burns
again, sthrengthenin' into a sword of light. Like in th' song
we sung together th' other night. [*He sings softly.*]

> Our courage so many have thought to be agein',
>   Now flames like a brilliant new star in th' sky;
> And Danger is proud to be call'd a good brother,
>   For Freedom has buckled her sword on her thigh.

AYAMONN [*joining in*].

> Then out to th' place where th' battle is bravest,
> Where th' noblest an' meanest fight fierce in th'
>   fray,
> There Republican banners shall mock at th'
>   foemen,
> An' Fenians shall turn th' dark night into day!

[*A pause as the two of them stand silent, each clasping the other's hand.* AYAMONN *opens the door to pass out.*]

ROORY [*in a tense whisper*]. Th' Fenians are in force again, Ayamonn; th' Sword o' Light is shinin'!

[*They go out, and* AYAMONN *closes the door as the Curtain falls.*]

ACT TWO

SCENE: *The same as in Act I.*

It is about ten o'clock at night. The rain has stopped, and there is a fine moon sailing through the sky. Some of its rays come in through the window at the side.

AYAMONN, *in his shirt-sleeves, is sitting at the table. He has an ordinary tin money-box in his hand, and a small pile of coppers, mixed with a few sixpences, are on the table beside him. He is just taking the last coin from the slit in the box with the aid of a knife-blade. His mother is by the dresser piling up the few pieces of crockery used for a recent meal. The old one-wick lamp is alight, and stands on the table near to* AYAMONN. *Several books lie open there, too.*

AYAMONN. There's th' last one out, now. It's quite a job getting them out with a knife.

MRS. BREYDON. Why don't you put them in a box with a simple lid on?

AYAMONN. The harder it is to get at, the less chance of me spending it on something more necessary than what I seek. [*He counts the money on the table.*] One bob—two—three —an' sixpence—an' nine—three an' ninepence; one an' threepence to get yet—a long way to go.

MRS. BREYDON. Maybe, now, th' bookseller would give you it for what you have till you can give him th' rest.

AYAMONN [*in agony*]. Aw, woman, if you can't say sense, say nothing! Constable's reproductions are five shillings second-hand, an' he that's selling is the bastard that nearly got me jailed for running off with his Shakespeare. It's touch an go if he'll let me have it for the five bob.

MRS. BREYDON [*philosophically*]. Well, seein' you done without it so long, you can go without it longer.

AYAMONN [*with firm conviction*]. I'll have it the first week we get the extra shilling the men are demandin'.

MRS. BREYDON. I shouldn't count your chickens before they're hatched.

AYAMONN [*joking a little bitterly*]. Perhaps our blessed Lady of Eblana's poor will work a miracle for me.

MRS. BREYDON [*a little anxiously*]. Hush, don't say that! Jokin' or serious, Ayamonn, I wouldn't say that. We don't believe in any of their Blessed Ladies, but as it's somethin' sacred, it's best not mentioned. [*She shuffles into her shawl.*] Though it's a queer thing, Her goin' off out of Her niche without a one in th' house knowin' why. They're all out huntin' for Her still.

[*The door opens, and* BRENNAN *comes in slowly, with a cute grin on his face. He has a large package, covered with paper, under an arm.*]

BRENNAN. Out huntin' still for Her they are, are they? Well, let them hunt; she's here! A prisoner under me arm!

MRS. BREYDON [*indignantly*]. Well, Mr. Brennan Moore, it's ashamed of yourself you should be yokin' th' poor people to throubled anxiety over their treasure; and little Ursula breakin' her heart into th' bargain.

AYAMONN. It's god-damned mean of you, Brennan! What good d'ye think you'll do by this rowdy love of your own opinions—forcing tumult into the minds of ignorant, anxious people?

BRENNAN [*calmly*]. Wait till yous see, wait till yous see, before yous are sorry for sayin' more.

[*He removes the paper and shows the lost image transfigured into a figure looking as if it had come straight from the shop: the white dress is spotless, the blue robe radiant, and the gold along its border and on the crown is gleaming. He holds it up for admiration.*]

BRENNAN [*triumphantly*]. There, what d'ye think of Her now? Fair as th' first grand tinge of th' dawn, She is, an' bright as th' star of the evenin'.

MRS. BREYDON. Glory be to God, isn't She lovely! But hurry Her off, Brennan, for She's not a thing for Protestant eyes to favour.

AYAMONN [*a little testily*]. Put it back, Brennan, put it back, and don't touch it again.

BRENNAN. Isn't that what I'm goin' to do? Oh, boy alive, won't they get th' shock o' their lives when they see Her shinin' in th' oul' spot. [*He becomes serious.*] Though, mind you, me thrue mind misgives me for decoratin' what's a charm to the people of Judah in th' worship of idols; but th' two of you is witness I did it for the sake of the little one, and not in any tilt towards honour to a graven image.

MRS. BREYDON [*resignedly*]. It's done now, God forgive us both, an' me for sayin' She's lovely. Touchin' a thing forbidden with a startled stir of praise!

AYAMONN. Put it back, put it back, man, and leave it quiet where you got it first.

[BRENNAN *goes out, looking intently out, and listening, before he does so.*]

MRS. BREYDON. He meant well, poor man, but he's done a dangerous thing. I'll be back before you start for work. [*With a heavy sigh.*] It won't take us long to tend her for the last time. The white sheets have come, th' fall candles wait to be lit, an' th' coffin's ordhered, an' th' room'll look sacred with the bunch of violets near her head. [*She goes out slowly—as she goes.*] Dear knows what'll happen to th' three childrhen.

[AYAMONN *sits silent for a few moments, reading a book, his elbows resting on the table.*]

AYAMONN [*with a deep sigh—murmuringly*]. Sheila, Sheila, my heart cries out for you! [*After a moment's pause, he reads.*]

But I am pigeon-livered, an' lack gall
   To make oppression bitther; or, ere this,
I should have fatted all th' region kites
With this slave's offal: Bloody, bawdy villain!
Oh, Will, you were a boyo; a brave boyo, though, and a
beautiful one!

[*The door opens and* OLD BRENNAN *comes in, showing by
his half-suppressed chuckles that he is enjoying himself. He
wanders over the room to stand by the fire.*]

BRENNAN [*chuckling*]. In Her old place she is, now, in Her new
coronation robe; and funny it is to think it's the last place
they'll look for Her.

AYAMONN. I'm busy, now.

BRENNAN [*sitting down by the fire*]. Ay, so you are; so I see;
busy readin'. Read away, for I won't disturb you; only have
a few quiet puffs at th' oul' pipe. [*A pause.*] Ah, then, don't
I wish I was young enough to bury meself in th' joy of
readin' all th' great books of th' world. Ah! but when I was
young, I had to work hard.

AYAMONN. I work hard, too.

BRENNAN. Course you do! Isn't that what I'm sayin'? An' all
th' more credit, too, though it must be thryin' to have
thoughtless people comin' in an' intherferin' with the gold-
en movements of your thoughts.

AYAMONN. It's often a damned nuisance!

BRENNAN. 'Course it is. Isn't that what I'm sayin'? [*As the door
opens.*] An' here's another o' th' boobies entherin' now.
[ROORY *comes in, and shuts the door rather noisily*.] Eh, go
easy, there—can't you see Ayamonn's busy studyin'?

ROORY [*coming and bending over* AYAMONN]. Are you still
lettin' oul' Ruskin tease you?

AYAMONN [*angrily*]. No, no; Shakespeare, Shakespeare, this
time! [*Springing from his chair.*] Damn it, can't you let a
man alone a minute? What th' hell d'ye want now?

BRENNAN [*warningly*]. I told you he was busy.

ROORY [*apologetically*]. Aw, I only came with the tickets you

asked me to bring you for the comin' National Anniversary
of Terence Bellew MacManus.

AYAMONN. All right, all right; let's have them.

ROORY. How many d'ye want? How many can you sell?

AYAMONN. Give me twelve sixpennies; if the sthrike doesn't
come off I'll easily sell that number.

ROORY [*counting out the tickets which* AYAMONN *gathers up
and puts into his pocket*]. I met that Mullcanny on the way
with a book for you; but he stopped to tell a couple of railwaymen that the story of Adam an' Eve was all a cod.

BRENNAN [*indignantly*]. He has a lot o' the people here in a
state o' steamin' anger, goin' about with his bitther belief
that the patthern of a man's hand is nearly at one with a
monkey's paw, a horse's foot, th' flipper of a seal, or th' wing
of a bat!

AYAMONN. Well, each of them is as wonderful as the hand of
a man.

ROORY. No, Ayamonn, not from the Christian point of view.
D'ye know what they're callin' him round here? Th' New
Broom, because he's always sayin' he'll sweep th' idea of
God clean outa th' mind o' man.

BRENNAN [*excited*]. There'll be dire damage done to him yet!
He was goin' to be flattened out be a docker th' other day
for tellin' him that a man first formin' showed an undoubted
sign of a tail.

AYAMONN. Ay, and when he's fully formed, if he doesn't show
the tail, he shows most signs of all that goes along with it.

ROORY. But isn't that a nice dignity to put on th' sacredness of
a man's conception!

BRENNAN [*whisperingly*]. An' a lot o' them are sayin', Ayamonn,
that your encouragement of him should come to an end.

AYAMONN. Indeed? Well, let them. I'll stand by any honest man
seekin' th' truth, though his way isn't my way. [*To* BREN-
NAN.] You, yourself, go about deriding many things beloved by your Catholic neighbours.

BRENNAN. I contest only dangerous deceits specified be the
Council o' Thrent, that are nowhere scheduled in th' pages

of the Holy Scriptures.

ROORY. Yes, Ayamonn, it's altogether different; he just goes about blatherin' in his ignorant Protestant way.

BRENNAN [*highly indignant*]. Ignorant, am I? An' where would a body find an ignorance lustier than your own, eh? If your Council o' Thrent's ordher for prayers for the dead who are past help, your dismal veneration of Saints an' Angels, your images of wood an' stone, carved an' coloured, have given you the image an' superscription of a tail, th' pure milk of the gospel has made a man of me, Godfearin', but stately, with a mind garlanded to th' steady an' eternal thruth!

[*While they have been arguing,* MULLCANNY *has peeped round the door, and now comes into the room, eyeing the two disputants with a lot of amusement and a little scorn. They take no notice of him.*]

ROORY. Sure, man, you have the neighbourhood hectored with your animosity against Catholic custom an' Catholic thought, never hesitatin' to give th' Pope even a deleterious name.

BRENNAN [*lapsing, in his excitement, into a semi-Ulster dialect*]. We dud ut tae yeh in Durry, on' sent your bravest floatin' down dud in th' wathers of th' Boyne, like th' hosts of Pharaoh tumblin' in the rush of th' Rud Sea! Thut was a slup in th' puss tae your Pope!

MULLCANNY. You pair of damned fools, don't you know that the Pope wanted King Billy to win, and that the Vatican was ablaze with lights of joy afther King James' defeat over the wathers of the Boyne?

ROORY. You're a liar, he didn't!

BRENNAN. You're a liar, it wasn't!

[*They turn from* MULLCANNY *to continue the row with themselves.*]

BRENNAN. Looksee, if I believed in the ministhration of Saints on' Angels, I'd say thut th' good Protestant St. Puthrick

was at the hud of what fell out at Durry, Aughrim, on' th'
Boyne.

ROORY [*stunned with the thought of St. Patrick as a Protestant*].
Protestant St. Pathrick? Is me hearin' sound, or what? What
name did you mention?

BRENNAN. I said St. Puthrick—th' evangelical founder of our
thrue Church.

ROORY. Is it dhreamin' I am? Is somethin' happenin' to me, or
is it happenin' to you? O, man, it's mixin' mirth with madness you are at thinkin' St. Pathrick ever looped his neck
in an orange sash, or tapped out a tune on a Protestant
dhrum! Let us only keep silent for a minute or two, an'
we'll hear him sayin' that th' hymn St. Pathrick sung an'
he on th' way to meet King Laeghaire, an' quench th' fire
o' Tara, was Lilly Bullero Bullen a Law!

BRENNAN [*contemptuously*]. I refuse to argue with a one who's
no' a broadminded mon. Abuse is no equivalent for lugic—
—so I say God save th' King, an' tae hull with th' Pope!

ROORY [*indignantly*]. You damned bigot—to hell with th' King,
an' God save th' Pope!

MULCANNY [*to* AYAMONN]. You see how they live in bitther-
ness, the one with the other. Envy, strife, and malice crawl
from the coloured slime of the fairy-tales that go to make
what is called religion. [*Taking a book from his pocket.*]
Here's something can bear a thousand tests, showing neatly
how the world and all it bears upon it came into slow existence over millions of years, doing away for ever with the
funny wonders of the seven days' creation set out in the
fairy book of the Bible.

AYAMONN [*taking the book from* MULLCANNY]. Thanks, Pether,
oul' son; I'm bound to have a good time reading it.

MULLCANNY. It'll give you the true and scientific history of
man as he was before Adam.

BRENNAN [*in a woeful voice*]. It's a darkened mind that thries
tae lower us to what we were before th' great an' good God
fashioned us. What does ony sensible person want to know
what we were like before the creation of th' first man?

AYAMONN [*murmuringly*]. To know the truth, to seek the truth, is good, though it lead to th' danger of eternal death.

ROORY [*horror-stricken—crossing himself*]. Th' Lord between us an' all harm!

BRENNAN [*whispering prayerfully*]. Lord, I believe, help Thou mine unbelief.

MULLCANNY [*pointing out a picture in the book*]. See? The human form unborn. The tail—look; the os coccyx sticking a mile out; there's no getting away from it!

BRENNAN [*shaking his head woefully*]. An' this is holy Ireland!

ROORY [*lifting his eyes to the ceiling—woefully*]. Poor St. Pathrick!

MULLCANNY [*mockingly*]. He's going to be a lonely man soon, eh? [*To* AYAMONN.] Keep it safe for me, Ayamonn. When you've read it, you'll be a different man. [*He goes to the door.*] Well, health with the whole o' you, and goodbye for the present. [*He goes out.*]

ROORY. Have nothin' to do with that book, Ayamonn, for that fellow gone out would rip up the floor of Heaven to see what was beneath it. It's clapped in jail he ought to be!

BRENNAN. An' th' book banned!

AYAMONN. Roory, Roory, is that th' sort o' freedom you'd bring to Ireland with a crowd of green branches an' th' joy of shouting? If we give no room to men of our time to question many things, all things, ay, life itself, then freedom's but a paper flower, a star of tinsel, a dead lass with gay ribbons at her breast an' a gold comb in her hair. Let us bring freedom here, not with sounding brass an' tinkling cymbal, but with silver trumpets blowing, with a song all men can sing, with a palm branch in our hand, rather than with a whip at our belt, and a headsman's axe on our shoulders.

[*There is a gentle knock at the door, and the voice of* SHEILA *is heard speaking.*]

SHEILA [*outside*]. Ayamonn, are you there? Are you in?

BRENNAN [*whispering*]. The little lass; I knew she'd come back.

AYAMONN. I don't want her to see you here. Go into the other room—quick. [*He pushes them towards it.*] An' keep still.

ROORY [*to* BRENNAN]. An' don't you go mockin' our Pope, see?

BRENNAN [*to* ROORY]. Nor you go singlin' out King Billy for a jeer.

AYAMONN. In with yous, quick!

BRENNAN. I prophesied she'd come back, didn't I, Ayamonn? that she'd come back, didn't I?

AYAMONN. Yes, yes; in you go.

[*He puts them in the other room and shuts the door. Then he crosses the room and opens the door to admit* SHEILA. *She comes in, and he and* SHEILA *stand silently for some moments, she trying to look at him, and finding it hard.*]

SHEILA [*at last*]. Well, haven't you anything to say to me?

AYAMONN [*slowly and coldly*]. I waited for you at the bridge today; but you didn't come.

SHEILA. I couldn't come; I told you why.

AYAMONN. I was very lonely.

SHEILA [*softly*]. So was I, Ayamonn, lonely even in front of God's holy face.

AYAMONN. Sheila, we've gone a long way in a gold canoe, over many waters, bright and surly, sometimes sending bitter spray asplash on our faces, forcing forward to the green glade of united work and united rest beyond the farther waves. But you were ever listening for the beat from the wings of the angel of fear. So you got out to walk safe on a crowded road.

SHEILA. This is a cold and cheerless welcome, Ayamonn.

AYAMONN. Change, if you want to, the burning kiss falling on the upturned, begging mouth for the chill caress of a bony, bearded Saint. [*Loudly.*] Go with th' yelling crowd, and keep them brave, and yell along with them!

SHEILA. Won't you listen, then, to the few words I have to say?

AYAMONN [*sitting down near the fire, and looking into it, though he leaves her standing*]. Go ahead! I won't fail to hear you.

SHEILA. God knows I don't mean to hurt you, but you must

know that we couldn't begin to live on what you're earning now—could we? [*He keeps silent.*] Oh, Ayamonn, why do you waste your time on doing foolish things?

AYAMONN. What foolish things?

[*A hubbub is heard in the street outside; voices saying loudly "Give him one in the bake" or "Down him with a one in th' belly"; then the sound of running footsteps, and silence.*]

SHEILA [*when she hears the voices—nervously*]. What's that?

AYAMONN [*without taking his gaze from the fire*]. Some drunken row or other. [*They listen silently for a few moments.*]

AYAMONN. Well, what foolish things?

SHEILA [*timid and hesitating*]. You know yourself, Ayamonn: trying to paint, going mad about Shakespeare, and consorting with a kind of people that can only do you harm.

AYAMONN [*mockingly prayerful—raising his eyes to the ceiling*]. O Lord, let me forsake the foolish, and live; and go in the way of Sheila's understanding!

SHEILA [*going over nearer to him*]. Listen, Ayamonn, my love; you know what I say is only for our own good, that we may come together all the sooner. [*Trying to speak jokingly.*] Now, really, isn't it comical I'd look if I were to go about in a scanty petticoat, covered in a sober black shawl, and my poor feet bare. [*Mocking.*] Wouldn't I look well that way!

AYAMONN [*quietly*]. With red roses in your hand, you'd look beautiful.

SHEILA [*desperately*]. Oh, for goodness' sake, Ayamonn, be sensible! I'm getting a little tired of all this. I can't bear the strain the way we're going on much longer. [*A short pause.*] You will either have to make good, or—— [*She pauses.*]

AYAMONN [*quietly*]. Or what?

SHEILA [*with a little catch in her voice*]. Or lose me; and you wouldn't like that to happen.

AYAMONN. I shouldn't like that to happen; but I could bear the sthrain.

SHEILA. I risked a big row tonight to come to tell you good

news: I've been told that the strike is bound to take place;
there is bound to be trouble; and, if you divide yourself
from the foolish men, and stick to your job, you'll soon be
a foreman of some kind or other.

AYAMONN [*rising from his seat and facing her for the first time*].
Who told you all this? The Inspector?

SHEILA. Never mind who; if he did, wasn't it decent of him?

AYAMONN. D'ye know what you're asking me to do, woman?
To be a blackleg; to blast with th' black frost of desertion
the gay hopes of my comrades. Whatever you may think
them to be, they are my comrades. Whatever they may say
or do, they remain my brothers and sisters. Go to hell, girl,
I have a soul to save as well as you. [*With a catch in his
voice.*] Oh, Sheila, you shouldn't have asked me to do this
thing!

SHEILA [*trying to come close, but he pushes her back*]. Oh,
Ayamonn, it is a chance; take it, do, for my sake!

[*Rapid footsteps are heard outside. The door flies open and
MULLCANNY comes in, pale, frightened, his clothes dishev-
elled, and a slight smear of blood on his forehead. His bowler
hat is crushed down on his head, his coat is torn, and his
waistcoat unbuttoned, showing his tie pulled out of its place.
He sinks into a chair.*]

AYAMONN. What's happened? Who did that to you?

MULLCANNY. Give's a drink, someone, will you?

[AYAMONN *gets him a drink from a jug on the dresser.*]

MULLCANNY. A gang of bowseys made for me, and I talking
to a man. Barely escaped with my life. Weekly communi-
cants, probably, the scoundrels! Only for some brave oul'
one, they'd have laid me out completely. She saved me from
worse.

AYAMONN. How th' hell did you bring all that on you?

MULLCANNY [*plaintively*]. Just trying to show a fellow the foolishness of faith in a hereafter, when something struck me
on the head, and I was surrounded by feet making kicks

at me!

[*A crash of breaking glass is heard from the other room, and* BRENNAN *and* ROORY *come running out of it.*]

ROORY. A stone has done for th' window! [*He sees* MULLCANNY.] Oh, that's how th' land lies, is it? Haven't I often said that if you go round leerin' at God an' His holy assistants, one day He's bound to have a rap at you!

BRENNAN. Keep away from that window, there, in case another one comes sailin' in.

[*Immediately he has spoken, a stone smashes in through the window.* BRENNAN *lies down flat on the floor;* MULLCANNY *slides from the chair and crouches on the ground;* ROORY *gets down on his hands and knees, keeping his head as low as possible, so that he resembles a Mohammedan at his devotions;* SHEILA *stands stiff in a corner, near the door; and* AYAMONN, *seizing up a hurley lying against the dresser, makes for the door to go out.*]

BRENNAN. I guessed this was comin'.

AYAMONN [*angrily*]. I'll show them!

SHEILA [*to* AYAMONN]. Stop where you are, you fool!

[*But* AYAMONN *pays no attention to the advice and hurries out of the door.*]

ROORY [*plaintively and with dignity—to* MULLCANNY]. This is what you bring down on innocent people, trimmed into a sane outlook on life with your obstinate association of man with th' lower animals.

MULLCANNY [*truculently*]. Only created impudence it is that strives to set yourselves above the ape's formation, genetically present in every person's body.

BRENNAN [*indignantly*]. String out life to where it started, an' you'll find no sign, let alone a proof, of the dignity, wisdom, an' civility of man ever having been associated with th' manners of a monkey.

MULLCANNY. And why do children like to climb trees, eh? Answer me that?

ROORY [*fiercely*]. They love it more where you come from than
they do here. Here's one wouldn't be surprised to hear that
waggin' tails followed all who jumped about th' waste o'
wild Killorglan!

SHEILA [*from her corner*]. It's surely to be pitied you are, young
man, lettin' yourself be bullied by ignorant books into believing that things are naught but what poor men are in-
clined to call them, blind to the glorious and eternal facts
that shine behind them.

MULLCANNY [*pityingly*]. Bullied be books—eternal facts—aw!
Yous are all scared stiff at the manifestation of a truth or
two. D'ye know that the contraction of catharrh, apoplexy,
consumption, and cataract of the eye is common to the monkeys? Knowledge you have now that you hadn't before; and
a lot of them even like beer.

ROORY. Well, that's something sensible, at last.

BRENNAN [*fiercely*]. Did they get their likin' for beer from us,
or did we get our likin' of beer from them? Answer me
that, you, now; answer me that!

ROORY. Answer him that. We're not Terra Del Fooaygeeans,
but sensible, sane, an' civilised souls.

MULLCANNY [*gleefully*]. Time's promoted reptiles—that's all;
yous can't do away with the os coccyges!

BRENNAN. Ladies present, ladies present.

ROORY [*creeping over rapidly till his face is close to that of*
MULLCANNY'S—*fiercely*]. We can get away from you, de-
spoiler of words comin' from th' mouth of men! We stand
on the earth, firm, upright, heads cocked, lookin' all men
in th' face, afraid o' nothin'; men o' goodwill we are,
abloom with th' blessin' o' charity, showin' in th' dust
we're made of, th' diamond-core of an everlastin' divinity!

SHEILA [*excitedly*]. Hung as high as Guilderoy he ought to be,
an' he deep in the evil of his rich illusions, spouting insults
at war with th' mysteries an' facts of our holy faith!

BRENNAN [*to* SHEILA]. Hush, pretty lady, hush. [*To the others.*]
Boys, boys, take example from a poor oul' Protestant here,

never lettin' himself be offended be a quiver of anger in any peaceable or terrified discussion. Now, let that last word finish it; finis—the end, see?

ROORY [*angrily—to* BRENNAN]. Finis youssell, you blurry-eyed, wither-skinned oul' greybeard, singin' songs in th' public streets for odd coppers, with all th' boys in th' Bank of Ireland workin' overtime countin' all you've got in their front room! Finis you!

BRENNAN [*indignantly*]. Bleatin' perjury out of you, y'are, about my possession of a few coins an office-boy, in a hurry, wouldn't stop to pick up from th' path before him! An' as for withered, soople as you I am, hands that can tinkle a thremblin' tune out of an oul' melodeon, legs that can carry me ten miles an' more, an' eyes that can still see without hardship a red berry shinin' from a distant bush!

[*The door opens and* AYAMONN *and his mother come in. She runs over to the blossoms at the window, tenderly examining the plants growing there—the musk, geranium, and the fuchsia.*]

MRS. BREYDON [*joyfully*]. Unharmed, th' whole of them. Th' stone passed them by, touchin' none o' them—thank God for that mercy!

AYAMONN. What th' hell are you doin' on your knees? Get up, get up. [*They rise from the floor shamefacedly.*] Th' rioters all dispersed. [*To* MULLCANNY.] Mother was th' oul' one who saved you from a sudden an' unprovided death. An' th' Blessed Image has come back again, all aglow in garments new. Listen!

[*A murmur of song has been heard while* AYAMONN *was speaking, and now* EEADA, DYMPNA, FINNOOLA, *and the* MEN *appear at the door—now wide open—half backing into the room singing part of a hymn softly, their pale faces still wearing the frozen look of resignation; staring at the Image shining bright and gorgeous as* BRENNAN *has made it for them, standing in a niche in the wall, directly opposite*] *the door.* EBADA, DYMPNA, FINNOOLA, *and the* MEN *singing softly—*]

> Oh! Queen of Eblana's poor children,
> Bear swiftly our woe away;
> An' give us a chance to live lightly
> An hour of our life's dark day!
> Lift up th' poor heads over bending,
> An' light a lone star in th' sky,
> To show thro' th' darkness, descending,
> A cheerier way to die.

EBADA [*coming forward a little*]. She came back to Her poor again, in raiment rich. She came back; of Her own accord. She came to abide with Her people.

DYMPNA. From her window, little Ursula looked, and saw Her come; in th' moonlight, along the street. She came, stately. Blinded be the coloured light that shone around about Her, the child fell back, in a swoon she fell full on the floor beneath her.

1ST MAN. My eyes caught a glimpse of Her too, glidin' back to where She came from. Regal an' proud She was, an' wondrous, so that me eyes failed; me knees thrembled an' bent low, an' me heart whispered a silent prayer to itself as th' vision passed me by, an' I fancied I saw a smile on Her holy face.

EBADA. Many have lived to see a strange thing this favoured night, an' blessin' will flow from it to all tempered into a lively belief; and maybe, too, to some who happen to be out of step with the many marchin' in the mode o' thruth. [*She comes a little closer to* MRS. BREYDON. *The others, backs turned towards the room, stand, most of them outside the door, a few just across the threshold, in a semicircle, heads bent as if praying, facing towards the Image.*] Th' hand of a black stranger it was who sent the stones flyin' through your windows; but ere tomorrow's sun is seen, they will be back again as shelther from th' elements. A blessin' generous on yous all—[*pause*]—except th' evil thing that stands, all stiff-necked, underneath th' roof!

MULLCANNY [*mockingly*]. Me!

SHEILA [*fiercely*]. Ay, you, that shouldn't find a smile or an unclenched hand in a decent man's house!

MULLCANNY. I'll go; there's too many here to deal with—I'll leave you with your miracle.

AYAMONN. You can stay if you wish, for whatever surety of shelther's here, it's open to th' spirit seeking to add another colour to whatever thruth we know already. Thought that has run from a blow will find a roof under its courage here, an' a fire to sit by, as long as I live an' th' oul' rooms last!

SHEILA [*with quiet bitterness*]. Well, shelter him, then, that by right should be lost in the night, a black night, an' bitterly lonely, without a dim ray from a half-hidden star to give him a far-away companionship; grey rain, in sodden showers, pouring over him; speary sleet slashing at his dead-cold face; numb limbs on him that must stir to keep alive, but can't move; with blanched fingers aching sorely from th' sting of a sharp wind; ay, an' a desolate rest under a thorny and dripping thicket of lean and twisted whins, too tired to thry to live longer against th' hate of the black wind and th' grey rain: Let him lie there, let him live there, forsaken, forgotten by all under a kindly roof and close to a cosy fire!

MULCANNY [*with pretended alarm*]. Good God, I'm done, now! I'm off before worse befall me. Good night, Ayamonn.

AYAMONN. Good night, my friend. [MULLCANNY *goes out.*]

BRENNAN. We're keepin' decent people out of their beds—so long, all.

ROORY. I'll be with you some o' th' way, an' we can finish that argument we had. Good night all.

[*He and* BRENNAN *go out together, closing the door after them.* SHEILA *stands where she was, sullen and silent.*]

MRS. BREYDON. Shame on you, Sheila, for such a smoky flame to come from such a golden lamp! [SHEILA *stays silent.*] Tired out I am, an' frightened be th' scene o' death I saw today. Dodge about how we may, we come to th' same end.

AYAMONN [*gently leading her towards the other room*]. Go an' lie down, lady; you're worn out. Time's a perjured jade, an' ever he moans a man must die. Who through every inch of life weaves a patthern of vigour an' elation can never taste death, but goes to sleep among th' stars, his withered arms outstretched to greet th' echo of his own shout. It will be for them left behind to sigh for an hour, an' then to sing their own odd songs, an' do their own odd dances, to give a lonely God a little company, till they, too, pass by on their bare way out. When a true man dies, he is buried in th' birth of a thousand worlds.

[MRS BREYDON *goes into the other room, and* AYAMONN *closes the door softly behind her. He comes back and stands pensive near the fire.*]

AYAMONN [*after a pause*]. Don't you think you should go too?

SHEILA [*a little brokenly*]. Let me have a few more words with you, Ayamonn, before we hurry to our separation.

AYAMONN [*quietly*]. There is nothing more to be said.

SHEILA. There's a lot to be said, but hasty time won't stretch an hour a little out to let the words be spoken. Goodbye.

AYAMONN [*without turning his head*]. Goodbye.

[SHEILA *is going slowly to the door when it partly opens, and half the head of* EEADA *peeps around it, amid an indistinct murmur as of praying outside.*]

EEADA [*in half a whisper*]. Th' Protestan' Rector to see Mr. Breydon. [*The half of her head disappears, but her voice is heard saying a little more loudly.*] This way, sir; shure you know th' way well, anyhow.

[*The door opening a little more, the* RECTOR *comes in. He is a handsome man of forty. His rather pale face wears a grave scholarly look, but there is kindness in his grey eyes, and humorous lines round his mouth, though these are almost hidden by a short, brown, pointed beard, here and there about to turn grey. His black clothes are covered by a warm black topcoat, the blackness brightened a little by a vivid green scarf he is wearing round his neck, the fringed ends falling over his shoulders. He carries a black, broad-brimmed, soft clerical hat and a walking-stick in his left hand. He hastens towards* AYAMONN, *smiling genially, hand outstretched in greeting.*]

RECTOR. My dear Ayamonn. [*They shake hands.*]

AYAMONN [*indicating* SHEILA]. A friend of mine, sir—Sheila Moorneen. [*Moving a chair.*] Sit down, sir.

[*The* RECTOR *bows to* SHEILA; *she returns it quietly, and the* RECTOR *sits down.*]

RECTOR. I've hurried from home in a cab, Ayamonn, to see you before the night was spent. [*His face forming grave lines.*] I've a message for you—and a warning.

[*The door again is partly opened, and again the half head of* EEADA *appears, mid the murmurs outside, unheard the moment the door closes.*]

EEADA. Two railwaymen to see you, Ayamonn; full house tonight you're havin', eh?

[*The half head goes, the door opens wider, and the two railwaymen come into the room. They are dressed drably as the other men are, but their peaked railway uniform caps* [*which they keep on their heads*] *have vivid scarlet bands around them. Their faces, too, are like the others, and stonily stare in front of them. They stand stock still when they see the* RECTOR.]

1ST RAILWAYMAN [*after a pause*]. 'Scuse us. Didn' know th' Protestan' Minister was here. We'll wait outside till he goes, Ayamonn.

AYAMONN. Th' Rector's a dear friend of mine, Bill; say what you want, without fear—he's a friend.

1ST RAILWAYMAN [*a little dubiously*]. Glad to hear it. You

know th' sthrike starts tomorrow?

AYAMONN. I know it now.

2ND. RAILWAYMAN. Wouldn' give's th' extra shillin'. Offered us thruppence instead—th' lowsers! [*Hastily—to* RECTOR.] 'Scuse me, sir.

1ST RAILWAYMAN [*taking a document from his breast pocket*]. An' th' meetin's proclaimed.

RECTOR [*to* AYAMONN.] That's part of what I came to tell you.

1ST RAILWAYMAN [*handing document to* AYAMONN]. They handed that to our Committee this evening, a warrant of warning.

RECTOR [*earnestly—to* AYAMONN]. I was advised to warn you, Ayamonn, that the Authorities are prepared to use all the force they have to prevent the meeting.

AYAMONN. Who advised you, sir—th' Inspector?

RECTOR. My churchwarden, Ayamonn. Come, even he has good in him.

AYAMONN. I daresay he has, sir; I've no grudge against him.

RECTOR [*convinced*]. I know that, Ayamonn.

AYAMONN [*indicating document—to* 1ST RAILWAYMAN]. What are th' Committee going to do with this?

1ST RAILWAYMAN. What would you do with it, Ayamonn?

AYAMONN [*setting it alight at the fire and waiting till it falls to ashes*]. That!

2ND RAILWAYMAN [*gleefully*]. Exactly what we said you'd do!

SHEILA [*haughtily*]. It's not what any sensible body would think he'd do.

1ST RAILWAYMAN [*ignoring her*]. Further still, Ayamonn, me son, we want you to be one of the speakers on the platform at the meeting.

SHEILA [*bursting forward and confronting the railwaymen*]. He'll do nothing of the kind—hear me? Nothing of the kind. Creepers, dead-faced desirers of a life that can never enter into you, go! Cinder-tongued moaners, who's to make any bones about what you suffer, or how you die? Ayamonn's his reading and his painting to do, and his mother to mind, more than lipping your complaints in front of gun muzzles, ready to sing a short and sudden death-song!

1ST RAILWAYMAN [*a little awed*]. To see Ayamonn we came, an' not you, Miss.

2ND RAILWAYMAN [*roughly*]. Let th' man speak for himself.

AYAMONN [*catching* SHEILA's *arm and drawing her back*]. It's my answer they're seeking. [*To railwaymen*]. Tell the Committee, Bill, I'll be there; and that they honour me when they set me in front of my brothers. The Minstrel Show must be forgotten.

SHEILA [*vehemently—to the* RECTOR]. You talk to him; you're his friend. You can influence him. Get him to stay away, man!

RECTOR. It's right for me to warn you, Ayamonn, and you, men, that the Authorities are determined to prevent the meeting; and that you run a grave risk in defying them.

2ND MAN [*growling*]. We'll chance it.

SHEILA [*to* RECTOR]. That's no good; that's not enough—forbid him to go. Show him God's against it!

RECTOR [*standing up*]. Who am I to say that God's against it? You are too young by a thousand years to know the mind of God. If they be his brothers, he does well among them.

SHEILA [*wildly*]. I'll get his mother to bar his way. She'll do more than murmur grand excuses.

[*She runs to the door of the other room, opens it, and goes in. After a few moments, she comes out slowly, goes to the chair left idle by the* RECTOR, *sits down on it, leans her arms on the table, and lets her head rest on them.*]

AYAMONN. Well?

SHEILA [*brokenly*]. She's stretched out, worn and wan, fast asleep, and I hadn't the heart to awaken her.

RECTOR [*holding out a hand to* AYAMONN]. Come to see me before you go, Ayamonn. Be sure, wherever you may be, whatever you may do, a blessing deep from my breast is all around you. Goodbye. [*To the railwaymen.*] Goodbye, my friends.

RAILWAYMEN. Goodbye, sir.

[*The* RECTOR *glances at* SHEILA, *decides to say nothing, and goes towards the door;* AYAMONN *opens it for him, and he goes out through the semicircle of men and women, still singing softly before the Statue of the Queen of Eblana's poor.* SHEILA'S *quiet crying heard as a minor note through the singing.*]

Oh, Queen of Eblana's poor children,
Bear swiftly our woe away,
An' give us a chance to live lightly,
An hour of our life's dark day!

ACT THREE

SCENE: *A part of Dublin City flowering into a street and a bridge across the river Liffey. The parapets are seen to the right and left so that the bridge fills most of the scene before the onlooker. The distant end of the bridge leads to a street flowing on to a point in the far distance; and to the right and left of this street are tall gaunt houses, mottled with dubious activities, with crowds of all sorts of men and women burrowing in them in a pathetic search for a home. These houses stand along another street running parallel with the river. In the distance, where the street, leading from the bridge, ends in a point of space, to the right, soars the tapering silver spire of a church; and to the left, Nelson's Pillar, a deep red, pierces the sky, with Nelson, a deep black, on its top, looking over everything that goes on around him. A gloomy grey sky is over all, so that the colours of the scene are made up of the dark houses, the brown parapets of the bridge, the grey sky, the silver spire, the red pillar, and Nelson's black figure.*

On one of the bridge parapets a number of the men seen in the previous scenes are gathered together, their expressionless faces hidden by being bent down towards their breasts. Some sit on the parapets, some lounge against the gaunt houses at the corner of the street leading from the bridge, and, in one corner, a man stands wearily against the parapet, head bent, an unlit pipe drooping from his mouth, apparently forgotten. The sun shines on pillar and church spire, but there is no sign of sun where these people are.

On the pavement, opposite to where the men sit, nearer to this end of the bridge, sit EEADA, DYMPNA, *and* FINNOOLA, *dressed so in black that they appear to be enveloped in the blackness of a dark night. In front of* EEADA *is a drab-coloured basket in which cakes and apples are spending an idle and uneasy time.* DYMPNA *has a shallower basket holding decadent blossoms, and a drooping bunch of violets hangs from a listless hand.*

EEADA [*drowsily*]. This spongy leaden sky's Dublin; those tomby houses is Dublin too—Dublin's scurvy body; an' we're Dublin's silver soul. [*She spits vigorously into the street.*] An' that's what Eeada thinks of th' city's soul an' body!

DYMPNA. You're more than right, Eeada, but I wouldn't be too harsh. [*Calling out in a sing-song way.*] Violets, here, on'y tuppence a bunch; tuppence a bunch, th' fresh violets!

EEADA [*calling out in a sing-song voice*]. Apples an' cakes, on'y tuppence a head here for th' cakes; ripe apples a penny apiece!

DYMPNA. Th' sun is always at a distance, an' th' chill grey is always here.

FINNOOLA. Half-mournin' skies for ever over us, frownin' out any chance of merriment that came staggerin' to us for a little support.

EEADA. That's Dublin, Finnoola, an' th' sky over it. Sorrow's a slush under our feet, up to our ankles, an' th' deep drip of it constant overhead.

DYMPNA. A graveyard where th' dead are all above th' ground.

EEADA. Without a blessed blink of rest to give them hope. An' she cockin' herself up that she stands among other cities as a queen o' counsel, laden with knowledge, afire with th' song of great men, enough to overawe all livin' beyond th' salty sea, undher another sun be day, an' undher a different moon be night.

[*They drowse, with heads bent lower.*]

IST MAN [*leaning wearily against the parapet*]. Golden Gander'll do it, if I'm e'er a thrue prophet. [*Raising his voice a little.*] He'll flash past th' winnin' post like an arra from th'

bow, in the five hundhred guinea West's Awake Steeple
chase Championship.

2ND MAN [*drowsily contradicting*]. In me neck he will! He'
have a chance if it was a ramble. Copper Goose'll leave hir
standin', if I'm e'er a thrue prophet.

EEADA [*waking up slightly*]. Prophets? Do my ears deceive me
or am I afther hearin' somebody say prophets?

DYMPNA. You heard a murmur of it, Eeada, an' it's a bad wor
to hear, remindin' us of our low estate at th' present junc
ture. Th' prophets we once had are well hidden behind Go
be now, an' no wondher, for we put small pass on them, ar
God in His generous anger's showin' us what it is to be sad
dled with Johnnies-come-marchin'-home, all song an' shin
an' no surety.

FINNOOLA [*shaking her head sadly*]. A gold-speckled candle
white as snow, was Dublin once; yellowish now, leanin' side
ways, an' guttherin' down to a last shaky glimmer in th
wind o' life.

EEADA. Well, we've got Guinness's Brewery still, giv in us
needy glimpse of a betther life an hour or so on a Saturda
night, though I hold me hand at praisin' th' puttin' of Bria
Boru's golden harp on every black porther bottle, destine
to give outsiders a false impression of our pride in th
tendher an' dauntless memories of th' past. But it's mesel
should whisper little against th' bottles, havin' used them a
cunnin' candlesticks, year in an' year out, since I lost mesel
in marriage; an' a fine conthrast is a tall white candle, se
firm in th' neck of a slender black bottle, givin' light to a
in th' room, an' showin' up th' blessed St. Anthony himsel
watchin' over us from a cosy corner in th' breast of th
chimney.

[*The* RECTOR *and the* INSPECTOR *appear at the farther en
of the bridge, and come over it towards where the men an
women are. The* RECTOR *is dressed in immaculate black
wears a glossy tall hat, and carries a walking-stick. He ha
shed his topcoat, but wears his green scarf round his neck
The* INSPECTOR *is clad in a blue uniform, slashed with silve*

*epaulettes on the shoulders, and silver braid on collar and
cuffs. He wears a big blue helmet, back and front peaks sil-
ver-bordered, and from a long silver spike on the top flows
a graceful plume of crimson hair. On the front is a great
silver crown, throned on a circle of red velvet. A sword, in
a silver scabbard, hangs by his side. He is wearing highly-
polished top-boots. They both pause on the bridge, the REC-
TOR looking pensively down over the parapet at the flowing
river.]*

INSPECTOR. It was a great wedding, sir. A beautiful bride and
an elegant bridegroom; a distinguished congregation, and
the Primate in his fine sermon did justice to the grand occasion, sir. Fittingly ended, too, by the organ with *The Voice
that Breathed o'er Eden.*

RECTOR [*apparently not very interested*]. Oh yes, yes; quite.

INSPECTOR. Historic disthrict, this, round heres headquarters
of a Volunteer Corp in Grattan's time—not, of course, that
I agree with Grattan. A great-great-grandfather of mine
was one of the officers.

RECTOR. Oh yes; was he?

INSPECTOR. Yes. Strange uniform he wore: richly black, with
sky-blue facings, a yellow breast-piece, ribbed with red
braid, and, capping all, a huge silver helmet having a yellow
plume soaring over it from the right-hand side.

RECTOR [*smiling*]. Your own's not too bad, Mr. Churchwarden.

INSPECTOR. Smart; but a bit too sombre, I think, sir.

EEADA [*whining towards them*]. On'y a penny each, th' rosy
apples, lovely for th' chiselurs—Jasus! what am I sayin'?
Lovely for th' little masters an' little misthresses, stately,
in their chandeliered an' carpeted dwellin'-houses; or a
cake—on'y tuppence a piece—daintily spiced, an' tastin'
splendid.

DYMPNA [*whining towards them*]. Tuppence, here, th' bunch
o' violets, fit for to go with th' white an' spotless cashmere
gown of our radiant Lady o' Fair Dealin'.

EEADA [*deprecatingly*]. What are you sayin', woman? That's a

Protestan' ministher, indeed, gentleman, Dympna!

DYMPNA. Me mind slipped for a poor minute; but it's pity he'll have on us, an' regulate our lives with what'll bring a sudden cup o' tea within fair reach of our hands.

BEADA. Apples, here, penny each, rosy apples picked hardly an hour ago from a laden three; cakes tuppence on'y, baked over scented turf as th' dawn stepped over th' blue-gowned backs o' th' Dublin Mountains.

DYMPNA. Tuppence a bunch, th' violets, shy an' dhrunk with th' dew o' th' mornin'; fain to lie in the white bosom of a highborn lady, or fit into th' lapel of a genuine gentleman's Sunday courtin' coat.

[*The* RECTOR *takes a few coins from his pocket and throws them to the women, who pick them up and sink into silence again.*]

INSPECTOR. Swift, too, must have walked about here with the thorny crown of madness pressing ever deeper into his brain.

RECTOR [*indicating the men and women*]. Who are these?

INSPECTOR [*indifferent*]. Those? Oh, flotsam and jetsam. A few of them dangerous at night, maybe; but harmless during the day.

RECTOR. I've read that tens of thousands of such as those followed Swift to the grave.

INSPECTOR. Indeed, sir? A queer man, the poor demented Dean, a right queer man.

[*A sleepy lounger suddenly gives a cough, gives his throat a hawk, and sends a big spit to one of the* INSPECTOR'*s polished boots, then sinks back into sleep again.*]

INSPECTOR [*springing back with an angry exclamation*]. Wha' th' hell are you after doing, you rotten lizard! Looka wha' you've done, you mangy rat!

[*He takes hold of the lounger and shakes his sharply.*]

2ND MAN [*sleepily resentful*]. Eh, there! Wha' th' hell?

INSPECTOR [*furiously*]. You spat on my boots, you tousled toad
—my boots, boots, boots!

2ND MAN [*frightened and bewildered*]. Boots, sir? Is it me, sir?
Not me, sir. Musta been someone else, sir.

INSPECTOR [*shaking him furiously*]. You, you, you!

2ND MAN. Me, sir? Never spit in public in me life, sir. Makin'
a mistake, sir. Musta been someone else.

RECTOR. Inspector Finglas! Remember you wear the King's
uniform! Quiet, quiet, man!

INSPECTOR [*subsiding*]. Pardon me. I lost my temper. I'm more
used to a blow from a stone than a dirty spit on my boot.

RECTOR [*shuddering a little*]. Let us go from here. Things here
frighten me, for they seem to look with wonder on our ease
and comfort.

INSPECTOR. Frighten you? Nonsense—and with me!

RECTOR. Things here are of a substance I dare not think about,
much less see and handle. Here, I can hardly bear to look
upon the same thing twice.

INSPECTOR. There you are, and as I've said so often, Breydon's
but a neat slab of a similar slime.

RECTOR. You wrong yourself to say so: Ayamonn Breydon has
within him the Kingdom of Heaven. [*He pauses.*] And so,
indeed, may these sad things we turn away from.

[*They pass out.*]

EEADA [*thinking of the coins given*]. Two tiny sixpences—four-
pence a head. Oh, well, beggars can't be choosers. But isn't
it a hard life to be grindin' our poor bums to powder, for
ever squattin' on the heartless pavements of th' Dublin
streets!

DYMPNA. Ah, what is it all to us but a deep-written testament
o' gloom: grey sky over our heads, brown an' dusty streets
undher our feet, with th' black an' bitther Liffey flowin'
through it all.

EEADA [*mournfully*]. We've dhrifted down to where there's
nothin'. Younger I was when every quiet-clad evenin' carried a jaunty jewel in her bosom. Tormented with joy I was

then as to whether I'd parade th' thronged sthreets on th' arm of a 16th Lancer, his black-breasted crimson coat a sight to see, an' a black plume droopin' from his haughty helmet; or lay claim to a red-breasted Prince o' Wales's Own, th' red plume in his hat a flame over his head.

DYMPNA. It was a 15th King's Own Hussar for me, Eeada, with his rich blue coat an' its fairyland o' yellow braid, two yellow sthripes down his trousers, an' a red bag an' plume dancin' on his busby.

EEADA. Lancers for me, Dympna.

DYMPNA. Hussars for me, Eeada.

EEADA. An' what for you, Finnoola?

FINNOOLA. What would a girl, born in a wild Cork valley, among mountains, brought up to sing the songs of her fathers, what would she choose but the patched coat, shaky shoes, an' white hungry face of th' Irish rebel? But their shabbiness was threaded with th' colours from the garments of Finn Mac Cool of th' golden hair, Goll Mac Morna of th' big blows, Caoilte of th' flyin' feet, an' Oscar of th' invincible spear.

EEADA [nudging DYMPNA]. That was some time ago, if y'ask me.

[BRENNAN comes slowly over the bridge from the far side. His melodeon is hanging on his back. He looks around for a likely place to play. He leans against a parapet, some distance off, and unslings his melodeon from his back.]

EEADA. Here's that oul' miser creepin' after coppers, an' some bank bulgin' with what he has in it already.

2ND MAN [waking suddenly, spitting out vigorously, and speaking venomously]. Rowlin' in th' coin o' th' realm—bastard!

[He sinks into a coma again.]

BRENNAN [giving himself confidence]. Evenin', ladies an' gentlemen. Good thing to be alive when th' sun's kind. [They take no heed of what he says.]

[BRENNAN *sighs; then plays a few preliminary notes on the melodeon to make sure it is in tune. He begins to sing in a voice that was once a mellow baritone, but now is a little husky with age, now and again quavering a little on the higher notes in the song.*]

BRENNAN [*singing*].
 I stroll'd with a fine maid far out in th' counthry,
 Th' blossoms around us all cryin' for dew;
 On a violet-clad bench, sure, I sat down beside her,
 An' tucked up my sleeves for to tie up her shoe.
 An' what's that to anyone whether or no,
 If I came to th' fore when she gave me th' cue?
 She clos'd her eyes tight as she murmur'd full low,
 Be good enough, dear, for to tie up by shoe.

EEADA [*with muttered indignation*]. Isn't that outrageous, now; on a day like this, too, an' in a sober mood!

DYMPNA. In front o' decent women as well!

1ST MAN [*waking up suddenly*]. Disturbin' me dhreams of Golden Gandher gallopin' home to win in a canther!

BRENNAN [*singing*].
 Th' hawthorn shook all her rich perfume upon us,
 Red poppies saluted, wherever they grew,
 Th' joyous exertion that flaunted before me,
 When I tuck'd up my sleeves for to fasten her shoe.
 An' what's it to anyone, whether or no?
 I learn'd in that moment far more than I knew,
 As she lifted her petticoat, shyly an' slow,
 An' I tucked up my sleeves for to fasten her shoe.

 The heathery hills were all dancin' around us,
 False things in th' world turn'd out to be thrue,
 When she put her arms round me, an' kiss'd me an' murmur'd,
 You've neatly an' tenderly tied up my shoe.
 What's that to anyone whether or no?
 I ventur'd quite gamely to see th' thing through,
 When she lifted her petticoat, silent an' slow,

An' I tuck' up my sleeves for to tie up her shoe.

[*Some pennies have been thrown from the windows of the houses.* BRENNAN *picks them up and, taking off a shabby, wide-brimmed hat, bestows a sweeping bow on the houses. During the singing of the last verse of the song,* AYAMONN *and* ROORY *have strolled in, and have listened to the old man singing while they leant against the balustrade of the bridge. The scene has grown darker as the old man is singing his song for the sun is setting.*]

2ND MAN [*waking up suddenly*]. Off with you, old man, thinkin' to turn our thoughts aside from th' way we are, an' th' wornout hope in front of us.

1ST MAN [*waking up—wrathfully*]. Get to hell outa that, with your sootherin' songs o' gaudy idleness!

EEADA. Makin' his soul, at his age, he ought to be, instead o' chantin' ditties th' way you'd fear what would come upon you in th' darkness o' th' night, an' ne'er a sword be your side either.

3RD MAN. Away with you an' your heathen songs to parts renowned for ignorance an' shame!

FINNOOLA. Away to where light women are plenty, an' free to open purple purses to throw you glitterin' coins!

[BRENNAN *slings his melodeon on to his back, puts his hat back on his head, and wends his way across the bridge.*]

ROORY [*as he passes*]. Isn't it a wondher, now, you wouldn't sing an Irish song, free o' blemish, instead o' one thickly speckled with th' lure of foreign enthertainment?

[BRENNAN *heeds him not, but crosses the bridge and goes out. The men and women begin to sink into drowsiness again.*]

AYAMONN. Let him be, man; he sang a merry song well, and should have got a fairer greeting.

ROORY [*taking no notice of* AYAMONN'S *remark—to the men and women*]. Why didn't yous stop him before he began?

Pearl of th' White Breasts, now, or *Battle Song o' Munster* that would pour into yous Conn's battle-fire of th' hundhred fights. Watchman o' Tara he was, his arm reachin' over deep rivers an' high hills, to dhrag out a host o' sthrong enemies shiverin' in shelthers. Leadher of Magh Femon's Host he was, Guardian of Moinmoy, an' Vetheran of our river Liffey, flowin' through a city whose dhrinkin' goblets once were made of gold, e'er wise men carried it with frankincense an' myrrh to star-lit Bethlehem.

EEADA [*full of sleep—murmuring low*]. Away you, too, with your spangled memories of battle-mad warriors buried too deep for words to find them. Penny, here, each, th' ripe apples.

DYMPNA [*sleepily—in a low murmur*]. Away, an' leave us to saunter in sleep, an' crave out a crust in the grey kingdom of quietness. Tuppence a bunch the fresh violets.

FINNOOLA [*sleepily*]. Run away, son, to where bright eyes can see no fear, an' white hands, idle, are willin' to buckle a sword on a young man's thigh.

1ST MAN [*with a sleepy growl*]. Get to hell where gay life has room to move, an' hours to waste, an' white praise is sung to coloured shadows. Time is precious here.

2ND AND 3RD MEN [*together—murmuringly*]. Time is precious here.

AYAMONN. Rouse yourselves; we hold a city in our hands!

EEADA [*in a very low, but bitter voice*]. It's a bitther city.

DYMPNA [*murmuring the same way*]. It's a black an' bitther city.

FINNOOLA [*speaking the same way*]. It's a bleak, black, an' bitther city.

1ST MAN. Like a batthered, tatthered whore, bullied by too long a life.

2ND MAN. An' her three gates are castles of poverty, penance, an' pain.

AYAMONN. She's what our hands have made her. We pray too much and work too little. Meanness, spite, and common pattherns are woven thick through all her glory; but her glory's there for open eyes to see.

EEADA [*bitterly—in a low voice*]. Take your fill of her glory, then; for it won't last long with your headin' against them who hold the kingdom an' who wield th' power.

DYMPNA [*reprovingly*]. He means well, Eeada, an' he knows things hid from us; an' we know his poor oul' mother's poor feet has worn out a pathway to most of our tumbling doorways, seekin' out ways o' comfort for us she sadly needs herself.

EEADA [*in a slightly livelier manner*]. Don't I know that well! A shabby sisther of ceaseless help she is, blind to herself for seein' so far into th' needs of others. May th' Lord be restless when He loses sight of her!

FINNOOLA. For all her tired look an' wrinkled face, a pure white candle she is, blessed this minute by St. Colmkille of th' gentle manner, or be Aidan, steeped in th' lore o' Heaven, or be Lausereena of th' silver voice an' snowy vestments— th' blue cloak o' Brigid be a banner over her head for ever!

THE OTHER TWO WOMEN [*together*]. Amen.

ROORY [*impatiently*]. We waste our time here—come on!

AYAMONN. Be still, man; it was dark when th' spirit of God first moved on th' face of th' waters.

ROORY. There's nothin' movin' here but misery. Gun peal an' slogan cry are th' only things to startle them. We're useless here. I'm off, if you're not.

AYAMONN. Wait a moment, Roory. No-one knows what a word may bring forth. Th' leaves an' blossoms have fallen, but th' three isn't dead.

ROORY [*hotly*]. An' d'ye think talkin' to these tatthered second-ghosts'll bring back Heaven's grace an' Heaven's beauty to Kaithleen ni Houlihan?

AYAMONN. Roory, Roory, your Kaithleen ni Houlihan has th' bent back of an oul' woman as well as th' walk of a queen. We love th' ideal Kaithleen ni Houlihan, not because she is false, but because she is beautiful; we hate th' real Kaithleen ni Houlihan, not because she is true, but because she is ugly.

ROORY [*disgusted*]. Aw, for God's sake, man!

[*He hurries off angrily.*]

EEADA [*calling scornfully after him*]. God speed you, scut!

AYAMONN [*placing a hand softly on* EEADA'S *head*]. Forget him,
an' remember ourselves, an' think of what we can do to
pull down th' banner from dusty bygones, an' fix it up in
th' needs an' desires of today.

[*The scene has now become so dark that things are but
dimly seen, save the silver spire and the crimson pillar in
the distance; and* AYAMONN'S *head set in a streak of sunlight, looking like the severed head of Dunn-Bo speaking
out of the darkness.*]

FINNOOLA. Songs of Osheen and Sword of Oscar could do nothing to tire this city of its shame.

AYAMONN. Friend, we would that you should live a greater life;
we will that all of us shall live a greater life. Our sthrike is
yours. A step ahead for us today; another one for you to-
morrow. We who have known, and know, the emptiness of
life shall know its fullness. All men and women quick with
life are fain to venture forward. [*To* EEADA.] The apple
grows for you to eat. [*To* DYMPNA.] The violet grows for you
to wear. [*To* FINNOOLA.] Young maiden, another world is in
your womb.

EEADA [*still a little gloomily*]. Th' soldiers will be chasin' us with
gunfire; th' polis hoppin' batons off our heads; our sons an'
husbands hurried off to prison, to sigh away th' time in
gloomier places than those they live in now.

AYAMONN. Don't flinch in th' first flare of fight. [*He looks away
from them and gazes meditatively down the river.*] Take
heart of grace from your city's hidden splendour. [*He points
with an outstretched hand.*] Oh, look! Look there! Th' sky
has thrown a gleaming green mantle over her bare shoulders,
bordhered with crimson, an' with a hood of gentle magenta
over her handsome head—look!

[*The scene has brightened, and bright and lovely colours are being brought to them by the caress of the setting sun. The houses on the far side of the river now bow to the visible world, decked in mauve and burnished bronze; and the men that have been lounging against them now stand stalwart, looking like fine bronze statues, slashed with scarlet.*]

AYAMONN. Look! Th' vans an' lorries rattling down th' quays, turned to bronze an' purple by th' sun, look like chariots forging forward to th' battlefront.

[EEADA, *rising into the light, now shows a fresh and virile face, and she is garbed in a dark-green robe, with a silvery mantle over her shoulders.*]

EEADA [*gazing intently before her*]. Shy an' lovely, as well as battle-minded!

[DYMPNA *rises now to look where* AYAMONN *is pointing. She is dressed like* EEADA, *and her face is aglow. The men have slid from the parapets of the bridge, turning, too, to look where* AYAMONN *is pointing. Their faces are aglow, like the women's, and they look like bronze statues, slashed with a vivid green.* FINNOOLA *rises, last, and stands a little behind the others, to look at the city showing her melody of colours.* FINNOOLA *is dressed in a skirt of a brighter green than the other two women, a white bodice slashed with black, and a flowing silvery scarf is round her waist.*]

FINNOOLA. She's glowin' like a song sung be Osheen himself, with th' golden melody of his own harp helpin'!

1ST MAN [*puzzled*]. Something funny musta happened, for, 'clare to God, I never noticed her shinin' that way before.

2ND MAN. Looka the loungers opposite have changed to sturdy men of bronze, and th' houses themselves are gay in purple an' silver!

3RD MAN. Our tired heads have always haunted far too low a level.

AYAMONN. There's th' great dome o' th' Four Courts lookin'

like a golden rose in a great bronze bowl! An' th' river
flowin' below it, a purple flood, marbled with ripples o'
scarlet; watch th' seagulls glidin' over it—like restless white
pearls astir on a royal breast. Our city's in th' grip o' God!

1ST MAN [*emotionally*]. Oh, hell, it's grand!

EEADA. Blessed be our city for ever an' ever.

AYAMONN [*lifting his right hand high*]. Home of th' Ostmen, of
th' Norman, an' th' Gael, we greet you! Greet you as you
catch a passing hour of loveliness, an' hold it tightly to your
panting breast! [*He sings.*]
Fair city, we tell thee our souls shall not slumber
Within th' warm folds of ambition or gain;
Our hands shall stretch out to th' fullness of labour,
Till wondher an' beauty within thee shall reign.

THE REST [*singing together*].
We vow to release thee from anger an' envy,
To dhrive th' fierce wolf an' sly fox from thy gate,
Till wise men an' matrons an' virgins shall murmur
O city of splendour, right fair is thy fate!

AYAMONN [*singing*].
Fair city, I tell thee that children's white laughter,
An' all th' red joy of grave youth goin' gay,
Shall make of thy streets a wild harp ever sounding,
Touch'd by th' swift fingers of young ones at play!

THE REST [*singing*].
We swear to release thee from hunger an' hardship,
From things that are ugly an' common an' mean;
Thy people together shall build a brave city,
Th' fairest an' finest that ever was seen!

[FINNOOLA *has been swaying her body to the rhythm of the
song, and now, just as the last part is ending, she swings out
on to the centre of the bridge in a dance. The tune, played
on a flute by someone, somewhere, is that of a Gavotte, or
an air of some dignified and joyous dance, and, for a while,
it is played in fairly slow time. After some time it gets
quicker, and* AYAMONN *dances out to meet her. They dance*

opposite each other, the people around clapping their hands to the tap of the dancers' feet. The two move around in this spontaneous dance, she in a golden pool of light, he in a violet-coloured shadow, now and again changing their movements so that she is in the violet-coloured shadow, and he in the golden pool.]

EEADA [*loudly*]. The finest colours God has to give are all around us now.

FINNOOLA [*as she dances*]. The Sword of Light is shining!

1ST MAN [*exultantly*]. Sons an' daughters of princes are we all, an' one with th' race of Melesius!

[*The dances comes to an end with* AYAMONN *and* FINNOOLA *having their arms round each other.*]

EEADA. Praise God for th' urge of jubilation in th' heart of th' young.

1ST MAN. An' for th' swiftness of leg an' foot in th' heart of a dance.

2ND MAN. An' for th' dhream that God's right hand still holds all things firmly.

[*The scene darkens slightly.* AYAMONN *loosens his hold on* FINNOOLA *and raises his head to listen to something. In the distance can be heard the sound of many feet marching in unison.*]

FINNOOLA [*a little anxiously*]. What is it you're listenin' to?

AYAMONN. I must go; goodbye, fair maid, goodbye.

FINNOOLA. Is it goin' to go you are, away from the fine things shinin' around us? Amn't I good enough for you?

AYAMONN [*earnestly*]. You're lovely stayin' still, an' brimmin' over with a wilder beauty when you're dancin'; but I must go. May you marry well, an' rear up children fair as Emer was, an' fine as Oscar's son; an' may they be young when Spanish ale foams high on every hand, an' wine from th' royal Pope's a common dhrink! Goodbye.

[*He kisses her, and goes across the bridge, passing out of sight on the farther bank of the river. The figures left behind have shrunk a little; the colours have faded a good deal, and all look a little puzzled and bewildered. The loungers have fallen back to the walls of the houses, and, though they do not lie against them, they stand close to them, as if seeking their shelter. There is a fairly long pause before anyone speaks. They stand apart, as if shy of each other's company.*]

EEADA [*murmuringly*]. Penny each, th' ripe apples. Who was that spoke that time? Jasus! I musta been dhreamin'.

DYMPNA [*in a bewildered voice*]. So must I, th' way I thought I was lost in a storm of joy, an' many colours, with gay clothes adornin' me.

FINNOOLA [*puzzled and dreamy*]. Dhreamin' I musta been when I heard strange words in a city nearly smothered be stars, with God guidin' us along th' banks of a purple river, all of us clad in fresh garments, fit to make Osheen mad to sing a song of the revelry dancin' in an' out of God's own vision.

EEADA [*murmuringly, but a little peevishly*]. For God's sake give over dwellin' on oul' songs sung be Osheen, th' way you'd be kindlin' a fire o' glory round some poor bog-warbler chantin' hoarse ditties in a sheltered corner of a windy street. [*Very sleepily.*] Th' dewy violets, here, on'y tuppence a bunch.

[*Now the tramp-tramp of marching men is heard more plainly.*]

DYMPNA [*a little more awake*]. What can that be, now?

1ST MAN [*gloomily, but with a note of defiance in his voice*]. Th' thramp of marchin' soldiers out to prevent our meetin' an' to stop our sthrike.

2ND MAN [*in a burst of resolution*]. We'll have both, in spite of them!

[*The scene darkens deeply now. In the pause following the*

2ND MAN'S *remark, nothing is heard but the sound of the tramping feet; then through this theatening sound comes the sound of voices singing quietly, voices that may be of those on and around the bridge, or of those singing some little distance away.*]

VOICES [*singing quietly*].
　　We swear to release thee from hunger and hardship,
　　From things that are ugly and common and mean;
　　The people together shall build a great city,
　　The finest and fairest that ever was seen.

ACT FOUR

SCENE: *Part of the grounds surrounding the Protestant church of St. Burnupus. The grounds aren't very beautiful, for they are in the midst of a poor and smoky district; but they are trim, and, considering the surroundings, they make a fair show. An iron railing running along the back is almost hidden by a green and golden hedge, except where, towards the centre, a fairly wide wooden gate gives admittance to the grounds. Beyond this gateway, on the pathway outside, is a street lamp. Shrubs grow here and there, and in the left corner, close to the hedge, are lilac and laburnum trees in bloom. To the right is the porch of the church, and part of the south wall, holding a long, rather narrow window, showing, in coloured glass, the figures of SS. Peter and Paul. Some distance away from the porch is a rowan tree, also in blossom, its white flowers contrasting richly with the gay yellow of the laburnum and the royal purple of the lilac. The rest of the grounds are laid out in grass, except for the path leading from the gateway to the entrance of the church. It is a warm, sunny evening, the Vigil of Easter, and the* RECTOR *is sitting on a deck-chair, before a table, on which are some books and papers. He is evidently considering the services that are to be held in the church on the following day.*

The RECTOR *is wearing a thick black cassock lined with red cloth, and at the moment is humming a verse of a hymn softly to himself, as he marks down notes on a slip of paper before him. A square black skull-cap covers his head.*

RECTOR [*singing to himself, softly*].
As Thou didst rise from Thy grim grave,
So may we rise and stand to brave

Th' power bestow'd on fool or knave;
We beseech Thee!

[*The verger comes out from the porch and walks towards the*
RECTOR. *He is bald as an egg, and his yellowish face is
parched and woebegone-looking. He is a man of sixty, and
shows it. His ordinary clothes are covered with a long black
mantle of thin stuff, with a small cape-like addition or inser-
tion of crimson velvet on the shoulders.*]

RECTOR [*noticing the verger beside him*]. Hymn 625: we must
have that as our opening hymn, Samuel.

SAMUEL. It's got to go in, sir.

RECTOR. As you say—it's got to go in. Did you want to speak
to me, Samuel?

SAMUEL. Excuse me, sir, for what I'm agoin' to say.

RECTOR [*encouragingly*]. Yes, yes, Samuel, go on.

SAMUEL [*mysteriously*]. Somethin's afther happenin', sir, that
I don't like.

RECTOR [*turning a little in his chair*]. Oh! What's that, Sam?

SAMUEL. Mr. Fosther was here this mornin' runnin' a hand
through th' daffodils sent for Easther, an' found somethin'
he didn't like.

RECTOR. Yes?

SAMUEL. It's not for me to remark on anything that manœuvres
out in front o' me, or to slip in a sly word on things done,
said, or thought on, be th' pastors, masthers, or higher indi-
viduals of th' congregation; but, sometimes, sir, there comes
a time when a true man should, must speak out.

RECTOR [*with a sigh*]. And the time has come to say something
now—what is it, Sam?

SAMUEL [*in a part whisper*]. This mornin', sir, and th' dear
spring sun shinin' through th' yellow robes of Pether an' th'
purple robes o' Paul, an' me arrangin' the books in th' pews,
who comes stealin' in, but lo and behold you, Fosther an'
Dowzard to have a squint round. Seein' they're Select Ves-
thrymen, I couldn't ask them why they were nosin' about
in the silence of th' church on an ordinary week-day

mornin'.

RECTOR [*patiently*]. Yes; but a long time ago, you said something about daffodils.

SAMUEL. I'm comin' at a gallop to them, sir.

RECTOR. Good; well, let's hear about the daffodils.

SAMUEL. Aha, says I, when I seen th' two prowlers with their heads close together, whisperin', aha, says I, there's somethin' on the carpet.

RECTOR. Is what you have to tell me something to do with Dowzard and Foster, or the daffodils?

SAMUEL. Wait till you hear; sometimes Fosther an' Dowzard'll be to th' fore, an' sometimes th' daffodils. What can these two oul' codgers be up to, says I, sidlin' up to where they were, hummin' a hymn.

RECTOR. Humming a hymn? I'm glad to hear it; for I'd be surprised to hear either of them humming a hymn.

SAMUEL. Me it was, sir, who was hummin' th' hymn; for in a church, I like me thoughts to go with th' work I'm doin', if you know what I mean.

RECTOR [*impatiently*]. It'll be nightfall before you get to the daffodils, man.

SAMUEL. Wait till you hear, sir. There I was gettin' close to them be degrees, when, all of a sudden, didn't Fosther turn on me, shoutin' "Are you goin' to be a party to th' plastherin' of Popish emblems over a Protestan' church?

RECTOR. Popish emblems?

SAMUEL. Th' daffodils, sir.

RECTOR. The daffodils? But they simply signify the new life that Spring gives; and we connect them in a symbolic way, quite innocently, with our Blessed Lord's Rising. And a beautiful symbol they are: daffodils that come before the swallow dares, and take the winds of March with beauty. Shakespeare, Sam.

SAMUEL [*lifting his eyes skywards and pointing upwards*]. Altogether too high up for poor me, sir. [*He bends down close to the* RECTOR's *ear.*] When he seen the cross of daffodils made be Breydon, he near went daft. [*A pause, as if* SAMUEL *ex-*

pected the RECTOR *to speak, but he stays silent.*] God knows what'll be th' upshot if it's fixed to the Communion Table, sir. [*Another slight pause.*] Is it really to go there, sir? Wouldn't it look a little more innocent on th' pulpit, sir?

RECTOR [*in a final voice*]. I will place it myself in front of the Communion Table, and, if Mr. Foster or Mr. Dowzard ask anything more about it, say that it has been placed there by me. And, remember, when you say Mr. Foster and Mr. Dowzard, it's to be Mr. Breydon too. [*He hands some leaflets to* SAMUEL.] Distribute these through the pews, Sam, please. The arranging of the flowers is finished, is it?

SAMUEL. Yessir; all but the cross.

RECTOR. I will see to that myself. Thanks, Sam.

[SAMUEL *goes off into the church, and the* RECTOR, *leaning back in his chair with a book in his hand, chants softly.*]

RECTOR [*chanting*].
May wonders cease when we grow tame,
Or worship greatness in a name;
May love for man be all our fame,
We beseech Thee!

[*As he pauses to meditate for a moment,* MRS. BREYDON *is seen coming along, outside the hedge. She enters by the gate, and comes over to the* RECTOR. SHEILA *has come with her, but lags a little behind when they enter the grounds. The* RECTOR *rises quickly from his chair to greet* MRS. BREYDON.]

RECTOR [*warmly*]. My dear Mrs. Breydon! Hasn't it been a lovely day? The weather promises well for Easter.

MRS. BREYDON. It would be good if other things promised as well as the weather, sir.

RECTOR. We must be patient, and more hopeful, my friend. From the clash of life new life is born.

MRS. BREYDON. An' often new life dies in th' clash too. Ah, when he comes, sir, speak th' word that will keep my boy safe at home, or here.

RECTOR [*laying a gentle hand on her arm*]. I wish I could, dear friend; I wish I could.

MRS. BREYDON. His mind, like his poor father's, hates what he sees as a sham; an' shams are powerful things, mustherin' at their broad backs guns that shoot, big jails that hide their foes, and high gallows to choke th' young cryin' out against them when th' stones are silent.

RECTOR. Let those safely sheltered under the lawn of the bishop, the miniver of the noble, the scarlet and ermine of the judge, say unto him, this thing you must not do; I won't, for sometimes out of the mouths of even babes and sucklings cometh wisdom.

SHEILA. If what's against him be so powerful, he is helpless; so let this power go on its way of darkened grandeur, and let Ayamonn sit safe by his own fireside.

[*To the left, on the path outside the hedge, the* INSPECTOR, *in full uniform, appears, evidently coming to see the* RECTOR; *on the right, followed by the men and women of the previous scenes, appears* AYAMONN. *He and the* INSPECTOR *meet at the gate. The* INSPECTOR *and he halt. The* INSPECTOR *indicates he will wait for* AYAMONN *to pass, and* AYAMONN *comes into the grounds towards the* RECTOR. *The* INSPECTOR *follows, but, in the grounds, stands a little apart, nearer the hedge. The men and women spread along the path outside, and stay still watching those in the grounds from over the hedge. They hold themselves erect, now; their faces are still pale, but are set with seams of resolution. Each is wearing in the bosom a golden-rayed sun.* BRENNAN *comes in and, crossing the grass, sidles over to sit down on the step of the porch.*]

RECTOR [*shaking* AYAMONN'S *hand*]. Ah, I'm so glad you've come; I hope you'll stay.

AYAMONN [*hastily*]. I come but to go. You got the cross of daffodils?

RECTOR. Your mother brought it to us; it will hang in front of our church's greatest promise. Come and place it there with your own loyal hands, Ayamonn.

INSPECTOR. Loyal hands engaged in rough rending of the law and the rumpling-up of decency and order; and all for what? For what would but buy blacking for a pair of boots, or a sheet of glass to mend a broken window!

BRENNAN [*from his seat on the porch's step*]. He's right, Ayamonn, me son, he's right: money's the root of all evil.

AYAMONN [*to the* INSPECTOR]. A shilling's little to you, and less to many; to us it is our Shechinah, showing us God's light is near; showing us the way in which our feet must go; a sun-ray on our face; the first step taken in the march of a thousand miles.

INSPECTOR [*threateningly*]. I register a lonely warning here that the people of power today will teach a lesson many will remember for ever; though some fools may not live long enough to learn it.

MRS. BREYDON. Stay here, my son, where safety is a green tree with a kindly growth.

MEN AND WOMEN [*in chorus—above*]. He comes with us!

SHEILA. Stay here where time goes by in sandals soft, where days fall gently as petals from a flower, where dark hair, growing grey, is never noticed.

MEN AND WOMEN [*above*]. He comes with us!

AYAMONN [*turning towards them*]. I go with you!

INSPECTOR [*vehemently*]. Before you go to carry out all your heated mind is set to do, I warn you for the last time that today swift horses will be galloping, and swords will be out of their scabbards!

RECTOR [*reprovingly—to* INSPECTOR]. I hope you, at least, will find not reason to set your horses moving.

INSPECTOR [*stiffly*]. I'll do my duty sir; and it would be a good thing if someone we all know did his in that state of life unto which it has pleased God to call him.

RECTOR [*losing his temper*]. Oh, damn it, man, when you repeat the Church's counsel, repeat it right! Not *unto which it has pleased God to call him*, but *unto which it shall please God* to call him.

INSPECTOR [*losing his temper too*]. Damn it, man, do you believe that what the fellow's doing now is the state of life unto which it has pleased God to call him?

RECTOR [*hotly*]. I have neither the authority nor the knowledge to deny it, though I have more of both than you, sir!

[*The* INSPECTOR *is about to answer angrily, but* SHEILA *catches his arm.*]

SHEILA. Oh, cancel from your mind the harder things you want to say, an' do your best to save us from another sorrow!

INSPECTOR [*shaking off* SHEILA'S *hand roughly, and going to the gateway, where he turns to speak again*]. Remember, all! When swords are drawn and horses charge, the kindly Law, so fat with hesitation, swoons away, and sees not, hears not, cares not what may happen.

MRS. BREYDON [*angrily—up to the* INSPECTOR]. Look at th' round world, man, an' all its wondhers, God made, flaming in it, an' what are you among them, standing here, or on a charging horse, but just a braided an' a tasselled dot!

[*The* INSPECTOR *hurries off, to pause, and stands outside the hedge, to the right, the men and women shrinking back a little in awe to give him a passage.*]

MRS. BREYDON [*to* AYAMONN]. Go on your way, my son, an' win. We'll welcome another inch of the world's welfare.

RECTOR [*shaking his hand*]. Go, and may the Lord direct you! [*He smiles.*] The Inspector's bark is louder than his bite is deep.

AYAMONN. For the present—goodbye!

[AYAMONN *hurries away through the gate, pausing, outside the hedge to the left, turning to give a last look at the* INSPECTOR.]

INSPECTOR. Bear back, my boy, when you see the horsemen charging!

[*He goes out by the right, and* AYAMONN *goes out left, followed by the men and the women. There is a slight pause.*]

RECTOR [*briskly—to banish a gloomy feeling*]. Now, Mrs. Breydon, you run along to the vestry, and make us a good cup of tea—I'm dying for one. [*To* SHEILA.] You'll join us, Miss Moorneen, won't you?

SHEILA [*immediately anxious*]. Oh no, thanks. I . . . I shouldn't even be here. I'm a Catholic, you know.

RECTOR. I know, and I'd be the last to ask you do anything you shouldn't; but rest assured there's no canonical law against taking tea made by a Protestant. Off you go, and help Mrs. Breydon. I'll join you in a moment.

[SHEILA *and* MRS. BREYDON *go off by the south wall of the church.*]

BRENNAN [*as the* RECTOR *is gathering his books and papers from the table*]. Hey, sir; hey there, sir: It won't shatther th' community at large this disturbance, will it, eh?

RECTOR. I hope not.

BRENNAN [*with a forced laugh*]. No, no, of course not. Bank of Ireland'll still stand, eh? Ay. Ravenous to break in, some of them are, eh? Ay, ay. Iron doors, iron doors are hard to open, eh?

RECTOR [*going off to get his tea*]. I suppose so.

BRENNAN. Ay, are they. He supposes so; only supposes—there's a responsible man for you!

[*The verger comes into the porch and bends over* BRENNAN.]

SAMUEL [*in a hoarse whisper*]. Come in an' have a decko at our grand cross.

BRENNAN. Cross? What cross?

SAMUEL. One o' daffodils; for Easther; to be put in front o' th' Communion Table.

BRENNAN [*climbing as quick as he can from the porch step*].

Popery, be God! We'll put a spoke in that wheel. Lemme in to see.

[*He goes into the church with the verger, who closes the door. After a pause, the sound of running feet is heard at a distance, and some stones hop off the path outside the hedge. In a few moments* DOWZARD *and* FOSTER *come running along, hurry through the gateway and pause, breathless, beside the porch.* DOWZARD *is a big, beefy, red-faced man, rolls of flesh pouring out over the collar of his coat. His head is massive and bald, with jet-black tufts behind his ear, and a tiny fringe of it combed across high over his forehead.* FOSTER *is small and scraggy, with aggression for ever lurking in his cranky face, ready to leap into full view at the slightest opportunity. His cheeks and lips are shaven, but spikes of yellowish whiskers point defiantly out from under his chin. His voice is squeaky and, when it is strengthened in anger, it rises into a thin piping scream. Both are dressed in the uniforms of railway foremen, blue cloth, with silver buttons, and silver braid on* DOWZARD'S *peaked hat and coatsleeves, and gold braid on those of* FOSTER. *Both have their coats tightly buttoned up on them. They take off their peaked caps and wipe sweat from their foreheads.* DOWZARD *pushes the door.*]

DOWZARD [*panting*]. Door shut, blast it! We're safe here, though, in th' grounds; Church grounds sacred. Unguarded, verminous villains—Papists, th' lot o' them!

FOSTER [*venomously*]. On' one o' their leaders a Select Vestryman. On' thot domned Rector stondin' by him. Steeped in Popery: sign o' th' cross; turnin' eastward sayin' th' Creed; sung Communion—be Gud, it's a public scondal!

DOWZARD. Some o' them stones scorched me ear passin' by. We shouldn't have worn our uniforms. Gave us away. I knew we were in for it when they called us scabs.

FOSTER [*going over and sitting down by the table*]. Scobs themselves! Smoky, vonomous bastards! Sut down, mon, on' calm yourself. I tull you I'd wear me uniform in th' Vutican. [*He unbuttons his coat and shows that he is wearing a vivid orange sash, bordered with blue.*] Thor's me sash for all tae see. You should ha' stud with me, mon; stud like th' heroes o' Dully's Brae!

[*The men and women run in, crouchingly, from right and left. They make the movement of throwing stones at the two men, who are hit on the head, and fall over the table as if they had been stunned, while the men and women raise their voices in a song, led by the* 1ST MAN, *all standing behind the hedge.*]

1ST MAN [*singing*].
   If we can't fire a gun, we can fire a hard stone,
   Till th' life of th' scab shrivels into a moan.
REST [*in chorus*].
   Let it sink in what I say,
   Let me say it again—
   Though th' Lord God made an odd scab, sure,
      He also made men!
1ST MAN [*singing*].
   There's room in this big world for Gentile an' Jew,
   For th' Bashibazouk, but there's no room for you;
REST [*in chorus*].
   Let it sink in what I say,
   Let it sink in what I tell—
   You'll be lucky to find a spare place down in hell!
1ST MAN [*singing*].
   Th' one honour you'll get is a dusty black plume.
   On th' head of th' nag taking you to th' tomb.
REST [*in chorus*].
   Let it sink in what I say,
   Let it sink in what I tell—
   Th' scab's curs'd be th' workers, book, candle, an' bell!

[*As they sing the last part of the last verse, they move way, those on the right, to the left; and those on the left, to the right. After a short pause,* DOWZARD, *holding a hand to his head, staggers over to the church door and kicks violently at it.*]

DOWZARD [*shouting*]. Ey, there, in there, come out, open th' blasted door an' help a half-dead man!

[*The church door is opened, and the* RECTOR, *followed by the verger and* BRENNAN, *comes out into the grounds.*]

RECTOR. What's wrong; what has happened?

DOWZARD. Th' Pope's bullies with hard stones have smitten us sore. Honest men, virtuous an' upright, loyal to th' law an' constitution, have this day been smitten sore with Popish stones—oh, me poor head!

FOSTER. St. Bartholomew's Day's dawnin' again, I'm tullin' yous, an' dismumbered Protestants'll lie on all th' sthreets!

RECTOR [*to the verger*]. Run in and fetch a basin of water, and tear a few strips from the old surplice hanging in the press. [*The verger goes back to the church, and the* RECTOR *turns to the two men.*] You can't be badly hurt when you complain so grandly.

FOSTER [*indignantly*]. Thot's right—pooh-pooh away a loyal Protestant skull all but shotthered to buts be a Popish stone!

RECTOR. Let me see the damage done. [*He examines the wound.*] Ah, a slight contusion. You won't die a martyr yet. [*The verger returns with basin of water and strips of linen, and the* RECTOR *bathes and bandages* FOSTER's *head.*] There, you'll do nicely. [*To* DOWZARD.] Now for yours. [*He examines the wound.*] Not even as bad as Mr. Foster's. [*He bathes and bandages* DOWZARD's *wound.*] Your caps saved you both from worse injuries.

FOSTER. Stand up for th' ruffians be makin' luttle of our hurts, so do, ay, do. [*Noticing* BRENNAN *who has edged towards the gate and is about to go away.*] Eh, you, aren't you goin' to stay an' put tustimony to the fullness o' th' Protestan' feth?

BRENNAN [*with slight mockery*]. Ay, I would, an' welcome, if I hodn't to go, forbye, at this hour of on uvery day, I mak' ut a rule tae be sturdy in th' readin' of a chapther o' God's word so's I won't hold on tae worldly things too strongly. [*He goes out.*]

FOSTER [*fiercely*]. A jully-fush Protestant! [*To the* RECTOR.] Look see, I tull you th' fires o' Smithfield 'ull be blazin' round Protestant bodies again, an' coloured lights 'ull be shown in th' Vatican windows soon!

DOWZARD. An' we'll be th' first to go up in th' flames.

RECTOR *laughing contemptuously*]. Nonsense, oh, nonsense.

FOSTER [*almost screaming*]. It's not nonsense, mon! Every sable-robed Jesuit's goin' about chucklin', his honds twitchin' to pounce out on men like me here, an' Eddie Dowzard there, tae manacle us, head, hond, and fut, for th' wheel, th' thumbscrew, an' th' rack, an' then finish us up at th' stake in a hoppy Romish auto-dey-fey! The Loyola boyos are out to fight another buttle with th' men o' King Bully!

RECTOR [*amused*]. Well, let the Loyola boyos and King Bully fight it out between them. I'm too busy to join either side. Goodbye.

FOSTER [*catching his arm as he is going—viciously*]. You're no' goin' tae be lut slide off like thot, now, with your guilty conscience, mon. There's things to be done, and things tae be ondone in yon church, there; ay, ay.

RECTOR [*quietly*]. Indeed?

FOSTER [*angrily—to* DOWZARD]. Uh, speak, speak a word, mon, on' don't leave ut all tae me.

DOWZARD. First, sir, we want you to get rid o' Breydon from the Vesthry an' from th' church.

RECTOR. Oh, indeed?

FOSTER [*almost screaming*]. It's no' oh, indeed; answer th' question—plain yes or no!

RECTOR [*coldly*]. Gentlemen, Mr. Breydon stays in the Vestry till the parishioners elect someone else; as for the church, God has seen fit to make him a member of Christ, and it is not for me, or even for you, gentlemen, to say that God did wrong.

DOWZARD [*sneeringly*]. An' when did that wondherful thing hoppen?

RECTOR. At his baptism, as you yourself should know.

FOSTER [*with an agonised squeal*]. Popery, popery, nothin' but popery! Th' whole place's infusted with it!

[*The verger appears at the porch door with the cross of daffodils in his hand. It has a Keltic shape, the shafts made of the flowers, and the circle of vivid green moss. The verger shows it to* DOWZARD, *behind the* RECTOR'S *back, and* DOWZARD *sidling over, takes it from him, the verger returning into the church again.*]

RECTOR. And now be good enough, Mr. Foster, to let go my arm.

FOSTER [*still gripping the* RECTOR'S *arm, and now thrusting his distorted face closer to the* RECTOR'S]. You're thryin' to make a Mass-house of God's tumple; you'd like to do a donce with th' whore o' Babylon, if we'd lot yeh, th' whore in purple an' scorlet, an' dhrunk with th' blood o' th' saints, if we lot yeh!

DOWZARD [*dancing out in front of them holding out the cross— with exultant anger*]. There y'are, see? Caught in the very act—red-handed—a popish symbol flourished in th' faces of Protestant people! [*With a shout.*] Ichabod, Ichabod!

FOSTER [*dancing about as if he were a dancing dervish*]. Things done behind our bocks are done in front of our faces! Oh, th' sly, sleek, sacerdutal, jesuitical worshippers of a wafer god! I'll no' stick it, no; I'll no stick it. Looksee, the rage godly, kindling Luther, kindles me! Down with them that inflame th' hearts o' th' congregation with th' sight o' Romish images! Here, go gimme a holt o' thot. [*He snatches the cross of flowers from* DOWZARD, *flings it on the ground, and dances wildly on it.*] Th' Bible on' th' Crown; th' twa on a half; th' orange on' blue; on' th' Dagon o' Popery ondher our feet! Protestonts, Protestonts, up on' be doin'!

DOWZARD [*wildly shouting*]. Th' dhrum, th' dhrum, th' Protestant drhum!

[*While* FOSTER *and* DOWZARD *have been dancing about and shouting their last few words, the men and women have run frightened along the path, behind the hedge. Those running from the right, turn, and run back to the left; those running from the left, turn, and run back to the left again, passing each other as they run.*]

FOSTER [*frantically*]. We'll die, give up th' ghost, suffer onything tae save ceevil on' reeligious liberty! [*He suddenly sees the men and women running about behind the hedge, and at once plunges into the porch, almost knocking the* RECTOR *down, and is followed, just as swiftly, by* DOWZARD. *As he flies—to the* RECTOR.] Out uh th' way, mon, out uh th' way!

[EEADA *comes running through the gate, into the garden, over to the* RECTOR.]

EEADA [*beseechingly*]. Oh, sir, please let me into the church, till all th' sthrife is over—no place's safe with the soldiers firin' an' th' police runnin' mad in a flourish o' batons!

RECTOR [*reassuringly*]. Be calm, be quiet, they won't touch a woman. They remain men, however furious they may be for the moment.

EEADA. Ara, God help your innocence! You should ha' seen them sthrikin' at men, women, an' childher. An' me own friend, Dympna, in hospital gettin' her face laced with stitches, th' way you'd lace a shoe! An' all along of followin' that mad fool, Breydon!

RECTOR. Go in, then. [*To the verger, who has come to the entrance.*] See her safe.

[EEADA *and the verger go into the church. A man, led by the* 1ST MAN, *whose face is full of fright and strain, comes through the gate into the grounds. The man has a huge brass tuba hammered down over his head, and, now and again, a faint moan is heard coming from beneath it.]*

1ST MAN [*irritably—to man whose head is covered by the tuba*]. Oh, for God's sake lift your feet an' look where you're goin'. Show your paces, or we'll both be ornaments for the morgue! [*Dragging him into the grounds.*] Here, in here, till the danger's past.

FOSTER [*exultantly, coming out of porch with DOWZARD*]. Aha, you're no' firin' stones, now, at decent Christian people!

DOWZARD [*standing pompously in their path*]. Off with you somewhere else, you Papish ruffians! Away with you from where men honour love, peace, ordher, an' a Christian life.

RECTOR [*coming forward and quietly setting DOWZARD aside*]. I'd better take control here; these ignorant people would never understand the purity of your Christian affection. [*Firmly.*] They will find shelter here, till the law regains its temper. [*To 1ST MAN—indicating tuba.*] Who did this to that poor man?

1ST MAN [*trying to repress amusement*]. Horse police, sir: chargin' th' band, one o' them stooped over, whipped th' big bugle out of his hand, brought it down with a wallop over his head, an' dhrove it home with his baton; an' th' rest, in passin', each had a skelp to fix it tighter. [*Bending over to whisper in the RECTOR's ear, he explodes into a laugh.*] 'Clare to God, it'll take a charge o' dynamite to get it off comfortable!

RECTOR [*severely*]. It's nothing to joke about, my man. Are we to make merry over another man's misery?

1ST MAN [*apologetically*]. Oh, no; no, no. Sure, he can't hear me, sir. A man makin' a joke of it deserves hangin'. [*Breaking out again.*] Doesn't he look, for all th' world, like an oulden knight in golden armour goin' out to conquer haythen kingdoms!

RECTOR [*trying to move the tuba, and failing*]. I don't know what to do.

[*The man with the tuba sinks down on the grass and lies*

*there. Along the path, outside the hedge, another frightened
man comes running, and when he enters the gateway it is
seen that the shell of a drum is fixed round his body. From
his shoulders to his waist, his arms wedged within the shell
as if in a vice, a green flag, with a golden harp on it, is laced
to the drum's rim, so that it forms a kind of a short skimpy
skirt down to the man's knees. He runs as quick as he can
across the grounds, bumping against* FOSTER *as he passes,
into the porch, and he can be heard kicking at the inner
door; then he comes to the outer door, to stand there and
glare at all who are looking at him.*]

MAN [*with drum round him*]. Eh, there, will yous get this other
door opened, if yous don't want to see a man murdhered.
Quit your starin', will yous? Oh, isn't there one decent, honest, dear Christian left livin' to set me free from this help-
lessness before any oncomin' emergency!

1ST MAN [*choking with suppressed enjoyment*]. He's like th'
Lady of th' Lake on th' banks of Loch Lomond—oh, th'
polis's doin' mighty things today for the glory o' God an'
th' honour of Ireland!

[*As the* 2ND MAN *leans helplessly against the side of the
porch,* FINNOOLA *comes slowly along the path outside the
hedge, holding on to the railings as she moves, step by step.
When she comes to the gateway, she sinks down to the
ground and turns a white and distorted face towards those
in the grounds.*]

FINNOOLA [*painfully*]. For th' love o' God, one of you tell me if
th' Reverend something Clinton's here, or have I to crawl
a long way further?

RECTOR [*hurrying over to her*]. He's here; I'm here, my good
woman. What is it you want of me?

FINNOOLA. I've a message for you from Ayamonn Breydon.

RECTOR [*eagerly*]. Yes, yes; where is he?

FINNOOLA. He's gone.

RECTOR. Gone? Gone where?

FINNOOLA. Gone to God, I hope. [*A rather long pause.*]

RECTOR [*in a low voice*]. May he rest in peace! And the message?

FINNOOLA. Yes. He whispered it in me ear as his life fled
through a bullet-hole in his chest—th' soldiers, th' soldiers.
He said this day's but a day's work done, an' it'll be begun
again tomorrow. You're to keep an eye on th' oul' woman.
He wants to lie in th' church tonight, sir. Me hip's hurt; th'
fut of a plungin' horse caught me, an' I flat on th' ground.
He sent a quick an' a long farewell to you. Oh, for Christ's
sake get's a dhrink o' wather! [*The verger runs for a drink.*]
We stood our groun' well, though. [*The verger comes back
with the water, and she drinks.*] Now I can have a thrickle
of rest at last. [*She stretches herself out on the ground.*]

RECTOR. Where did you leave him? Where is he lying now?

[*She lies there, and makes no answer. He picks up the
broken cross of flowers and is silent for a few moments.*]

RECTOR [*with head bent low—sorrowfully*]. Oh, Ayamonn,
Ayamonn, my dear, dear friend. Oh, Lord, open Thou mine
eyes that I may see Thee, even as in a glass, darkly, in all
this mischief and all this woe!

[*The curtain comes down to indicate the passing of some
hours. When it rises again, it is evening. The lamp over the
porch door is lighted, and so is the church, the light shining
through the yellow robe of St. Peter and the purple robe of
St. Paul from the window in the church's wall. The church
organ is playing, very softly, a dead march. The lamp on the
path, outside the hedge, isn't yet lighted. The dark figures
of men and women can be faintly seen lining themselves
along the hedge.* MRS. BREYDON *is standing in the grounds,
near the gateway.* FOSTER *and* DOWZARD *stand on the steps
of the porch. A little in front, with his back turned towards
them, stands the* RECTOR, *now with white surplice over his
cassock, his stole around his neck, and the crimson-lined*

hood of a Doctor of Divinity on his shoulders. SHEILA, *holding a bunch of crimson roses in her hand, stands under the rowan tree. Partly behind the tree, the* INSPECTOR *is standing alone. A* LAMPLIGHTER *comes along the path, carrying his pole with the little flower of light in the brass top. He lights the lamp on the path, then comes over to peer across the hedge.*]

LAMPLIGHTER. What's up? What's on? What's happenin' here? What'r they all doin' now?

1ST MAN. Bringin' th' body o' Breydon to th' church.

LAMPLIGHTER. Aw, is that it? Guessed somethin' was goin' on.

1ST MAN. He died for us.

LAMPLIGHTER. Looka that, now! An' they're all accouthered in their best to welcome him home, wha'? Aw, well, th' world's got to keep movin', so I must be off; so long! [*He goes.*]

DOWZARD [*speaking to the* RECTOR'S *back*]. For th' last time, sir, I tell you half of the Vestry's against him comin' here; they don't want our church mixed up with this venomous disturbance.

RECTOR [*without moving, and keeping his eyes looking towards the gateway*]. All things in life, the evil and the good, the orderly and disorderly, are mixed with the life of the Church Militant here on earth. We honour our brother, not for what may have been an error in him, but for the truth for ever before his face. We dare not grudge him God's forgiveness and rest eternal because he held no banner above a man-made custom.

FOSTER [*savagely*]. Aw, looksee, I'm no' a mon to sut down on' listen to a tumblin' blether o' words—wull ye, or wull ye not, give intil us?

[*In the distance a bagpipe is heard playing* Flowers of the Forest. MRS. BREYDON'S *body stiffens, and* SHEILA'S *head bends lower on her breast.*]

RECTOR. It is a small thing that you weary me, but you weary my God also. Stand aside, and go your way of smoky ignorance, leaving me to welcome him whose turbulence has sunken into a deep sleep, and who cometh now as the waters of Shiloah that go softly, and sing sadly of peace.

[*As he is speaking, the lament ceases, and a moment after, a stretcher bier, bearing the covered-up body of* AYAMONN, *appears at the gateway. It is carried down towards the church, and the* RECTOR *goes to meet it.*]

RECTOR [*intoning*]. Lord, Thou hast been our refuge from one generation to another. For a thousand years in Thy sight are but as yesterday. [*He chants.*]

> All our brother's mordant strife,
> Fought for more abundant life;
> For this, and more—oh, hold him dear.
> Jesu, Son of Mary, hear!
>
> Gather to Thy loving breast
> Ev'ry laughing thoughtful jest,
> Gemm'd with many a thoughtful tear.
> Jesu, Son of Mary, hear!
>
> When Charon rows him nigh to shore,
> To see a land, ne'er seen before,
> Him to rest eternal steer.
> Jesu, Son of Mary, hear!

[*The bier is carried into the church, and, as it passes,* SHEILA *lays the bunch of crimson roses on the body's breast.*]

SHEILA. Ayamonn, Ayamonn, my own poor Ayamonn!

[*The* RECTOR *precedes the bier, and* MRS. BREYDON *walks beside it, into the church, the rest staying where they are. There is a slight pause.*]

DOWZARD. We'd betther be goin'. Th' man's a malignant Romaniser. Keep your eye on th' rabble goin' out.

FOSTER [*contemptuously*]. There's little fight left in thom, th'
now. I'll no' forgive thot Inspector fur refusin' to back our
demond.

[*They swagger out through the gateway and disappear along
the path outside the hedge, as those who carried the bier
come out of the church.*]

2ND MAN. That's the last, th' very last of him—a core o' darkness stretched out in a dim church.

3RD MAN. It was a noble an' a mighty death.

INSPECTOR [*from where he is near the tree*]. It wasn't a very
noble thing to die for a single shilling.

SHEILA. Maybe he saw the shilling in th' shape of a new world.

[*The 2ND and 3RD MEN go out by the gateway and mingle
with the rest gathered there. The INSPECTOR comes closer
to SHEILA.*]

INSPECTOR. Oughtn't you to go from this gloom, Sheila? Believe
me, I did my best. I thought the charge would send them flying, but they wouldn't budge; wouldn't budge, till the soldiers fired, and he was hit. Believe me, I did my best. I tried
to force my horse between them and him.

SHEILA [*calmly*]. I believe you, Inspector Finglas.

INSPECTOR [*gently catching her by the arm*]. Tom to you, dear.
Come, Sheila, come, and let us put these things away from
us as we saunter slowly home.

SHEILA [*with a quiver in her voice*]. Oh, not now; oh not tonight! Go your own way, and let me go mine, alone tonight.

INSPECTOR [*taking her hand in his*]. Sheila, Sheila, be sparing
in your thought for death, and let life smile before you. Be
sparing in thought of death on one who spent his life too
rashly and lost it all too soon. Ill-gotten wealth of life, ill-
gone for ever!

SHEILA [*withdrawing her hand from his gently*]. Oh, Tom, I
hope you're right; you are right, you must be right.

[*They have walked to the gateway, and now stand there together, the men and women along the hedge eyeing them, though pretending to take no notice.*]

INSPECTOR. You'll see it clearer, dear, when busy Time in space has set another scene of summer's glory, and new-born spring's loud voice of hope hushes to silence th' intolerant dead.

SHEILA [*musingly*]. He said that roses red were never meant for me; before I left him last, that's what he said. Dear loneliness tonight must help me think it out, for that's just what he said. [*Suddenly—with violence.*] Oh, you dusky-minded killer of more worthy men!

[*She runs violently away from him, and goes out, leaving him with the men and women, who stand idly by as if noticing nothing.*]

INSPECTOR [*after a pause*]. What are ye doing here? Get home! Home with you, you lean rats, to your holes and haunts! D'ye think th' like o' you alone are decked with th' dark honour of trouble? [*Men and women scatter, slowly and sullenly, till only* BRENNAN, *with his melodeon on his back, is left, leaning by the gate. To* BRENNAN.] Heard what I said? Are you deaf, or what?

BRENNAN [*calmly*]. I'm a Protestant, an' a worshipper in this church.

INSPECTOR. One of the elect! So was Breydon. Well, keep clear of unruly crowds—my men don't wait to ask the way you worship when they raise their arms to strike.

[*He goes slowly away down the path. A few moments pass, then the* RECTOR *and* MRS. BREYDON *come out of the church. He arranges a shawl round her shoulders.*]

RECTOR. There; that's better! My wife insists you stay the night with us, so there's no getting out of it.

MRS. BREYDON. She's kind. [*She pauses to look at the rowan tree.*] There's th' three he loved, bare, or dhrenched with blossom. Like himself, for fine things grew thick in his nature; an' lather come the berries, th' red berries, like the blood that flowed today out of his white body. [*Suddenly— turning to face the church.*] Is it puttin' out th' lights he is?

RECTOR. Yes, before he goes home for the night.

MRS. BREYDON. Isn't it a sad thing for him to be lyin' lonesome in th' cheerless darkness of th' livelong night!

RECTOR [*going to the porch and calling out*]. Sam, leave the lights on tonight.

[*The church, which had dimmed, lights up again.*]

RECTOR. He's not so lonesome as you think, dear friend, but alive and laughing in the midst of God's gay welcome. Come.

[*They slowly go through the gate and pass out. The verger comes from the church and swings the outer door to, to lock up for the night.* BRENNAN *comes down into the grounds.*]

SAMUEL [*grumbling*]. Light on all night—more of his Roman-isin' manœuvres.

BRENNAN. Eh, eh, there; houl' on a second!

SAMUEL. What th' hell do you want?

BRENNAN. Just to sing a little song he liked as a sign of respect an' affection; an' as a finisher-off to a last farewell.

SAMUEL [*locking the door*]. An' what d'ye take me for? You an' your song an' your last farewell!

BRENNAN [*giving him a coin*]. For a bare few minutes, an' leave th' door open so's th' sound'll have a fair chance to go in to him. [*The verger opens the door.*] That's it. You're a kind man, really.

[BRENNAN *stands facing into the porch, the verger leaning against the side of it.* BRENNAN *unslings his melodeon, plays a few preliminary notes on it, and then sings softly.*]

A sober, black shawl hides her body entirely,
Touch'd be th' sun an' th' salt spray of th' sea;
But deep in th' darkness a slim hand, so lovely,
Carries a rich bunch of red roses for me!

[*The rest of the song is cut off by the ending of the play.*]

RED ROSES FOR ME

A sober black shawl hides her body entirely Touch'd by the sun and th' salt spray of th' sea; But down in th' darkness a slim hand so love-ly, Car-ries a rich bunch of red ro-ses for me.—

TH' BOULD FENIAN MEN

Our cour-age so ma-ny have thought to be ag-in', Now flames like a bril-liant new star in the sky; An' Dan-ger is proud to be call'd a new bro-ther, Since Freedom has buckled her sword on her thigh. Then out to th' place where the bat-tle is brav-est, Where th' noblest an' meanest fight fierce in th' fray, Re-pub-lic-an ban-ners shall mock at th' foe-men, An' Fen-ians shall turn a dark night in-to day!

OH, QUEEN OF EBLANA'S POOR CHILDREN

Oh, Queen of Eb - la - na's poor child - ren, Bear swift - ly our woe a -

way; An' give us a chance to live light - ly An hour of our life's dark

day; Lift up th' poor heads ev - er bend - ing, An' light a lone star in th'

sky, To show thro' th' dark-ness, de-scend-ing, A cheer-i-er way to die.

I TUCK'D UP MY SLEEVES

I stroll'd with a fine maid far out in th' coun-try, Th'

blos-soms a - round us all cry - in' for dew;— On a

dai-sy deckt bench, sure, I sat down be-side her And tuck'd up my sleeves for to

tie up her shoe; An' what's that to a - ny one wheth-er or no, If I

came to th' fore when she gave me th' cue? She clos'd her eyes tight as she

mur-mured full low, Be good e-nough, dear, for to tie up my shoe.

BROTHERS

All our bro-ther's mord-ant strife,

Fought for more a-bund-ant life: For

this, and more, oh, hold him dear:

Je-su, Son of Ma-ry, hear!

ALL MY SONS [1947]

---

by Arthur Miller
[1915-   ]

For Elia Kazan

CHARACTERS

JOE KELLER, *a factory owner*
KATE KELLER, *his wife*
CHRIS KELLER, *their son*
ANN DEEVER, *their house-guest*
GEORGE DEEVER, *her brother*
DR. JIM BAYLISS, *friend of the Kellers*
SUE BAYLISS, *his wife*
FRANK LUBEY $\Big\}$ *the Kellers' next-door neighbors*
LYDIA LUBEY
BERT, *a neighborhood eight-year-old*

SYNOPSIS OF SCENES

ACT I: The back yard of the Keller home in the outskirts of an American town. August of our era.

ACT II: Scene, as before. The same evening, as twilight falls.

ACT III: Scene, as before. Two o'clock the following morning.

ACT ONE

The back yard of the KELLER *home in the outskirts of an American town. August of our era.*

The stage is hedged on right and left by tall, closely planted poplars which lend the yard a secluded atmosphere. Upstage is filled with the back of the house and its open, unroofed porch which extends into the yard some six feet. The house is two stories high and has seven rooms. It would have cost perhaps fifteen thousand in the early twenties when it was built. Now it is nicely painted, looks tight and comfortable, and the yard is green with sod, here and there plants whose season is gone. At the right, beside the house, the entrance of the driveway can be seen, but the poplars cut off view of its continuation downstage. In the left corner, downstage, stands the four-foot high stump of a slender apple tree whose upper trunk and branches lie toppled beside it, fruit still clinging to its branches.

Downstage right is a small, trellised arbor, shaped like a sea-shell, with a decorative bulb hanging from its forward-curving roof. Garden chairs and a table are scattered about. A garbage pail on the ground next to the porch steps, a wire leaf-burner near it.

ON THE RISE: *It is early Sunday morning.* JOE KELLER *is sitting in the sun reading the want ads of the Sunday paper, the other sections of which lie neatly on the ground beside*

him. Behind his back, inside the arbor, DOCTOR JIM BAYLISS
is reading part of the paper at the table.

KELLER *is nearing sixty. A heavy man of stolid mind and
build, a business man these many years, but with the imprint
of the machine-shop worker and boss still upon him. When
he reads, when he speaks, when he listens, it is with the terrible concentration of the uneducated man for whom there
is still wonder in many commonly known things, a man
whose judgments must be dredged out of experience and a
peasant-like common sense. A man among men.*

DOCTOR BAYLISS *is nearing forty. A wry self-controlled
man, an easy talker, but with a wisp of sadness that clings
even to his self-effacing humor.*

AT CURTAIN, JIM *is standing at left, staring at the broken
tree. He taps a pipe on it, blows through the pipe, feels in
his pockets for tobacco, then speaks.*

JIM. Where's your tobacco?
KELLER. I think I left it on the table. [JIM *goes slowly to table
on the arbor at right, finds a pouch, and sits there on the
bench, filling his pipe.*] Gonna rain tonight.
JIM. Paper says so?
KELLER. Yeah, right here.
JIM. Then it can't rain.

[FRANK LUBEY *enters, from right, through a small space
between the poplars.* FRANK *is thirty-two but balding. A
pleasant, opinionated man, uncertain of himself, with a
tendency toward peevishness when crossed, but always wanting it pleasant and neighborly. He rather saunters in, leisurely, nothing to do. He does not notice* JIM *in the arbor.
On his greeting,* JIM *does not bother looking up.*]

FRANK. Hya.
KELLER. Hello, Frank. What's doin'?
FRANK. Nothin'. Walking off my breakfast. [*Looks up at the
sky.*] That beautiful? Not a cloud.
KELLER [*looks up*]. Yeah, nice.

FRANK. Every Sunday ought to be like this.

KELLER [*indicating the sections beside him*]. Want the paper?

FRANK. What's the difference, it's all bad news. What's today's calamity?

KELLER. I don't know, I don't read the news part any more. It's more interesting in the want ads.

FRANK. Why, you trying to buy something?

KELLER. No, I'm just interested. To see what people want, y'know? For instance, here's a guy is lookin' for two Newfoundland dogs. Now what's he want with two Newfoundland dogs?

FRANK. That is funny.

KELLER. Here's another one. Wanted—Old Dictionaries. High prices paid. Now what's a man going to do with an old dictionary?

FRANK. Why not? Probably a book collector.

KELLER. You mean he'll make a living out of that?

FRANK. Sure, there's a lot of them.

KELLER [*shakes his head*]. All the kind of business goin' on. In my day, either you were a lawyer, or a doctor, or you worked in a shop. Now . . .

FRANK. Well, I was going to be a forester once.

KELLER. Well, that shows you; in my day, there was no such thing. [*Scanning the page, sweeping it with his hand.*] You look at a page like this you realize how ignorant you are. [*Softly, with wonder, as he scans page.*] Psss!

FRANK [*noticing tree*]. Hey, what happened to your tree?

KELLER. Ain't that awful? The wind must've got it last night. You heard the wind, didn't you?

FRANK. Yeah, I got a mess in my yard, too. [*Goes to tree.*] What a pity. [*Turns to* KELLER.] What'd Kate say?

KELLER. They're all asleep yet. I'm just waiting for her to see it.

FRANK [*struck*]. You know?— It's funny.

KELLER. What?

FRANK. Larry was born in August. He'd been twenty-seven this month. And his tree blows down.

KELLER [*touched*]. I'm surprised you remember his birthday,

Frank. That's nice.

FRANK. Well, I'm working on his horoscope.

KELLER. How can you make him a horoscope? That's for the future, ain't it?

FRANK. Well, what I'm doing is this, see. Larry was reported missing on November 25th, right?

KELLER. Yeah?

FRANK. Well, then, we assume that if he was killed it was on November 25th. Now, what Kate wants . . .

KELLER. Oh, Kate asked you to make a horoscope?

FRANK. Yeah, what she wants to find out is whether November 25th was a favorable day for Larry.

KELLER. What is that, favorable day?

FRANK. Well, a favorable day for a person is a fortunate day, according to his stars. In other words it would be practically impossible for him to have died on his favorable day.

KELLER. Well, was that his favorable day?—November 25th?

FRANK. That's what I'm working on to find out. It takes time! See, the point is, if November 25th was his favorable day, then it's completely possible he's alive somewhere, because . . . I mean it's possible. [*He notices* JIM *now.* JIM *is looking at him as though at an idiot. To* JIM—*with an uncertain laugh.*] I didn't even see you.

KELLER [*to* JIM]. Is he talkin' sense?

JIM. Him? He's all right. He's just completely out of his mind, that's all.

FRANK [*peeved*]. The trouble with you is, you don't *believe* in anything.

JIM. And your trouble is that you believe in *anything. You* didn't see my kid this morning, did you?

FRANK. No.

KELLER. Imagine? He walked off with his thermometer. Right out of his bag.

JIM [*gets up*]. What a problem. One look at a girl and he takes her temperature. [*Goes to driveway, looks upstage toward street.*]

FRANK. That boy's going to be a real doctor; he's smart.

JIM. Over my dead body he'll be a doctor. A good beginning, too.

FRANK. Why? It's an honorable profession.

JIM [*looks at him tiredly*]. Frank, will you stop talking like a civics book? [KELLER *laughs.*]

FRANK. Why, I saw a movie a couple of weeks ago, reminded me of you. There was a doctor in that picture . . .

KELLER. Don Ameche!

FRANK. I think it was, yeah. And he worked in his basement discovering things. That's what you ought to do; you could help humanity, instead of . . .

JIM. I would love to help humanity on a Warner Brothers salary.

KELLER [*points at him, laughing*]. That's very good, Jim.

JIM [*looks toward house*]. Well, where's the beautiful girl was supposed to be here?

FRANK [*excited*]. Annie came?

KELLER. Sure, sleepin' upstairs. We picked her up on the one o'clock train last night. Wonderful thing. Girl leaves here, a scrawny kid. Couple of years go by, she's a regular woman. Hardly recognized her, and she was running in and out of this yard all her life. That was a very happy family used to live in your house, Jim.

JIM. Like to meet her. The block can use a pretty girl. In the whole neighborhood there's not a damned thing to look at. [*Enter* SUE, JIM's *wife, from left. She is rounding forty, an overweight woman who fears it. On seeing her* JIM *wryly adds:*] . . . Except my wife, of course.

SUE [*in same spirit*]. Mrs. Adams is on the phone, you dog.

JIM [*to* KELLER]. Such is the condition which prevails, [*Going to his wife.*] my love, my light. . . .

SUE. Don't sniff around me. [*Points to their house, left.*] And give her a nasty answer. I can smell her perfume over the phone.

JIM. What's the matter with her now?

SUE. I don't know, dear. She sounds like she's in terrible pain—unless her mouth is full of candy.

JIM. Why don't you just tell her to lay down?

SUE. She enjoys it more when you tell her to lay down. And when are you going to see Mr. Hubbard?

JIM. My dear; Mr. Hubbard is not sick, and I have better things to do than to sit there and hold his hand.

SUE. It seems to me that for ten dollars you could hold his hand.

JIM [to KELLER]. If your son wants to play golf tell him I'm ready. [Going left.] Or if he'd like to take a trip around the world for about thirty years. [He exits left.]

KELLER. Why do you needle him? He's a doctor, women are supposed to call him up.

SUE. All I said was Mrs. Adams is on the phone. Can I have some of your parsley?

KELLER. Yeah, sure. [She goes left to parsley box and pulls some parsley.] You were a nurse too long, Susie. You're too . . . too . . . realistic.

SUE [laughing, points at him]. Now you said it! [Enter LYDIA LUBEY from right. She is a robust, laughing girl of twenty-seven.]

LYDIA. Frank, the toaster . . . [Sees the others.] Hya.

KELLER. Hello!

LYDIA [to FRANK]. The toaster is off again.

FRANK. Well, plug it in, I just fixed it.

LYDIA [kindly, but insistently]. Please, dear, fix it back like it was before.

FRANK. I don't know why you can't learn to turn on a simple thing like a toaster! [FRANK exits right.]

SUE [laughs]. Thomas Edison.

LYDIA [apologetically]. He's really very handy. [She sees broken tree.] Oh, did the wind get your tree?

KELLER. Yeah, last night.

LYDIA. Oh, what a pity. Annie get in?

KELLER. She'll be down soon. Wait'll you meet her, Sue, she's a knockout.

SUE. I should've been a man. People are always introducing me to beautiful women. [To JOE.] Tell her to come over later;

I imagine she'd like to see what we did with her house. And thanks. [SUE *exits left.*]

LYDIA. Is she still unhappy, Joe?

KELLER. Annie? I don't suppose she goes around dancing on her toes, but she seems to be over it.

LYDIA. She going to get married? Is there anybody . . . ?

KELLER. I suppose . . . say, it's a couple years already. She can't mourn a boy forever.

LYDIA. It's so strange . . . Annie's here and not even married. And I've got three babies. I always thought it'd be the other way around.

KELLER. Well, that's what a war does. I had two sons, now I got one. It changed all the tallies. In my day when you had sons it was an honor. Today a doctor could make a million dollars if he could figure out a way to bring a boy into the world without a trigger finger.

LYDIA. You know, I was just reading . . . [*Enter* CHRIS KELLER *from house, stands in doorway.*]

LYDIA. Hya, Chris . . . [FRANK *shouts from off right.*]

FRANK. Lydia, come in here! If you want the toaster to work don't plug in the malted mixer.

LYDIA [*embarrassed, laughs*]. Did I . . . ?

FRANK. And the next time I fix something don't tell me I'm crazy! Now come in here!

LYDIA [*to* KELLER]. I'll never hear the end of this one.

KELLER [*calling to* FRANK]. So what's the difference? Instead of toast have a malted!

LYDIA. Sh! sh! [*She exits right laughing.*]

[CHRIS *watches her off. He is thirty-two; like his father, solidly built, a listener. A man capable of immense affection and loyalty. He has a cup of coffee in one hand, part of a doughnut in other.*]

KELLER. You want the paper?

CHRIS. That's all right, just the book section. [*He bends down and pulls out part of paper on porch floor.*]

KELLER. You're always reading the book section and you never buy a book.

CHRIS [*coming down to settee*]. I like to keep abreast of my ignorance. [*He sits on settee.*]

KELLER. What is that, every week a new book comes out?

CHRIS. Lot of new books.

KELLER. All different.

CHRIS. All different.

KELLER [*shakes his head, puts knife down on bench, takes oilstone up to the cabinet.*] Psss! Annie up yet?

CHRIS. Mother's giving her breakfast in the dining-room.

KELLER [*crosses, downstage of stool, looking at broken tree*]. See what happened to the tree?

CHRIS [*without looking up*]. Yeah.

KELLER. What's Mother going to say? [BERT *runs on from driveway. He is about eight. He jumps on stool, then on* KELLER's *back.*]

BERT. You're finally up.

KELLER [*swinging him around and putting him down*]. Ha! Bert's here! Where's Tommy? He's got his father's thermometer again.

BERT. He's taking a reading.

CHRIS. What!

BERT. But it's only oral.

KELLER. Oh, well, there's no harm in oral. So what's new this morning, Bert?

BERT. Nothin'. [*He goes to broken tree, walks around it.*]

KELLER. Then you couldn't've made a complete inspection of the block. In the beginning, when I first made you a policeman you used to come in every morning with something new. Now, nothin's ever new.

BERT. Except some kids from Thirtieth Street. They started kicking a can down the block, and I made them go away because you were sleeping.

KELLER. Now you're talkin', Bert. Now you're on the ball. First thing you know I'm liable to make you a detective.

BERT [*pulls him down by the lapel and whispers in his ear*]. Can I see the jail now?

KELLER. Seein' the jail ain't allowed, Bert. You know that.

BERT. Aw, I betcha there isn't even a jail. I don't see any bars on the cellar windows.

KELLER. Bert, on my word of honor, there's a jail in the basement. I showed you my gun, didn't I?

BERT. But that's a hunting gun.

KELLER. That's an arresting gun!

BERT. Then why don't you ever arrest anybody? Tommy said another dirty word to Doris yesterday, and you didn't even demote him.

KELLER [*he chuckles and winks at* CHRIS, *who is enjoying all this*]. Yeah, that's a dangerous character, that Tommy. [*Beckons him closer.*] What word does he say?

BERT [*backing away quickly in great embarrassment*]. Oh, I can't say that.

KELLER [*grabs him by the shirt and pulls him back*]. Well, gimme an idea.

BERT. I can't. It's not a nice word.

KELLER. Just whisper it in my ear. I'll close my eyes. Maybe I won't even hear it.

BERT [*on tiptoe, puts his lips to* KELLER's *ear, then in unbearable embarrassment steps back*]. I can't Mr. Keller.

CHRIS [*laughing*]. Don't make him do that.

KELLER. Okay, Bert. I take your word. Now go out, and keep both eyes peeled.

BERT [*interested*]. For what?

KELLER. For what! Bert, the whole neighborhood is depending on you. A policeman don't ask questions. Now peel them eyes!

BERT [*mystified, but willing*]. Okay. [*He runs off right back of arbor*].

KELLER [*calling after him*]. And mum's the word Bert.

BERT [*stops and sticks his head thru the arbor*]. About what?

KELLER. Just in general. Be v-e-r-y careful.

BERT [*nods in bewilderment*]. Okay. [BERT *exits downstage right.*]

KELLER [*laughs*]. I got all the kids crazy!

CHRIS. One of these days, they'll all come in here and beat your brains out.

KELLER. What's she going to say? Maybe we ought to tell her before she sees it.

CHRIS. She saw it.

KELLER. How could she see it? I was the first one up. She was still in bed.

CHRIS. She was out here when it broke.

KELLER. When?

CHRIS. About four this morning. [*Indicating window above them.*] I heard it cracking and I woke up and looked out. She was standing right here when it cracked.

KELLER. What was she doing out here four in the morning?

CHRIS. I don't know. When it cracked she ran back into the house and cried in the kitchen.

KELLER. Did you talk to her?

CHRIS. No, I . . . I figured the best thing was to leave her alone.

[*Pause.*]

KELLER [*deeply touched*]. She cried hard?

CHRIS. I could hear her right through the floor of my room.

KELLER [*slight pause*]. What was she doing out here at that hour? [CHRIS *silent. An undertone of anger showing.*] She's dreaming about him again. She's walking around at night.

CHRIS. I guess she is.

KELLER. She's getting just like after he died. [*Slight pause*]. What's the meaning of that?

CHRIS. I don't know the meaning of it. [*Slight pause.*] But I know one thing, Dad. We've made a terrible mistake with Mother.

KELLER. What?

CHRIS. Being dishonest with her. That kind of thing always pays off, and now it's paying off.

KELLER. What do you mean, dishonest?

CHRIS. You know Larry's not coming back and I know it. Why do we allow her to go on thinking that we believe with her?

KELLER. What do you want to do, argue with her?

CHRIS. I don't want to argue with her, but it's time she realized that nobody believes Larry is alive any more. [KELLER *simply moves away, thinking, looking at the ground.*] Why shouldn't she dream of him, walk the nights waiting for him? Do we contradict her? Do we say straight out that we have no hope any more? That we haven't had any hope for years now?

KELLER [*frightened at the thought*]. You can't say that to her.

CHRIS. We've got to say it to her.

KELLER. How're you going to prove it? Can you prove it?

CHRIS. For God's sake, three years! Nobody comes back after three years. It's insane.

KELLER. To you it is, and to me. But not to her. You can talk yourself blue in the face, but there's no body and there's no grave, so where are you?

CHRIS. Sit down, Dad. I want to talk to you.

KELLER [*looks at him searchingly a moment, and sitting . . .*] The trouble is the Goddam newspapers. Every month some boy turns up from nowhere, so the next one is going to be Larry, so . . .

CHRIS. All right, all right, listen to me. [*Slight pause.* KELLER *sits on settee.*] You know why I asked Annie here, don't you?

KELLER [*he knows, but . . .*] Why?

CHRIS. You know.

KELLER. Well, I got an idea, but . . . What's the story?

CHRIS. I'm going to ask her to marry me. [*Slight pause.*]

KELLER [*nods*]. Well, that's only your business, Chris.

CHRIS. You know it's not only my business.

KELLER. What do you want me to do? You're old enough to know your own mind.

CHRIS [*asking, annoyed*]. Then it's all right, I'll go ahead with it?

KELLER. Well, you want to be sure Mother isn't going to . . .

CHRIS. Then it isn't just my business.

KELLER. I'm just sayin'. . . .

CHRIS. Sometimes you infuriate me, you know that? Isn't it your business, too, if I tell this to Mother and she throws a fit about it? You have such a talent for ignoring things.

KELLER. I ignore what I gotta ignore. The girl is Larry's girl . . .

CHRIS. She's not Larry's girl.

KELLER. From Mother's point of view he is not dead and you have no right to take his girl. [*Slight pause.*] Now you can go on from there if you know where to go, but I'm tellin' you I don't know where to go. See? I don't know. Now what can I do for you?

CHRIS. I don't know why it is, but every time I reach out for something I want, I have to pull back because other people will suffer. My whole bloody life, time after time after time.

KELLER. You're a considerate fella, there's nothing wrong in that.

CHRIS. To hell with that.

KELLER. Did you ask Annie yet?

CHRIS. I wanted to get this settled first.

KELLER. How do you know she'll marry you? Maybe she feels the same way Mother does?

CHRIS. Well, if she does, then that's the end of it. From her letters I think she's forgotten him. I'll find out. And then we'll thrash it out with Mother? Right? Dad, don't avoid me.

KELLER. The trouble is, you don't see enough women. You never did.

CHRIS. So what? I'm not fast with women.

KELLER. I don't see why it has to be Annie. . . .

CHRIS. Because it is.

KELLER. That's a good answer, but it don't answer anything. You haven't seen her since you went to war. It's five years.

CHRIS. I can't help it. I know her best. I was brought up next door to her. These years when I think of someone for my wife, I think of Annie. What do you want, a diagram?

KELLER. I don't want a diagram . . . I . . . I'm . . . She thinks he's coming back, Chris. You marry that girl and you're pronouncing him dead. Now what's going to happen to Mother? Do you know? I don't! [*Pause.*]

CHRIS. All right, then, Dad.

KELLER [*thinking Chris has retreated*]. Give it some more thought.

CHRIS. I've given it three years of thought. I'd hoped that if I waited, Mother would forget Larry and then we'd have a regular wedding and everything happy. But if that can't happen here, then I'll have to get out.

KELLER. What the hell is *this*?

CHRIS. I'll get out. I'll get married and live some place else. Maybe in New York.

KELLER. Are you crazy?

CHRIS. I've been a good son too long, a good sucker. I'm through with it.

KELLER. You've got a business here, what the hell is this?

CHRIS. The business! The business doesn't inspire me.

KELLER. Must you be inspired?

CHRIS. Yes. I like it an hour a day. If I have to grub for money all day long at least at evening I want it beautiful. I want a family, I want some kids, I want to build something I can give myself to. Annie is in the middle of that. Now . . . where do I find it?

KELLER. You mean . . . [*Goes to him.*] Tell me something, you mean you'd leave the business?

CHRIS. Yes. On this I would.

KELLER [*pause*]. Well . . . you don't want to think like that.

CHRIS. Then help me stay here.

KELLER. All right, but . . . but don't think like that. Because what the hell did I work for? That's only for you, Chris, the whole shootin'-match is for you!

CHRIS. I know that, Dad. Just you help me stay here.

KELLER [*puts a fist up to* CHRIS' *jaw*]. But don't think that way, you hear me?

CHRIS. I am thinking that way.

KELLER [*lowering his hand*]. I don't understand you, do I?

CHRIS. No, you don't. I'm a pretty tough guy.

KELLER. Yeah. I can see that. [MOTHER *appears on porch. She is in her early fifties, a woman of uncontrolled inspirations, and an overwhelming capacity for love.*]

MOTHER. Joe?

CHRIS [*going toward porch*]. Hello, Mom.

MOTHER [*indicating house behind her. To* KELLER]. Did you take a bag from under the sink?

KELLER. Yeah. I put it in the pail.

MOTHER. Well, get it out of the pail. That's my potatoes. [CHRIS *bursts out laughing—goes up into alley*.]

KELLER [*laughing*]. I thought it was garbage.

MOTHER. Will you do me a favor, Joe? Don't be helpful.

KELLER. I can afford another bag of potatoes.

MOTHER. Minnie scoured that pail in boiling water last night. It's cleaner than your teeth.

KELLER. And I don't understand why, after I worked forty years and I got a maid, why I have to take out the garbage.

MOTHER. If you would make up your mind that every bag in the kitchen isn't full of garbage you wouldn't be throwing out your vegetables. Last time it was the onions. [CHRIS *comes on, hands her bag*.]

KELLER. I don't like garbage in the house.

MOTHER. Then don't eat. [*She goes into the kitchen with bag*.]

CHRIS. That settles you for today.

KELLER. Yeah, I'm in last place again. I don't know, once upon a time I used to think that when I got money again I would have a maid and my wife would take it easy. Now I got money, and I got a maid, and my wife is workin' for the maid. [*He sits in one of the chairs.* MOTHER *comes out on last line. She carries a pot of stringbeans*.]

MOTHER. It's her day off, what are you crabbing about?

CHRIS [*to mother*]. Isn't Annie finished eating?

MOTHER [*looking around preoccupiedly at yard*]. She'll be right out. [*Moves.*] That wind did some job on this place. [*Of the tree.*] So much for that, thank God.

KELLER [*indicating chair beside him*]. Sit down, take it easy.

MOTHER [*she presses her hand to top of her head*]. I've got such a funny pain on the top of my head.

CHRIS. Can I get you an aspirin?

MOTHER [*picks a few petals off ground, stands there smelling them in her hand, then sprinkles them over plants*]. No more roses. It's so funny . . . everything decides to happen at the same time. This month is his birthday; his tree blows down, Annie comes. Everything that happened seems to be coming back. I was just down the cellar, and what do I stumble over? His baseball glove. I haven't seen it in a century.

CHRIS. Don't you think Annie looks well?

MOTHER. Fine. There's no question about it. She's a beauty . . . I still don't know what brought her here. Not that I'm not glad to see her, but . . .

CHRIS. I just thought we'd all like to see each other again. [MOTHER *just looks at him, nodding ever so slightly—almost as though admitting something.*] And I wanted to see her myself.

MOTHER [*her nods halt. To* KELLER]. The only thing is I think her nose got longer. But I'll always love that girl. She's one that didn't jump into bed with somebody else as soon as it happened with her fella.

KELLER [*as though that were impossible for Annie*]. Oh, what're you . . . ?

MOTHER. Never mind. Most of them didn't wait till the telegrams were opened. I'm just glad she came, so you can see I'm not *completely* out of my mind. [*Sits, and rapidly breaks stringbeans in the pot.*]

CHRIS. Just because she isn't married doesn't mean she's been mourning Larry.

MOTHER [*with an undercurrent of observation*]. Why then isn't she?

CHRIS [*a little flustered*]. Well . . . it could've been any number of things.

MOTHER [*directly at him*]. Like what, for instance?

CHRIS [*embarrassed, but standing his ground*]. I don't know. Whatever it is. Can I get you an aspirin? [MOTHER *puts her hand to her head.*]

MOTHER [*she gets up and goes aimlessly toward the trees on rising*]. It's not like a headache.

KELLER. You don't sleep, that's why. She's wearing out more

bedroom slippers than shoes.

MOTHER. I had a terrible night. [*She stops moving.*] I never had a night like that.

CHRIS [*looks at* KELLER]. What was it, Mom? Did you dream?

MOTHER. More, more than a dream.

CHRIS [*hesitantly*]. About Larry?

MOTHER. I was fast asleep, and . . . [*Raising her arm over the audience.*] Remember the way he used to fly low past the house when he was in training? When we used to see his face in the cockpit going by? That's the way I saw him. Only high up. Way, way up, where the clouds are. He was so real I could reach out and touch him. And suddenly he started to fall. And crying, crying to me . . . Mom, Mom! I could hear him like he was in the room. Mom! . . . it was his voice! If I could touch him I knew I could stop him, if I could only . . . [*Breaks off, allowing her outstretched hand to fall.*] I woke up and it was so funny . . . The wind . . . it was like the roaring of his engine. I came out here . . . I must've still been half asleep. I could hear that roaring like he was going by. The tree snapped right in front of me . . . and I like . . . came awake. [*She is looking at tree. She suddenly realizes something, turns with a reprimanding finger shaking slightly at* KELLER.] See? We should never have planted that tree. I said so in the first place; It was too soon to plant a tree for him.

CHRIS [*alarmed*]. Too soon!

MOTHER [*angering*]. We rushed into it. Everybody was in such a hurry to bury him. I *said* not to plant it yet. [*To* KELLER.] I *told* you to . . . !

CHRIS. Mother, Mother! [*She looks into his face.*] The wind blew it down. What significance has that got? What are you talking about? Mother, please . . . Don't go through it all again, will you? It's no good, it doesn't accomplish anything. I've been thinking y'know?—maybe we ought to put our minds to forgetting him?

MOTHER. That's the third time you've said that this week.

CHRIS. Because it's not right; we never took up our lives again.

We're like at a railroad station waiting for a train that never comes in.

MOTHER [*presses top of her head*]. Get me an aspirin, heh?

CHRIS. Sure, and let's break out of this, heh, Mom? I thought the four of us might go out to dinner a couple of nights, maybe go dancing out at the shore.

MOTHER. Fine. [*To* KELLER.] We can do it tonight.

KELLER. Swell with me!

CHRIS. Sure, let's have some fun. [*To* MOTHER.] You'll start with this aspirin. [*He goes up and into house with new spirit. Her smile vanishes.*]

MOTHER [*with an accusing undertone*]. Why did he invite her here?

KELLER. Why does that bother you?

MOTHER. She's been in New York three and a half years, why all of a sudden . . . ?

KELLER. Well, maybe . . . maybe he just wanted to see her . . .

MOTHER. Nobody comes seven hundred miles "just to see."

KELLER. What do you mean? He lived next door to the girl all his life, why shouldn't he want to see her again? [MOTHER *looks at him critically.*] Don't look at me like that, he didn't tell me any more than he told you.

MOTHER [*a warning and a question*]. He's not going to marry her.

KELLER. How do you know he's even thinking of it?

MOTHER. It's got that about it.

KELLER [*sharply watching her reaction*]. Well? So what?

MOTHER [*alarmed*]. What's going on here, Joe?

KELLER. Now listen, kid . . .

MOTHER [*avoiding contact with him*]. She's not his girl, Joe; she knows she's not.

KELLER. You can't read her mind.

MOTHER. Then why is she still single? New York is full of men, why isn't she married? [*Pause.*] Probably a hundred people told her she's foolish, but she's waited.

KELLER. How do you know why she waited?

MOTHER. She knows what I know, that's why. She's faithful as a rock. In my worst moments, I think of her waiting, and I know again that I'm right.

KELLER. Look, it's a nice day. What are we arguing for?

MOTHER [*warningly*]. Nobody in this house dast take her faith away, Joe. Strangers might. But not his father, not his brother.

KELLER [*exasperated*]. What do you want me to do? What do you want?

MOTHER. I want you to act like he's coming back. Both of you. Don't think I haven't noticed you since Chris invited her. I won't stand for any nonsense.

KELLER. But, Kate . . .

MOTHER. Because if he's not coming back, then I'll kill myself! Laugh. Laugh at me. [*She points to tree.*] But why did that happen the very night she came back? Laugh, but there are meanings in such things. She goes to sleep in his room and his memorial breaks in pieces. Look at it; look. [*She sits on bench at his left.*] Joe . . .

KELLER. Calm yourself.

MOTHER. Believe with me, Joe. I can't stand all alone.

KELLER. Calm yourself.

MOTHER. Only last week a man turned up in Detroit, missing longer than Larry. You read it yourself.

KELLER. All right, all right, calm yourself.

MOTHER. You above all have got to believe, you . . .

KELLER [*rises*]. Why me above all?

MOTHER. . . . Just don't stop believing . . .

KELLER. What does that mean, me above all? [BERT *comes rushing on from left.*]

BERT. Mr. Keller! Say, Mr. Keller . . . [*Pointing up driveway.*] Tommy just said it again!

KELLER [*not remembering any of it*]. Said what? . . . Who? . .

BERT. The dirty word.

KELLER. Oh. Well . . .

BERT. Gee, aren't you going to arrest him? I warned him.

MOTHER [*with suddenness*]. Stop that, Bert. Go home. [BERT *backs up, as she advances.*] There's no jail here.

KELLER [*as though to say, "Oh-what-the-hell-let-him-believe-there-is.*"] Kate . . .

MOTHER [*turning on* KELLER, *furiously*]. There's no jail here! I want you to stop that jail business! [*He turns, shamed, but peeved.*]

BERT [*past her to* KELLER]. He's right across the street.

MOTHER. Go home, Bert. [BERT *turns around and goes up drive-way. She is shaken. Her speech is bitten off, extremely urgent.*] I want you to stop that, Joe. That whole jail business!

KELLER [*alarmed, therefore angered*]. Look at you, look at you shaking.

MOTHER [*trying to control herself, moving about clasping her hands*]. I can't help it.

KELLER. What have I got to hide? What the hell is the matter with you, Kate?

MOTHER. I didn't say you had anything to hide, I'm just telling you to stop it; Now stop it! [*As* ANN *and* CHRIS *appear on porch.* ANN *is twenty-six, gentle but despite herself capable of holding fast to what she knows.* CHRIS *opens door for her.*]

ANN. Hya, Joe! [*She leads off a general laugh that is not self-conscious because they know one another too well.*]

CHRIS [*bringing* ANN *down, with an outstretched, chivalric arm*]. Take a breath of that air, kid. You never get air like that in New York.

MOTHER [*genuinely overcome with it*]. Annie, where did you get that dress!

ANN. I couldn't resist. I'm taking it right off before I ruin it. [*Swings around.*] How's that for three weeks' salary?

MOTHER [*to* KELLER]. Isn't she the most . . . ? [*To* ANN.] It's gorgeous, simply gor . . .

CHRIS [*to* MOTHER]. No kidding, now, isn't she the prettiest gal you ever saw?

MOTHER [*caught short by his obvious admiration, she finds herself reaching out for a glass of water and aspirin in his hand, and . . .*] You gained a little weight, didn't you, dar-ling? [*She gulps pill and drinks.*]

ANN. It comes and goes.

KELLER. Look how nice her legs turned out!

ANN [*she runs to fence, left*]. Boy, the poplars got thick, didn'
they?

KELLER [*moves upstage to settee and sits*]. Well, it's three years
Annie. We're gettin' old, kid.

MOTHER. How does Mom like New York? [ANN *keeps lookin,*
through trees.]

ANN [*a little hurt*]. Why'd they take our hammock away?

KELLER. Oh, no, it broke. Couple of years ago.

MOTHER. What broke? He had one of his light lunches an
flopped into it.

ANN [*she laughs and turns back toward* JIM's *yard. . . .*] Oh
excuse me! [JIM *has come to fence and is looking over it*
He is smoking a cigar. As she cries out, he comes on around
on stage.]

JIM. How do you do. [*To* CHRIS.] She looks very intelligent!

CHRIS. Ann, this is Jim . . . Doctor Bayliss.

ANN [*shaking* JIM's *hand*]. Oh sure, he writes a lot about you

JIM. Don't believe it. He likes everybody. In the Battalion h
was known as Mother McKeller.

ANN. I can believe it . . . You know——? [*To* MOTHER.] It's s
strange seeing him come out of that yard. [*To* CHRIS.] I gues
I never grew up. It almost seems that Mom and Pop ar
in there now. And you and my brother doing Algebra, an
Larry trying to copy my home-work. Gosh, those dear dea
days beyond recall.

JIM. Well, I hope that doesn't mean you want me to move out

SUE [*calling from off left*]. Jim, come in here! Mr. Hubbard
is on the phone!

JIM. I told you I don't want . . .

SUE [*commandingly sweet*]. Please, dear! Please!!

JIM [*resigned*]. All right, Susie, [*Trailing off.*] all right, a
right . . . [*To* ANN.] I've only met you, Ann, but if I may
offer you a piece of advice— When you marry, never—ever
in your mind—never count your husband's money.

SUE [*from off*]. Jim?!

JIM. At once! [*Turns and goes left.*] At once. [*He exits left.*]

MOTHER [ANN *is looking at her. She speaks meaningfully*]. I told her to take up the guitar. It'd be a common interest for them. [*They laugh.*] Well, he loves the guitar!

ANN [*as though to overcome* MOTHER, *she becomes suddenly lively, crosses to* KELLER *on settee, sits on his lap*]. Let's eat at the shore tonight! Raise some hell around here, like we used to before Larry went!

MOTHER [*emotionally*]. You think of him! You see? [*Triumphantly.*] She thinks of him!

ANN [*with an uncomprehending smile*]. What do you mean, Kate?

MOTHER. Nothing. Just that you . . . remember him, he's in your thoughts.

ANN. That's a funny thing to say; how could I help remembering him?

MOTHER [*it is drawing to a head the wrong way for her; she starts anew. She rises and comes to* ANN]. Did you hang up your things?

ANN. Yeah . . . [*To* CHRIS.] Say, you've sure gone in for clothes. I could hardly find room in the closet.

MOTHER. No, don't you remember? That's Larry's room.

ANN. You mean . . . they're Larry's?

MOTHER. Didn't you recognize them?

ANN [*slowly rising, a little embarrassed*]. Well, it never occurred to me that you'd . . . I mean the shoes are all shined.

MOTHER. Yes, dear. [*Slight pause.* ANN *can't stop staring at her.* MOTHER *breaks it by speaking with the relish of gossip, putting her arm around* ANN *and walking stage left with her.*] For so long I've been aching for a nice conversation with you, Annie. Tell me something.

ANN. What?

MOTHER. I don't know. Something nice.

CHRIS [*wryly*]. She means do you go out much?

MOTHER. Oh, shut up.

KELLER. And are any of them serious?

MOTHER [*laughing, sits in her chair*]. Why don't you both choke?

KELLER. Annie, you can't go into a restaurant with that woman any more. In five minutes thirty-nine strange people are sitting at the table telling her their life story.

MOTHER. If I can't ask Annie a personal question . . .

KELLER. Askin' is all right, but don't beat her over the head. You're beatin' her, you're beatin' her. [*They are laughing.*]

ANN [*to* MOTHER. *Takes pan of beans off stool, puts them on floor under chair and sits*]. Don't let them bulldoze you. Ask me anything you like. What do you want to know, Kate? Come on, let's gossip.

MOTHER [*to* CHRIS *and* KELLER]. She's the only one is got any sense. [*To* Ann.] Your mother . . . She's not getting a divorce, heh?

ANN. No, she's calmed down about it now. I think when he gets out they'll probably live together. In New York, of course.

MOTHER. That's fine. Because your father is still . . . I mean he's a decent man after all is said and done.

ANN. I don't care. She can take him back if she likes.

MOTHER. And you? You . . . [*Shakes her head negatively.*] . . . go out much? [*Slight pause.*]

ANN [*delicately*]. You mean am I still waiting for him?

MOTHER. Well, no, I don't expect you to wait for him but . . .

ANN [*kindly*]. But that's what you mean, isn't it?

MOTHER. . . Well . . . yes.

ANN. Well, I'm not, Kate.

MOTHER [*faintly*]. You're not?

ANN. Isn't it ridiculous? You don't really imagine he's . . . ?

MOTHER. I know, dear, but don't say it's ridiculous, because the papers were full of it; I don't know about New York but there was half a page about a man missing even longer than Larry, and he turned up from Burma.

CHRIS [*coming to* ANN]. He couldn't have wanted to come home very badly, Mom.

MOTHER. Don't be so smart.

CHRIS. You can have a helluva time in Burma.

ANN [*rises and swings around in back of* CHRIS]. So I've heard.

CHRIS. Mother, I'll bet you money that you're the only woma▪

in the country who after three years is still . . .

MOTHER. You're sure?

CHRIS. Yes, I am.

MOTHER. Well, if you're sure then you're sure. [*She turns her head away an instant.*] They don't say it on the radio but I'm sure that in the dark at night they're still waiting for their sons.

CHRIS. Mother, you're absolutely——

MOTHER [*waving him off*]. Don't be so damned smart! Now stop it! [*Slight pause.*] There are just a few things you *don't* know. All of you. And I'll tell you one of them, Annie. Deep, deep in your heart you've always been waiting for him.

ANN [*resolutely*]. No, Kate.

MOTHER [*with increasing demand*]. But deep in your heart, Annie!

CHRIS. She ought to know, shouldn't she?

MOTHER. Don't let them tell you what to think. Listen to your heart. Only your heart.

ANN. Why does your heart tell you he's alive?

MOTHER. Because he has to be.

ANN. But why, Kate?

MOTHER [*going to her*]. Because certain things have to be, and certain things can never be. Like the sun has to rise, it has to be. That's why there's God. Otherwise anything could happen. But there's God, so certain things can never happen. I would know, Annie—just like I knew the day he [*indicates* CHRIS.] went into that terrible battle. Did he write me? Was it in the papers? No, but that morning I couldn't raise my head off the pillow. Ask Joe. Suddenly, I knew. I knew! And he was nearly killed that day. Ann, you *know* I'm right!

ANN [*she stands there in silence, then turns trembling, going upstage*]. No, Kate.

MOTHER. I have to have some tea. [FRANK *appears from left, carrying ladder.*]

FRANK. Annie! [*Coming down.*] How are you, gee whiz!

ANN [*taking his hand*]. Why, Frank, you're losing your hair.

KELLER. He's got responsibility.

FRANK. Gee whiz!

KELLER. Without Frank the stars wouldn't know when to come out.

FRANK [*laughs. To* ANN]. You look more womanly. You've matured. You . . .

KELLER. Take it easy, Frank, you're a married man.

ANN [*as they laugh*]. You still haberdashering?

FRANK. Why not? Maybe I too can get to be president. How's your brother? Got his degree, I hear.

ANN. Oh, George has his own office now!

FRANK. Don't say! [*Funereally.*] And your dad? Is he . . . ?

ANN [*abruptly*]. Fine. I'll be in to see Lydia.

FRANK [*sympathetically*]. How about it, does Dad expect a parole soon?

ANN [*with growing ill-ease*]. I really don't know, I . . .

FRANK [*staunchly defending her father for her sake*]. I mean because I feel, y'know, that if an intelligent man like your father is put in prison, there ought to be a law that says either you execute him, or let him go after a year.

CHRIS [*interrupting*]. Want a hand with that ladder, Frank?

FRANK [*taking cue*]. That's all right, I'll . . . [*picks up ladder.*] I'll finish the horoscope tonight, Kate. [*Embarrassed.*] See you later, Ann, you look wonderful. [*He exits right. They look at* ANN.]

ANN [*to* CHRIS, *sits slowly on stool*]. Haven't they stopped talking about Dad?

CHRIS [*comes down and sits on arm of chair*]. Nobody talks about him any more.

KELLER [*rises and comes to her*]. Gone and forgotten, kid.

ANN. Tell me. Because I don't want to meet anybody on the block if they're going to . . .

CHRIS. I don't want you to worry about it.

ANN [*to* KELLER]. Do they still remember the case, Joe? Do they talk about you?

KELLER. The only one still talks about it is my wife.

MOTHER. That's because you keep on playing policeman with

the kids. All their parents hear out of you is jail, jail, jail.

KELLER. Actually what happened was that when I got home from the penitentiary the kids got very interested in me. You know kids. I was [*Laughs.*] like the expert on the jail situation. And as time passed they got it confused and . . . I ended up a detective. [*Laughs.*]

MOTHER. Except that *they* didn't get it confused. [*To* ANN.] He hands out police badges from the Post Toasties boxes. [*They laugh.*]

ANN [*wondrously at them, happily. She rises and comes to* KELLER, *putting her arm around his shoulder*]. Gosh, it's wonderful to hear you laughing about it.

CHRIS. Why, what'd you expect?

ANN. The last thing I remember on this block was one word—"Murderers!" Remember that, Kate? . . . Mrs. Hammond standing in front of our house and yelling that word . . . She's still around, I suppose?

MOTHER. They're all still around.

KELLER. Don't listen to her. Every Saturday night the whole gang is playin' poker in this arbor. All the ones who yelled murderer takin' my money now.

MOTHER. Don't, Joe, she's a sensitive girl, don't fool her. [*To* ANN.] They still remember about Dad. It's different with him—[*Indicates* JOE.]—he was exonerated, your father's still there. That's why I wasn't so enthusiastic about your coming. Honestly, I know how sensitive you are, and I told Chris, I said . . .

KELLER. Listen, you do like I did and you'll be all right. The day I come home, I got out of my car;—but not in front of the house . . . on the corner. You should've been here, Annie, and you too, Chris; you'd-a seen something. Everybody knew I was getting out that day; the porches were loaded. Picture it now; none of them believed I was innocent. The story was, I pulled a fast one getting myself exonerated. So I get out of my car, and I walk down the street. But very slow. And with a smile. The beast! I was the beast; the guy who sold cracked cylinder heads to the Army Air Force;

the guy who made twenty-one P-40's crash in Australia. Kid, walkin' down the street that day I was guilty as hell. Except I wasn't, and there was a court paper in my pocket to prove I wasn't, and I walked . . . past . . . the porches. Result? Fourteen months later I had one of the best shops in the state again, a respected man again; bigger than ever.

CHRIS [*with admiration*]. Joe McGuts.

KELLER [*now with great force*]. That's the only way you lick 'em is guts! [*To* ANN.] The worst thing you did was to move away from here. You made it tough for your father when he gets out. That's why I tell you, I like to see him move back right on this block.

MOTHER [*pained*]. How could they move back?

KELLER. It ain't gonna end *till* they move back! [*To* ANN.] Till people play cards with him again, and talk with him, and smile with him—you play cards with a man you know he can't be a murderer. And the next time you write him I like you to tell him just what I said. [ANN *simply stares at him.*] You hear me?

ANN [*surprised*]. Don't you hold anything against him?

KELLER. Annie, I never believed in crucifying people.

ANN [*mystified*]. But he was your partner, he dragged you through the mud . . .

KELLER. Well, he ain't my sweetheart, but you gotta forgive, don't you?

ANN. You, either, Kate? Don't you feel any . . . ?

KELLER [*to* ANN]. The next time you write Dad . . .

ANN. I don't write him.

KELLER [*struck*]. Well every now and then you . . .

ANN [*a little ashamed, but determined*]. No, I've *never* written to him. Neither has my brother. [*To* CHRIS.] Say, do you feel this way, too?

CHRIS. He murdered twenty-one pilots.

KELLER. What the hell kinda talk is that?

MOTHER. That's not a thing to say about a man.

ANN. What else can you say? When they took him away I followed him, went to him every visiting day. I was crying al

the time. Until the news came about Larry. Then I realized.
It's wrong to pity a man like that. Father or no father,
there's only one way to look at him. He knowingly shipped
out parts that would crash an airplane. And how do you
know Larry wasn't one of them?

MOTHER. I was waiting for that. [*Going to her.*] As long as
you're here, Annie, I want to ask you never to say that again.

ANN. You surprise me. I thought you'd be mad at him.

MOTHER. What your father did had nothing to do with Larry.
Nothing.

ANN. But we can't know that.

MOTHER [*striving for control*]. As long as you're here!

ANN [*perplexed*]. But, Kate . . .

MOTHER. Put that out of your head!

KELLER. Because . . .

MOTHER [*quickly to* KELLER]. That's all, that's enough. [*Places
her hand on her head.*] Come inside now, and have some tea
with me. [*She turns and goes up steps.*]

KELLER [*to* ANN]. The one thing you . . .

MOTHER [*sharply*]. He's not dead, so there's no argument! Now
come!

KELLER [*angrily*]. In a minute! [MOTHER *turns and goes into
house.*] Now look, Annie . . .

CHRIS. All right, Dad, forget it.

KELLER. No, she dasn't feel that way. Annie . . .

CHRIS. I'm sick of the whole subject, now cut it out.

KELLER. You want her to go on like this? [*To* ANN.] Those cylinder heads went into P-40's only. What's the matter with
you? You know Larry never flew a P-40.

CHRIS. So who flew those P-40's, pigs?

KELLER. The man was a fool, but don't make a murderer out
of him. You got no sense? Look what it does to her! [*To*
ANN.] Listen, you gotta appreciate what was doin' in that shop
in the war. The both of you! It was a madhouse. Every half
hour the Major callin' for cylinder heads, they were whippin'
us with the telephone. The trucks were hauling them away
hot, damn near. I mean just try to see it human, see it human.

All of a sudden a batch comes out with a crack. That happens, that's the business. A fine, hairline crack. All right, so . . . so he's a little man, your father, always scared of loud voices. What'll the Major say?—Half a day's production shot. . . . What'll I say? You know what I mean? Human. [*He pauses.*] So he takes out his tools and he . . . covers over the cracks. All right . . . that's bad, it's wrong, but that's what a little man does. If I could have gone in that day I'd a told him—junk 'em, Herb, we can afford it. But alone he was afraid. But I know he meant no harm. He believed they'd hold up a hundred percent. That's a mistake, but it ain't murder. You mustn't feel that way about him. You understand me? It ain't right.

ANN [*she regards him a moment*]. Joe, let's forget it.

KELLER. Annie, the day the news came about Larry he was in the next cell to mine . . . Dad. And he cried, Annie . . . he cried half the night.

ANN [*touched*]. He shoulda cried all night. [*Slight pause.*]

KELLER [*almost angered*]. Annie, I do not understand why you . . . !

CHRIS [*breaking in—with nervous urgency*]. Are you going to stop it?!

ANN. Don't yell at him. He just wants everybody happy.

KELLER [*clasps her around waist, smiling*]. That's my sentiments. Can you stand steak?

CHRIS. And champagne!

KELLER. Now you're operatin'! I'll call Swanson's for a table! Big time tonight, Annie!

ANN. Can't scare me.

KELLER [*to CHRIS, pointing at ANN*]. I like that girl. Wrap her up. [*They laugh. Goes up porch.*] You got nice legs, Annie! . . . I want to see everybody drunk tonight. [*Pointing to CHRIS.*] Look at him, he's blushin'! [*He exits, laughing, into house.*]

CHRIS [*calling after him*]. Drink your tea, Casanova. [*He turns to ANN.*] Isn't he a great guy?

ANN. You're the only one I know who loves his parents!

CHRIS. I know. It went out of style, didn't it?

ANN [*with a sudden touch of sadness*]. It's all right. It's a good thing. [*She looks about.*] You know? It's lovely here. The air is sweet.

CHRIS [*hopefully*]. You're not sorry you came?

ANN. Not sorry, no. But I'm . . . not going to stay . . .

CHRIS. Why?

ANN. In the first place, your mother as much as told me to go.

CHRIS. Well . . .

ANN. You saw that . . . and then you . . . you've been kind of . . .

CHRIS. What?

ANN. Well . . . kind of embarrassed ever since I got here.

CHRIS. The trouble is I planned on kind of sneaking up on you over a period of a week or so. But they take it for granted that we're all set.

ANN. I knew they would. Your mother anyway.

CHRIS. How did you know?

ANN. From *her* point of view, why else would I come?

CHRIS. Well . . . would you want to? [ANN *studies him.*] I guess you know this is why I asked you to come.

ANN. I guess this is why I came.

CHRIS. Ann, I love you. I love you a great deal. [*Finally.*] I love you [*Pause. She waits.*] I have no imagination . . . that's all I know to tell you. [ANN, *waiting, ready.*] I'm embarrassing you. I didn't want to tell it to you here. I wanted some place we'd never been; a place where we'd be brand new to each other. . . . You feel it's wrong here, don't you? This yard, this chair? I want you to be ready for me. I don't want to win you away from anything.

ANN [*putting her arms around him*]. Oh, Chris, I've been ready a long, long time!

CHRIS. Then he's gone forever. You're sure.

ANN. I almost got married two years ago.

CHRIS. . . . why didn't you?

ANN. You started to write to me . . . [*Slight pause.*]

CHRIS. You felt something that far back?

ANN. Every day since!

CHRIS. Ann, why didn't you let me know?

ANN. I was waiting for you Chris. Till then you never wrote. And when you did, what did you say? You sure can be ambiguous, you know.

CHRIS [*he looks towards house, then at her, trembling*]. Give me a kiss, Ann. Give me a . . . [*They kiss.*] God, I kissed you, Annie, I kissed Annie. How long, how long I've been waiting to kiss you!

ANN. I'll never forgive you. Why did you wait all these years? All I've done is sit and wonder if I was crazy for thinking of you.

CHRIS. Annie, we're going to live now! I'm going to make you so happy. [*He kisses her, but without their bodies touching.*]

ANN [*a little embarrassed*]. Not like that you're not.

CHRIS. I kissed you . . .

ANN. Like Larry's brother. Do it like you, Chris. [*He breaks away from her abruptly.*] What is it, Chris?

CHRIS. Let's drive some place . . . I want to be alone with you.

ANN. No . . . what is it, Chris, your mother?

CHRIS. No . . . nothing like that . . .

ANN. Then what's wrong? . . . Even in your letters, there was something ashamed.

CHRIS. Yes. I suppose I have been. But it's going from me.

ANN. You've got to tell me—

CHRIS. I don't know how to start. [*He takes her hand. He speaks quietly, factually at first.*]

ANN. It wouldn't work this way. [*Slight pause.*]

CHRIS. It's all mixed up with so many other things. . . . You remember, overseas, I was in command of a company?

ANN. Yeah, sure.

CHRIS. Well, I lost them.

ANN. How many?

CHRIS. Just about all.

ANN. Oh, gee!

CHRIS. It takes a little time to toss that off. Because they weren't just men. For instance, one time it'd been raining several days and this kid came to me, and gave me his last pair of dry socks. Put them in my pocket. That's only a little thing . . . but . . . that's the kind of guys I had. They didn't die; they killed themselves for each other. I mean that exactly; a little more selfish and they'd've been here today. And I got an idea—watching them go down. Everything was being destroyed, see, but it seemed to me that one new thing was made. A kind of . . . responsibility. Man for man. You understand me?— To show that, to bring that on to the earth again like some kind of a monument and everyone would feel it standing there, behind him, and it would make a difference to him. [*Pause.*] And then I came home and it was incredible. I . . . there was no meaning in it here; the whole thing to them was a kind of a—bus accident. I went to work with Dad, and that rat-race again. I felt . . . what you said . . . ashamed somehow. Because nobody was changed at all. It seemed to make suckers out of a lot of guys. I felt wrong to be alive, to open the bank-book, to drive the new car, to see the new refrigerator. I mean you can take those things out of a war, but when you drive that car you've got to know that it came out of the love a man can have for a man, you've got to be a little better because of that. Otherwise what you have is really loot, and there's blood on it. I didn't want to take any of it. And I guess that included you.

ANN. And you still feel that way?

CHRIS. I want you now, Annie.

ANN. Because you mustn't feel that way any more. Because you have a right to whatever you have. Everything, Chris, understand that? To me, too . . . And the money, there's nothing wrong in your money. Your father put hundreds of planes in the air, you should be proud. A man should be paid for that . . .

CHRIS. Oh Annie, Annie . . . I'm going to make a fortune for you!

KELLER [*offstage*]. Hello . . . Yes. Sure.

ANN [*laughing softly*]. What'll I do with a fortune . . . ? [*They kiss. KELLER enters from house.*]

KELLER [*thumbing toward house*]. Hey, Ann, your brother . . .

[*They step apart shyly.* KELLER *comes down, and wryly* . . .]
What is this, Labor Day?

CHRIS [*waving him away, knowing the kidding will be endless.*]
All right, all right . . .

ANN. You shouldn't burst out like that.

KELLER. Well, nobody told me it was Labor Day. [*Looks around.*] Where's the hot dogs?

CHRIS [*loving it*]. All right. You said it once.

KELLER. Well, as long as I know it's Labor Day from now on, I'll wear a bell around my neck.

ANN [*affectionately*]. He's so subtle!

CHRIS. George Bernard Shaw as an elephant.

KELLER. George—hey, you kissed it out of my head—your brother's on the phone.

ANN [*surprised*]. My brother?

KELLER. Yeah, George. Long distance.

ANN. What's the matter, is anything wrong?

KELLER. I don't know, Kate's talking to him. Hurry up, she'll cost him five dollars.

ANN. [*She takes a step upstage, then comes down toward* CHRIS.]
I wonder if we ought to tell your mother yet? I mean I'm not very good in an argument.

CHRIS. We'll wait till tonight. After dinner. Now don't get tense, just leave it to me.

KELLER. What're you telling·her?

CHRIS. Go ahead, Ann. [*With misgivings,* ANN *goes up and into house.*] We're getting married, Dad. [KELLER *nods indecisively.*] Well, don't you say anything?

KELLER [*distracted*]. I'm glad, Chris, I'm just . . . George is calling from Columbus.

CHRIS. Columbus!

KELLER. Did Annie tell you he was going to see his father today?

CHRIS. No, I don't think she knew anything about it.

KELLER [*asking uncomfortably*]. Chris! You . . . you think you know her pretty good?

CHRIS [*hurt and apprehensive*]. What kind of a question . . . ?

KELLER. I'm just wondering. All these years George don't go to see his father. Suddenly he goes . . . and she comes here.

CHRIS. Well, what about it?

KELLER. It's crazy, but it comes to my mind. She don't hold nothin' against me, does she?

CHRIS [angry]. I don't know what you're talking about.

KELLER [a little more combatively]. I'm just talkin'. To his last day in court the man blamed it all on me; and this is his daughter. I mean if she was sent here to find out something?

CHRIS. [angered]. Why? What is there to find out?

ANN [on phone, offstage]. Why are you so excited, George? What happened there?

KELLER. I mean if they want to open up the case again, for the nuisance value, to hurt us?

CHRIS. Dad . . . how could you think that of her? ⎫
ANN. [still on phone]. But what did he say to ⎬ [Together.]
you, for God's sake? ⎭

KELLER. It couldn't be, heh. You know.

CHRIS. Dad, you amaze me . . .

KELLER [breaking in]. All right, forget it, forget it. [With great force, moving about.] I want a clean start for you, Chris. I want a new sign over the plant—Christopher Keller, Incorporated.

CHRIS [a little uneasily]. J. O. Keller is good enough.

KELLER. We'll talk about it. I'm going to build you a house, stone, with a driveway from the road. I want you to spread out, Chris, I want you to use what I made for you . . . [He is close to him now.] . . . I mean, with joy, Chris, without shame . . . with joy.

CHRIS [touched]. I will, Dad.

KELLER [with deep emotion]. . . . . Say it to me.

CHRIS. Why?

KELLER. Because sometimes I think you're . . . ashamed of the money.

CHRIS. No, don't feel that.

KELLER. Because it's good money, there's nothing wrong with that money.

CHRIS [*a little frightened*]. Dad, you don't have to tell me this.

KELLER [*with overriding affection and self-confidence now. He grips* CHRIS *by the back of the neck, and with laughter between his determined jaws:*]. Look, Chris, I'll go to work on Mother for you. We'll get her so drunk tonight we'll all get married! [*Steps away, with a wide gesture of his arm*]. There's gonna be a wedding, kid, like there never was seen! Champagne, tuxedoes . . . !

[*He breaks off as* ANN's *voice comes out loud from the house where she is still talking on phone.*]

ANN. Simply because when you get excited you don't control yourself. . . . [MOTHER *comes out of house.*] Well, what did he tell you for God's sake? [*Pause.*] All right, come then. [*Pause.*] Yes, they'll all be here. Nobody's running away from you. And try to get hold of yourself, will you? [*Pause.*] All right, all right. Goodbye. [*There is a brief pause as* ANN *hangs up receiver, then comes out of kitchen.*]

CHRIS. Something happen?

KELLER. He's coming here?

ANN. On the seven o'clock. He's in Columbus. [*To* MOTHER.] I told him it would be all right.

KELLER. Sure, fine! Your father took sick?

ANN [*mystified*]. No, George didn't say he was sick. I . . . [*Shaking it off.*] I don't know, I suppose it's something stupid, you know my brother . . . [*She comes to* CHRIS.] Let's go for a drive, or something . . .

CHRIS. Sure. Give me the keys, Dad.

MOTHER. Drive through the park. It's beautiful now.

CHRIS. Come on, Ann. [*To them.*] Be back right away.

ANN [*as she and* CHRIS *exit up driveway*]. See you. [MOTHER *comes down toward* KELLER, *her eyes fixed on him.*]

KELLER. Take your time. [*To* MOTHER.] What does George want?

MOTHER. He's been in Columbus since this morning with Steve. He's gotta see Annie right away, he says.

KELLER. What for?

MOTHER. I don't know. [*She speaks with warning.*] He's a lawyer now, Joe. George is a lawyer. All these years he never even sent a postcard to Steve. Since he got back from the war, not a postcard.

KELLER. So what?

MOTHER [*her tension breaking out*]. Suddenly he takes an airplane from New York to see him. An airplane!

KELLER. Well? So?

MOTHER [*trembling*]. Why?

KELLER. I don't read minds. Do you?

MOTHER. Why, Joe? What has Steve suddenly got to tell him that he takes an airplane to see him?

KELLER. What do I care what Steve's got to tell him?

MOTHER. You're sure, Joe?

KELLER [*frightened, but angry*]. Yes, I'm sure.

MOTHER [*she sits stiffly in a chair*]. Be smart now, Joe. The boy is coming. Be smart.

KELLER [*desperately*]. Once and for all, did you hear what I said? I said I'm sure!

MOTHER [*she nods weakly*]. All right, Joe. [*He straightens up.*] Just . . . be smart. [KELLER, *in hopeless fury, looks at her, turns around, goes up to porch and into house, slamming screen door violently behind him.* MOTHER *sits in chair downstage, stiffly, staring, seeing.*]

ACT TWO

As twilight falls, that evening.

On the rise, CHRIS *is discovered at right, sawing the broken-off tree, leaving stump standing alone. He is dressed in good pants, white shoes, but without a shirt. He disappears with tree up the alley when* MOTHER *appears on porch. She comes down and stands watching him. She has on a dressing-gown, carries a tray of grape-juice drink in a pitcher, and glasses with sprigs of mint in them.*

MOTHER [*calling up alley*]. Did you have to put on good pants to do that? [*She comes downstage and puts tray on table in the arbor. Then looks around uneasily, then feels pitcher for coolness.* CHRIS *enters from alley brushing off his hands.*] You notice there's more light with that thing gone?

CHRIS. Why aren't you dressing?

MOTHER. It's suffocating upstairs. I made a grape drink for Georgie. He always liked grape. Come and have some.

CHRIS [*impatiently*]. Well, come on, get dressed. And what's Dad sleeping so much for? [*He goes to table and pours a glass of juice.*]

MOTHER. He's worried. When he's worried he sleeps. [*Pauses. Looks into his eyes.*] We're dumb, Chris. Dad and I are stupid people. We don't know anything. You've got to protect us.

CHRIS. You're silly; what's there to be afraid of?

MOTHER. To his last day in court Steve never gave up the idea that Dad made him do it. If they're going to open the case again I won't live through it.

CHRIS. George is just a damn fool, Mother. How can you take him seriously?

MOTHER. That family hates us. Maybe even Annie. . . .

CHRIS. Oh, now, Mother . . .

MOTHER. You think just because you like everybody, they like you!

CHRIS. All right, stop working yourself up. Just leave everything to me.

MOTHER. When George goes home tell her to go with him.

CHRIS [non-committally]. Don't worry about Annie.

MOTHER. Steve is her father, too.

CHRIS. Are you going to cut it out? Now, come.

MOTHER [going upstage with him]. You don't realize how people can hate, Chris, they can hate so much they'll tear the world to pieces. . . . [ANN, dressed up, appears on porch.]

CHRIS. Look! She's dressed already. [As he and MOTHER mount porch.] I've just got to put on a shirt.

ANN [in a preoccupied way]. Are you feeling well, Katie?

MOTHER. What's the difference, dear. There are certain people, y'know, the sicker they get the longer they live. [She goes into house.]

CHRIS. You look nice.

ANN. We're going to tell her tonight.

CHRIS. Absolutely, don't worry about it.

ANN. I wish we could tell her now. I can't stand scheming. My stomach gets hard.

CHRIS. It's not scheming, we'll just get her in a better mood.

MOTHER [offstage, in the house]. Joe, are you going to sleep all day!

ANN [laughing]. The only one who's relaxed is your father. He's fast asleep.

CHRIS. I'm relaxed.

ANN. Are you?

CHRIS. Look. [He holds out his hand and makes it shake.] Let me know when George gets here. [He goes into the house. She moves aimlessly, and then is drawn toward tree stump. She goes to it, hesitantly touches broken top in the hush of her thoughts. Offstage LYDIA calls, "Johnny! Come get your supper!" SUE enters from left, and calls, seeing ANN.]

SUE. Is my husband . . . ?

ANN [turns, startled]. Oh!

SUE. I'm terribly sorry.

ANN. It's all right, I . . . I'm a little silly about the dark.

SUE [*looks about*]. It is getting dark.

ANN. Are you looking for your husband?

SUE. As usual. [*Laughs tiredly.*] He spends so much time here, they'll be charging him rent.

ANN. Nobody was dressed so he drove over to the depot to pick up my brother.

SUE. Oh, your brother's in?

ANN. Yeah, they ought to be here any minute now. Will you have a cold drink?

SUE. I will, thanks. [ANN *goes to table and pours.*] My husband. Too hot to drive me to beach.— Men are like little boys; for the neighbors they'll always cut the grass.

ANN. People like to do things for the Kellers. Been that way since I can remember.

SUE. It's amazing. I guess your brother's coming to give you away, heh?

ANN [*giving her drink*]. I don't know. I suppose.

SUE. You must be all nerved up.

ANN. It's always a problem getting yourself married, isn't it?

SUE. That depends on your shape, of course. I don't see why you should have had a problem.

ANN. I've had chances—

SUE. I'll bet. It's romantic . . . it's very unusual to me, marrying the brother of your sweetheart.

ANN. I don't know. I think it's mostly that whenever I need somebody to tell me the truth I've always thought of Chris. When he tells you something you know it's so. He relaxes me.

SUE. And he's got money. That's important, you know.

ANN. It wouldn't matter to me.

SUE. You'd be surprised. It makes all the difference. I married an interne. On my salary. And that was bad, because as soon as a woman supports a man he owes her something. You can never owe somebody without resenting them. [ANN *laughs.*] That's true, you know.

ANN. Underneath, I think the doctor is very devoted.

SUE. Oh, certainly. But it's bad when a man always sees the bars in front of him. Jim thinks he's in jail all the time.

ANN. Oh . . .

SUE. That's why I've been intending to ask you a small favor, Ann . . . it's something very important to me.

ANN. Certainly, if I can do it.

SUE. You can. When you take up housekeeping, try to find a place away from here.

ANN. Are you fooling?

SUE. I'm very serious. My husband is unhappy with Chris around.

ANN. How is that?

SUE. Jim's a successful doctor. But he's got an idea he'd like to do medical research. Discover things. You see?

ANN. Well, isn't that good?

SUE. Research pays twenty-five dollars a week minus laundering the hair shirt. You've got to give up your life to go into it.

ANN. How does Chris?

SUE [*with growing feeling*]. Chris makes people want to be better than it's possible to be. He does that to people.

ANN. Is that bad?

SUE. My husband has a family, dear. Every time he has a session with Chris he feels as though he's compromising by not giving up everything for research. As though Chris or anybody else isn't compromising. It happens with Jim every couple of years. He meets a man and makes a statue out of him.

ANN. Maybe he's right. I don't mean that Chris is a statue, but . . .

SUE. Now darling, you know he's not right.

ANN. I don't agree with you. Chris . . .

SUE. Let's face it, dear. Chris is working with his father, isn't he? He's taking money out of that business every week in the year.

ANN. What of it?

SUE. You ask me what of it?

ANN. I certainly do ask you. [*She seems about to burst out.*]
  You oughtn't cast aspersions like that, I'm surprised at you.

SUE. You're surprised at me!

ANN. He'd never take five cents out of that plant if there was
  anything wrong in it.

SUE. You know that.

ANN. I know it. I resent everything you've said.

SUE [*moving toward her*]. You know what I resent, dear?

ANN. Please, I don't want to argue.

SUE. I resent living next door to the Holy Family. It makes me
  look like a bum, you understand?

ANN. I can't do anything about that.

SUE. Who is he to ruin a man's life? Everybody knows Joe
  pulled a fast one to get out of jail.

ANN. That's not true!

SUE. Then why don't you go out and talk to people? Go on, talk
  to them. There's not a person on the block who doesn't know
  the truth.

ANN. That's a lie. People come here all the time for cards
  and . . .

SUE. So what? They give him credit for being smart. I do, too,
  I've got nothing against Joe. But if Chris wants people to
  put on the hair shirt let him take off his broadcloth. He's
  driving my husband crazy with that phony idealism of his,
  and I'm at the end of my rope on it! [CHRIS *enters on porch,
  wearing shirt and tie now. She turns quickly, hearing. With
  a smile.*] Hello, darling. How's Mother?

CHRIS. I thought George came.

SUE. No, it was just us.

CHRIS [*coming down to them*]. Susie, do me a favor, heh? Go
  up to Mother and see if you can calm her. She's all worked
  up.

SUE. She still doesn't know about you two?

CHRIS [*laughs a little*]. Well, she senses it, I guess. You know
  my mother.

SUE [*going up to porch*]. Oh, yeah, she's psychic.

CHRIS. Maybe there's something in the medicine chest.

SUE. I'll give her one of everything. [*On porch.*] Don't worry
about Kate; couple of drinks, dance her around a little . . .
she'll love Ann. [*To* ANN.] Because you're the female version
of him. [CHRIS *laughs.*] Don't be alarmed, I said version.
[*She goes into house.*]

CHRIS. Interesting woman, isn't she?

ANN. Yeah, she's very interesting.

CHRIS. She's a great nurse, you know, she . . .

ANN [*in tension, but trying to control it*]. Are you still doing
that?

CHRIS [*sensing something wrong, but still smiling*]. Doing what?

ANN. As soon as you get to know somebody you find a distinction for them. How do you know she's a great nurse?

CHRIS. What's the matter, Ann?

ANN. The woman hates you. She despises you!

CHRIS. Hey . . . what's hit you?

ANN. Gee, Chris . . .

CHRIS. What happened here?

ANN. You never . . . Why didn't you tell me?

CHRIS. Tell you what?

ANN. She says they think Joe is guilty.

CHRIS. What difference does it make what they think?

ANN. I don't care what they think, I just don't understand why
you took the trouble to deny it. You said it was all forgotten.

CHRIS. I didn't want you to feel there was anything wrong in
you coming here, that's all. I know a lot of people think my
father was guilty, and I assumed there might be some question in your mind.

ANN. But I never once said I suspected him.

CHRIS. Nobody says it.

ANN. Chris, I know how much you love him, but it could
never . . .

CHRIS. Do you think I could forgive him if he'd done that thing?

ANN. I'm not here out of a blue sky, Chris. I turned my back on
my father, if there's anything wrong here now . . .

CHRIS. I know that, Ann.

ANN. George is coming from Dad, and I don't think it's with a blessing.

CHRIS. He's welcome here. You've got nothing to fear from George.

ANN. Tell me that . . . just tell me that.

CHRIS. The man is innocent, Ann. Remember he was falsely accused once and it put him through hell. How would you behave if you were faced with the same thing again? Annie, believe me, there's nothing wrong for you here, believe me, kid.

ANN. All right, Chris, all right. [*They embrace as* KELLER *appears quietly on porch.* ANN *simply studies him.*]

KELLER. Every time I come out here it looks like Playland!

[*They break and laugh in embarrassment.*]

CHRIS. I thought you were going to shave?

KELLER [*sitting on bench*]. In a minute. I just woke up, I can't see nothin'.

ANN. You look shaved.

KELLER. Oh, no. [*Massages his jaw.*] Gotta be extra special tonight. Big night, Annie. So how's it feel to be a married woman?

ANN [*laughs*]. I don't know, yet.

KELLER [*to* CHRIS]. What's the matter, you slippin'? [*He takes a little box of apples from under the bench as they talk.*]

CHRIS. The great roué!

KELLER. What is that, roué?

CHRIS. It's French.

KELLER. Don't talk dirty. [*They laugh.*]

CHRIS [*to* ANN]. You ever meet a bigger ignoramus?

KELLER. Well, somebody's got to make a living.

ANN [*as they laugh*]. That's telling him.

KELLER. I don't know, everybody's gettin' so Goddam educated in this country there'll be nobody to take away the garbage. [*They laugh.*] It's gettin' so the only dumb ones left are the bosses.

ANN. You're not so dumb, Joe.

KELLER. I know, but you go into our plant, for instance. I got

so many lieutenants, majors and colonels that I'm ashamed
to ask somebody to sweep the floor. I gotta be careful I'll
insult somebody. No kiddin'. It's a tragedy: you stand on
the street today and spit, you're gonna hit a college man.

CHRIS. Well, don't spit.

KELLER [*breaks apple in half, passing it to* ANN *and* CHRIS]. I
mean to say, it's comin' to a pass. [*He takes a breath.*] I
been thinkin', Annie . . . your brother, George. I been
thinkin' about your brother George. When he comes I like
you to *brooch* something to him.

CHRIS. Broach.

KELLER. What's the matter with brooch?

CHRIS [*smiling*]. It's not English.

KELLER. When I went to night school it was brooch.

ANN [*laughing*]. Well, in day school it's broach.

KELLER. Don't surround me, will you? Seriously, Ann . . . You
say he's not well. George, I been thinkin', why should he
knock himself out in New York with that cut-throat compe-
tition, when I got so many friends here; I'm very friendly
with some big lawyers in town. I could set George up here.

ANN. That's awfully nice of you, Joe.

KELLER. No, kid, it ain't nice of me. I want you to understand
me. I'm thinking of Chris. [*Slight pause.*] See . . . this is
what I mean. You get older, you want to feel that you . . . accomplished something. My only accomplishment is my son.
I ain't brainy. That's all I accomplished. Now, a year, eighteen months, your father'll be a free man. Who is he going to
come to Annie? His baby. You. He'll come, old, mad, into
your house.

ANN. That can't matter any more, Joe.

KELLER. I don't want that hate to come between us. [*Gestures
between* CHRIS *and himself.*]

ANN. I can only tell you that that could never happen.

KELLER. You're in love now, Annie, but believe me, I'm older
than you and I know—a daughter is a daughter, and a father
is a father. And it could happen. [*He pauses.*] I like you and
George to go to him in prison and tell him. . . . "Dad, Joe

wants to bring you into the business when you get out."

ANN [*surprised, even shocked*]. You'd have him as a partner?

KELLER. No, no partner. A good job. [*Pause. He sees she is shocked, a little mystified. He gets up, speaks more nervously.*] I want him to know, Annie . . . while he's sitting there I want him to know that when he gets out he's got a place waitin' for him. It'll take his bitterness away. To know you got a place . . . it sweetens you.

ANN. Joe, you owe him nothing.

KELLER. I owe him a good kick in the teeth, but he's your father. . . .

CHRIS. Then kick him in the teeth! I don't want him in the plant, so that's that! You understand? And besides, don't talk about him like that. People misunderstand you!

KELLER. And I don't understand why she has to crucify the man.

CHRIS. Well, it's her father, if she feels . . .

KELLER. No, no. . . .

CHRIS [*almost angrily*]. What's it to you? Why . . . ?

KELLER [*a commanding outburst in his high nervousness*]. A father is a father! [*As though the outburst had revealed him, he looks about, wanting to retract it. His hand goes to his cheek.*] I better . . . I better shave. [*He turns and a smile is on his face. To* ANN.] I didn't mean to yell at you, Annie.

ANN. Let's forget the whole thing, Joe.

KELLER. Right. [*To* CHRIS.] She's likable.

CHRIS [*a little peeved at the man's stupidity*]. Shave, will you?

KELLER. Right again.

[*As he turns to porch* LYDIA *comes hurrying from her house, right.*]

LYDIA. I forgot all about it . . . [*Seeing* CHRIS *and* ANN.] Hya. [*To* JOE.] I promised to fix Kate's hair for tonight. Did she comb it yet?

KELLER. Always a smile, hey, Lydia?

LYDIA. Sure, why not?

KELLER [*going up on porch*]. Come on up and comb my Katie's hair. [LYDIA *goes up on porch.*] She's got a big night, make her beautiful.

LYDIA. I will.

KELLER [*he holds door open for her and she goes into kitchen. To* CHRIS *and* ANN]. Hey, that could be a song. [*He sings softly.*]

"Come on up and comb my Katie's hair . . .
Oh, come on up, 'cause she's my lady fair—"

[*To* ANN.] How's that for one year of night school? [*He continues singing as he goes into kitchen.*]

"Oh, come on up, come on up, and comb my lady's hair——"

[JIM BAYLISS *rounds corner of driveway, walking rapidly.* JIM *crosses to* CHRIS, *motions him up and pulls him down to stage left, excitedly.* KELLER *stands just inside kitchen door, watching them.*]

CHRIS. What's the matter? Where is he?

JIM. Where's your mother?

CHRIS. Upstairs, dressing.

ANN [*crossing to them rapidly*]. What happened to George?

JIM. I asked him to wait in the car. Listen to me now. Can you take some advice? [*They wait.*] Don't bring him in here.

ANN. Why?

JIM. Kate is in bad shape, you can't explode this in front of her.

ANN. Explode what?

JIM. You know why he's here, don't try to kid it away. There's blood in his eye; drive him somewhere and talk to him alone.

[ANN *turns to go up drive, takes a couple of steps, sees* KELLER *and stops. He goes quietly on into house.*]

CHRIS [*shaken, and therefore angered*]. Don't be an old lady.

JIM. He's come to take her home. What does that mean? [*To* ANN.] You know what that means. Fight it out with him some place else.

ANN [*she comes back down toward* CHRIS]. I'll drive . . . him somewhere.

CHRIS [*goes to her*]. No.

JIM. Will you stop being an idiot?

CHRIS. Nobody's afraid of him here. Cut that out! [*He starts for driveway, but is brought up short by* GEORGE, *who enters there.* GEORGE *is* CHRIS' *age, but a paler man, now on the edge of his self-restraint. He speaks quietly, as though afraid to find himself screaming. An instant's hesitation and* CHRIS *steps up to him, hand extended, smiling.*] Helluva way to do; what're you sitting out there for?

GEORGE. Doctor said your mother isn't well, I . . .

CHRIS. So what? She'd want to see you, wouldn't she? We've been waiting for you all afternoon. [*He puts his hand on* GEORGE'S *arm, but* GEORGE *pulls away, coming across toward* ANN.]

ANN [*touching his collar*]. This is filthy, didn't you bring another shirt? [GEORGE *breaks away from her, and moves down and left, examining the yard. Door opens, and he turns rapidly, thinking it is* KATE, *but it's* SUE. *She looks at him, he turns away and moves on left, to fence. He looks over it at his former home.* SUE *comes down stage.*]

SUE [*annoyed*]. How about the beach, Jim?

JIM. Oh, it's too hot to drive.

SUE. How'd you get to the station—Zeppelin?

CHRIS. This is Mrs. Bayliss, George. [*Calling, as* GEORGE *pays no attention, staring at house off left.*] George! [GEORGE *turns.*] Mrs. Baylis.

SUE. How do you do.

GEORGE [*removing his hat*]. You're the people who bought our house, aren't you?

SUE. That's right. Come and see what we did with it before you leave.

GEORGE [*he walks down and away from her*]. I liked it the way it was.

SUE [*after a brief pause*]. He's frank, isn't he?

JIM [*pulling her off left*]. See you later. . . . Take it easy, fella. [*They exit, left.*]

CHRIS [*calling after them*]. Thanks for driving him! [*Turning to* GEORGE.] How about some grape juice? Mother made it especially for you.

GEORGE [*with forced appreciation*]. Good old Kate, remembered my grape juice.

CHRIS. You drank enough of it in this house. How've you been, George?— Sit down.

GEORGE [*he keeps moving*]. It takes me a minute. [*Looking around.*] It seems impossible.

CHRIS. What?

GEORGE. I'm back here.

CHRIS. Say, you've gotten a little nervous, haven't you?

GEORGE. Yeah, toward the end of the day. What're you, big executive now?

CHRIS. Just kind of medium. How's the law?

GEORGE. I don't know. When I was studying in the hospital it seemed sensible, but outside there doesn't seem to be much of a law. The trees got thick, didn't they? [*Points to stump.*] What's that?

CHRIS. Blew down last night. We had it there for Larry. You know.

GEORGE. Why, afraid you'll forget him?

CHRIS [*starts for* GEORGE]. Kind of a remark is that?

ANN [*breaking in, putting a restraining hand on* CHRIS]. When did you start wearing a hat?

GEORGE [*discovers hat in his hand*]. Today. From now on I decided to look like a lawyer, anyway. [*He holds it up to her.*] Don't you recognize it?

ANN. Why? Where . . . ?

GEORGE. Your father's . . . he asked me to wear it.

ANN. . . . How is he?

GEORGE. He got smaller.

ANN. Smaller?

GEORGE. Yeah, little. [*Holds out his hand to measure.*] He's a little man. That's what happens to suckers, you know. It's good I went to him in time—another year there'd be nothing left but his smell.

CHRIS. What's the matter, George, what's the trouble?

GEORGE. The trouble? The trouble is when you make suckers out of people once, you shouldn't try to do it twice.

CHRIS. What does that mean?

GEORGE [to ANN]. You're not married yet, are you?

ANN. George, will you sit down and stop—?

GEORGE. Are you married yet?

ANN. No, I'm not married yet.

GEORGE. You're not going to marry him.

ANN. Why am I not going to marry him?

GEORGE. Because his father destroyed your family.

CHRIS. Now look, George . . .

GEORGE. Cut it short, Chris. Tell her to come home with me. Let's not argue, you know what I've got to say.

CHRIS. George, you don't want to be the voice of God, do you?

GEORGE. I'm . . .

CHRIS. That's been your trouble all your life, George, you dive into things. What kind of a statement is that to make? You're a big boy now.

GEORGE. I'm a big boy now.

CHRIS. Don't come bulling in here. If you've got something to say, be civilized about it.

GEORGE. Don't civilize me!

ANN. Shhh!

CHRIS [ready to hit him]. Are you going to talk like a grown man or aren't you?

ANN [quickly, to forestall an outburst]. Sit down, dear. Don't be angry, what's the matter? [He allows her to seat him, looking at her.] Now what happened? You kissed me when I left, now you . . .

GEORGE [breathlessly]. My life turned upside down since then. I couldn't go back to work when you left. I wanted to go to Dad and tell him you were going to be married. It seemed impossible not to tell him. He loved you so much . . . [He pauses.] Annie . . . we did a terrible thing. We can never be forgiven. Not even to send him a card at Christmas. I didn't see him once since I got home from the war! Annie, you don't know what was done to that man. You don't know what happened.

ANN [*afraid*]. Of course I know.

GEORGE. You can't know, you wouldn't be here. Dad came to work that day. The night foreman came to him and showed him the cylinder heads . . . they were coming out of the process with defects. There was something wrong with the process. So Dad went directly to the phone and called here and told Joe to come down right away. But the morning passed. No sign of Joe. So Dad called again. By this time he had over a hundred defectives. The Army was screaming for stuff and Dad didn't have anything to ship. So Joe told him . . . on the phone he told him to weld, cover up the cracks in any way he could, and ship them out.

CHRIS. Are you through now?

GEORGE [*surging up at him*]. I'm not through now! [*Back to* ANN.] Dad was afraid. He wanted Joe there if he was going to do it. But Joe can't come down . . . he's sick. Sick! He suddenly gets the flu! Suddenly! But he promised to take responsibility. Do you understand what I'm saying? On the telephone you can't have responsibility! In a court you can always deny a phone call and that's exactly what he did. They knew he was a liar the first time, but in the appeal they believed that rotten lie and now Joe is a big shot and your father is the patsy. [*He gets up.*] Now what're you going to do? Eat his food, sleep in his bed? Answer me; what're you going to do?

CHRIS. What're you going to do, George?

GEORGE. He's too smart for me, I can't prove a phone call.

CHRIS. Then how dare you come in here with that rot?

ANN. George, the court . . .

GEORGE. The court didn't know your father! But you know him. You know in your heart Joe did it.

CHRIS [*whirling him around*]. Lower your voice or I'll throw you out of here!

GEORGE. She knows. She knows.

CHRIS [*to* ANN]. Get him out of here, Ann. Get him out of here.

ANN. George, I know everything you've said. Dad told that whole thing in court, and they . . .

GEORGE [*almost a scream*]. The court did not know him, Annie!

ANN. Shhh!— But he'll say anything, George. You know how quick he can lie.

GEORGE [*turning to* CHRIS, *with deliberation*]. I'll ask you something, and look me in the eye when you answer me.

CHRIS. I'll look you in the eye.

GEORGE. You know your father . . .

CHRIS. I know him well.

GEORGE. And he's the kind of boss to let a hundred and twenty-one cylinder heads be repaired and shipped out of his shop without even knowing about it?

CHRIS. He's that kind of boss.

GEORGE. And that's the same Joe Keller who never left his shop without first going around to see that all the lights were out.

CHRIS [*with growing anger*]. The same Joe Keller.

GEORGE. The same man who knows how many minutes a day his workers spend in the toilet.

CHRIS. The same man.

GEORGE. And my father, that frightened mouse who'd never buy a shirt without somebody along—that man would dare do such a thing on his own?

CHRIS. On his own. And because he's a frightened mouse this is another thing he'd do;—throw the blame on somebody else because he's not man enough to take it himself. He tried it in court but it didn't work, but with a fool like you it works!

GEORGE. Oh, Chris, you're a liar to yourself!

ANN [*deeply shaken*]. Don't talk like that!

CHRIS [*sits facing* GEORGE]. Tell me, George. What happened? The court record was good enough for you all these years, why isn't it good now? Why did you believe it all these years?

GEORGE [*after a slight pause*]. Because you believed it. . . . That's the truth, Chris. I believed everything, because I thought you did. But today I heard it from his mouth. From his mouth it's altogether different than the record. Anyone who knows him, and knows your father, will believe it from

his mouth. Your Dad took everything we have. I can't beat
that. But she's one item he's not going to grab. [*He turns to*
ANN.] Get your things. Everything they have is covered
with blood. You're not the kind of a girl who can live with
that. Get your things.

CHRIS. Ann . . . you're not going to believe that, are you?

ANN [*she goes to him*]. You know it's not true, don't you?

GEORGE. How can he tell you? It's his father. [*To* CHRIS.] None
of these things ever even cross your mind?

CHRIS. Yes, they crossed my mind. Anything can cross your
mind!

GEORGE. *He knows,* Annie. He knows!

CHRIS. The Voice of God!

GEORGE. Then why isn't your name on the business? Explain
that to her!

CHRIS. What the hell has that got to do with . . . ?

GEORGE. Annie, why isn't his name on it?

CHRIS. Even when I don't own it!

GEORGE. Who're you kidding? Who gets it when he dies? [*To*
ANN.] Open your eyes, you know the both of them, isn't
that the first thing they'd do, the way they love each other?
—J. O. Keller & Son? [*Pause.* ANN *looks from him to* CHRIS.]
I'll settle it. Do you want to settle it, or are you afraid to?

CHRIS. . . . What do you mean?

GEORGE. Let me go up and talk to your father. In ten minutes
you'll have the answer. Or are you afraid of the answer?

CHRIS. I'm not afraid of the answer. I know the answer. But
my mother isn't well and I don't want a fight here now.

GEORGE. Let me go to him.

CHRIS. You're not going to start a fight here now.

GEORGE [*to* ANN]. What more do you want!!! [*There is a sound
of footsteps in the house.*]

ANN [*turns her head suddenly toward the house*]. Someone's
coming.

CHRIS [*to* GEORGE, *quietly*]. You won't say anything now.

ANN. You'll go soon. I'll call a cab.

GEORGE. You're coming with me.

ANN. And don't mention marriage, because we haven't told her yet.

GEORGE. You're coming with me.

ANN. You understand? Don't . . . George, you're not going to start anything now! [*She hears footsteps.*] Shsh! [MOTHER *enters on porch. She is dressed almost formally, her hair is fixed. They are all turned toward her. On seeing* GEORGE *she raises both hands, comes down toward him.*]

MOTHER. Georgie, Georgie.

GEORGE [*he has always liked her*]. Hello, Kate.

MOTHER [*she cups his face in her hands*]. They made an old man out of you. [*Touches his hair.*] Look, you're gray.

GEORGE [*her pity, open and unabashed, reaches into him, and he smiles sadly*]. I know, I . . .

MOTHER. I told you when you went away, don't try for medals.

GEORGE [*he laughs, tiredly*]. I didn't try, Kate. They made it very easy for me.

MOTHER [*actually angry*]. Go on. You're all alike. [*To* ANN.] Look at him, why did you say he's fine? He looks like a ghost.

GEORGE [*relishing her solicitude*]. I feel all right.

MOTHER. I'm sick to look at you. What's the matter with your mother, why don't she feed you?

ANN. He just hasn't any appetite.

MOTHER. If he ate in my house he'd have an appetite. [*To* ANN.] I pity your husband! [*To* GEORGE.] Sit down. I'll make you a sandwich.

GEORGE [*sits with an embarrassed laugh*]. I'm really not hungry.

MOTHER. Honest to God, it breaks my heart to see what happened to all the children. How we worked and planned for you, and you end up no better than us.

GEORGE [*with deep feeling for her*]. You . . . you haven't changed at all, you know that, Kate?

MOTHER. None of us changed, Georgie. We all love you. Joe was just talking about the day you were born and the water got shut off. People were carrying basins from a block away —a stranger would have thought the whole neighborhood was on fire! [*They laugh. She sees the juice. To* ANN.] Why didn't you give him some juice!

ANN [*defensively*]. I offered it to him.

MOTHER [*scoffingly*]. You offered it to him! [*Thrusting glass into* GEORGE's *hand.*] Give it to him! [*To* GEORGE, *who is laughing.*] And now you're going to sit here and drink some juice . . . and look like something!

GEORGE [*sitting*]. Kate, I feel hungry already.

CHRIS [*proudly*]. She could turn Mahatma Ghandi into a heavy-weight!

MOTHER [*to* CHRIS, *with great energy*]. Listen, to hell with the restaurant! I got a ham in the icebox, and frozen strawberries, and avocados, and . . .

ANN. Swell, I'll help you!

GEORGE. The train leaves at eight-thirty, Ann.

MOTHER [*to* ANN]. You're leaving?

CHRIS. No, Mother, she's not . . .

ANN [*breaking through it, going to* GEORGE]. You hardly got here; give yourself a chance to get acquainted again.

CHRIS. Sure, you don't even know us any more.

MOTHER. Well, Chris, if they can't stay, don't . . .

CHRIS. No, it's just a question of George, Mother, he planned on . . .

GEORGE [*he gets up politely, nicely, for* KATE's *sake*]. Now wait a minute, Chris . . .

CHRIS. [*smiling and full of command, cutting him off*]. If you want to go, I'll drive you to the station now, but if you're staying, no arguments while you're here.

MOTHER [*at last confessing the tension*]. Why should he argue? [*She goes to him, and with desperation and compassion, stroking his hair.*] Georgie and us have no argument. How could we have an argument, Georgie? We all got hit by the same lightning, how can you . . . ? Did you see what happened to Larry's tree, Georgie? [*She has taken his arm, and unwillingly he moves across stage with her.*] Imagine? While I was dreaming of him in the middle of the night, the wind came along and . . . [LYDIA *enters on porch. As soon as she sees him.*]

LYDIA. Hey, Georgie! Georgie! Georgie! Georgie! Georgie!
[*She comes down to him eagerly. She has a flowered hat in
her hand, which* KATE *takes from her as she goes to* GEORGE.]

GEORGE. [*They shake hands eagerly, warmly.*] Hello, Laughy.
What'd you do, grow?

LYDIA. I'm a big girl now.

MOTHER [*taking hat from her*]. Look what she can do to a hat!

ANN [*to* LYDIA, *admiring the hat*]. Did you make that?

MOTHER. In ten minutes! [*She puts it on.*]

LYDIA [*fixing it on her head*]. I only rearranged it.

GEORGE. You still make your own clothes?

CHRIS [*of* MOTHER]. Ain't she classy! All she needs now is a
Russian wolfhound.

MOTHER [*moving her head from left to right*]. It feels like somebody is sitting on my head.

ANN. No, it's beautiful, Kate.

MOTHER [*kisses* LYDIA—*to* GEORGE]. She's a genius! You
should've married her. [*They laugh.*] This one can feed you!

LYDIA [*strangely embarrassed*]. Oh, stop that, Kate.

GEORGE [*to* LYDIA]. Didn't I hear you had a baby?

MOTHER. You don't hear so good. She's got three babies.

GEORGE [*a little hurt by it—to* LYDIA]. No kidding, three?

LYDIA. Yeah, it was one, two, three— You've been away a long
time, Georgie.

GEORGE. I'm beginning to realize.

MOTHER [*to* CHRIS *and* GEORGE]. The trouble with you kids is
you *think* too much.

LYDIA. Well, we think, too.

MOTHER. Yes, but not all the time.

GEORGE [*with almost obvious envy*]. They never took Frank,
heh?

LYDIA [*a little apologetically*]. No, he was always one year ahead
of the draft.

MOTHER. It's amazing. When they were calling boys twenty-
seven Frank was just twenty-eight, when they made it twenty-eight he was just twenty-nine. That's why he took up

astrology. It's all in when you were born, it just goes to show.

CHRIS. What does it go to show?

MOTHER [*to* CHRIS]. Don't be so intelligent. Some superstitions are very nice! [*To* LYDIA.] Did he finish Larry's horoscope?

LYDIA. I'll ask him now, I'm going in. [*To* GEORGE, *a little sadly, almost embarrassed.*] Would you like to see my babies? Come on.

GEORGE. I don't think so, Lydia.

LYDIA [*understanding*]. All right. Good luck to you, George.

GEORGE. Thanks. And to you . . . And Frank. [*She smiles at him, turns and goes off right to her house.* GEORGE *stands staring after her.*]

LYDIA [*as she runs off*]. Oh, Frank!

MOTHER [*reading his thoughts*]. She got pretty, heh?

GEORGE [*sadly*]. Very pretty.

MOTHER [*as a reprimand*]. She's beautiful, you damned fool!

GEORGE [*looks around longingly; and softly, with a catch in his throat*]. She makes it seem so nice around here.

MOTHER [*shaking her finger at him*]. Look what happened to you because you wouldn't listen to me! I told you to marry that girl and stay out of the war!

GEORGE [*laughs at himself*]. She used to laugh too much.

MOTHER. And you didn't laugh enough. While you were getting mad about Fascism, Frank was getting into her bed.

GEORGE [*to* CHRIS]. He won the war, Frank.

CHRIS. All the battles.

MOTHER [*in pursuit of this mood*]. The day they started the draft, Georgie, I told you you loved that girl.

CHRIS [*laughs*]. And truer love hath no man!

MOTHER. I'm smarter than any of you.

GEORGE [*laughing*]. She's wonderful!

MOTHER. And now you're going to listen to me, George. You had big principles, Eagle Scouts the three of you; so now I got a tree, and this one, [*Indicating* CHRIS.] when the weather gets bad he can't stand on his feet; and that big dope, [*Pointing to* LYDIA'S *house.*] next door who never reads anything but Andy Gump has three children and his house paid off.

Stop being a philosopher, and look after yourself. Like Joe was just saying—you move back here, he'll help you get set, and I'll find you a girl and put a smile on your face.

GEORGE. Joe? Joe wants me here?

ANN [*eagerly*]. He asked me to tell you, and I think it's a good idea.

MOTHER. Certainly. Why must you make believe you hate us? Is that another principle?—that you have to hate us? You don't hate us, George, I know you, you can't fool me, I diapered you. [*Suddenly to* ANN.] You remember Mr. Marcy's daughter?

ANN [*laughing, to* GEORGE]. She's got you hooked already!

[GEORGE *laughs, is excited.*]

MOTHER. You look her over, George; you'll see she's the most beautiful . . .

CHRIS. She's got warts, George.

MOTHER [*to* CHRIS]. She hasn't got warts! [*To* GEORGE.] So the girl has a little beauty mark on her chin . . .

CHRIS. And two on her nose.

MOTHER. You remember. Her father's the retired police inspector.

CHRIS. Sergeant, George.

MOTHER. He's a very kind man!

CHRIS. He looks like a gorilla.

MOTHER [*to* GEORGE]. He never shot anybody [*They all burst out laughing, as* KELLER *appears in doorway.* GEORGE *rises abruptly, stares at* KELLER, *who comes rapidly down to him.*]

KELLER [*the laughter stops. With strained joviality*]. Well! Look who's here! [*Extending his hand.*] Georgie, good to see ya.

GEORGE [*shakes hands—somberly*]. How're you, Joe?

KELLER. So-so. Gettin' old. You comin' out to dinner with us?

GEORGE. No, got to be back in New York.

ANN. I'll call a cab for you. [*She goes up into the house.*]

KELLER. Too bad you can't stay, George. Sit down. [*To* MOTHER.] He looks fine.

MOTHER. He looks terrible.

KELLER. That's what I said, you look terrible, George. [*They laugh.*] I wear the pants and she beats me with the belt.

GEORGE. I saw your factory on the way from the station. It looks like General Motors.

KELLER. I wish it was General Motors, but it ain't. Sit down, George. Sit down. [*Takes cigar out of his pocket.*] So you finally went to see your father, I hear?

GEORGE. Yes, this morning. What kind of stuff do you make now?

KELLER. Oh, little of everything. Pressure cookers, an assembly for washing machines. Got a nice, flexible plant now. So how'd you find Dad? Feel all right?

GEORGE [*searching* KELLER, *he speaks indecisively*]. No, he's not well, Joe.

KELLER [*lighting his cigar*]. Not his heart again, is it?

GEORGE. It's everything, Joe. It's his soul.

KELLER [*blowing out smoke*]. Uh huh——

CHRIS. How about seeing what they did with your house?

KELLER. Leave him be.

GEORGE [*to* CHRIS, *indicating* KELLER]. I'd like to talk to him.

KELLER. Sure, he just got here. That's the way they do, George. A little man makes a mistake and they hang him by the thumbs; the big ones become ambassadors. I wish you'd-a told me you were going to see Dad.

GEORGE [*studying him*]. I didn't know you were interested.

KELLER. In a way, I am. I would like him to know, George, that as far as I'm concerned, any time he wants, he's got a place with me. I would like him to know that.

GEORGE. He hates your guts, Joe. Don't you know that?

KELLER. I imagined it. But that can change, too.

MOTHER. Steve was never like that.

GEORGE. He's like that now. He'd like to take every man who made money in the war and put him up against a wall.

CHRIS. He'll need a lot of bullets.

GEORGE. And he'd better not get any.

KELLER. That's a sad thing to hear.

GEORGE [*with bitterness dominant*]. Why? What'd you expect him to think of you?

KELLER [*the force of his nature rising, but under control*]. I'm sad to see he hasn't changed. As long as I know him, twenty-five years, the man never learned how to take the blame. You know that, George.

GEORGE [*he does*]. Well, I . . .

KELLER. But you do know it. Because the way you come in here you don't look like you remember it. I mean like in 1937 when we had the shop on Flood Street. And he damn near blew us all up with that heater he left burning for two days without water. He wouldn't admit that was his fault, either. I had to fire a mechanic to save his face. You remember that.

GEORGE. Yes, but . . .

KELLER. I'm just mentioning it, George. Because this is just another one of a lot of things. Like when he gave Frank that money to invest in oil stock.

GEORGE [*distressed*]. I know that, I . . .

KELLER [*driving in, but restrained*]. But it's good to remember those things, kid. The way he cursed Frank because the stock went down. Was that Frank's fault? To listen to him Frank was a swindler. And all the man did was give him a bad tip.

GEORGE [*gets up, moves away*]. I know those things . . .

KELLER. Then remember them, remember them. [ANN *comes out of house.*] There are certain men in the world who rather see everybody hung before they'll take blame. You understand me, George? [*They stand facing each other,* GEORGE *trying to judge him.*]

ANN [*coming downstage*]. The cab's on its way. Would you like to wash?

MOTHER [*with the thrust of hope*]. Why must he go? Make the midnight, George.

KELLER. Sure, you'll have dinner with us!

ANN. How about it? Why not? We're eating at the lake, we could have a swell time.

GEORGE [*long pause, as he looks at* ANN, CHRIS, KELLER, *then back to her*]. All right.

MOTHER. Now you're talking.

CHRIS. I've got a shirt that'll go right with that suit.

MOTHER. Size fifteen and a half, right, George?

GEORGE. Is Lydia . . . ? I mean—Frank and Lydia coming?

MOTHER. I'll get you a date that'll make her look like a . . . [*She starts upstage.*]

GEORGE [*laughs*]. No, I don't want a date.

CHRIS. I know somebody just for you! Charlotte Tanner! [*He starts for the house.*]

KELLER. Call Charlotte, that's right.

MOTHER. Sure, call her up. [CHRIS *goes into house.*]

ANN. You go up and pick out a shirt and tie.

GEORGE [*he stops, looks around at them and the place*]. I never felt at home anywhere but here. I feel so . . . [*He nearly laughs, and turns away from them.*] Kate, you look so young, you know? You didn't change at all. It . . . rings an old bell. [*Turns to* KELLER.] You too, Joe, you're amazingly the same. The whole atmosphere is.

KELLER. Say, I ain't got time to get sick.

MOTHER. He hasn't been laid up in fifteen years. . . .

KELLER. Except my flu during the war.

MOTHER. Huhh?

KELLER. My flu, when I was sick during . . . the war.

MOTHER. Well, sure . . . [*To* GEORGE.] I meant except for that flu. [GEORGE *stands perfectly still.*] Well, it slipped my mind, don't look at me that way. He wanted to go to the shop but he couldn't lift himself off the bed. I thought he had pneumonia.

GEORGE. Why did you say he's never . . . ?

KELLER. I know how you feel, kid, I'll never forgive myself. If I could've gone in that day I'd never allow Dad to touch those heads.

GEORGE. She said you've never been sick.

MOTHER. I said he was sick, George.

GEORGE [*going to* ANN]. Ann, didn't you hear her say . . . ?

MOTHER. Do you remember every time you were sick?

GEORGE. I'd remember pneumonia. Especially if I got it just the day my partner was going to patch up cylinder heads . . . What happened that day, Joe?

FRANK [enters briskly from driveway, holding LARRY's horoscope in his hand. He comes to KATE]. Kate! Kate!

MOTHER. Frank, did you see George?

FRANK [extending his hand]. Lydia told me, I'm glad to . . . you'll have to pardon me. [Pulling MOTHER over right.] I've got something amazing for you, Kate, I finished Larry's horoscope.

MOTHER. You'd be interested in this, George. It's wonderful the way he can understand the . . .

CHRIS [entering from house]. George, the girl's on the phone . . .

MOTHER [desperately]. He finished Larry's horoscope!

CHRIS. Frank, can't you pick a better time than this?

FRANK. The greatest men who ever lived believed in the stars!

CHRIS. Stop filling her head with that junk!

FRANK. Is it junk to feel that there's a greater power than ourselves? I've studied the stars of his life! I won't argue with you, I'm telling you. Somewhere in this world your brother is alive!

MOTHER [instantly to CHRIS]. Why isn't it possible?

CHRIS. Because it's insane.

FRANK. Just a minute now. I'll tell you something and you can do as you please. Just let me say it. He was supposed to have died on November twenty-fifth. But November twenty-fifth was his favorable day.

CHRIS. Mother!

MOTHER. Listen to him!

FRANK. It was a day when everything good was shining on him, the kind of day he should've married on. You can laugh at a lot of it, I can understand you laughing. But the odds are a million to one that a man won't die on his favorable day. That's known, that's known, Chris!

MOTHER. Why isn't it possible, why isn't it possible, Chris!

GEORGE [to ANN]. Don't you understand what she's saying?

She just told you to go. What are you waiting for now?

CHRIS. Nobody can tell her to go. [*A car horn is heard.*]

MOTHER [*to* FRANK]. Thank you, darling, for your trouble. Will you tell him to wait, Frank?

FRANK [*as he goes*]. Sure thing.

MOTHER [*calling out*]. They'll be right out, driver!

CHRIS. She's not leaving, Mother.

GEORGE. You heard her say it, he's never been sick!

MOTHER. He misunderstood me, Chris! [CHRIS *looks at her, struck.*]

GEORGE [*to* ANN]. He simply told your father to kill pilots, and covered himself in bed!

CHRIS. You'd better answer him, Annie. Answer him.

MOTHER. I packed your bag, darling . . .

CHRIS. What?

MOTHER. I packed your bag. All you've got to do is close it.

ANN. I'm not closing anything. He asked me here and I'm staying till he tells me to go. [*To* GEORGE.] Till Chris tells me!

CHRIS. That's all! Now get out of here, George!

MOTHER [*to* CHRIS]. But if that's how he feels . . .

CHRIS. That's all, nothing more till Christ comes, about the case or Larry as long as I'm here! [*To* ANN.] Now get out of here, George!

GEORGE [*to* ANN]. You tell me. I want to hear you tell me.

ANN. Go, George! [*They disappear up the driveway,* ANN *saying "Don't take it that way, George! Please don't take it that way."*]

[CHRIS *turns to his mother.*]

CHRIS. What do you mean, you packed her bag? How dare you pack her bag?

MOTHER. Chris . . .

CHRIS. How dare you pack her bag?

MOTHER. She doesn't belong here.

CHRIS. Then I don't belong here.

MOTHER. She's Larry's girl.

CHRIS. And I'm his brother and he's dead, and I'm marrying his girl.

MOTHER. Never, never in this world!

KELLER. You lost your mind?

MOTHER. You have nothing to say!

KELLER [*cruelly*]. I got plenty to say. Three and a half years you been talking like a maniac—

MOTHER [*she smashes him across the face*]. Nothing. You have nothing to say. Now I say. He's coming back, and everybody has got to wait.

CHRIS. Mother, Mother . . .

MOTHER. Wait, wait . . .

CHRIS. How long? How long?

MOTHER [*rolling out of her*]. Till he comes; forever and ever till he comes!

CHRIS. [*as an ultimatum*]. Mother, I'm going ahead with it.

MOTHER. Chris, I've never said no to you in my life, now I say no!

CHRIS. You'll never let him go till I do it.

MOTHER. I'll never let him go and you'll never let him go . . . !

CHRIS. I've let him go. I've let him go a long . . .

MOTHER [*with no less force, but turning from him*]. Then let your father go. [*Pause.* CHRIS *stands transfixed.*]

KELLER. She's out of her mind.

MOTHER. Altogether! [*To* CHRIS, *but not facing them.*] Your brother's alive, darling, because if he's dead, your father killed him. Do you understand me now? As long as you live, that boy is alive. God does not let a son be killed by his father. Now you see, don't you? Now you see. [*Beyond control, she hurries up and into house.*]

KELLER [CHRIS *has not moved. He speaks insinuatingly, questioningly*]. She's out of her mind.

CHRIS [*a broken whisper*]. Then . . . you did it?

KELLER [*the beginning of plea in his voice*]. He never flew a P-40—

CHRIS [*struck. Deadly*]. But the others.

KELLER [*insistently*]. She's out of her mind. [*He takes a step toward* CHRIS, *pleadingly.*]

CHRIS [*unyielding*]. Dad . . . you did it?

KELLER. He never flew a P-40, what's the matter with you?

CHRIS [*still asking, and saying*]. Then you did it. To the others.

[*Both hold their voices down.*]

KELLER [*afraid of him, his deadly insistence*]. What's the matter with you? What the hell is the matter with you?

CHRIS [*quietly, incredibly*]. How could you do that? How?

KELLER. What's the matter with you?

CHRIS. Dad . . . Dad, you killed twenty-one men!

KELLER. What, killed?

CHRIS. You killed them, you murdered them.

KELLER [*as though throwing his whole nature open before* CHRIS]. How could I kill anybody?

CHRIS. Dad! Dad!

KELLER [*trying to hush him*]. I didn't kill anybody!

CHRIS. Then explain it to me. What did you do? Explain it to me or I'll tear you to pieces!

KELLER [*horrified at his overwhelming fury*]. Don't Chris, don't . . .

CHRIS. I want to know what you did, now what did you do? You had a hundred and twenty cracked engine-heads, now what did you do?

KELLER. If you're going to hang me then I . . .

CHRIS. I'm listening, God Almighty, I'm listening!

KELLER [*their movements now are those of subtle pursuit and escape.* KELLER *keeps a step out of* CHRIS' *range as he talks*]. You're a boy, what could I do! I'm in business, a man is in business; a hundred and twenty cracked, you're out of business; you got a process, the process don't work you're out of business; you don't know how to operate, your stuff is no good; they close you up, they tear up your contracts, what the hell's it to them? You lay forty years into a business and they knock you out in five minutes, what could I do, let them take forty years, let them take my life away? [*His voice cracking.*] I never thought they'd install them. I swear to

God. I thought they'd stop 'em before anybody took off.

CHRIS. Then why'd you ship them out?

KELLER. By the time they could spot them I thought I'd have the process going again, and I could show them they needed me and they'd let it go by. But weeks passed and I got no kick-back, so I was going to tell them.

CHRIS. They why didn't you tell them?

KELLER. It was too late. The paper, it was all over the front page, twenty-one went down, it was too late. They came with handcuffs into the shop, what could I do? [*He sits on bench at center.*] Chris . . . Chris, I did it for you, it was a chance and I took it for you. I'm sixty-one years old, when would I have another chance to make something for you? Sixty-one years old you don't get another chance, do ya?

CHRIS. You even knew they wouldn't hold up in the air.

KELLER. I didn't say that . . .

CHRIS. But you were going to warn them not to use them . . .

KELLER. But that don't mean . . .

CHRIS. It means you knew they'd crash.

KELLER. It don't mean that.

CHRIS. Then you *thought* they'd crash.

KELLER. I was afraid maybe . . .

CHRIS. You were afraid maybe! God in heaven, what kind of a man are you? Kids were hanging in the air by those heads. You knew that!

KELLER. For you, a business for you!

CHRIS [*with burning fury*]. For me! Where do you live, where have you come from? For me!—I was dying every day and you were killing my boys and you did it for me? What the hell do you think I was thinking of, the Goddam business? Is that as far as your mind can see, the business? What is that, the world—the business? What the hell do you mean, you did it for me? Don't you have a country? Don't you live in the world? What the hell are you? You're not even an animal, no animal kills his own, what are you? What must I do to you? I ought to tear the tongue out of your mouth, what must I do? [*With his fist he pounds down upon his father's shoulder. He stumbles away, covering his face as he weeps.*] What must I do, Jesus God, what must I do?

KELLER. Chris . . . My Chris . . .

ACT THREE

Two o'clock the following morning, MOTHER *is discovered on the rise, rocking ceaselessly in a chair, staring at her thoughts. It is an intense, slight, sort of rocking. A light shows from upstairs bedroom, lower floor windows being dark. The moon is strong and casts its bluish light.*
Presently JIM, *dressed in jacket and hat, appears from the left, and seeing her, goes up beside her.*

JIM. Any news?

MOTHER. No news.

JIM [*gently*]. You can't sit up all night, dear, why don't you go to bed?

MOTHER. I'm waiting for Chris. Don't worry about me, Jim, I'm perfectly all right.

JIM. But it's almost two o'clock.

MOTHER. I can't sleep. [*Slight pause.*] You had an emergency?

JIM [*tiredly*]. Somebody had a headache and thought he was dying. [*Slight pause.*] Half of my patients are quite mad. Nobody realizes how many people are walking around loose, and they're cracked as coconuts. Money. Money-money-money-money. You say it long enough it doesn't mean anything. [*She smiles, makes a silent laugh.*] Oh, how I'd love to be around when that happens!

MOTHER [*shakes her head*]. You're so childish, Jim! Sometimes you are.

JIM [*looks at her a moment*]. Kate. [*Pause.*] What happened?

KATE. I told you. He had an argument with Joe. Then he got in the car and drove away.

JIM. What kind of an argument?

MOTHER. An argument, Joe . . . he was crying like a child, before.

JIM. They argued about Ann?

MOTHER [*slight hesitation*]. No, not Ann. Imagine? [*Indicates lighted window above.*] She hasn't come out of that room since he left. All night in that room.

JIM [*looks at window, then at her*]. What'd Joe do, tell him?

MOTHER [*she stops rocking*]. Tell him what?

JIM. Don't be afraid, Kate, I know. I've always known.

MOTHER. How?

JIM. It occurred to me a long time ago.

MOTHER. I always had the feeling that in the back of his head, Chris . . . almost knew. I didn't think it would be such a shock.

JIM [*gets up*]. Chris would never know how to live with a thing like that. It takes a certain talent . . . for lying. You have it, and I do. But not him.

MOTHER. What do you mean . . . he's not coming back?

JIM. Oh, no, he'll come back. We all come back, Kate. These private little revolutions always die. The compromise is always made. In a peculiar way. Frank is right—every man does have a star. The star is one's honesty. And you spend your life groping for it, but once it's out it never lights again. I don't think he went very far. He probably just wanted to be alone to watch his star go out.

MOTHER. Just as long as he comes back.

JIM. I wish he wouldn't, Kate. One year I simply took off, went to New Orleans; for two months I lived on bananas and milk, and studied a certain disease. It was beautiful. And then she came, and she cried. And I went back home with her. And now I live in the usual darkness; I can't find myself; it's even hard sometimes to remember the kind of man I wanted to be. I'm a good husband; Chris is a good son— he'll come back. [KELLER *comes out on porch in dressing-gown and slippers. He goes upstage—to alley.* JIM *goes to him.*]

JIM. I have a feeling he's in the park. I'll look around for him. Put her to bed, Joe; this is no good for what she's got. [JIM *exits up driveway.*]

KELLER [*coming down*]. What does he want here?

MOTHER. His friend is not home.

KELLER [*his voice is husky. Comes down to her*]. I don't like him mixing in so much.

MOTHER. It's too late, Joe. He knows.

KELLER [*apprehensively*]. How does he know?

MOTHER. He guessed a long time ago.

KELLER. I don't like that.

MOTHER [*laughs dangerously, quietly into the line*]. What you don't like . . .

KELLER. Yeah, what I don't like.

MOTHER. You can't bull yourself through this one, Joe, you better be smart now. This thing—this thing is not over yet.

KELLER [*indicating lighted window above*]. And what is she doing up there? She don't come out of the room.

MOTHER. I don't know, what is she doing? Sit down, stop being mad. You want to live? You better figure out your life.

KELLER. She don't know, does she?

MOTHER. She saw Chris storming out of here. It's one and one—she knows how to add.

KELLER. Maybe I ought to talk to her?

MOTHER. Don't ask me, Joe.

KELLER [*almost an outburst*]. Then who do I ask? But I don't think she'll do anything about it.

MOTHER. You're asking me again.

KELLER. I'm askin' you. What am I, a stranger? I thought I had a family here. What happened to my family?

MOTHER. You've got a family. I'm simply telling you that I have no strength to think anymore.

KELLER. You have no strength. The minute there's trouble you have no strength.

MOTHER. Joe, you're doing the same thing again; all your life whenever there's trouble you yell at me and you think that settles it.

KELLER. Then what do I do? Tell me, talk to me, what do I do?

MOTHER. Joe . . . I've been thinking this way. If he comes back . . .

KELLER. What do you mean "if"? . . . he's comin' back!

MOTHER. I think if you sit him down and you . . . explain your-self. I mean you ought to make it clear to him that you know you did a terrible thing. [*Not looking into his eyes.*] I mean if he saw that you realize what you did. You see?

KELLER. What ice does that cut?

MOTHER [*a little fearfully*]. I mean if you told him that you want to pay for what you did.

KELLER [*sensing . . . quietly*]. How can I pay?

MOTHER. Tell him . . . you're willing to go to prison. [*Pause.*]

KELLER [*struck, amazed*]. I'm willing to . . . ?

MOTHER [*quickly*]. You wouldn't go, he wouldn't ask you to go. But if you told him you wanted to, if he could feel that you wanted to pay, maybe he would forgive you.

KELLER. He would forgive me! For what?

MOTHER. Joe, you know what I mean.

KELLER. I don't know what you mean! You wanted money, so I made money. What must I be forgiven? You wanted money, didn't you?

MOTHER. I didn't want it that way.

KELLER. I didn't want it that way, either! What difference is it what you want? I spoiled the both of you. I should've put him out when he was ten like I was put out, and made him earn his keep. Then he'd know how a buck is made in this world. Forgiven! I could live on a quarter a day myself, but I got a family so I . . .

MOTHER. Joe, Joe . . . it don't excuse it that you did it for the family.

KELLER. It's got to excuse it!

MOTHER. There's something bigger than the family to him.

KELLER. Nothin' is bigger!

MOTHER. There is to him.

KELLER. There's nothin' he could do that I wouldn't forgive. Because he's my son. Because I'm his father and he's my son.

MOTHER. Joe, I tell you . . .

KELLER. Nothin's bigger than that. And you're goin' to tell him, you understand? I'm his father and he's my son, and if there's something bigger than that I'll put a bullet in my head!

MOTHER. You stop that!

KELLER. You heard me. Now you know what to tell him. [*Pause. He moves from her—halts.*] But he wouldn't put me away though . . . He wouldn't do that . . . Would he?

MOTHER. He loved you, Joe, you broke his heart.

KELLER. But to put me away . . .

MOTHER. I don't know. I'm beginning to think we don't really know him. They say in the war he was such a killer. Here he was always afraid of mice. I don't know him. I don't know what he'll do.

KELLER. Goddamn, if Larry was alive he wouldn't act like this. He understood the way the world is made. He listened to me. To him the world had a forty-foot front, it ended at the building line. This one, everything bothers him. You make a deal, overcharge two cents, and his hair falls out. He don't understand money. Too easy, it came too easy. Yes sir. Larry. That was a boy we lost. Larry. Larry. [*He slumps on chair in front of her.*] What am I gonna do, Kate . . .

MOTHER. Joe, Joe please . . . you'll be all right, nothing is going to happen . . .

KELLER [*desperately, lost*]. For you, Kate, for both of you, that's all I ever lived for . . .

MOTHER. I know, darling, I know . . . [ANN *enters from house. They say nothing, waiting for her to speak.*]

ANN. Why do you stay up? I'll tell you when he comes.

KELLER [*rises, goes to her*]. You didn't eat supper, did you? [*To* MOTHER.] Why didn't you make her eat something?

MOTHER. Sure, I'll . . .

ANN. Never mind, Kate, I'm all right. [*They are unable to speak to each other.*] There's something I want to tell you. [*She starts, then halts.*] I'm not going to do anything about it. . . .

MOTHER. She's a good girl! [*To* KELLER.] You see? She's a . . .

ANN. I'll do nothing about Joe, but you're going to do something for me. [*Directly to* MOTHER.] You made Chris feel guilty with me. Whether you wanted to or not, you've crip-

pled him in front of me. I'd like you to tell him that Larry
is dead and that you know it. You understand me? I'm not
going out of here alone. There's no life for me that way. I
want you to set him free. And then I promise you, everything
will end, and we'll go away, and that's all.

KELLER. You'll do that. You'll tell him.

ANN. I know what I'm asking, Kate. You had two sons. But
you've only got one now.

KELLER. You'll tell him . . .

ANN. And you've got to say it to him so he knows you mean it.

MOTHER. My dear, if the boy was dead, it wouldn't depend on
my words to make Chris know it. . . . The night he gets
into your bed, his heart will dry up. Because he knows and
you know. To his dying day he'll wait for his brother! No,
my dear, no such thing. You're going in the morning, and
you're going alone. That's your life, that's your lonely life.

[*She goes to porch, and starts in.*]

ANN. Larry is dead, Kate.

MOTHER [*she stops*]. Don't speak to me.

ANN. I said he's dead. I know! He crashed off the coast of
China November twenty-fifth! His engine didn't fail him.
But he died. I know . . .

MOTHER. How did he die? You're lying to me. If you know,
how did he die?

ANN. I loved him. You know I loved him. Would I have looked
at anyone else if I wasn't sure? That's enough for you.

MOTHER [*moving on her*]. What's enough for me? What're you
talking about? [*She grasps* ANN'S *wrists.*]

ANN. You're hurting my wrists.

MOTHER. What are you talking about! [*Pause. She stares at* ANN
a moment, then turns and goes to KELLER.]

ANN. Joe, go in the house . . .

KELLER. Why should I . . .

ANN. Please go.

KELLER. Lemme know when he comes. [KELLER *goes into
house.*]

MOTHER [*she sees* ANN *take a letter from her pocket*]. What's that?

ANN. Sit down . . . [MOTHER *moves left to chair, but does not sit.*] First you've got to understand. When I came, I didn't have any idea that Joe . . . I had nothing against him or you. I came to get married. I hoped . . . So I didn't bring this to hurt you. I thought I'd show it to you only if there was no other way to settle Larry in your mind.

MOTHER. Larry? [*Snatches letter from* ANN's *hand.*]

ANN. He wrote it to me just before he—[MOTHER *opens and begins to read letter.*] I'm not trying to hurt you, Kate. You're making me do this, now remember you're—— Remember. I've been so lonely, Kate . . . I can't leave here alone again. [*A long, low moan comes from* MOTHER's *throat as she reads.*] You made me show it to you. You wouldn't believe me. I told you a hundred times, why wouldn't you believe me!

MOTHER. Oh, my God . . .

ANN [*with pity and fear*]. Kate, please, please . . .

MOTHER. My God, my God . . .

ANN. Kate, dear, I'm so sorry . . . I'm so sorry. [CHRIS *enters from driveway. He seems exhausted.*]

CHRIS. What's the matter . . . ?

ANN. Where were you? . . . you're all perspired. [MOTHER *doesn't move.*] Where were you?

CHRIS. Just drove around a little. I thought you'd be gone.

ANN. Where do I go? I have nowhere to go.

CHRIS [*to* MOTHER]. Where's Dad?

ANN. Inside lying down.

CHRIS. Sit down, both of you. I'll say what there is to say.

MOTHER. I didn't hear the car . . .

CHRIS. I left it in the garage.

MOTHER. Jim is out looking for you.

CHRIS. Mother . . . I'm going away. There are a couple of firms in Cleveland, I think I can get a place. I mean, I'm going away for good. [*To* ANN *alone.*] I know what you're thinking Annie. It's true. I'm yellow. I was made yellow in this house because I suspected my father and I did nothing about it, but if I knew that night when I came home what I know now, he'd be in the district attorney's office by this time, and I'd have brought him there. Now if I look at him, all I'm able to do is cry.

MOTHER. What are you talking about? What else can you do?

CHRIS. I could jail him! I could jail him, if I were human any more. But I'm like everybody else now. I'm practical now. You made me practical.

MOTHER. But you have to be.

CHRIS. The cats in that alley are practical, the bums who ran away when we were fighting were practical. Only the dead ones weren't practical. But now I'm practical, and I spit on myself. I'm going away. I'm going now.

ANN [goes up to stop him]. I'm coming with you. . . .

CHRIS. No, Ann.

ANN. Chris, I don't ask you to do anything about Joe.

CHRIS. You do, you do . . .

ANN. I swear I never will.

CHRIS. In your heart you always will.

ANN. Then do what you have to do!

CHRIS. Do what? What is there to do? I've looked all night for a reason to make him suffer.

ANN. There's reason, there's reason!

CHRIS. What? Do I raise the dead when I put him behind bars? Then what'll I do it for? We used to shoot a man who acted like a dog, but honor was real there, you were protecting something. But here? This is the land of the great big dogs, you don't love a man here, you eat him! That's the principle; the only one we live by—it just happened to kill a few people this time, that's all. The world's that way, how can I take it out on him? What sense does that make? This is a zoo, a zoo!

ANN [to MOTHER]. You know what he's got to do! Tell him!

MOTHER. Let him go.

ANN. I won't let him go. You'll tell him what he's got to do . . .

MOTHER. Annie!

ANN. Then I will! [KELLER *enters from house.* CHRIS *sees him, goes down right near arbor.*]

KELLER. What's the matter with you? I want to talk to you.

CHRIS. I've got nothing to say to you.

KELLER [*taking his arm*]. I want to talk to you!

CHRIS [*pulling violently away from him*]. Don't do that, Dad. I'm going to hurt you if you do that. There's nothing to say, so say it quick.

KELLER. Exactly what's the matter? What's the matter? You got too much money? Is that what bothers you?

CHRIS [*with an edge of sarcasm*]. It bothers me.

KELLER. If you can't get used to it, then throw it away. You hear me? Take every cent and give it to charity, throw it in the sewer. Does that settle it? In the sewer, that's all. You think I'm kidding? I'm tellin' you what to do, if it's dirty then burn it. It's your money, that's not my money. I'm a dead man, I'm an old dead man, nothing's mine. Well, talk to me!—what do you want to do!

CHRIS. It's not what I want to do. It's what you want to do.

KELLER. What should I want to do? [CHRIS *is silent.*] Jail? You want me to go to jail? If you want me to go, say so! Is that where I belong?—then tell me so! [*Slight pause.*] What's the matter, why can't you tell me? [*Furiously.*] You say everything else to me, say that! [*Slight pause.*] I'll tell you why you can't say it. Because you know I don't belong there. Because you know! [*With growing emphasis and passion, and a persistent tone of desperation.*] Who worked for nothin' in that war? When they work for nothin', I'll work for nothin'. Did they ship a gun or a truck outa Detroit before they got their price? Is that clean? It's dollars and cents, nickels and dimes; war and peace, it's nickels and dimes, what's clean? Half the Goddamn country is gotta go if I go! That's why you can't tell me.

CHRIS. That's exactly why.

KELLER. Then . . . why am *I* bad?

CHRIS. *I* know you're no worse than most men but I thought you were better. I never saw you as a man. I saw you as my father. [*Almost breaking.*] I can't look at you this way, I can't look at myself! [*He turns away unable to face* KELLER. ANN *goes quickly to* MOTHER, *takes letter from her and starts for* CHRIS. MOTHER *instantly rushes to intercept her.*]

MOTHER. Give me that!

ANN. He's going to read it! [*She thrusts letter into* CHRIS' *hand.*] Larry. He wrote it to me the day he died. . . .

KELLER. Larry!?

MOTHER. Chris, it's not for you. [*He starts to read.*] Joe . . . go away . . .

KELLER [*mystified, frightened*]. Why'd she say, Larry, what . . . ?

MOTHER. [*She desperately pushes him toward alley, glancing at* CHRIS.] Go to the street Joe, go to the street! [*She comes down beside* KELLER.] Don't, Chris . . . [*Pleading from her whole soul.*] Don't tell him . . .

CHRIS [*quietly*]. Three and one half years . . . talking, talking. Now you tell me what you must do. . . . This is how he died, now tell me where you belong.

KELLER [*pleading*]. Chris, a man can't be a Jesus in this world!

CHRIS. I know all about the world. I know the whole crap story. Now listen to this, and tell me what a man's got to be! [*Reads.* "My dear Ann: . . ." You listening? He wrote this the day he died. Listen, don't cry . . . listen! "My dear Ann: It is impossible to put down the things I feel. But I've got to tell you something. Yesterday they flew in a load of papers from the States and I read about Dad and your father being convicted. I can't express myself. I can't tell you how I feel—I can't bear to live any more. Last night I circled the base for twenty minutes before I could bring myself in. How could he have done that? Every day three or four men never come back and he sits back there doing business. . . . I don't know how to tell you what I feel . . . I can't face anybody . . . I'm going out on a mission in a few minutes. They'll probably report me missing. If they do, I want you to know that you mustn't wait for me. I tell you, Ann, if I had him here now I could kill him—" [KELLER *grabs letter from* CHRIS' *hand and reads it.*] [*After a long pause.*] Now blame the world. Do you understand that letter?

KELLER [*he speaks almost inaudibly*]. I think I do. Get the car, I'll put on my jacket. [*He turns and starts slowly for the house.* MOTHER *rushes to intercept him.*]

MOTHER. Why are you going? You'll sleep, why are you going?

KELLER. I can't sleep here. I'll feel better if I go.

MOTHER. You're so foolish. Larry was your son too, wasn't he? You know he'd never tell you to do this.

KELLER [*looking at letter in his hand*]. Then what is this if it isn't telling me? Sure, he was my son. But I think to him they were all my sons. And I guess they were, I guess they were. I'll be right down. [*Exits into house.*]

MOTHER [*to* CHRIS, *with determination*]. You're not going to take him!

CHRIS. I'm taking him.

MOTHER. It's up to you, if you tell him to stay he'll stay. Go and tell him!

CHRIS. Nobody could stop him now.

MOTHER. You'll stop him! How long will he live in prison?— are you trying to kill him?

CHRIS [*holding out letter*]. I thought you read this!

MOTHER [*of Larry, the letter*]. The war is over! Didn't you hear? ——it's over!

CHRIS. Then what was Larry to you? A stone that fell into the water? It's not enough for him to be sorry. Larry didn't kill himself to make you and Dad sorry.

MOTHER. What more can we be!

CHRIS. You can be better! Once and for all you can know there's a universe of people outside and you're responsible to it, and unless you know that you threw away your son because that's why he died.

[*A shot is heard in the house. They stand frozen for a brief second.* CHRIS *starts for porch, pauses at step, turns to* ANN.]

CHRIS. Find Jim! [*He goes on into the house and* ANN *runs up* driveway. MOTHER *stands alone, transfixed.*]

MOTHER [*softly, almost moaning*]. Joe . . . Joe . . . Joe . . .
Joe . . . [CHRIS *comes out of house, down to* MOTHER'S *arms.*]

CHRIS [*almost crying*]. Mother, I didn't mean to . . .

MOTHER. Don't dear. Don't take it on yourself. Forget now.
Live. [CHRIS *stirs as if to answer.*] Shhh . . . [*She puts his
arms down gently and moves towards porch.*] Shhh . . . [*As
she reaches porch steps she begins sobbing, as the curtain
falls.*]

THE GLASS MENAGERIE   [*1945*]

---

by Tennessee Williams
[1914-   ]

Nobody, not even the rain, has such small hands.
E. E. CUMMINGS

CHARACTERS

AMANDA WINGFIELD, *the mother*

LAURA WINGFIELD, *her daughter*

TOM WINGFIELD, *her son*

JIM O'CONNOR, *the gentleman caller*

SCENE: AN ALLEY IN ST. LOUIS

PART I. Preparation for a Gentleman Caller.
PART II. The Gentleman calls.

TIME: Now and the Past.

SCENE ONE

[*The Wingfield apartment is in the rear of the building, one of those vast hive-like conglomerations of cellular living-units that flower as warty growths in overcrowded urban centers of lower middle-class population and are symptomatic of the impulse of this largest and fundamentally enslaved section of American society to avoid fluidity and differentiation and to exist and function as one interfused mass of automatism.*

The apartment faces an alley and is entered by a fire-escape, a structure whose name is a touch of accidental poetic truth, for all of these huge buildings are always burning with the slow and implacable fires of human desperation. The fire-escape is included in the set—that is, the landing of it and steps descending from it.

The scene is memory and is therefore nonrealistic. Memory takes a lot of poetic license. It omits some details; others are exaggerated, according to the emotional value of the articles it touches, for memory is seated predominantly in the heart. The interior is therefore rather dim and poetic.

At the rise of the curtain, the audience is faced with the dark, grim rear wall of the Wingfield tenement. This building, which runs parallel to the footlights, is flanked on both sides by dark, narrow alleys which run into murky canyons of tangled clotheslines, garbage cans and the sinister lattice-

*work of neighboring fire-escapes. It is up and down these
side alleys that exterior entrances and exits are made, during
the play. At the end of* TOM'S *opening commentary, the
dark tenement wall slowly reveals (by means of a transparency)
the interior of the ground floor Wingfield apartment.*

*Downstage is the living room, which also serves as a
sleeping room for* LAURA, *the sofa unfolding to make her
bed. Upstage, center, and divided by a wide arch or second
proscenium with transparent faded portieres (or second
curtain), is the dining room. In an old-fashioned what-not in
the living room are seen scores of transparent glass animals.
A blown-up photograph of the father hangs on the wall of
the living room, facing the audience, to the left of the archway.
It is the face of a very handsome young man in a
doughboy's First World War cap. He is gallantly smiling,
ineluctably smiling, as if to say, "I will be smiling forever."*

*The audience hears and sees the opening scene in the dining
room through both the transparent fourth wall of the
building and the transparent gauze portieres of the dining-
room arch. It is during this revealing scene that the fourth
wall slowly ascends, out of sight. This transparent exterior
wall is not brought down again until the very end of the
play, during* TOM'S *final speech.*

*The narrator is an undisguised convention of the play. He
takes whatever license with dramatic convention as is convenient
to his purposes.*

TOM *enters dressed as a merchant sailor from alley, stage
left, and strolls across the front of the stage to the fire-
escape. There he stops and lights a cigarette. He addresses
the audience.*]

TOM. Yes, I have tricks in my pocket, I have things up my
sleeve. But I am the opposite of a stage magician. He gives
you illusion that has the appearance of truth. I give you
truth in the pleasant disguise of illusion. To begin with, I
turn back time. I reverse it to that quaint period, the thirties,

when the huge middle class of America was matriculating in a school for the blind. Their eyes had failed them, or they had failed their eyes, and so they were having their fingers pressed forcibly down on the fiery Braille alphabet of a dissolving economy. In Spain there was revolution. Here there was only shouting and confusion. In Spain there was Guernica. Here there were disturbances of labor, sometimes pretty violent, in otherwise peaceful cities such as Chicago, Cleveland, Saint Louis . . . This is the social background of the play.

[MUSIC.]

The play is memory. Being a memory play, it is dimly lighted, it is sentimental, it is not realistic. In memory everything seems to happen to music. That explains the fiddle in the wings. I am the narrator of the play, and also a character in it. The other characters are my mother, Amanda, my sister, Laura, and a gentleman caller who appears in the final scenes. He is the most realistic character in the play, being an emissary from a world of reality that we were somehow set apart from. But since I have a poet's weakness for symbols, I am using this character also as a symbol; he is the long delayed but always expected something that we live for. There is a fifth character in the play who doesn't appear except in this larger-than-life photograph over the mantel. This is our father who left us a long time ago. He was a telephone man who fell in love with long distances; he gave up his job with the telephone company and skipped the light fantastic out of town . . . The last we heard of him was a picture post-card from Mazatlan, on the Pacific coast of Mexico, containing a message of two words— "Hello— Good-bye!" and no address. I think the rest of the play will explain itself. . . .

[AMANDA'S *voice becomes audible through the portieres.*]

[LEGEND ON SCREEN: "OU SONT LES NEIGES."]

[*He divides the portieres and enters the upstage area.*]

[AMANDA *and* LAURA *are seated at a drop-leaf table. Eating is indicated by gestures without food or utensils.* AMANDA *faces the audience.* TOM *and* LAURA *are seated in profile.*]

[*The interior has lit up softly and through the scrim we see* AMANDA *and* LAURA *seated at the table in the upstage area.*]

AMANDA [*calling*]. Tom?

TOM. Yes, Mother.

AMANDA. We can't say grace until you come to the table!

TOM. Coming, Mother. [*He bows slightly and withdraws, reappearing a few moments later in his place at the table.*]

AMANDA [*to her son*]. Honey, don't *push* with your *fingers*. If you have to push with something, the thing to push with is a crust of bread. And chew——chew! Animals have sections in their stomachs which enable them to digest food without mastication, but human beings are supposed to chew their food before they swallow it down. Eat food leisurely, son, and really enjoy it. A well-cooked meal has lots of delicate flavors that have to be held in the mouth for appreciation. So chew your food and give your salivary glands a chance to function!

[TOM *deliberately lays his imaginary fork down and pushes his chair back from the table.*]

TOM. I haven't enjoyed one bite of this dinner because of your constant directions on how to eat it. It's you that make me rush through meals with your hawk-like attention to every bite I take. Sickening——spoils my appetite——all this discussion of animals' secretion——salivary glands——mastication!

AMANDA [*lightly*]. Temperament like a Metropolitan star! [*He rises and crosses downstage.*] You're not excused from the table.

TOM. I'm getting a cigarette.

AMANDA. You smoke too much.

[LAURA *rises.*]

LAURA. I'll bring in the blanc mange.

[*He remains standing with his cigarette by the portieres during the following.*]

AMANDA [*rising*]. No, sister, no, sister—you be the lady this time and I'll be the darky.

LAURA. I'm already up.

AMANDA. Resume your seat, little sister—I want you to stay fresh and pretty—for gentlemen callers!

LAURA. I'm not expecting any gentlemen callers.

AMANDA [*crossing out to kitchenette. Airily*]. Sometimes they come when they are least expected! Why, I remember one Sunday afternoon in Blue Mountain— [*Enters kitchenette.*]

TOM. I know what's coming!

LAURA. Yes. But let her tell it.

TOM. Again?

LAURA. She loves to tell it.

[AMANDA *returns with bowl of dessert.*]

AMANDA. One Sunday afternoon in Blue Mountain—your mother received—*seventeen!*—gentlemen callers! Why, sometimes there weren't chairs enough to accommodate them all. We had to send the nigger over to bring in folding chairs from the parish house.

TOM [*remaining at portieres*]. How did you entertain those gentlemen callers?

AMANDA. I understood the art of conversation!

TOM. I bet you could talk.

AMANDA. Girls in those days *knew* how to talk, I can tell you.

TOM. Yes?

[IMAGE: AMANDA AS A GIRL ON A PORCH, GREETING CALLERS.]

AMANDA. They knew how to entertain their gentlemen callers. It wasn't enough for a girl to be possessed of a pretty face and a graceful figure—although I wasn't slighted in either respect. She also needed to have a nimble wit and a tongue to meet all occasions.

TOM. What did you talk about?

AMANDA. Things of importance going on in the world! Never
anything coarse or common or vulgar. [*She addresses* TOM
*as though he were seated in the vacant chair at the table
though he remains by portieres. He plays this scene as though
he held the book.*] My callers were gentlemen—all! Among
my callers were some of the most prominent young planters
of the Mississippi Delta—planters and sons of planters!

[TOM *motions for music and a spot of light on* AMANDA.]

[*Her eyes lift, her face glows, her voice becomes rich and
elegiac.*]

[SCREEN LEGEND: "OÙ SONT LES NEIGES."]

There was young Champ Laughlin who later became vice
president of the Delta Planters Bank. Hadley Stevenson who
was drowned in Moon Lake and left his widow one hundred and fifty thousand in Government bonds. There were
the Cutrere brothers, Wesley and Bates. Bates was one of
my bright particular beaux! He got in a quarrel with that wild
Wainwright boy. They shot it out on the floor of Moon
Lake Casino. Bates was shot through the stomach. Died in
the ambulance on his way to Memphis. His widow was also
well-provided for, came into eight or ten thousand acres—
that's all. She married him on the rebound—never loved
her—carried my picture on him the night he died! And
there was that boy that every girl in the Delta had set her
cap for! That beautiful, brilliant young Fitzhugh boy from
Greene County!

TOM. What did he leave his widow?

AMANDA. He never married! Gracious, you talk as though all
of my old admirers had turned up their toes to the daisies!

TOM. Isn't this the first you've mentioned that still survives?

AMANDA. That Fitzhugh boy went North and made a fortune—
came to be known as the Wolf of Wall Street! He had the
Midas touch, whatever he touched turned to gold! And I
could have been Mrs. Duncan J. Fitzhugh, mind you! But—

I picked your *father!*

LAURA [*rising*]. Mother, let me clear the table.

AMANDA. No, dear, you go in front and study your typewriter chart. Or practice your shorthand a little. Stay fresh and pretty!— It's almost time for our gentlemen callers to start arriving. [*She flounces girlishly toward the kitchenette.*] How many do you suppose we're going to entertain this afternoon?

[TOM *throws down the paper and jumps up with a groan.*]

LAURA [*alone in the dining room*]. I don't believe we're going to receive any, Mother.

AMANDA [*reappearing, airily*]. What? No one—not one? You must be joking! [LAURA *nervously echoes her laugh. She slips in a fugitive manner through the half-open portieres and draws them gently behind her. A shaft of very clear light is thrown on her face against the faded tapestry of the curtains.* MUSIC: "THE GLASS MENAGERIE" UNDER FAINTLY. *Lightly:*] Not one gentleman caller? It can't be true! There must be a flood, there must have been a tornado!

LAURA. It isn't a flood, it's not a tornado, Mother. I'm just not popular like you were in Blue Mountain. . . . [TOM *utters another groan.* LAURA *glances at him with a faint, apologetic smile. Her voice catching a little.*] Mother's afraid I'm going to be an old maid.

THE SCENE DIMS OUT WITH "GLASS MENAGERIE" MUSIC.

SCENE TWO

["*Laura, Haven't You Ever Liked Some Boy?*"]

On the dark stage the screen is lighted with the image of blue roses.

Gradually LAURA'S *figure becomes apparent and the screen goes out.*

The music subsides.

LAURA *is seated in the delicate ivory chair at the small claw-foot table.*

She wears a dress of soft violet material for a kimono— her hair tied back from her forehead with a ribbon.

She is washing and polishing her collection of glass.

AMANDA *appears on the fire-escape steps. At the sound of her ascent,* LAURA *catches her breath, thrusts the bowl of ornaments away and seats herself stiffly before the diagram of the typewriter keyboard as though it held her spellbound. Something has happened to* AMANDA. *It is written in her face as she climbs to the landing: a look that is grim and hopeless and a little absurd.*

She has on one of those cheap or imitation velvety-looking cloth coats with imitation fur collar. Her hat is five or six years old, one of those dreadful cloche hats that were worn in the late twenties and she is clasping an enormous black patent-leather pocketbook with nickel clasps and initials. This is her full-dress outfit, the one she usually wears to the D.A.R.

Before entering she looks through the door.

She purses her lips, opens her eyes wide, rolls them upward and shakes her head.

Then she slowly lets herself in the door. Seeing her mother's expression LAURA *touches her lips with a nervous gesture.*]

LAURA. Hello, Mother, I was— [*She makes a nervous gesture toward the chart on the wall.* AMANDA *leans against the shut door and stares at* LAURA *with a martyred look.*]

AMANDA. Deception? Deception? [*She slowly removes her hat and gloves, continuing the sweet suffering stare. She lets the hat and gloves fall on the floor—a bit of acting.*]

LAURA [*shakily*]. How was the D.A.R. meeting? [AMANDA *slowly opens her purse and removes a dainty white handkerchief which she shakes out delicately and delicately touches to her lips and nostrils.*] Didn't you go to the D.A.R. meeting, Mother?

AMANDA [*faintly, almost inaudibly*]. —No.—No. [*Then more forcibly:*] I did not have the strength—to go to the D.A.R. In fact, I did not have the courage! I wanted to find a hole in the ground and hide myself in it forever! [*She crosses slowly to the wall and removes the diagram of the typewriter keyboard. She holds it in front of her for a second, staring at it sweetly and sorrowfully—then bites her lips and tears it in two pieces.*]

LAURA [*faintly*]. Why did you do that, Mother? [AMANDA *repeats the same procedure with the chart of the Gregg Alphabet.*] Why are you—

AMANDA. Why? Why? How old are you, Laura?

LAURA. Mother, you know my age.

AMANDA. I thought that you were an adult; it seems that I was mistaken. [*She crosses slowly to the sofa and sinks down and stares at* LAURA.]

LAURA. Please don't stare at me, Mother.

[AMANDA *closes her eyes and lowers her head. Count ten.*]

AMANDA. What are we going to do, what is going to become of us, what is the future?

[*Count ten.*]

LAURA. Has something happened, Mother? [AMANDA *draws a long breath and takes out the handkerchief again. Dabbing process.*] Mother, has—something happened?

AMANDA. I'll be all right in a minute. I'm just bewildered—
[*Count five*]—by life. . . .

LAURA. Mother, I wish that you would tell me what's happened!

AMANDA. As you know, I was supposed to be inducted into
my office at the D.A.R. this afternoon. [IMAGE: A SWARM
OF TYPEWRITERS.] But I stopped off at Rubicam's business
college to speak to your teachers about your having a cold
and ask them what progress they thought you were making
down there.

LAURA. Oh. . . .

AMANDA. I went to the typing instructor and introduced myself as your mother. She didn't know who you were. Wingfield, she said. We don't have any such student enrolled at
the school! I assured her she did, that you had been going to
classes since early in January. "I wonder," she said, "if you
could be talking about that terribly shy little girl who dropped
out of school after only a few days' attendance?" "No," I
said, "Laura, my daughter has been going to school every
day for the past six weeks!" "Excuse me," she said.
She took the attendance book out and there was your
name, unmistakably printed, and all the dates you were
absent until they decided that you had dropped out of
school. I still said, "No, there must have been some mistake! There must have been some mix-up in the records!"
And she said, "No—I remember her perfectly now. Her
hands shook so that she couldn't hit the right keys! The
first time we gave a speed-test, she broke down completely
—was sick at the stomach and almost had to be carried
into the wash-room! After that morning she never showed
up any more. We phoned the house but never got any
answer—while I was working at Famous and Barr, I suppose, demonstrating those— Oh!" I felt so weak I could
barely keep on my feet! I had to sit down while they got me
a glass of water! Fifty dollars' tuition, all of our plans—
my hopes and ambitions for you—just gone up the spout,

just gone up the spout like that. [LAURA *draws a long breath and gets awkwardly to her feet. She crosses to the victrola and winds it up.*] What are you doing?

LAURA. Oh! [*She releases the handle and returns to her seat.*]

AMANDA. Laura, where have you been going when you've gone out pretending that you were going to business college?

LAURA. I've just been going out walking.

AMANDA. That's not true.

LAURA. It is. I just went walking.

AMANDA. Walking? Walking? In winter? Deliberately courting pneumonia in that light coat? Where did you walk to, Laura?

LAURA. All sorts of places—mostly in the park.

AMANDA. Even after you'd started catching that cold?

LAURA. It was the lesser of two evils, Mother. [IMAGE: WINTER SCENE IN PARK.] I couldn't go back up. I—threw up—on the floor!

AMANDA. From half past seven till after five every day you mean to tell me you walked around in the park, because you wanted to make me think that you were still going to Rubicam's Business College?

LAURA. It wasn't as bad as it sounds. I went inside places to get warmed up.

AMANDA. Inside where?

LAURA. I went in the art museum and the bird-houses at the Zoo. I visited the penguins every day! Sometimes I did without lunch and went to the movies. Lately I've been spending most of my afternoons in the Jewel-box, that big glass house where they raise the tropical flowers.

AMANDA. You did all this to deceive me, just for deception? [LAURA *looks down.*] Why?

LAURA. Mother, when you're disappointed, you get that awful suffering look on your face, like the picture of Jesus' mother in the museum!

AMANDA. Hush!

LAURA. I couldn't face it.

[*Pause. A whisper of strings.*]

[LEGEND: "THE CRUST OF HUMILITY."]

AMANDA [*hopelessly fingering the huge pocketbook*]. So what are we going to do the rest of our lives? Stay home and watch the parades go by? Amuse ourselves with the glass menagerie, darling? Eternally play those worn-out phonograph records your father left as a painful reminder of him? We won't have a business career—we've given that up because it gave us nervous indigestion! [*Laughs wearily.*] What is there left but dependency all our lives? I know so well what becomes of unmarried women who aren't prepared to occupy a position. I've seen such pitiful cases in the South—barely tolerated spinsters living upon the grudging patronage of sister's husband or brother's wife!—stuck away in some little mouse-trap of a room—encouraged by one in-law to visit another—little birdlike women without any nest—eating the crust of humility all their life! Is that the future that we've mapped out for ourselves? I swear it's the only alternative I can think of! It isn't a very pleasant alternative, is it? Of course—some girls *do marry*. [*LAURA twists her hands nervously.*] Haven't you ever liked some boy?

LAURA. Yes. I liked one once. [*Rises.*] I came across his picture a while ago.

AMANDA [*with some interest*]. He gave you his picture?

LAURA. No, it's in the year-book.

AMANDA [*disappointed*]. Oh—a high-school boy.

[SCREEN IMAGE: JIM AS HIGH-SCHOOL HERO BEARING A SILVER CUP.]

LAURA. Yes. His name was Jim. [LAURA *lifts the heavy annual from the claw-foot table.*] Here he is in *The Pirates of Penzance.*

LAURA. The operetta the senior class put on. He had a wonderful voice and we sat across the aisle from each other Mondays, Wednesdays and Fridays in the Aud. Here he is with the silver cup for debating! See his grin?

AMANDA [*absently*]. He must have had a jolly disposition.

LAURA. He used to call me— Blue Roses.

[IMAGE: BLUE ROSES.]

AMANDA. Why did he call you such a name as that?

LAURA. When I had that attack of pleurosis—he asked me what was the matter when I came back. I said pleurosis— he thought that I said Blue Roses! So that's what he always called me after that. Whenever he saw me, he'd holler, "Hello, Blue Roses!" I didn't care for the girl that he went out with. Emily Meisenbach. Emily was the best-dressed girl at Soldan. She never struck me, though, as being sincere . . . It says in the Personal Section—they're engaged. That's—six years ago! They must be married by now.

AMANDA. Girls that aren't cut out for business careers usually wind up married to some nice man. [*Gets up with a spark of revival.*] Sister, that's what you'll do!

[LAURA *utters a startled, doubtful laugh. She reaches quickly for a piece of glass.*]

LAURA. But, Mother—

AMANDA. Yes? [*Crossing to photograph.*]

LAURA [*in a tone of frightened apology*]. I'm—crippled!

[IMAGE: SCREEN.]

AMANDA. Nonsense! Laura, I've told you never, never to use that word. Why, you're not crippled, you just have a little defect—hardly noticeable, even! When people have some slight disadvantage like that, they cultivate other things to make up for it—develop charm—and vivacity—and— *charm!* That's all you have to do! [*She turns again to the photograph.*] One thing your father had *plenty of*—was *charm!*

[TOM *motions to the fiddle in the wings.*]

THE SCENE FADES OUT WITH MUSIC

SCENE THREE

[TOM *speaks from the fire-escape landing.*]

TOM. After the fiasco at Rubicam's Business College, the idea of getting a gentleman caller for Laura began to play a more important part in Mother's calculations. It became an obsession. Like some archetype of the universal unconscious, the image of the gentleman caller haunted our small apartment. . . . [IMAGE: YOUNG MAN AT DOOR WITH FLOWERS.] An evening at home rarely passed without some allusion to this image, this spectre, this hope. . . . Even when he wasn't mentioned, his presence hung in Mother's preoccupied look and in my sister's frightened, apologetic manner—hung like a sentence passed upon the Wingfields! Mother was a woman of action as well as words. She began to take logical steps in the planned direction. Late that winter and in the early spring—realizing that extra money would be needed to properly feather the nest and plume the bird—she conducted a vigorous campaign on the telephone, roping in subscribers to one of those magazines for matrons called *The Home-maker's Companion,* the type of journal that features the serialized sublimations of ladies of letters who think in terms of delicate cup-like breasts, slim, tapering waists, rich, creamy thighs, eyes like wood-smoke in autumn, fingers that soothe and caress like strains of music, bodies as powerful as Etruscan sculpture.

[SCREEN IMAGES: GLAMOR MAGAZINE COVER.]

[AMANDA *enters with phone on long extension cord. She is spotted in the dim stage.*]

AMANDA. Ida Scott? This is Amanda Wingfield! We *missed* you at the D.A.R. last Monday! I said to myself: She's probably suffering with that sinus condition! How is that sinus condition? Horrors! Heaven have mercy!— You're a Christian martyr, yes, that's what you are, a Christian martyr! Well, I just now happened to notice that your subscription to the *Companion's* about to expire! Yes, it expires with the next issue, honey!—just when that wonderful new serial by Bessie Mae Hopper is getting off to such an exciting start. Oh, honey, it's something that you can't miss! You remember how *Gone With the Wind* took everybody by storm? You simply couldn't go out if you hadn't read it. All everybody *talked* was Scarlett O'Hara. Well, this is a book that critics already compare to *Gone With the Wind*. It's the *Gone With the Wind* of the post-World War generation!— What?— Burning?— Oh, honey, don't let them burn, go take a look in the oven and I'll hold the wire! Heavens— I think she's hung up!

DIM OUT

[LEGEND ON SCREEN: "YOU THINK I'M IN LOVE WITH CONTINENTAL SHOEMAKERS?"]

[*Before the stage is lighted, the violent voices of* TOM *and* AMANDA *are heard.*]

[*They are quarreling behind the portieres. In front of them stands* LAURA *with clenched hands and panicky expression.*]

[*A clear pool of light on her figure throughout this scene.*]

TOM. What in Christ's name am I—
AMANDA [*shrilly*]. Don't you use that—
TOM. Supposed to do!
AMANDA. Expression! Not in my—
TOM. Ohhh!
AMANDA. Presence! Have you gone out of your senses?
TOM. I have, that's true, *driven* out!

AMANDA. What is the matter with you, you—big—big—IDIOT!

TOM. Look—I've got *no thing*, no single thing—

AMANDA. Lower your voice!

TOM. In my life here that I can call my OWN! Everything is—

AMANDA. Stop that shouting!

TOM. Yesterday you confiscated my books! You had the nerve to—

AMANDA. I took that horrible novel back to the library—yes! That hideous book by that insane Mr. Lawrence. [TOM *laughs wildly*.] I cannot control the output of diseased minds or people who cater to them— [TOM *laughs still more wildly*.] BUT I WON'T ALLOW SUCH FILTH BROUGHT INTO MY HOUSE! No, no, no, no, no!

TOM. House, house! Who pays rent on it, who makes a slave of himself to—

AMANDA [*fairly screeching*]. Don't you DARE to—

TOM. No, no, *I* mustn't say things! *I've* got to just—

AMANDA. Let me tell you—

TOM. I don't want to hear any more! [*He tears the portieres open. The upstage area is lit with a turgid smoky red glow.*]

[AMANDA'S *hair is in metal curlers and she wears a very old bathrobe, much too large for her slight figure, a relic of the faithless Mr. Wingfield.*]

[*An upright typewriter and a wild disarray of manuscripts is on the drop-leaf table. The quarrel was probably precipitated by* AMANDA'S *interruption of his creative labor. A chair lying overthrown on the floor.*]

[*Their gesticulating shadows are cast on the ceiling by the fiery glow.*]

AMANDA. You *will* hear more, you—

TOM. No, I won't hear more, I'm going out!

AMANDA. You come right back in—

TOM. Out, out out! Because I'm—

AMANDA. Come back here, Tom Wingfield! I'm not through talking to you!

TOM. Oh, go——

LAURA [*desperately*]. —Tom!

AMANDA. You're going to listen, and no more insolence from you! I'm at the end of my patience! [*He comes back toward her.*]

TOM. What do you think I'm at? Aren't I suppose to have any patience to reach the end of, Mother? I know, I know. It seems unimportant to you, what I'm *doing*—what I *want* to do—having a little *difference* between them! You don't think that—

AMANDA. I think you've been doing things that you're ashamed of. That's why you act like this. I don't believe that you go every night to the movies. Nobody goes to the movies night after night. Nobody in their right minds goes to the movies as often as you pretend to. People don't go to the movies at nearly midnight, and movies don't let out at two A.M. Come in stumbling. Muttering to yourself like a maniac! You get three hours' sleep and then go to work. Oh, I can picture the way you're doing down there. Moping, doping, because you're in no condition.

TOM [*wildly*]. No, I'm in no condition!

AMANDA. What right have you got to jeopardize your job? Jeopardize the security of us all? How do you think we'd manage if you were—

TOM. Listen! You think I'm crazy *about* the *warehouse*? [*He bends fiercely toward her slight figure.*] You think I'm in love with the Continental Shoemakers? You think I want to spend fifty-five *years* down there in that—*celotex interior!* with—*fluorescent*—*tubes!* Look! I'd rather somebody picked up a crowbar and battered out my brains—than go back mornings! I *go!* Every time you come in yelling that God damn *"Rise and Shine!"* *"Rise and Shine!"* I say to myself, "How *lucky dead* people are!" But I get up. I *go!* For sixty-five dollars a month I give up all that I dream of doing and being *ever!* And you say self—*self's* all I ever think of. Why, listen, if self is what I thought of, Mother, I'd be where he is—GONE! [*Pointing to father's picture.*] As far as the system of transportation reaches! [*He starts past her. She grabs his arm.*] Don't grab at me, Mother!

AMANDA. Where are you going?

TOM. I'm going to the *movies!*

AMANDA. I don't believe that lie!

TOM [*crouching toward her, overtowering her tiny figure. She backs away, gasping*]. I'm going to opium dens! Yes, opium dens, dens of vice and criminals' hang-outs, Mother. I've joined the Hogan gang, I'm a hired assassin, I carry a tommy-gun in a violin case! I run a string of cat-houses in the Valley! They call me Killer, Killer Wingfield, I'm leading a double-life, a simple, honest warehouse worker by day, by night, a dynamic *czar* of the *underworld, Mother.* I go to gambling casinos, I spin away fortunes on the roulette table! I wear a patch over one eye and a false mustache, sometimes I put on green whiskers. On those occasions they call me—*El Diablo!* Oh, I could tell you things to make you sleepless! My enemies plan to dynamite this place. They're going to blow us all sky-high some night! I'll be glad, very happy, and so will you! You'll go up, up on a broomstick, over Blue Mountain with seventeen gentlemen callers! You ugly—babbling old—*witch.* . . . [*He goes through a series of violent, clumsy movements, seizing his overcoat, lunging to the door, pulling it fiercely open. The women watch him, aghast. His arm catches in the sleeve of the coat as he struggles to pull it on. For a moment he is pinioned by the bulky garment. With an outraged groan he tears the coat off again, splitting the shoulder of it, and hurls it across the room. It strikes against the shelf of* LAURA'S *glass collection, there is a tinkle of shattering glass.* LAURA *cries out as if wounded.*]

[MUSIC LEGEND: "THE GLASS MENAGERIE."]

LAURA [*shrilly*]. *My glass!*—menagerie. . . . [*She covers her face and turns away.*]

[*But* AMANDA *is still stunned and stupefied by the "ugly*

witch" so that she barely notices this occurrence. Now she recovers her speech.]

AMANDA [*in an awful voice*]. I won't speak to you—until you apologize! [*She crosses through portieres and draws them together behind her.* TOM *is left with* LAURA. LAURA *clings weakly to the mantel with her face averted.* TOM *stares at her stupidly for a moment. Then he crosses to shelf. Drops awkwardly on his knees to collect the fallen glass, glancing at* LAURA *as if he would speak but couldn't.*]

"The Glass Menagerie" steals in as

THE SCENE DIMS OUT

SCENE FOUR

[*The interior is dark. Faint light in the alley.*

A deep-voice bell in a church is tolling the hour of five as the scene commences.

TOM *appears at the top of the alley. After each solemn boom of the bell in the tower, he shakes a little noise-maker or rattle as if to express the tiny spasm of man in contrast to the sustained power and dignity of the Almighty. This and the unsteadiness of his advance make it evident that he has been drinking.*

As he climbs the few steps to the fire-escape landing light steals up inside. LAURA *appears in night-dress, observing* TOM'S *empty bed in the front room.*

TOM *fishes in his pockets for door-key, removing a motley assortment of articles in the search, including a perfect shower of movie-ticket stubs and an empty bottle. At last he finds the key, but just as he is about to insert it, it slips from his fingers. He strikes a match and crouches below the door.*]

TOM [*bitterly*]. One crack—and it falls through!

[LAURA *opens the door.*]

LAURA. Tom! Tom, what are you doing?
TOM. Looking for a door-key.
LAURA. Where have you been all this time?
TOM. I have been to the movies.
LAURA. All this time at the movies?
TOM. There was a very long program. There was a Garbo picture and a Mickey Mouse and a travelogue and a newsreel and a preview of coming attractions. And there was an organ solo and a collection for the milk-fund—simultaneously—which ended up in a terrible fight between a fat

lady and an usher!

LAURA [*innocently*]. Did you have to stay through everything?

TOM. Of course! And, oh, I forgot! There was a big stage show! The headliner on this stage show was Malvolio the Magician. He performed wonderful tricks, many of them, such as pouring water back and forth between pitchers. First it turned to wine and then it turned to beer and then it turned to whiskey. I know it was whiskey it finally turned into because he needed somebody to come up out of the audience to help him, and I came up—both shows! It was Kentucky Straight Bourbon. A very generous fellow, he gave souvenirs. [*He pulls from his back pocket a shimmering rainbow-colored scarf*.] He gave me this. This is his magic scarf. You can have it, Laura. You wave it over a canary cage and you get a bowl of gold-fish. You wave it over the gold-fish bowl and they fly away canaries. . . . But the wonderfullest trick of all was the coffin trick. We nailed him into a coffin and he got out of the coffin without removing one nail. [*He has come inside*.] There is a trick that would come in handy for me—get me out of this 2 by 4 situation! [*Flops onto bed and starts removing shoes*.]

LAURA. Tom—Shhh!

TOM. What're you shushing me for?

LAURA. You'll wake up Mother.

TOM. Goody, goody! Pay 'er back for all those "Rise an' Shines." [*Lies down, groaning*.] You know it don't take much intelligence to get yourself into a nailed-up coffin, Laura. But who in hell ever got himself out of one without removing one nail?

[*As if in answer, the father's grinning photograph lights up*.]

SCENE DIMS OUT

[*Immediately following: The church bell is heard striking six. At the sixth stroke the alarm clock goes off in* AMANDA's *room, and after a few moments we hear her calling: "Rise and Shine! Rise and Shine! Laura, go tell your brother to rise and shine!"*]

TOM [*Sitting up slowly*]. I'll rise—but I won't shine.

[*The light increases.*]

AMANDA. Laura, tell your brother his coffee is ready.

[LAURA *slips into front room.*]

LAURA. Tom it's nearly seven. Don't make Mother nervous. [*He stares at her stupidly. Beseechingly.*] Tom, speak to Mother this morning. Make up with her, apologize, speak to her!

TOM. She won't to me. It's her that started not speaking.

LAURA. If you just say you're sorry she'll start speaking.

TOM. Her not speaking—is that such a tragedy?

LAURA. Please—please!

AMANDA [*calling from kitchenette*]. Laura, are you going to do what I asked you to do, or do I have to get dressed and go out myself?

LAURA. Going, going—soon as I get on my coat! [*She pulls on a shapeless felt hat with nervous, jerky movement, pleadingly glancing at* TOM. *Rushes awkwardly for coat. The coat is one of* AMANDA'S, *inaccurately made-over, the sleeves too short for* LAURA.] Butter and what else?

AMANDA [*entering upstage*]. Just butter. Tell them to charge it.

LAURA. Mother, they make such faces when I do that.

AMANDA. Sticks and stones can break our bones, but the expression on Mr. Garfinkel's face won't harm us! Tell your brother his coffee is getting cold.

LAURA [*at door*]. Do what I asked you, will you, will you, Tom?

[*He looks sullenly away.*]

AMANDA. Laura, go now or just don't go at all!

LAURA [*rushing out*]. Going—going! [*A second later she cries out.* TOM *springs up and crosses to door.* AMANDA *rushes anxiously in.* TOM *opens the door.*]

TOM. Laura?

LAURA. I'm all right. I slipped, but I'm all right.

AMANDA [*peering anxiously after her*]. If anyone breaks a leg on those fire-escape steps, the landlord ought to be sued for every cent he possesses! [*She shuts door. Remembers she isn't speaking and returns to other room.*]

[*As* TOM *enters listlessly for his coffee, she turns her back to him and stands rigidly facing the window on the gloomy gray vault of the areaway. Its light on her face with its aged but childish features is cruelly sharp, satirical as a Daumier print.*]

[MUSIC UNDER: "AVE MARIA."]

TOM *glances sheepishly but sullenly at her averted figure and slumps at the table. The coffee is scalding hot; he sips it and gasps and spits it back in the cup. At his gasp,* AMANDA *catches her breath and half turns. Then catches herself and turns back to window.*]

[TOM *blows on his coffee, glancing sidewise at his mother. She clears her throat.* TOM *clears his. He starts to rise. Sinks back down again, scratches his head, clears his throat again.* AMANDA *coughs.* TOM *raises his cup in both hands to blow on it, his eyes staring over the rim of it at his mother for several moments. Then he slowly sets the cup down and awkwardly and hesitantly rises from the chair.*]

TOM [*hoarsely*]. Mother. I—I apologize. Mother. [AMANDA *draws a quick, shuddering breath. Her face works grotesquely. She breaks into childlike tears.*] I'm sorry for what I said, for everything that I said, I didn't mean it.

AMANDA [*sobbingly*]. My devotion has made me a witch and so I make myself hateful to my children!

TOM. *No*, you *don't*.

AMANDA. I worry so much, don't sleep, it makes me nervous!

TOM [*gently*]. I understand that.

AMANDA. I've had to put up a solitary battle all these years. But you're my right-hand bower! Don't fall down, don't fail!

TOM [*gently*]. I try, Mother.

AMANDA [*with great enthusiasm*]. Try and you will SUCCEED! [*The notion makes her breathless.*] Why, you—you're just *full* of natural endowments! Both of my children—they're *unusual* children! Don't you think I know it? I'm so— *proud!* Happy and—feel I've—so much to be thankful for but— Promise me one thing, son!

TOM. What, Mother?

AMANDA. Promise, son, you'll—never be a drunkard!

TOM [*turns to her grinning*]. I will never be a drunkard, Mother.

AMANDA. That's what frightened me so, that you'd be drinking! Eat a bowl of Purina!

TOM. Just coffee, Mother.

AMANDA. Shredded wheat biscuit?

TOM. No. No, Mother, just coffee.

AMANDA. You can't put in a day's work on an empty stomach. You've got ten minutes—don't gulp! Drinking too-hot liquids makes cancer of the stomach. . . . Put cream in.

TOM. No, thank you.

AMANDA. To cool it.

TOM. No! No, thank you, I want it black.

AMANDA. I know, but it's not good for you. We have to do all that we can to build ourselves up. In these trying times we live in, all that we have to cling to is—each other. . . . That's why it's so important to— Tom, I— I sent out your sister so I could discuss something with you. If you hadn't spoken I would have spoken to you. [*Sits down.*]

TOM [*gently*]. What is it, Mother, that you want to discuss?

AMANDA. *Laura!*

[TOM *puts his cup down slowly.*]

[LEGEND ON SCREEN: "LAURA."]

[MUSIC: "THE GLASS MENAGERIE."]

TOM. —Oh.—Laura . . .

AMANDA [*touching his sleeve*]. You know how Laura is. So

quiet but—still water runs deep! She notices things and I think she—broods about them. [TOM *looks up*]. A few days ago I came in and she was crying.

TOM. What about?

AMANDA. You.

TOM. Me?

AMANDA. She has an idea that you're not happy here.

TOM. What gave her that idea?

AMANDA. What gives her any idea? However, you do act strangely. I—I'm not criticizing, understand *that!* I know your ambitions do not lie in the warehouse, that like everybody in the whole wide world—you've had to—make sacrifices, but—Tom—Tom—life's not easy, it calls for—Spartan endurance! There's so many things in my heart that I cannot describe to you! I've never told you but I—*loved* your father. . . .

TOM [*gently*]. I know that, Mother.

AMANDA. And you—when I see you taking after his ways! Staying out late—and—well, you *had* been drinking the night you were in that—terrifying condition! Laura says that you hate the apartment and that you go out nights to get away from it! Is that true, Tom?

TOM. No. You say there's so much in your heart that you can't describe to me. That's true of me, too. There's so much in my heart that I can't describe to *you!* So let's respect each other's—

AMANDA. But, why—*why*, Tom—are you always so *restless?* Where do you *go* to, nights?

TOM. I—go to the movies.

AMANDA. Why do you go to the movies so much, Tom?

TOM. I go to the movies because—I like adventure. Adventure is something I don't have much of at work, so I go to the movies.

AMANDA. But, Tom, you go to the movies *entirely* too *much!*

TOM. I like a lot of adventure.

[AMANDA *looks baffled, then hurt. As the familiar inquisi-*

tion resumes he becomes hard and impatient again. AMANDA
slips back into her querulous attitude toward him.]

[IMAGE ON SCREEN: SAILING VESSEL WITH JOLLY ROGER.]

AMANDA. Most young men find adventure in their careers.

TOM. Then most young men are not employed in a warehouse.

AMANDA. The world is full of young men employed in ware-
houses and offices and factories.

TOM. Do all of them find adventure in their careers?

AMANDA. They do or they do without it! Not everybody has a
craze for adventure.

TOM. Man is by instinct a lover, a hunter, a fighter, and none
of those instincts are given much play at the warehouse!

AMANDA. Man is by instinct! Don't quote instinct to me! Instinct is something that people have got away from! It
belongs to animals! Christian adults don't want it!

TOM. What do Christian adults want, then, Mother?

AMANDA. Superior things! Things of the mind and the spirit!
Only animals have to satisfy instincts! Surely your aims
are somewhat higher than theirs! Than monkeys—pigs—

TOM. I reckon they're not.

AMANDA. You're joking. However, that isn't what I wanted to
discuss.

TOM [*rising*]. I haven't much time.

AMANDA [*pushing his shoulders*]. Sit down.

TOM. You want me to punch in red at the warehouse, Mother?

AMANDA. You have five minutes. I want to talk about Laura.

[LEGEND: "PLANS AND PROVISIONS."]

TOM. All right! What about Laura?

AMANDA. We have to be making plans and provisions for her.
She's older than you, two years, and nothing has happened.
She just drifts along doing nothing. It frightens me terribly
how she just drifts along.

TOM. I guess she's the type that people call home girls.

AMANDA. There's no such type, and if there is, it's a pity! That
is unless the home is hers, with a husband!

TOM. What?

AMANDA. Oh, I can see the handwriting on the wall as plain as I see the nose in front of my face! It's terrifying! More and more you remind me of your father! He was out all hours without explanation—Then *left! Good-bye!* And me with the bag to hold. I saw that letter you got from the Merchant Marine. I know what you're dreaming of. I'm not standing here blindfolded. Very well, then. Then *do* it! But not till there's somebody to take your place.

TOM. What do you mean?

AMANDA. I mean that as soon as Laura has got somebody to take care of her, married, a home of her own, independent— why, then you'll be free to go wherever you please, on land, on sea, whichever way the wind blows you! But until that time you've got to look out for your sister. I don't say me because I'm old and don't matter! I say for your sister because she's young and dependent. I put her in business college—a dismal failure! Frightened her so it made her sick to her stomach. I took her over to the Young People's League at the church. Another fiasco. She spoke to nobody, nobody spoke to her. Now all she does is fool with those pieces of glass and play those worn-out records. What kind of a life is that for a girl to lead?

TOM. What can I do about it?

AMANDA. Overcome selfishness! Self, self, self is all that you ever think of! [TOM *springs up and crosses to get his coat. It is ugly and bulky. He pulls on a cap with earmuffs.*] Where is your muffler? Put your wool muffler on! [*He snatches it angrily from the closet and tosses it around his neck and pulls both ends tight.*] Tom! I haven't said what I had in mind to ask you.

TOM. I'm too late to—

AMANDA [*catching his arm—very importunately. Then shyly*]. Down at the warehouse, aren't there some—nice young men?

TOM. No!

AMANDA. There *must* be—*some* . . .

TOM. Mother—

[*Gesture.*]

AMANDA. Find out one that's clean-living—doesn't drink and—ask him out for sister!

TOM. What?

AMANDA. For *sister!* To *meet!* Get *acquainted!*

TOM [*stamping to door*]. Oh, my *go-osh!*

AMANDA. Will you? [*He opens door. Imploringly.*] Will you? [*He starts down.*] Will you? *Will* you, dear?

TOM [*calling back*]. YES!

[AMANDA *closes the door hesitantly and with a troubled but faintly hopeful expression.*]

[SCREEN IMAGE: GLAMOR MAGAZINE COVER.]

[*Spot* AMANDA *at phone.*]

AMANDA. Ella Cartwright? This is Amanda Wingfield! How are you, honey? How is that kidney condition? [*Count five.*] Horrors! [*Count five.*] You're a Christian martyr, yes, honey, that's what you are, a Christian martyr! Well, I just happened to notice in my little red book that your subscription to the *Companion* has just run out! I knew that you wouldn't want to miss out on the wonderful serial starting in this new issue. It's by Bessie Mae Hopper, the first thing she's written since *Honeymoon for Three.* Wasn't that a strange and interesting story? Well, this one is even lovelier, I believe. It has a sophisticated, society background. It's all about the horsey set on Long Island!

FADE OUT

SCENE FIVE

LEGEND ON SCREEN: "ANNUNCIATION." *Fade with music.*

[*It is early dusk of a spring evening. Supper has just been finished in the Wingfield apartment.* AMANDA *and* LAURA *in light colored dresses are removing dishes from the table, in the upstage area, which is shadowy, their movements formalized almost as a dance or ritual, their moving forms as pale and silent as moths.*

TOM, *in white shirt and trousers, rises from the table and crosses toward the fire-escape.*]

AMANDA [*as he passes her*]. Son, will you do me a favor?

TOM. What?

AMANDA. Comb your hair! You look so pretty when your hair is combed! [TOM *slouches on sofa with evening paper. Enormous caption "Franco Triumphs".*] There is only one respect in which I would like you to emulate your father.

TOM. What respect is that?

AMANDA. The care he always took of his appearance. He never allowed himself to look untidy. [*He throws down the paper and crosses to fire-escape.*] Where are you going?

TOM. I'm going out to smoke.

AMANDA. You smoke too much. A pack a day at fifteen cents a pack. How much would that amount to in a month? Thirty times fifteen is how much, Tom? Figure it out and you will be astounded at what you could save. Enough to give you a night-school course in accounting at Washington U! Just think what a wonderful thing that would be for you, son!

[TOM *is unmoved by the thought.*]

TOM. I'd rather smoke. [*He steps out on landing, letting the screen door slam.*]

AMANDA [*sharply*]. I know! That's the tragedy of it. . . . [*Alone, she turns to look at her husband's picture.*]

[DANCE MUSIC: "ALL THE WORLD IS WAITING FOR THE SUN- RISE!"]

TOM [*to the audience*]. Across the alley from us was the Para- dise Dance Hall. On evenings in spring the windows and doors were open and the music came outdoors. Sometimes the lights were turned out except for a large glass sphere that hung from the ceiling. It would turn slowly about and filter the dusk with delicate rainbow colors. Then the or- chestra played a waltz or a tango, something that had a slow and sensuous rhythm. Couples would come outside, to the relative privacy of the alley. You could see them kiss- ing behind ash-pits and telephone poles. This was the com- pensation for lives that passed like mine, without any change or adventure. Adventure and change were imminent in this year. They were waiting around the corner for all these kids. Suspended in the mist over Berchtesgaden, caught in the folds of Chamberlain's umbrella—In Spain there was Guer- nica! But here there was only hot swing music and liquor, dance halls, bars, and movies, and sex that hung in the gloom like a chandelier and flooded the world with brief, deceptive rainbows. . . . All the world was waiting for bombardments!

[AMANDA *turns from the picture and comes outside.*]

AMANDA [*Sighing*]. A fire-escape landing's a poor excuse for a porch. [*She spreads a newspaper on a step and sits down, gracefully and demurely as if she were settling into a swing on a Mississippi veranda.*] What are you looking at?

TOM. The moon.

AMANDA. Is there a moon this evening?

TOM. It's rising over Garfinkel's Delicatessen.

AMANDA. So it is! A little silver slipper of a moon. Have you made a wish on it yet?

TOM. Um-hum.

AMANDA. What did you wish for?

TOM. That's a secret.

AMANDA. A secret, huh? Well, I won't tell mine either. I will be just as mysterious as you.

TOM. I bet I can guess what yours is.

AMANDA. Is my head so transparent?

TOM. You're not a sphinx.

AMANDA. No, I don't have secrets. I'll tell you what I wished for on the moon. Success and happiness for my precious children! I wish for that whenever there's a moon, and when there isn't a moon, I wish for it, too.

TOM. I thought perhaps you wished for a gentleman caller.

AMANDA. Why do you say that?

TOM. Don't you remember asking me to fetch one?

AMANDA. I remember suggesting that it would be nice for your sister if you brought home some nice young man from the warehouse. I think that I've made that suggestion more than once.

TOM. Yes, you have made it repeatedly.

AMANDA. Well?

TOM. We are going to have one.

AMANDA. *What?*

TOM. A gentleman caller!

[THE ANNUNCIATION IS CELEBRATED WITH MUSIC.]

[AMANDA *rises.*]

[IMAGE ON SCREEN: CALLER WITH BOUQUET.]

AMANDA. You mean you have asked some nice young man to come over?

TOM. Yep. I've asked him to dinner.

AMANDA. You really did?

TOM. I did!

AMANDA. You did, and did he—*accept?*

TOM. He did!

AMANDA. Well, well—well, well! That's—lovely!

TOM. I thought that you would be pleased.

AMANDA. It's definite, then?

TOM. Very definite.

AMANDA. Soon?

TOM. Very soon.

AMANDA. For heaven's sake, stop putting on and tell me some things, will you?

TOM. What things do you want me to tell you?

AMANDA. *Naturally* I would like to know when he's *coming!*

TOM. He's coming tomorrow.

AMANDA. *Tomorrow?*

TOM. Yep. Tomorrow.

AMANDA. But, Tom!

TOM. Yes, Mother?

AMANDA. Tomorrow gives me no time!

TOM. Time for what?

AMANDA. Preparations! Why didn't you phone me at once, as soon as you asked him, the minute that he accepted? Then, don't you see, I could have been getting ready!

TOM. You don't have to make any fuss.

AMANDA. Oh, Tom, Tom, Tom, of course I have to make a fuss! I want things nice, not sloppy! Not thrown together. I'll certainly have to do some fast thinking, won't I?

TOM. I don't see why you have to think at all.

AMANDA. You just don't know. We can't have a gentleman caller in a pig-sty! All my wedding silver has to be polished, the monogrammed table linen ought to be laundered! The windows have to be washed and fresh curtains put up. And how about clothes? We have to *wear* something, don't we?

TOM. Mother, this boy is no one to make a fuss over!

AMANDA. Do you realize he's the first young man we've introduced to your sister? It's terrible, dreadful, disgraceful that poor little sister has never received a single gentleman caller! Tom, come inside! [*She opens the screen door.*]

TOM. What for?

AMANDA. I want to ask you some things.

TOM. If you're going to make such a fuss, I'll call it off, I'll tell him not to come!

AMANDA. You certainly won't do anything of the kind. Nothing offends people worse than broken engagements. It simply means I'll have to work like a Turk! We won't be brilliant, but we will pass inspection. Come on inside. [TOM *follows, groaning.*] Sit down.

TOM. Any particular place you would like me to sit?

AMANDA. Thank heavens I've got that new sofa! I'm also making payments on a floor lamp I'll have sent out! And put the chintz covers on, they'll brighten things up! Of course I'd hoped to have these walls re-papered. . . . What is the young man's name?

TOM. His name is O'Connor.

AMANDA. That, of course, means fish—tomorrow is Friday! I'll have that salmon loaf—with Durkee's dressing! What does he do? He works at the warehouse?

TOM. Of course! How else would I—

AMANDA. Tom, he—doesn't drink?

TOM. Why do you ask me that?

AMANDA. Your father *did!*

TOM. Don't get started on that!

AMANDA. He *does* drink, then?

TOM. Not that I know of!

AMANDA. Make sure, be certain! The last thing I want for my daughter's a boy who drinks!

TOM. Aren't you being a little bit premature? Mr. O'Connor has not yet appeared on the scene!

AMANDA. But will tomorrow. To meet your sister, and what do I know about his character? Nothing! Old maids are better off than. wives of drunkards!

TOM. Oh, my God!

AMANDA. Be still!

TOM [*leaning forward to whisper*]. Lots of fellows meet girls whom they don't marry!

AMANDA. Oh,. talk sensibly, Tom—and don't be sarcastic! [*She has gotten a hairbrush.*]

TOM. What are you doing?

AMANDA. I'm brushing that cow-lick down! What is this young man's position at the warehouse?

TOM [*submitting grimly to the brush and the interrogation*]. This young man's position is that of a shipping clerk, Mother.

AMANDA. Sounds to me like a fairly responsible job, the sort of a job *you* would be in if you just had more *get-up*. What is his salary? Have you any idea?

TOM. I would judge it to be approximately eighty-five dollars a month.

AMANDA. Well—not princely, but—

TOM. Twenty more than I make.

AMANDA. Yes, how well I know! But for a family man, eighty-five dollars a month is not much more than you can just get by on. . . .

TOM. Yes, but Mr. O'Connor is not a family man.

AMANDA. He might be, mightn't he? Some time in the future?

TOM. I see. Plans and provisions.

AMANDA. You are the only young man that I know of who ignores the fact that the future becomes the present, the present the past, and the past turns into everlasting regret if you don't plan for it!

TOM. I will think that over and see what I can make of it.

AMANDA. Don't be supercilious with your mother! Tell me some more about this—what do you call him?

TOM. James D. O'Connor. The D. is for Delaney.

AMANDA. Irish on *both* sides! *Gracious!* And doesn't drink?

TOM. Shall I call him up and ask him right this minute?

AMANDA. The only way to find out about those things is to make discreet inquiries at the proper moment. When I was a girl in Blue Mountain and it was suspected that a young man drank, the girl whose attentions he had been receiving, if any girl *was*, would sometimes speak to the minister of his church, or rather her father would if her father was living, and sort of feel him out on the young man's character. That is the way such things are discreetly handled to keep a young woman from making a tragic mistake!

TOM. Then how did you happen to make a tragic mistake?

AMANDA. That innocent look of your father's had everyone

fooled! He *smiled*—the world was *enchanted!* No girl can do worse than put herself at the mercy of a handsome appearance! I hope that Mr. O'Connor is not too good-looking.

TOM. No, he's not too good-looking. He's covered with freckles and hasn't too much of a nose.

AMANDA. He's not right-down homely, though?

TOM. Not right-down homely. Just medium homely, I'd say.

AMANDA. Character's what to look for in a man.

TOM. That's what I've always said, Mother.

AMANDA. You've never said anything of the kind and I suspect you would never give it a thought.

TOM. Don't be so suspicious of me.

AMANDA. At least I hope he's the type that's up and coming.

TOM. I think he really goes in for self-improvement.

AMANDA. What reason have you to think so?

TOM. He goes to night school.

AMANDA [*beaming*]. Splendid! What does he do, I mean study?

TOM. Radio engineering and public speaking!

AMANDA. Then he has visions of being advanced in the world! Any young man who studies public speaking is aiming to have an executive job some day! And radio engineering? A thing for the future! Both of these facts are very illuminating. Those are the sort of things that a mother should know concerning any young man who comes to call on her daughter. Seriously or—not.

TOM. One little warning. He doesn't know about Laura. I didn't let on that we had dark ulterior motives. I just said, why don't you come and have dinner with us? He said okay and that was the whole conversation.

AMANDA. I bet it was! You're eloquent as an oyster. However, he'll know about Laura when he gets here. When he sees how lovely and sweet and pretty she is, he'll thank his lucky stars he was asked to dinner.

TOM. Mother, you mustn't expect too much of Laura.

AMANDA. What do you mean?

TOM. Laura seems all those things to you and me because she's ours and we love her. We don't even notice she's crippled any more.

AMANDA. Don't say crippled! You know that I never allow that word to be used!

TOM. But face facts, Mother. She is and—that's not all—

AMANDA. What do you mean "not all"?

TOM. Laura is very different from other girls.

AMANDA. I think the difference is all to her advantage.

TOM. Not quite all—in the eyes of others—strangers—she's terribly shy and lives in a world of her own and those things make her seem a little peculiar to people outside the house.

AMANDA. Don't say peculiar.

TOM. Face the facts. She is.

[THE DANCE-HALL MUSIC CHANGES TO A TANGO THAT HAS A MINOR AND SOMEWHAT OMINOUS TONE.]

AMANDA. In what way is she peculiar—may I ask?

TOM [gently]. She lives in a world of her own—a world of— little glass ornaments, Mother. . . . [Gets up. AMANDA remains holding brush, looking at him, troubled.] She plays old phonograph records and—that's about all— [He glances at himself in the mirror and crosses to door.]

AMANDA [sharply]. Where are you going?

TOM. I'm going to the movies. [Out screen door.]

AMANDA. Not to the movies, every night to the movies! [Follows quickly to screen door.] I don't believe you always go to the movies! [He is gone. AMANDA looks worriedly after him for a moment. Then vitality and optimism return and she turns from the door. Crossing to portieres.] Laura! Laura! [LAURA answers from kitchenette.]

LAURA. Yes, Mother.

AMANDA. Let those dishes go and come in front! [LAURA appears with dish towel. Gaily.] Laura, come here and make a wish on the moon!

LAURA [entering]. Moon—moon?

AMANDA. A little silver slipper of a moon. Look over your left shoulder, Laura, and make a wish! [LAURA looks faintly puzzled as if called out of sleep. AMANDA seizes her shoulders *and turns her at an angle by the door.*] No! Now, darling, wish!

LAURA. What shall I wish for, Mother?

AMANDA [*her voice trembling and her eyes suddenly filling with tears*]. Happiness! Good Fortune!

[*The violin rises and the stage dims out.*]

SCENE SIX

[IMAGE: HIGH SCHOOL HERO.]

TOM. And so the following evening I brought Jim home to dinner. I had known Jim slightly in high school. In high school Jim was a hero. He had tremendous Irish good nature and vitality with the scrubbed and polished look of white chinaware. He seemed to move in a continual spotlight. He was a star in basketball, captain of the debating club, president of the senior class and the glee club and he sang the male lead in the annual light operas. He was always running or bounding, never just walking. He seemed always at the point of defeating the law of gravity. He was shooting with such velocity through his adolescence that you would logically expect him to arrive at nothing short of the White House by the time he was thirty. But Jim apparently ran into more interference after his graduation from Soldan. His speed had definitely slowed. Six years after he left high school he was holding a job that wasn't much better than mine.

[IMAGE: CLERK.]

He was the only one at the warehouse with whom I was on friendly terms. I was valuable to him as someone who could remember his former glory, who had seen him win basketball games and the silver cup in debating. He knew of my secret practice of retiring to a cabinet of the washroom to work on poems when business was slack in the warehouse. He called me Shakespeare. And while the other boys in the warehouse regarded me with suspicious hostility, Jim took a humorous attitude toward me. Gradually his attitude affected the others, their hostility wore off and they also began to smile at me as people smile at an oddly fashioned dog who trots across their path at some distance.

I knew that Jim and Laura had known each other at Soldan, and I had heard Laura speak admiringly of his voice. I didn't know if Jim remembered her or not. In high school Laura had been as unobtrusive as Jim had been astonishing. If he did remember Laura, it was not as my sister, for when I asked him to dinner, he grinned and said, "You know, Shakespeare, I never thought of you as having folks!"

He was about to discover that I did. . . .

[LIGHT UP STAGE.]

[LEGEND ON SCREEN: "THE ACCENT OF A COMING FOOT."]

[*Friday evening. It is about five o'clock of a late spring evening which comes "scattering poems in the sky."*]
[*A delicate lemony light is in the Wingfield apartment.*]

[AMANDA *has worked like a Turk in preparation for the gentleman caller. The results are astonishing. The new floor lamp with its rose-silk shade is in place, a colored paper lantern conceals the broken light fixture in the ceiling, new billowing white curtains are at the windows, chintz covers are on chairs and sofa, a pair of new sofa pillows make their initial appearance.*]

[*Open boxes and tissue paper are scattered on the floor.*]

[LAURA *stands in the middle with lifted arms while* AMANDA *crouches before her, adjusting the hem of the new dress, devout and ritualistic. The dress is colored and designed by memory. The arrangement of* LAURA'S *hair is changed; it is softer and more becoming. A fragile, unearthly prettiness has come out in* LAURA: *she is like a piece of translucent glass touched by light, given a momentary radiance, not actual, not lasting.*]

AMANDA [*impatiently*]. Why are you trembling?
LAURA. Mother, you've made me so nervous!
AMANDA. How have I made you nervous?
LAURA. By all this fuss! You make it seem so important!
AMANDA. I don't understand you, Laura. You couldn't be satis-

fied with just sitting home, and yet whenever I try to arrange something for you, you seem to resist it. [*She gets up.*] Now take a look at yourself. No, wait! Wait just a moment—I have an idea!

LAURA. What is it now?

[AMANDA *produces two powder puffs which she wraps in hankerchiefs and stuffs in* LAURA'S *bosom.*]

LAURA. Mother, what are you doing?

AMANDA. They call them "Gay Deceivers"!

LAURA. I won't wear them!

AMANDA. You will!

LAURA. Why should I?

AMANDA. Because, to be painfully honest, your chest is flat.

LAURA. You make it seem like we were setting a trap.

AMANDA. All pretty girls are a trap, a pretty trap, and men expect them to be. [LEGEND: "A PRETTY TRAP."] Now look at yourself, young lady. This is the prettiest you will ever be! I've got to fix myself now! You're going to be surprised by your mother's appearance! [*She crosses through portieres, humming gaily.*]

[LAURA *moves slowly to the long mirror and stares solemnly at herself.*]

[*A wind blows the white curtains inward in a slow, graceful motion and with a faint, sorrowful sighing.*]

AMANDA [*off stage*]. It isn't dark enough yet. [*She turns slowly before the mirror with a troubled look.*]

[LEGEND ON SCREEN: "THIS IS MY SISTER: CELEBRATE HER WITH STRINGS!" MUSIC.]

AMANDA [*laughing, off*]. I'm going to show you something. I'm going to make a spectacular appearance!

LAURA. What is it, Mother?

AMANDA. Possess your soul in patience—you will see! Something I've resurrected from that old trunk! Styles haven't changed so terribly much after all. . . . [*She parts the por-*

tieres.] Now just look at your mother! [*She wears a girlish frock of yellowed voile with a blue silk sash. She carries a bunch of jonquils—the legend of her youth is nearly revived. Feverishly*] This is the dress in which I led the cotillion. Won the cakewalk twice at Sunset Hill, wore one spring to the Governor's ball in Jackson! See how I sashayed around the ballroom, Laura? [*She raises her skirt and does a mincing step around the room.*] I wore it on Sundays for my gentlemen callers! I had it on the day I met your father— I had malaria fever all that spring. The change of climate from East Tennessee to the Delta—weakened resistance— I had a little temperature all the time—not enough to be serious—just enough to make me restless and giddy! Invitations poured in—parties all over the Delta!—"Stay in bed," said Mother, "you have fever!"—but I just wouldn't. —I took quinine but kept on going, going!—Evenings, dances!—Afternoons, long, long rides! Picnics—lovely!— So lovely, that country in May.—All lacy with dogwood, literally flooded with jonquils!—That was the spring I had the craze for jonquils. Jonquils became an absolute obsession. Mother said, "Honey, there's no room for jonquils." And still I kept on bringing in more jonquils. Whenever, wherever I saw them, I'd say, "Stop! Stop! I see jonquils!" I made the young men help me gather the jonquils! It was a joke, Amanda and her jonquils! Finally there were no more vases to hold them, every available space was filled with jonquils. No vases to hold them? All right, I'll hold them myself! And then I—[*She stops in front of the picture.* MUSIC.] met your father! Malaria fever and jonquils and then—this—boy. . . . [*She switches on the rose-colored lamp.*] I hope they get here before it starts to rain. [*She crosses upstage and places the jonquils in bowl on table.*] I gave your brother a little extra change so he and Mr. O'Connor could take the service car home.

LAURA [*with altered look*]. What did you say his name was?

AMANDA. O'Connor.

LAURA. What is his first name?

AMANDA. I don't remember. Oh, yes, I do. It was—Jim!

[LAURA *sways slightly and catches hold of a chair.*]

[LEGEND ON SCREEN: "NOT JIM!"]

LAURA [*faintly*]. Not—Jim!

AMANDA. Yes, that was it, it was Jim! I've never known a Jim
that wasn't nice!

[MUSIC: OMINOUS.]

LAURA. Are you sure his name is Jim O'Connor?

AMANDA. Yes. Why?

LAURA. Is he the one that Tom used to know in high school?

AMANDA. He didn't say so. I think he just got to know him at
the warehouse.

LAURA. There was a Jim O'Connor we both knew in high school
—[*Then, with effort.*] If that is the one that Tom is bringing to dinner—you'll have to excuse me, I won't come to
the table.

AMANDA. What sort of nonsense is this?

LAURA. You asked me once if I'd ever liked a boy. Don't you
remember I showed you this boy's picture?

AMANDA. You mean the boy you showed me in the year book?

LAURA. Yes, that boy.

AMANDA. Laura, Laura, were you in love with that boy?

LAURA. I don't know, Mother. All I know is I couldn't sit at
the table if it was him!

AMANDA. It won't be him! It isn't the least bit likely. But
whether it is or not, you will come to the table. You will not
be excused.

LAURA. I'll have to be, Mother.

AMANDA. I don't intend to humor your silliness, Laura. I've
had too much from you and your brother, both! So just sit
down and compose yourself till they come. Tom has forgotten his key so you'll have to let them in, when they arrive.

LAURA [*panicky*]. Oh, Mother—*you* answer the door!

AMANDA [*lightly*]. I'll be in the kitchen—busy!

LAURA. Oh, Mother, please answer the door, don't make me do it!

AMANDA [*crossing into kitchenette*]. I've got to fix the dressing for the salmon. Fuss, fuss—silliness!—over a gentleman caller!

[*Door swings shut.* LAURA *is left alone.*]

[LEGEND: "TERROR!"]

[*She utters a low moan and turns off the lamp—sits stiffly on the edge of the sofa, knotting her fingers together.*]

[LEGEND ON SCREEN: "THE OPENING OF A DOOR!"]

[TOM *and* JIM *appear on the fire-escape steps and climb to landing. Hearing their approach,* LAURA *rises with a panicky gesture. She retreats to the portieres.*]

[*The doorbell.* LAURA *catches her breath and touches her throat. Low drums.*]

AMANDA [*calling.*] Laura, sweetheart! The door!

[LAURA *stares at it without moving.*]

JIM. I think we just beat the rain.

TOM. Uh-huh. [*He rings again, nervously.* JIM *whistles and fishes for a cigarette.*]

AMANDA [*very, very gaily*]. Laura, that is your brother and Mr. O'Connor! Will you let them in, darling?

[LAURA *crosses toward kitchenette door.*]

LAURA [*breathlessly*]. Mother—you go to the door!

[AMANDA *steps out of kitchenette and stares furiously at* LAURA. *She points imperiously at the door.*]

LAURA. Please, please!

AMANDA [*in a fierce whisper*]. What is the matter with you, you silly thing?

LAURA [*desperately*]. Please, you answer it, *please!*

AMANDA. I told you I wasn't going to humor you, Laura. Why

have you chosen this moment to lose your mind?

LAURA. Please, please, please, you go!

AMANDA. You'll have to go to the door because I can't!

LAURA [*despairingly*]. I can't either!

AMANDA. *Why?*

LAURA. I'm *sick!*

AMANDA. I'm sick, too—of your nonsense! Why can't you and your brother be normal people? Fantastic whims and behavior! [TOM *gives a long ring.*] Preposterous goings on! Can you give me one reason—[*Calls out lyrically:*] COMING! JUST ONE SECOND!—why you should be afraid to open a door? Now you answer it, Laura!

LAURA. Oh, oh, oh . . . [*She returns through the portieres. Darts to the victrola and winds it frantically and turns it on.*]

AMANDA. Laura Wingfield, you march right to that door!

LAURA. Yes—yes, Mother!

[*A faraway, scratchy rendition of "Dardanella" softens the air and gives her strength to move through it. She slips to the door and draws it cautiously open.*]

[TOM *enters with the caller,* JIM O'CONNOR.]

TOM. Laura, this is Jim. Jim, this is my sister, Laura.

JIM [*stepping inside*]. I didn't know that Shakespeare had a sister!

LAURA [*retreating stiff and trembling from the door*]. How—how do you do?

JIM [*heartily extending his hand*]. Okay!

[LAURA *touches it hesitantly with hers.*]

JIM. Your hand's *cold,* Laura!

LAURA. Yes, well—I've been playing the victrola. . . .

JIM. Must have been playing classical music on it! You ought to play a little hot swing music to warm you up!

LAURA. Excuse me—I haven't finished playing the victrola. . . .

[*She turns awkwardly and hurries into the front room. She pauses a second by the victrola. Then catches her breath and darts through the portieres like a frightened deer.*]

JIM [*grinning*]. What was the matter?

TOM. Oh—with Laura? Laura is—terribly shy.

JIM. Shy, huh? It's unusual to meet a shy girl nowadays. I don't believe you ever mentioned you had a sister.

TOM. Well, now you know. I have one. Here is the *Post Dispatch*. You want a piece of it?

JIM. Uh-huh.

TOM. What piece? The comics?

JIM. Sports! [*Glances at it.*] Ole Dizzy Dean is on his bad behavior.

TOM [*disinterest*]. Yeah? [*Lights cigarette and crosses back to fire-escape door.*]

JIM. Where are *you* going?

TOM. I'm going out on the terrace.

JIM [*goes after him*]. You know, Shakespeare—I'm going to sell you a bill of goods!

TOM. What goods?

JIM. A course I'm taking.

TOM. Huh?

JIM. In public speaking! You and me, we're not the warehouse type.

TOM. Thanks—that's good news. But what has public speaking got to do with it?

JIM. It fits you for—executive positions!

TOM. Awww.

JIM. I tell you it's done a helluva lot for me.

[IMAGE: EXECUTIVE AT DESK.]

TOM. In what respect?

JIM. In every! Ask yourself what is the difference between you an' me and men in the office down front? Brains?—No!—Ability?—No! Then what? Just one little thing—

TOM. What is that one little thing?

JIM. Primarily it amounts to—social poise! Being able to square up to people and hold your own on any social level!

AMANDA [*off stage*]. Tom?

TOM. Yes, Mother?

AMANDA. Is that you and Mr. O'Connor?

TOM. Yes, Mother.

AMANDA. Well, you just make yourselves comfortable in there.

TOM. Yes, Mother.

AMANDA. Ask Mr. O'Connor if he would like to wash his hands.

JIM. Aw, no—no—thank you—I took care of that at the warehouse. Tom—

TOM. Yes?

JIM. Mr. Mendoza was speaking to me about you.

TOM. Favorably?

JIM. What do you think?

TOM. Well—

JIM. You're going to be out of a job if you don't wake up.

TOM. I am waking up—

JIM. You show no signs.

TOM. The signs are interior.

[IMAGE ON SCREEN: THE SAILING VESSEL WITH JOLLY ROGER AGAIN.]

TOM. I'm planning to change. [*He leans over the rail speaking with quiet exhilaration. The incandescent marquees and signs of the first-run movie houses light his face from across the alley. He looks like a voyager.*] I'm right at the point of committing myself to a future that doesn't include the warehouse and Mr. Mendoza or even a night-school course in public speaking.

JIM. What are you gassing about?

TOM. I'm tired of the movies.

JIM. Movies!

TOM. Yes, movies! Look at them— [*A wave toward the marvels of Grand Avenue.*] All of those glamorous people—having adventures—hogging it all, gobbling the whole thing up! You know what happens? People go to the *movies* instead of *moving!* Hollywood characters are supposed to have all the adventures for everybody in America, while everybody in America sits in a dark room and watches them have them! Yes, until there's a war. That's when adventure becomes available to the masses! *Everyone's* dish, not only Gable's! Then the people in the dark room come out of the dark room to have some adventures themselves—Goody, goody!—It's our turn now, to go to the South Sea Island—to make a safari—to be exotic, far-off!—But I'm not patient. I don't want to wait till then. I'm tired of the *movies* and I am *about* to *move!*

JIM [*incredulously*]. Move?

TOM. Yes.

JIM. When?

TOM. Soon!

JIM. Where? Where?

[THEME THREE MUSIC SEEMS TO ANSWER THE QUESTION, WHILE TOM THINKS IT OVER. HE SEARCHES AMONG HIS POCKETS.]

TOM. I'm starting to boil inside. I know I seem dreamy, but inside—well, I'm boiling!—Whenever I pick up a shoe, I shudder a little thinking how short life is and what I am doing!—Whatever that means, I know it doesn't mean shoes—except as something to wear on a traveler's feet! [*Finds paper.*] Look—

JIM. What?

TOM. I'm a member.

JIM [*reading*]. The Union of Merchant Seamen.

TOM. I paid my dues this month, instead of the light bill.

JIM. You will regret it when they turn the lights off.

TOM. I won't be here.

JIM. How about your mother?

TOM. I'm like my father. The bastard son of a bastard! See how he grins? And he's been absent going on sixteen years!

JIM. You're just talking, you drip. How does your mother feel about it?

TOM. Shhh!—Here comes Mother! Mother is not acquainted with my plans!

AMANDA [*enters portieres*]. Where are you all?

TOM. On the terrace, Mother.

[*They start inside. She advances to them.* TOM *is distinctly shocked at her appearance. Even* JIM *blinks a little. He is making his first contact with girlish Southern vivacity and in spite of the night-school course in public speaking is somewhat thrown off the beam by the unexpected outlay of social charm.*]

[*Certain responses are attempted by* JIM *but are swept aside by* AMANDA's *gay laughter and chatter.* TOM *is embarrassed but after the first shock* JIM *reacts very warmly. Grins and chuckles, is altogether won over.*]

[IMAGE: AMANDA AS A GIRL.]

AMANDA [*coyly smiling, shaking her girlish ringlets*]. Well, well, well, so this is Mr. O'Connor. Introductions entirely unnecessary. I've heard so much about you from my boy. I finally said to him, Tom—good gracious!—why don't you bring this paragon to supper? I'd like to meet this nice young man at the warehouse!—Instead of just hearing him sing your praises so much! I don't know why my son is so standoffish—that's not Southern behavior! Let's sit down and—I think we could stand a little more air in here! Tom, leave the door open. I felt a nice fresh breeze a moment ago. Where has it gone to? Mmm, so warm already! And not quite summer, even. We're going to burn up when summer really gets started. However, we're having—we're having a very light supper. I think light things are better fo' this time of year. The same as light clothes are. Light clothes an' light food are what warm weather calls fo'. You know our blood gets so thick during th' winter—it takes a while fo' us to *adjust* ou'selves!—when the season changes . . . It's come so quick this year. I wasn't prepared. All of a sudden—heavens! Already summer!—I ran to the trunk an' pulled out this light dress— Terribly old! Historical almost! But feels so good—so good an' co-ol, y'know. . . .

TOM. Mother—

AMANDA. Yes, honey?

TOM. How about—supper?

AMANDA. Honey, you go ask Sister if supper is ready! You know that Sister is in full charge of supper! Tell her you hungry boys are waiting for it. [*To* JIM.] Have you met Laura?

JIM. She—

AMANDA. Let you in? Oh, good, you've met already! It's rare for a girl as sweet an' pretty as Laura to be domestic! But Laura is, thank heavens, not only pretty but also very domestic. I'm not at all. I never was a bit. I never could make a thing but angel-food cake. Well, in the South we had so many servants. Gone, gone, gone. All vestige of gracious living! Gone completely! I wasn't prepared for what the future brought me. All of my gentlemen callers were sons of planters and so of course I assumed that I would be married to one and raise my family on a large piece of land with plenty of servants. But man proposes—and woman accepts the proposal!—To vary that old, old saying a little bit—I married no planter! I married a man who worked for the telephone company!—That gallantly smiling gentleman over there! [*Points to the picture.*] A telephone man who—fell in love with long-distance!— Now he travels and I don't even know where!— But what am I going on for about my—tribulations? Tell me yours—I hope you don't have any! Tom?

TOM. [*returning*]. Yes, Mother?

AMANDA. Is supper nearly ready?

TOM. It looks to me like supper is on the table.

AMANDA. Let me look— [*She rises prettily and looks through portieres.*] Oh, lovely!— But where is Sister?

TOM. Laura is not feeling well and she says that she thinks she'd better not come to the table.

AMANDA. What?—Nonsense!—Laura? Oh, Laura!

LAURA [*off stage, faintly*]. Yes, Mother.

AMANDA. You really must come to the table. We won't be seated until you come to the table! Come in, Mr. O'Connor. You sit over there, and I'll— Laura? Laura Wingfield! You're keeping us waiting, honey! We can't say grace until you come to the table!

[*The back door is pushed weakly open and* LAURA *comes in. She is obviously quite faint, her lips trembling, her eyes wide and staring. She moves unsteadily toward the table.*]

[LEGEND: "TERROR!"]

[*Outside a summer storm is coming abruptly. The white curtains billow inward at the windows and there is a sorrowful murmur and deep blue dusk.*]

[LAURA *suddenly stumbles—she catches at a chair with a faint moan.*]

TOM. Laura!

AMANDA. Laura! [*There is a clap of thunder.*] [LEGEND: "AH!"] [*Despairingly*]. Why, Laura, you *are* sick, darling! Tom, help your sister into the living room, dear! Sit in the living room, Laura—rest on the sofa. Well! [*To the gentleman caller.*] Standing over the hot stove made her ill!—I told her that it was just too warm this evening, but— [TOM *comes back in.* LAURA *is on the sofa.*] Is Laura all right now?

TOM. Yes.

AMANDA. What *is* that? Rain? A nice cool rain has come up! [*She gives the gentleman caller a frightened look.*] I think we may—have grace—now . . . [TOM *looks at her stupidly.*] Tom, honey—you say grace!

TOM. Oh . . . "For these and all thy mercies—" [*They bow their heads,* AMANDA *stealing a nervous glance at* JIM. *In the living room* LAURA, *stretched on the sofa, clenches her hand to her lips, to hold back a shuddering sob.*] God's Holy Name be praised—

THE SCENE DIMS OUT

SCENE SEVEN

[A Souvenir.]

[*Half an hour later. Dinner is just being finished in the upstage area which is concealed by the drawn portieres.*

As the curtain rises LAURA *is still huddled upon the sofa,
her feet drawn under her, her head resting on a pale blue
pillow, her eyes wide and mysteriously watchful. The new
floor lamp with its shade of rose-colored silk gives a soft,
becoming light to her face, bringing out the fragile, unearthly prettiness which usually escapes attention. There
is a steady murmur of rain, but it is slackening and stops
soon after the scene begins; the air outside becomes pale
and luminous as the moon breaks out.*

*A moment after the curtain rises, the lights in both rooms
flicker and go out.*]

JIM. Hey, there, Mr. Light Bulb!

[AMANDA *laughs nervously.*]

[LEGEND: "SUSPENSION OF A PUBLIC SERVICE."]

AMANDA. Where was Moses when the lights went out? Ha-ha.
Do you know the answer to that one, Mr. O'Connor?
JIM. No, Ma'am, what's the answer?
AMANDA. In the dark! [JIM *laughs appreciably.*] Everybody
sit still. I'll light the candles: Isn't it lucky we have them
on the table? Where's a match? Which of you gentlemen
can provide a match?
JIM. Here.
AMANDA. Thank you, sir.
JIM. Not at all, Ma'am!
AMANDA. I guess the fuse has burnt out. Mr. O'Connor, can
you tell a burnt-out fuse? I know I can't and Tom is a total
loss when it comes to mechanics. [SOUND: GETTING UP:

VOICES RECEDE A LITTLE TO KITCHENETTE.] Oh, be careful you don't bump into something. We don't want our gentleman caller to break his neck. Now wouldn't that be a fine howdy-do?

JIM. Ha-ha! Where is the fuse-box?

AMANDA. Right here next to the stove. Can you see anything?

JIM. Just a minute.

AMANDA. Isn't electricity a mysterious thing? Wasn't it Benjamin Franklin who tied a key to a kite? We live in such a mysterious universe, don't we? Some people say that science clears up all the mysteries for us. In my opinion it only creates more! Have you found it yet?

JIM. No, Ma'am. All these fuses look okay to me.

AMANDA. Tom!

TOM. Yes, Mother?

AMANDA. That light bill I gave you several days ago. The one I told you we got the notices about?

TOM. Oh.—Yeah.

[LEGEND: "HA!"]

AMANDA. You didn't neglect to pay it by any chance?

TOM. Why, I—

AMANDA. Didn't! I might have known it!

JIM. Shakespeare probably wrote a poem on that light bill, Mrs. Wingfield.

AMANDA. I might have known better than to trust him with it! There's such a high price for negligence in this world!

JIM. Maybe the poem will win a ten-dollar prize.

AMANDA. We'll just have to spend the remainder of the evening in the nineteenth century, before Mr. Edison made the Mazda lamp!

JIM. Candlelight is my favorite kind of light.

AMANDA. That shows you're romantic! But that's no excuse for Tom. Well, we got through dinner. Very considerate of them to let us get through dinner before they plunged us into everlasting darkness, wasn't it, Mr. O'Connor?

JIM. Ha-ha!

AMANDA. Tom, as a penalty for your carelessness you can help me with the dishes.

JIM. Let me give you a hand.

AMANDA. Indeed you will not!

JIM. I ought to be good for something.

AMANDA. Good for something? [*Her tone is rhapsodic.*] *You?* Why, Mr. O'Connor, nobody, *nobody's* given me this much entertainment—as you have!

JIM. Aw, now, Mrs. Wingfield!

AMANDA. I'm not exaggerating, not one bit! But Sister is all by her lonesome. You go keep her company in the parlor! I'll give you this lovely old candelabrum that used to be on the altar at the church of the Heavenly Rest. It was melted a little out of shape when the church burnt down. Lightning struck it one spring. Gypsy Jones was holding a revival at the time and he intimated that the church was destroyed because the Episcopalians gave card parties.

JIM. Ha-ha.

AMANDA. And how about you coaxing Sister to drink a little wine? I think it would be good for her! Can you carry both at once?

JIM. Sure. I'm Superman!

AMANDA. Now, Thomas, get into this apron!

[*The door of kitchenette swings closed on* AMANDA'S *gay laughter; the flickering light approaches the portieres.*]

[LAURA *sits up nervously as he enters. Her speech at first is low and breathless from the almost intolerable strain of being alone with a stranger.*]

[THE LEGEND. "I DON'T SUPPOSE YOU REMEMBER ME AT ALL!"]

[*In her first speeches in this scene, before* JIM'S *warmth overcomes her paralyzing shyness,* LAURA'S *voice is thin and breathless as though she has just run up a steep flight of stairs.*]

[JIM'S *attitude is gently humorous. In playing this scene it*

*should be stressed that while the incident is apparently un-
important, it is to* LAURA *the climax of her secret life.*]

JIM. Hello, there, Laura.

LAURA [*faintly*]. Hello. [*She clears her throat.*]

JIM. How are you feeling now? Better?

LAURA. Yes. Yes, thank you.

JIM. This is for you. A little dandelion wine. [*He extends it
toward her with extravagant gallantry.*]

LAURA. Thank you.

JIM. Drink it—but don't get drunk! [*He laughs heartily.* LAURA
takes the glass uncertainly; laughs shyly.] Where shall I set
the candles?

LAURA. Oh—oh, anywhere . . .

JIM. How about here on the floor? Any objections?

LAURA. No.

JIM. I'll spread a newspaper under to catch the drippings. I like
to sit on the floor. Mind if I do?

LAURA. Oh, no.

JIM. Give me a pillow?

LAURA. What?

JIM. A pillow!

LAURA. Oh . . . [*Hands him one quickly.*]

JIM. How about you? Don't you like to sit on the floor?

LAURA. Oh—yes.

JIM. Why don't you, then?

LAURA. I—will.

JIM. Take a pillow! [LAURA *does. Sits on the other side of the
candelabrum.* JIM *crosses his legs and smiles engagingly at
her.*] I can't hardly see you sitting way over there.

LAURA. I can—see you.

JIM. I know, but that's not fair, I'm in the limelight. [LAURA
moves her pillow closer.] Good! Now I can see you! Comfortable?

LAURA. Yes.

JIM. So am I. Comfortable as a cow. Will you have some gum?

LAURA. No, thank you.

JIM. I think that I will indulge, with your permission. [*Musingly unwraps it and holds it up.*] Think of the fortune made by the guy that invented the first piece of chewing gum. Amazing, huh? The Wrigley Building is one of the sights of Chicago.—I saw it summer before last when I went up to the Century of Progress. Did you take in the Century of Progress?

LAURA. No, I didn't.

JIM. Well, it was quite a wonderful exposition. What impressed me most was the Hall of Science. Gives you an idea of what the future will be in America, even more wonderful than the present time is! [*Pause. Smiling at her.*] Your brother tells me you're shy. Is that right, Laura?

LAURA. I—don't know.

JIM. I judge you to be an old-fashioned type of girl. Well, I think that's a pretty good type to be. Hope you don't think I'm being too personal—do you?

LAURA [*hastily, out of embarrassment*]. I believe I *will* take a piece of gum, if you—don't mind. [*Clearing her throat.*] Mr. O'Connor, have you—kept up with your singing?

JIM. Singing? Me?

LAURA. Yes. I remember what a beautiful voice you had.

JIM. When did you hear me sing?

[VOICE OFF STAGE IN THE PAUSE.]

VOICE [*off stage*].

> O blow, ye winds, heigh-ho,
> A-roving I will go!
> I'm off to my love
> With a boxing glove—
> Ten thousand miles away!

JIM. You say you've heard me sing?

LAURA. Oh, yes! Yes, very often . . . I—don't suppose you remember me—at all?

JIM [*smiling doubtfully*]. You know I have an idea I've seen you before. I had that idea soon as you opened the door. It

seemed almost like I was about to remember your name.
But the name that I started to call you—wasn't a name! And
so I stopped myself before I said it.

LAURA. Wasn't it—Blue Roses?

JIM [*springs up. Grinning*]. Blue Roses! My gosh, yes—Blue
Roses! That's what I had on my tongue when you opened
the door! Isn't it funny what tricks your memory plays? I
didn't connect you with high school somehow or other. But
that's where it was; it was high school. I didn't even know
you were Shakespeare's sister! Gosh, I'm sorry.

LAURA. I didn't expect you to. You—barely knew me!

JIM. But we did have a speaking acquaintance, huh?

LAURA. Yes, we—spoke to each other.

JIM. When did you recognize me?

LAURA. Oh, right away!

JIM. Soon as I came in the door?

LAURA. When I heard your name I thought it was probably you.
I knew that Tom used to know you a little in high school.
So when you came in the door— Well, then I was—sure.

JIM. Why didn't you *say* something, then?

LAURA [*breathlessly*]. I didn't know what to say, I was—too
surprised!

JIM. For goodness' sakes! You know, this sure is funny!

LAURA. Yes! Yes, isn't it, though . . .

JIM. Didn't we have a class in something together?

LAURA. Yes, we did.

JIM. What class was that?

LAURA. It was—singing—Chorus!

JIM. Aw!

LAURA. I sat across the aisle from you in the Aud.

JIM. Aw.

LAURA. Mondays, Wednesdays and Fridays.

JIM. Now I remember—you always came in late.

LAURA. Yes, it was so hard for me, getting upstairs. I had that
brace on my leg—it clumped so loud!

JIM. I never heard any clumping.

LAURA [*wincing at the recollection*]. To me it sounded like—

thunder!

JIM. Well, well, well, I never even noticed.

LAURA. And everybody was seated before I came in. I had to walk in front of all those people. My seat was in the back row. I had to go clumping all the way up the aisle with everyone watching!

JIM. You shouldn't have been self-conscious.

LAURA. I know, but I was. It was always such a relief when the singing started.

JIM. Aw, yes, I've placed you now! I used to call you Blue Roses. How was it that I got started calling you that?

LAURA. I was out of school a little while with pleurosis. When I came back you asked me what was the matter. I said I had pleurosis—you thought I said Blue Roses. That's what you always called me after that!

JIM. I hope you didn't mind.

LAURA. Oh, no—I liked it. You see, I wasn't acquainted with many—people. . . .

JIM. As I remember you sort of stuck by yourself.

LAURA. I—I—never have had much luck at—making friends.

JIM. I don't see why you wouldn't.

LAURA. Well, I—started out badly.

JIM. You mean being—

LAURA. Yes, it sort of—stood between me—

JIM. You shouldn't have let it!

LAURA. I know, but it did, and—

JIM. You were shy with people!

LAURA. I tried not to be but never could—

JIM. Overcome it?

LAURA. No, I—I never could!

JIM. I guess being shy is something you have to work out of kind of gradually.

LAURA [sorrowfully]. Yes—I guess it—

JIM. Takes time!

LAURA. Yes—

JIM. People are not so dreadful when you know them. That's what you have to remember! And everybody has problems,

not just you, but practically everybody has got some problems. You think of yourself as having the only problems,
as being the only one who is disappointed. But just look
around you and you will see lots of people as disappointed
as you are. For instance, I hoped when I was going to high
school that I would be further along at this time, six years
later, than I am now— You remember that wonderful
write-up I had in *The Torch?*

LAURA. Yes! [*She rises and crosses to table.*]

JIM. It said I was bound to succeed in anything I went into!
[LAURA *returns with the annual.*] Holy Jeez! *The Torch!* [*He
accepts it reverently. They smile across it with mutual wonder.* LAURA *crouches beside him and they begin to turn
through it.* LAURA'S *shyness is dissolving in his warmth.*]

LAURA. Here you are in *Pirates of Penzance!*

JIM [*wistfully*]. I sang the baritone lead in that operetta.

LAURA [*rapidly*]. So—*beautifully!*

JIM [*protesting*]. Aw—

LAURA. Yes, yes—beautifully—beautifully!

JIM. You heard me?

LAURA. All three times!

JIM. No!

LAURA. Yes!

JIM. All three performances?

LAURA [*looking down*]. Yes.

JIM. Why?

LAURA. I—wanted to ask you to—autograph my program.

JIM. Why didn't you ask me to?

LAURA. You were always surrounded by your own friends so
much that I never had a chance to.

JIM. You should have just—

LAURA. Well, I—thought you might think I was—

JIM. Thought I might think you was—what?

LAURA. Oh—

JIM [*with reflective relish*]. I was beleaguered by females in
those days.

LAURA. You were terribly popular!

JIM. Yeah—

LAURA. You had such a—friendly way—

JIM. I was spoiled in high school.

LAURA. Everybody—liked you!

JIM. Including you?

LAURA. I—yes, I—I did, too— [*She gently closes the book in her lap.*]

JIM. Well, well, well!—Give me that program, Laura. [*She hands it to him. He signs it with a flourish.*] There you are— better late than never!

LAURA. Oh, I—what a—surprise!

JIM. My signature isn't worth very much right now. But some day—maybe—it will increase in value! Being disappointed is one thing and being discouraged is something else. I am disappointed but I am not discouraged. I'm twenty-three years old. How old are you?

LAURA. I'll be twenty-four in June.

JIM. That's not old age!

LAURA. No, but—

JIM. You finished high school?

LAURA [*with difficulty*]. I didn't go back.

JIM. You mean you dropped out?

LAURA. I made bad grades in my final examinations. [*She rises and replaces the book and the program. Her voice strained.*] How is—Emily Meisenbach getting along?

JIM. Oh, that kraut-head!

LAURA. Why do you call her that?

JIM. That's what she was.

LAURA. You're not still—going with her?

JIM. I never see her.

LAURA. It said in the Personal Section that you were—engaged!

JIM. I know, but I wasn't impressed by that—propaganda!

LAURA. It wasn't—the truth?

JIM. Only in Emily's optimistic opinion!

LAURA. Oh—

[LEGEND. "WHAT HAVE YOU DONE SINCE HIGH SCHOOL?"]

[JIM *lights a cigarette and leans indolently back on his el-bows smiling at* LAURA *with a warmth and charm which lights her inwardly with altar candles. She remains by the table and turns in her hands a piece of glass to cover her tumult.*]

JIM [*after several reflective puffs on a cigarette*]. What have you done since high school? [*She seems not to hear him.*] Huh? [LAURA *looks up.*] I said what have you done since high school, Laura?

LAURA. Nothing much.

JIM. You must have been doing something these six long years.

LAURA. Yes.

JIM. Well, then, such as what?

LAURA. I took a business course at business college—

JIM. How did that work out?

LAURA. Well, not very—well—I had to drop out, it gave me—indigestion—

[JIM *laughs gently.*]

JIM. What are you doing now?

LAURA. I don't do anything—much. Oh, please don't think I sit around doing nothing! My glass collection takes up a good deal of time. Glass is something you have to take good care of.

JIM. What did you say—about glass?

LAURA. Collection I said—I have one— [*She clears her throat and turns away again, acutely shy.*]

JIM [*abruptly*]. You know what I judge to be the trouble with you? Inferiority complex! Know what that is? That's what they call it when someone low-rates himself! I understand it because I had it, too. Although my case was not so ag-gravated as yours seems to be. I had it until I took up public speaking, developed my voice, and learned that I had an aptitude for science. Before that time I never thought of myself as being outstanding in any way whatsoever! Now I've never made a regular study of it, but I have a friend who says I can analyze people better than doctors that make a profession of it. I don't claim that to be necessarily true, but I can sure guess a person's psychology, Laura! [*Takes out his gum.*] Excuse me, Laura. I always take it out when the flavor is gone. I'll use this scrap of paper to wrap it in. I know how it is to get it stuck on a shoe. Yep—that's what I judge to be your principal trouble. A lack of confidence in yourself as a person. You don't have the proper amount of faith in yourself. I'm basing that fact on a number of your remarks and also on certain observations I've made. For instance that clumping you thought was so awful in high school. You say that you even dreaded to walk into class. You see what you did? You dropped out of school, you gave up an education because of a clump, which as far as I know was practically non-existent! A little physical defect is what you have. Hardly noticeable even! Magnified thousands of times by imagination! You know what my strong advice to you is? Think of yourself as *superior* in some way!

LAURA. In what way would I think?

JIM. Why, man alive, Laura! Just look about you a little. What do you see? A world full of common people! All of 'em born and all of 'em going to die! Which of them has one-tenth of your good points! Or mine! Or anyone else's, as far as that goes— Gosh! Everybody excels in some one thing. Some in many! [*Unconsciously glances at himself in the mirror.*] All you've got to do is discover in *what!* Take me, for instance. [*He adjusts his tie at the mirror.*] My interest happens to lie in electro-dynamics. I'm taking a course in radio engineering at night school, Laura, on top of a fairly responsible job at the warehouse. I'm taking that course and studying public speaking.

LAURA. Ohhhh.

JIM. Because I believe in the future of television! [*Turning back to her.*] I wish to be ready to go up right along with it. Therefore I'm planning to get in on the ground floor. In fact I've already made the right connections and all that remains is for the industry itself to get under way! Full steam—— [*His eyes are starry.*] *Knowledge*—Zzzzzp! *Money*—Zzzzzzp!— *Power!* That's the cycle democracy is built on! [*His attitude is convincingly dynamic.* LAURA *stares at him, even her shyness eclipsed in her absolute wonder. He suddenly grins.*] I guess you think I think a lot of myself!

LAURA. No——o-o-o, I——

JIM. Now how about you? Isn't there something you take more interest in than anything else?

LAURA. Well, I do—as I said—have my—glass collection—

[*A peal of girlish laughter from the kitchen.*]

JIM. I'm not right sure I know what you're talking about. What kind of glass is it?

LAURA. Little articles of it, they're ornaments mostly! Most of them are little animals made out of glass, the tiniest little animals in the world. Mother calls them a glass menagerie! Here's an example of one, if you'd like to see it! This one is one of the oldest. It's nearly thirteen. [MUSIC: "THE GLASS MENAGERIE."] [*He stretches out his hand.*] Oh, be careful— if you breathe, it breaks!

JIM. I'd better not take it. I'm pretty clumsy with things.

LAURA. Go on, I trust you with him! [*Places it in his palm.*] There now—you're holding him gently! Hold him over the light, he loves the light! You see how the light shines through him?

JIM. It sure does shine!

LAURA. I shouldn't be partial, but he is my favorite one.

JIM. What kind of a thing is this one supposed to be?

LAURA. Haven't you noticed the single horn on his forehead?

JIM. A unicorn, huh?

LAURA. Mmm-hmmm!

JIM. Unicorns, aren't they extinct in the modern world?

LAURA. I know!

JIM. Poor little fellow, he must feel sort of lonesome.

LAURA [*smiling*]. Well, if he does he doesn't complain about it. He stays on a shelf with some horses that don't have horns and all of them seem to get along nicely together.

JIM. How do you know?

LAURA [*lightly*]. I haven't heard any arguments among them!

JIM [*grinning*]. No arguments, huh? Well, that's a pretty good sign! Where shall I set him?

LAURA. Put him on the table. They all like a change of scenery once in a while!

JIM [*stretching*]. Well, well, well, well— Look how big my shadow is when I stretch!

LAURA. Oh, oh, yes—it stretches across the ceiling!

JIM [*crossing to door*]. I think it's stopped raining. [*Opens fire-escape door.*] Where does the music come from?

LAURA. From the Paradise Dance Hall across the alley.

JIM. How about cutting the rug a little, Miss Wingfield?

LAURA. Oh, I—

JIM. Or is your program filled up? Let me have a look at it. [*Grasps imaginary card.*] Why, every dance is taken! I'll just have to scratch some out. [WALTZ MUSIC: "LA GOLON-DRINA"] Ahhh, a waltz! [*He executes some sweeping turns by himself then holds his arms toward* LAURA.]

LAURA [*breathlessly*]. I—can't dance!

JIM. There you go, that inferiority stuff!

LAURA. I've never danced in my life!

JIM. Come on, try!

LAURA. Oh, but I'd step on you!

JIM. I'm not made out of glass.

LAURA. How—how—how do we start?

JIM. Just leave it to me. You hold your arms out a little.

LAURA. Like this?

JIM. A little bit higher. Right. Now don't tighten up, that's the main thing about it—relax.

LAURA [*laughing breathlessly*]. It's hard not to.

JIM. Okay.

LAURA. I'm afraid you can't budge me.

JIM. What do you bet I can't? [*He swings her into motion.*]

LAURA. Goodness, yes, you can!

JIM. Let yourself go, now, Laura, just let yourself go.

LAURA. I'm—

JIM. Come on!

LAURA. Trying!

JIM. Not so stiff— Easy does it!

LAURA. I know but I'm—

JIM. Loosen th' backbone! There now, that's a lot better.

LAURA. Am I?

JIM. Lots, lots better! [*He moves her about the room in a clumsy waltz.*]

LAURA. Oh, my!

JIM. Ha-ha!

LAURA. Oh, my goodness!

JIM. Ha-ha-ha! [*They suddenly bump into the table.* JIM *stops.*] What did we hit on?

LAURA. Table.

JIM. Did something fall off it? I think—

LAURA. Yes.

JIM. I hope that it wasn't the little glass horse with the horn!

LAURA. Yes.

JIM. Aw, aw, aw. Is it broken?

LAURA. Now it is just like all the other horses.

JIM. It's lost its—

LAURA. Horn! It doesn't matter. Maybe it's a blessing in disguise.

JIM. You'll never forgive me. I bet that that was your favorite piece of glass.

LAURA. I don't have favorites much. It's no tragedy, Freckles. Glass breaks so easily. No matter how careful you are. The traffic jars the shelves and things fall off them.

JIM. Still I'm awfully sorry that I was the cause.

LAURA [*smiling*]. I'll just imagine he had an operation. The horn was removed to make him feel less—freakish! [*They both laugh.*] Now he will feel more at home with the other horses, the ones that don't have horns. . .

JIM. Ha-ha, that's very funny! [*Suddenly serious.*] I'm glad to see that you have a sense of humor. You know—you're— well—very different! Surprisingly different from anyone else

I know! [*His voice becomes soft and hesitant with a genuine feeling.*] Do you mind me telling you that? [LAURA *is abashed beyond speech.*] I mean it in a nice way . . . [LAURA *nods shyly, looking away.*] You make me feel sort of—I don't know how to put it! I'm usually pretty good at expressing things, but— This is something that I don't know how to say! [LAURA *touches her throat and clears it—turns the broken unicorn in her hands.*] [*Even softer.*] Has anyone ever told you that you were pretty? [PAUSE: MUSIC.] [LAURA *looks up slowly, with wonder, and shakes her head.*] Well, you are! In a very different way from anyone else. And all the nicer because of the difference, too. [*His voice becomes low and husky.* LAURA *turns away, nearly faint with the novelty of her emotions.*] I wish that you were my sister. I'd teach you to have some confidence in yourself. The different people are not like other people, but being different is nothing to be ashamed of. Because other people are not such wonderful people. They're one hundred times one thousand. You're one times one! They walk all over the earth. You just stay here. They're common as—weeds, but—you—well, you're —*Blue Roses!*

[IMAGE ON SCREEN: BLUE ROSES.]

[MUSIC CHANGES.]

LAURA. But blue is wrong for—roses . . .

JIM. It's right for you— You're—pretty!

LAURA. In what respect am I pretty?

JIM. In all respects—believe me! Your eyes—your hair—are pretty! Your hands are pretty! [*He catches hold of her hand.*] You think I'm making this up because I'm invited to dinner and have to be nice. Oh, I could do that! I could put on an act for you, Laura, and say lots of things without being very sincere. But this time I am. I'm talking to you sincerely. I happened to notice you had this inferiority complex that keeps you from feeling comfortable with people. Somebody needs to build your confidence up and make you proud instead of shy and turning away and—blushing— Somebody ought to— Ought to—*kiss you, Laura!* [*His hand slips slowly up her arm to her shoulder.*] [MUSIC SWELLS TUMULTUOUSLY.] [*He suddenly turns her about and kisses her on the lips.*] [*When he releases her* LAURA *sinks on the sofa with a bright, dazed look.*] [JIM *backs away and fishes in his pocket for a cigarette.*] [LEGEND ON SCREEN: "SOUVENIR."] Stumble-john! [*He lights the cigarette, avoiding her look.*] [*There is a peal of girlish laughter from* AMANDA *in the kitchen.*] [LAURA *slowly raises and opens her hand. It still contains the little broken glass animal. She looks at it with a tender, bewildered expression.*] Stumble-john! I shouldn't have done that— That was way off the beam. You don't smoke, do you? [*She looks up, smiling, not hearing the question.*] [*He sits beside her a little gingerly. She looks at him speechlessly—waiting.*] [*He coughs decorously and moves a little farther aside as he considers the situation and senses her feelings, dimly, with perturbation.*] [*Gently.*] Would you—care for a—mint? [*She doesn't seem to hear him but her look grows brighter even.*] Peppermint—Life Saver? My pocket's a regular drug store—wherever I go . . . [*He pops a mint in his mouth. Then gulps and decides to make a clean breast of it. He speaks slowly and gingerly.*] Laura, you know, if I had a sister like you, I'd do the same thing as Tom. I'd bring out fellows and—introduce her to them. The right type of boys of a type to—appreciate her. Only—well—he made a mistake about me. Maybe I've got no call to be saying this. That may not have been the idea in having me over. But what if it was? There's nothing wrong about that. The only trouble is that in my case—I'm not in a situation to—do the right thing. I can't take down your number and say I'll phone. I can't call up next week and—ask for a date. I thought I had better explain the situation in case you misunderstood it and—hurt your feelings. . . . [*Pause.*] [*Slowly, very slowly,* LAURA'S *look changes, her eyes returning slowly from his to the ornament in her palm.*]

[AMANDA *utters another gay laugh in the kitchen.*]

LAURA [*faintly*]. You—won't—call again?

JIM. No, Laura, I can't. [*He rises from the sofa.*] As I was just explaining, I've—got strings on me, Laura, I've—been going steady! I go out all the time with a girl named Betty. She's a home-girl like you, and Catholic, and Irish, and in a great many ways we—get along fine. I met her last summer on a moonlight boat trip up the river to Alton, on the *Majestic.* Well—right away from the start it was—love! [LEGEND: LOVE!] [LAURA *sways slightly forward and grips the arm of the sofa. He fails to notice, now enrapt in his own comfortable being.*] Being in love has made a new man of me! [*Leaning stiffly forward, clutching the arm of the sofa,* LAURA *struggles visibly with her storm. But* JIM *is oblivious, she is a long way off.*] The power of love is really pretty tremendous! Love is something that—changes the whole world, Laura! [*The storm abates a little and* LAURA *leans back. He notices her again.*] It happened that Betty's aunt took sick, she got a wire and had to go to Centralia. So Tom—when he asked me to dinner—I naturally just accepted the invitation, not knowing that you—that he—that I— [*He stops awkwardly.*] Huh—I'm a stumble-john! [*He flops back on the sofa.*] [*The holy candles in the altar of* LAURA'S *face have been snuffed out. There is a look of almost infinite desolation.*] [JIM *glances at her uneasily.*] I wish that you would—say something. [*She bites her lip which was trembling and then bravely smiles. She opens her hand again on the broken glass ornament. Then she gently takes his hand and raises it level with her own. She carefully places the unicorn in the palm of his hand, then pushes his fingers closed upon it.*] What are you—doing that for? You want me to have him?—Laura? [*She nods.*] What for?

LAURA. A—souvenir . . .

[*She rises unsteadily and crouches beside the victrola to wind it up.*]

[LEGEND ON SCREEN: "THINGS HAVE A WAY OF TURNING OUT SO BADLY!"]

[OR IMAGE: "GENTLEMAN CALLER WAVING GOODBYE!—GAILY."]

[*At this moment* AMANDA *rushes brightly back in the front room. She bears a pitcher of fruit punch in an old-fashioned cut-glass pitcher and a plate of macaroons. The plate has a gold border and poppies painted on it.*]

AMANDA. Well, well, well! Isn't the air delightful after the shower? I've made you children a little liquid refreshment. [*Turns gaily to the gentleman caller.*] Jim, do you know that song about lemonade?
      "Lemonade, lemonade
         Made in the shade and stirred with a spade—
         Good enough for any old maid!"
JIM [*uneasily*]. Ha-ha! No—I never heard it.
AMANDA. Why, Laura! You look so serious!
JIM. We were having a serious conversation.
AMANDA. Good! Now you're better acquainted!
JIM [*uncertainly*]. Ha-ha! Yes.
AMANDA. You modern young people are much more serious-minded than my generation. I was so gay as a girl!
JIM. You haven't changed, Mrs. Wingfield.
AMANDA. Tonight I'm rejuvenated! The gaiety of the occasion, Mr. O'Connor! [*She tosses her head with a pearl of laughter. Spills lemonade.*] Oooo! I'm baptizing myself!
JIM. Here—let me—
AMANDA [*setting the pitcher down*]. There now. I discovered we had some maraschino cherries. I dumped them in, juice and all!
JIM. You shouldn't have gone to that trouble, Mrs. Wingfield.
AMANDA. Trouble, trouble? Why it was loads of fun! Didn't you hear me cutting up in the kitchen? I bet your ears were burning! I told Tom how outdone with him I was for keeping you to himself so long a time! He should have brought

you over much, much sooner! Well, now that you've found your way, I want you to be a very frequent caller! Not just occasional but all the time. Oh, we're going to have a lot of gay times together! I see them coming! Mmm, just breathe that air! So fresh, and the moon's so pretty! I'll skip back out—I know where my place is when young folks are having a—serious conversation!

JIM. Oh, don't go out, Mrs. Wingfield. The fact of the matter is I've got to be going.

AMANDA. Going, now? You're joking! Why, it's only the shank of the evening, Mr. O'Connor!

JIM. Well, you know how it is.

AMANDA. You mean you're a young workingman and have to keep workingmen's hours. We'll let you off early tonight. But only on the condition that next time you stay later. What's the best night for you? Isn't Saturday night the best night for you workingmen?

JIM. I have a couple of time-clocks to punch, Mrs. Wingfield. One at morning, another one at night!

AMANDA. My, but you *are* ambitious! You work at night, too?

JIM. No, Ma'am, not work but—Betty! [*He crosses deliberately to pick up his hat. The band at the Paradise Dance Hall goes into a tender waltz.*]

AMANDA. Betty? Betty? Who's—Betty! [*There is an ominous cracking sound in the sky.*]

JIM. Oh, just a girl. The girl I go steady with! [*He smiles charmingly. The sky falls.*]

[LEGEND: "THE SKY FALLS."]

AMANDA [*a long-drawn exhalation*]. Ohhhh . . . Is it a serious romance, Mr. O'Connor?

JIM. We're going to be married the second Sunday in June.

AMANDA. Ohhhh—how nice! Tom didn't mention that you were engaged to be married.

JIM. The cat's not out of the bag at the warehouse yet. You know how they are. They call you Romeo and stuff like that. [*He stops at the oval mirror to put on his hat. He carefully shapes the brim and the crown to give a discreetly dashing effect.*] It's been a wonderful evening, Mrs. Wingfield. I guess this is what they mean by Southern hospitality.

AMANDA. It really wasn't anything at all.

JIM. I hope it don't seem like I'm rushing off. But I promised Betty I'd pick her up at the Wabash depot, an' by the time I get my jalopy down there her train'll be in. Some women are pretty upset if you keep 'em waiting.

AMANDA. Yes, I know— The tyranny of women! [*Extends her hand.*] Good-bye, Mr. O'Connor. I wish you luck—and happiness—and success! All three of them, and so does Laura!— Don't you, Laura?

LAURA. Yes!

JIM [*taking her hand*]. Good-bye, Laura. I'm certainly going to treasure that souvenir. And don't you forget the good advice I gave you. [*Raises his voice to a cheery shout.*] So long, Shakespeare! Thanks again, ladies— Good night!

[*He grins and ducks jauntily out.*]

[*Still bravely grimacing,* AMANDA *closes the door on the gentleman caller. Then she turns back to the room with a puzzled expression. She and* LAURA *don't dare to face each other.* LAURA *crouches beside the victrola to wind it.*]

AMANDA [*faintly*]. Things have a way of turning out so badly. I don't believe that I would play the victrola. Well, well—well— Our gentleman caller was engaged to be married! Tom!

TOM [*from back*]. Yes, Mother?

AMANDA. Come in here a minute. I want to tell you something awfully funny.

TOM [*enters with macaroon and a glass of the lemonade*]. Has the gentleman caller gotten away already?

AMANDA. The gentleman caller has made an early departure. What a wonderful joke you played on us!

TOM. How do you mean?

AMANDA. You didn't mention that he was engaged to be married.

TOM. Jim? Engaged?

AMANDA. That's what he just informed us.

TOM. I'll be jiggered! I didn't know about that.

AMANDA. That seems very peculiar.

TOM. What's peculiar about it?

AMANDA. Didn't you call him your best friend down at the warehouse?

TOM. He is, but how did I know?

AMANDA. It seems extremely peculiar that you wouldn't know your best friend was going to be married!

TOM. The warehouse is where I work, not where I know things about people!

AMANDA. You don't know things anywhere! You live in a dream; you manufacture illusions! [*He crosses to door.*] Where are you going?

TOM. I'm going to the movies.

AMANDA. That's right, now that you've had us make such fools of ourselves. The effort, the preparations, all the expense! The new floor lamp, the rug, the clothes for Laura! All for what? To entertain some other girl's fiancé! Go to the movies, go! Don't think about us, a mother deserted, an unmarried sister who's crippled and has no job! Don't let anything interfere with your selfish pleasure! Just go, go, go—to the movies!

TOM. All right, I will! The more you shout about my selfishness to me the quicker I'll go, and I won't go to the movies!

AMANDA. Go, then! Then go to the moon—you selfish dreamer!

[TOM *smashes his glass on the floor. He plunges out on the fire-escape, slamming the door.* LAURA *screams—cut by door.*]

[*Dance-hall music up.* TOM *goes to the rail and grips it desperately, lifting his face in the chill white moonlight penetrating the narrow abyss of the alley.*]

[LEGEND ON SCREEN: "AND SO GOOD-BYE . . ."]

[TOM'S *closing speech is timed with the interior pantomime. The interior scene is played as though viewed through soundproof glass.* AMANDA *appears to be making a comforting speech to* LAURA *who is huddled upon the sofa. Now that we cannot hear the mother's speech, her silliness is gone and she has dignity and tragic beauty.* LAURA'S *dark hair hides her face until at the end of the speech she lifts it to smile at her mother.* AMANDA'S *gestures are slow and graceful, almost dancelike, as she comforts the daughter. At the end of her speech she glances a moment at the father's picture—then withdraws through the portieres. At close of* TOM'S *speech,* LAURA *blows out the candles, ending the play.*]

TOM. I didn't go to the moon, I went much further—for time is the longest distance between two places— Not long after that I was fired for writing a poem on the lid of a shoe-box. I left Saint Louis. I descended the steps of this fire-escape for a last time and followed, from then on, in my father's footsteps, attempting to find in motion what was lost in space— I traveled around a great deal. The cities swept about me like dead leaves, leaves that were brightly colored but torn away from the branches. I would have stopped, but I was pursued by something. It always came upon me unawares, taking me altogether by surprise. Perhaps it was a familiar bit of music. Perhaps it was only a piece of transparent glass— Perhaps I am walking along a street at night, in some strange city, before I have found companions. I pass the lighted window of a shop where perfume is sold. The window is filled with pieces of colored glass, tiny transparent bottles in delicate colors, like bits of a shattered rainbow. Then all at once my sister touches my shoulder. I turn around and look into her eyes . . . Oh, Laura, Laura, I tried to leave you behind me, but I am more faithful than I intended to be! I reach for a cigarette, I cross the street, I run into the movies or a bar, I buy a drink, I speak to the nearest stranger—anything that can blow your candles out!

[LAURA *bends over the candles.*]—for nowadays the world is lit by lightning! Blow out your candles, Laura—and so good-bye. . . .

[*She blows the candles out.*]

THE SCENE DISSOLVES

PRODUCTION NOTES

Being a "memory play," *The Glass Menagerie* can be presented with unusual freedom of convention. Because of its considerably delicate or tenuous material, atmospheric touches and subtleties of direction play a particularly important part. Expressionism and all other unconventional techniques in drama have only one valid aim, and that is a closer approach to truth. When a play employs unconventional techniques, it is not, or certainly shouldn't be, trying to escape its responsibility of dealing with reality, or interpreting experience, but is actually or should be attempting to find a closer approach, a more penetrating and vivid expression of things as they are. The straight realistic play with its genuine frigidaire and authentic ice-cubes, its characters that speak exactly as its audience speaks, corresponds to the academic landscape and has the same virtue of a photographic likeness. Everyone should know nowadays the unimportance of the photographic in art: that truth, life, or reality is an organic thing which the poetic imagination can represent or suggest, in essence, only through transformation, through changing into other forms than those which were merely present in appearance.

These remarks are not meant as comments only on this particular play. They have to do with a conception of a new, plastic theatre which must take the place of the exhausted theatre of realistic conventions if the theatre is to resume vitality as a part of our culture.

THE SCREEN DEVICE

There is *only one important difference between the original and acting version of the play* and that is the *omission* in the latter of the device which I tentatively included in my *original* script. This device was the use of a screen on which were projected magic-lantern slides bearing images or titles. I do not regret the omission of this device from the present Broadway production. The extraordinary power of Miss Taylor's performance made it suitable to have the utmost simplicity in the physical production. But I think it may be interesting to some readers to see how this device was conceived. So I am putting it into the published manuscript. These images and legends, projected from behind, were cast on a section of wall between the front-room and dining-room areas, which should be indistinguishable from the rest when not in use.

The purpose of this will probably be apparent. It is to give accent to certain values in each scene. Each scene contains a particular point (or several) which is structurally the most important. In an episodic play, such as this, the basic structure or narrative line may be obscured from the audience; the effect may seem fragmentary rather than architectural. This may not be the fault of the play so much as a lack of attention in the audience. The legend or image upon the screen will strengthen the effect of what is merely allusion in the writing and allow the primary point to be made more simply and lightly than if the entire responsibility were on the spoken lines. Aside from this structural value, I think the screen will have a definite emotional appeal, less definable but just as important. An imaginative producer or director may invent many other uses for this device than those indicated in the present script. In fact the possibilities of the device seem much larger to me than the instance of this play can possibly utilize.

THE MUSIC

Another extra-literary accent in this play is provided by the use of music. A single recurring tune, "The Glass Menagerie," is used to give emotional emphasis to suitable passages. This tune is like circus music, not when you are on the grounds or in the immediate vicinity of the parade, but when you are at some distance and very likely thinking of something else. It seems under those circumstances to continue almost interminably and it weaves in and out of your preoccupied consciousness; then it is the lightest, most delicate music in the world and perhaps the saddest. It expresses the surface vivacity of life with the underlying strain of immutable and inexpressible sorrow. When you look at a piece of delicately spun glass you think of two things: how beautiful it is and how easily it can be broken. Both of those ideas should be woven into the recurring tune, which dips in and out of the play as if it were carried on a wind that changes. It serves as a thread of connection and allusion between the narrator with his separate point in time and space and the subject of his story. Between each episode it returns as reference to the emotion, nostalgia, which is the first condition of the play. It is primarily Laura's music and therefore comes out most clearly when the play focuses upon her and the lovely fragility of glass which is her image.

THE LIGHTING

The lighting in the play is not realistic. In keeping with the atmosphere of memory, the stage is dim. Shafts of light are focused on selected areas or actors, sometimes in contradistinction to what is the apparent center. For instance, in the quarrel scene between Tom and Amanda, in which Laura has no active part, the clearest pool of light is on her figure. This is also true of the supper scene, when her silent figure on the sofa should remain the visual center. The light upon Laura should be distinct from the others, having a peculiar pristine clarity such as light used in early religious portraits of female saints or madonnas. A certain correspondence to light in religious paintings, such as El Greco's, where the figures are radiant in atmosphere that is relatively dusky, could be effectively used throughout the play. (It will also permit a more effective use of the screen.) A free, imaginative use of light can be of enormous value in giving a mobile, plastic quality to plays of a more or less static nature.   *T.W.*